of his career reveals him as a complex figure: to some "a benefactor to the cause of liberalism," to others a "wicked meddler," and to the *Times* of his day, "a misguided patriot."

Certainly he was a diplomat of ambition, purpose, and force, whose role was highly significant in an obscure area of British international involvement in the nineteenth century.

Mario Rodríguez, the author of this book, is a native Californian. He attended California schools and received both his undergraduate and graduate degrees from the University of California. He is at present pursuing investigation of the life and times of José Francisco Barrundia (1787–1854), a controversial politician and leading liberal whose career spans four decades of Central American history. To conduct this study, Professor Rodríguez was awarded a John Simon Guggenheim Fellowship in history and is spending the academic year, 1964–65, in Central America. He also held the Morse Fellowship in History from Yale University which provided a year (1958–59) of study in England, Belgium, and France.

Dr. Rodríguez is a member of the Department of History at the University of Arizona in Tucson, having joined the faculty in 1960. He is a frequent contributor to scholarly periodicals and now has in press a synthesis of Central American history to be published by Prentice-Hall and Company. He is also a contributing editor for the *Handbook of Latin American Studies*.

A Palmerstonian
Diplomat in
Central America

FREDERICK
CHATFIELD, ESQ.

Frederick Chatfield, Esq.

A Palmerstonian Diplomat

in

Central America

FREDERICK CHATFIELD, Esq.

by

MARIO RODRÍGUEZ

THE UNIVERSITY OF ARIZONA PRESS
TUCSON   1964

To
Amanda, Mildred, and Jacqueline

PREFACE

The nature of historical research and the fortunes of academic life often lead the historian down unfamiliar paths. Upon completing a doctoral dissertation on a seventeenth-century theme in South American history, the remotest thought from my mind was that before long I would be engaged in a full-scale research project concerning nineteenth-century Central America. It all started with an appointment to a university where scholarship in this particular field was well-established. As part of my teaching assignment at Tulane University in New Orleans, I attended the weekly sessions of a special inter-disciplinary seminar for graduate students and faculty. Impressed with the knowledgeable comments of my colleagues, I found their enthusiasm for Central American affairs to be infectious. The general theme of foreign influences upon the area especially appealed to me.

After reading widely in the field, there were certain topics which captured my attention. One of them was the ideological impact of the United States upon Central America. In Professor Joseph Byrne Lockey's work *Essays in Pan-Americanism* (Berkeley, 1939), I had learned that American representation in Central America before the 1840's, for one reason or another, was one of "Diplomatic Futility." So far as the physical presence of our agents was concerned, the evidence appeared convincing. It occurred to me, however, that the characterization was less valid in the ideological realm. A case in point was Guatemala's acceptance and implementation of a judicial experiment conceived by Edward Livingston, a prominent figure of the Jeffersonian and Jacksonian eras in American history. In Central America, I looked for the available documentation on this topic and subsequently published a brief study entitled *The Livingston Codes in the Guatemalan Crisis of 1837-1838* (Middle American Research Institute, New Orleans, 1955). In the process, I gained valuable insights into the political developments of that period. Convinced that the Central American Republic (1824-1839) represented basically an experiment in liberalism, or "Applied Enlightenment," it also seemed to me that the Guatemalan crisis of 1837 marked the beginning of the final secessionist movement. Moreover, I was amazed at the ignorance which prevailed concerning the real issues in the last years of the Republic's existence. By this time, my commitment to the Central American field was complete: I was determined to study the liberal movement in the first half of the nineteenth century. And as I collected materials throughout the world, I kept this in mind.

A second and related topic, which resulted from the Tulane seminar, dealt with the British impact on Central America. Along positive lines, I sought documents on the introduction of the Lancastrian system of education and on Jeremy Bentham's influence upon political thought and governmental developments. In addition, there was a statement made in 1849 by Ephraim George Squier, the American chargé d'affaires, which intrigued me. Although by no means a disinterested bystander, Squier claimed that English agents were largely responsible for the dissolution of the Central American Republic. If this were true, I reasoned, then Great Britain had also had a negative effect upon the development of Central American liberalism. At least this was an hypothesis worth checking. And, since Frederick Chatfield was the leading British representative in the area during those years, I focused attention upon him. Little did I suspect that a detailed study of his public career would result from my investigations. In short, a chain of circumstances as well as the direction of the documentation shaped my research interests.

Along the line, moreover, certain institutions and persons expedited and contributed to the present study. In the "Bibliographical Essay," I mention the various depositories and libraries that have graciously allowed me to use their materials. I am indeed grateful for the cooperation of their staffs. I am especially indebted to Yale University for awarding me a Morse Fellowship in History in 1958-1959 and for minor grants which enabled me to purchase microfilm. Among the individuals to whom I owe a special debt of gratitude are: Professor Engel Sluiter, my mentor and friend at the University of California at Berkeley, who taught me the skills of the historian; my erstwhile colleagues at Tulane University — William J. Griffith, Robert Wauchope, and Kalman H. Silvert — who inspired and cultivated my interest in Central America; Yale professors José Juan Arrom and Firuz Kazemzadeh whose critical comments on the style and content of the manuscript were invaluable; professors Andrew Lossky of the University of California at Los Angeles and J. Fred Rippy of the University of Chicago who also gave me the benefit of their wisdom; and my present colleagues at the University of Arizona — Russell C. Ewing, Herman E. Bateman, John A. Carroll, and Donald N. Lammers — who offered valuable advice on the final chapters of this study. My research assistants Vincent C. Peloso in Tucson and Walter Sterling in New Haven likewise performed yeoman service at various stages in the preparation of the manuscript. And last but not least, I wish to thank my wife and daughter — Mildred and Jacqueline — for their efforts in tracking down biographical material in Europe, for their help in the technical aspects of this work, and especially for their patience with an irritable author. To all of those mentioned, and to Frederick Chatfield too, I owe so much. It goes without saying that the final responsibility for this study rests with me.

Mario Rodríguez

Tucson, Arizona
January, 1964

CONTENTS

Abbreviations Used in the Text xii

Prologue: A Disfigured Face 1

One: The Upstart Spy 9

Two: Consul and Minister 31

Three: Minister Plenipotentiary 53

Four: Reciprocal Annoyance 89

Five: Rude and Uncivilised 121

Six: Macbeth's Cauldron 149

Seven: This Miserable Island 179

Eight: El Ominoso Chatfield 211

Nine: Quijano's Ransom 239

Ten: Old Predilections 269

Eleven: Brother Jonathan and the Tiger 295

Twelve: Prometheus and Hamlet 327

Epilogue: The Brighton Peabody 359

Bibliographical Essay 367

Index 379

MAPS

Central America . . . . fp 1

British Honduras, 1826 88

Mosquito Shore 148

Gulf of Fonseca Region . . . . fp 282

ABBREVIATIONS

A. Documents (Manuscript and Printed).

A.A.E.P.	Archives des Affaires Etrangères, Paris.
/CPAC	Correspondance Politique: Amerique Centrale.
/CCG	Correspondance Consulaire et Commerciale: Guatemala.
A.G.N.G.	Archivo General de la Nación, Guatemala.
/CLCA	Correspondencia de la Legación de Centro-América.
/CM	Comisión de Ministros.
/CMRE	Correspondencia del Ministerio de Relaciones Exteriores.
/LV	Libro Verde.
B.L.	Bancroft Library, Berkeley, California.
/CAP	Central American Pamphlets. 9 vols.
/CAMN	Central American Miscellaneous Newspapers. 5 vols.
B.N.G.	Biblioteca Nacional, Guatemala.
/HS	Hojas Sueltas.
/F	Folletos.
/V	Valenzuela Collection.
F.O.	Public Record Office, London. Foreign Office Documents.
/5	America, United States.
/10	Belgium.
/15	Central America.
/30	Germany.
/53	Mosquito Nation.
/64	Prussia.
/65	Russia.
/97	Guatemala: Affairs of Central America and Mosquito.
/252	Central American Consulate.
/254	Central American Cousulate. Miscellaneous.
HPD	Thomas C. Hansard, ed., *The Parliamentary Debates* (1st series, 41 vols., London, 1804–1820).
M.A.E.B.	Ministère des Affaires Étrangères et du Commerce Extérieur, Bruxelles.
/CPSG	Correspondance Politique. Série Generale. Amérique Centrale, 1823–61.
/CPC	Correspondance Politique: Consulats.
/CST	Colonisation, Santo Tomás, No. 2207.
MDCIA	William Ray Manning, ed., *Diplomatic Correspondence of the United States: Inter-American Affairs, 1831–1860* (12 vols., Washington, 1932–1939).
MTUSA	Hunter Miller, ed., *Treaties and Other International Acts of the United States of America, 1776–1863* (8 vols., Washington, 1931–1948).
R.P. 30/32	Public Record Office. Russell Papers.
T.P.C.G.	Arturo Taracena. Private Collection. Guatemala.

B. Special Abbreviations used in Footnotes.

conf.	—	confidential
C.O.	—	Colonial Office
cons.	—	consular
exp.	—	expediente
ext.	—	extract
F.O.	—	Foreign Office
leg.	—	legajo
mem.	—	memorandum
No.	—	Number
Nos.	—	Numbers
p. encl.	—	plus enclosure
p. encl.s	—	plus enclosures
pvt.	—	private
pvt./conf.	—	private and confidential
pvt./sep.	—	private and separate
sec.	—	secret
sep.	—	separate

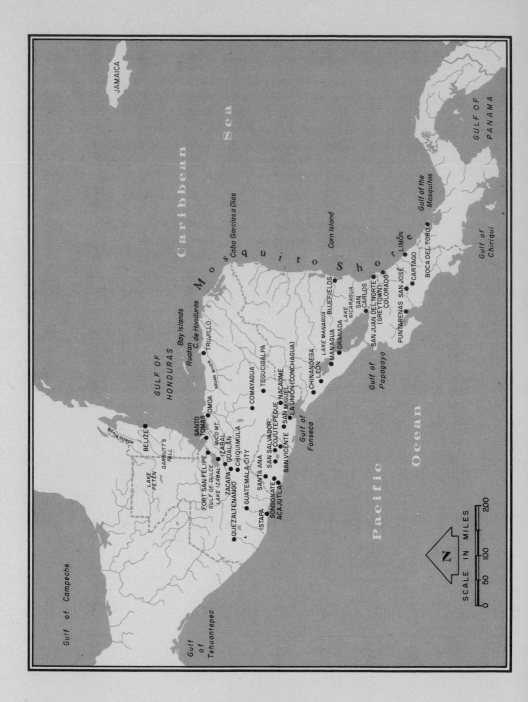

Central America

PROLOGUE

A Disfigured Face

Che sara sara.[1]
—Chatfield, Sussex

As he drank the natural waters of Aix la Chapelle during the summer months of 1830, Frederick Chatfield could well curse those four winters he spent as the British consul at Memel, a Baltic port in East Prussia. The extreme severity of the climate in the north exposed a marked weakness in his constitution—a sluggish circulation in the stomach vessels which in turn forced too much blood to the head and apparently caused the painful and unseemly eruptions on his face. When artificial waters failed to bring any relief, a professor of medicine at the University of Berlin strongly urged him to apply for a leave of absence from his consular post so that he might attend the "baths" in Rhenish Prussia for a season.[2]

But Frederick Chatfield, approaching thirty, was troubled by more than just a disfigured face. The experience at Memel raised certain doubts in his mind about a career in the foreign service. If only his superiors — he thought to himself — had been disposed to implement his frequent suggestions to enhance the prestige of the consulate, if they had but given him some indication that a promotion was in the offing, then perhaps the ugliness of his face — a passing disfigurement, after all — might not have been in vain. On the other hand, Superintendent John Bidwell of the Consular Department had listened sympathetically to his recommendations which would have compelled English ship-masters to register directly with their consul; and, in confidence, he had explained to Chatfield the opposition the Foreign Office faced on this measure from no less than three governmental agencies.[3] But young Frederick lacked the patience to wait for the obstacles to dissolve themselves; and it still infuriated and disillusioned him to think that fellow Englishmen, for whatever the reason, could condone a practice which degraded their representative at Memel and forced him to rely upon "inferior" customs officials of another nation for the type of commercial information desired by the Foreign Office. Under those conditions, he could be nothing more or nothing less than a counting

---

1. Motto, Chatfield or Chatfeild of Sussex County, James Fairbairn, *Fairbairn's Crests* (2 vols., London, n.d.), I, 104.
2. To John Bidwell, No. 2, pvt., March 10, 1830, F.O.64/165.
3. From Bidwell, pvt./conf., January 28, 1829; to Bidwell, pvt./conf., February 14, 1829, F.O. 64/160.

1

clerk, or a "police magistrate" settling fights among British seamen.[4] This was hardly what he had envisioned in July, 1826, when Foreign Secretary George Canning recommended him for the consular post at Memel. Was this the way to treat a man who had served as a cavalry officer in the second regiment of the exclusive Life Guards, the personal escort of His Britannic Majesty?

———•◦•———

Much of Chatfield's disappointment with the consular service stemmed from inability, as well as unwillingness, to reconcile himself to the fact that his primary function was commercial rather than political or diplomatic. He was not averse to commerce as such; he merely disliked the nature of the duties expected of him. Quite early in his career, young Frederick demonstrated an unusual capacity for research on economic matters, from which he enjoyed deducing in grand lines what British commercial policy and objectives should be in a given area. He preferred, in short, the role of the analyst and policy maker to that of the counting clerk, a function which he consistently refused to perform throughout his career even to the point of paying the salary of vice consuls, or clerks, out of his own pocket. Then he would stubbornly list those charges on the expenses of the consulate, only to have the Foreign Office refuse to accept them.[5]

The continual haggle with the Foreign Office over salary and living expenses was an important phase of Chatfield's one-man campaign to reform the consular service so that its primary function would be political. He perhaps had no illusions that he could succeed in this unequal contest, but — and he admitted this to Bidwell — by keeping his name before his superiors in this manner they would not tend to forget him when promotions were considered or new posts opened up in areas where the political function might predominate.[6] In dispatch after dispatch, with a regularity that smacked of impudence, the British consul at Memel complained that he could not maintain his consulate on a paltry five hundred pounds a year, that sundry expenses alone — and he could document this with vouchers — consumed at least twenty percent of his salary, and that, furthermore, it was unreasonable to expect him to pay traveling expenses to Memel, especially since the Foreign Office had instructed

4. To George Shee, No. 15, p.encl. s, April 1, 1831; to Bidwell, pvt./conf., April 14, 1831, F.O. 64/176.
5. To Earl of Dudley, No. 18, December 31, 1827, F.O. 64/151; from Bidwell, February 20, 1828, F.O. 64/155; to Shee, No. 15, April 1, 1831, F.O. 64/176.
6. To Bidwell, February 14, 1829, F.O. 64/160.

him to take the circuitous route through Berlin. Secretaries Canning, Dudley, and Aberdeen all read Chatfield's dispatches on this subject and were not convinced by them. When he received the standard reply that consuls were authorized to collect port dues to meet most of these expenses, the British agent at Memel was beside himself at the penny-pinching methods of the service. His superiors apparently wanted him to live like a counting clerk.[7]

Although Memel was on the road from St. Petersburg to Berlin, its geographical location was discouraging to a young man with political ambitions.[8] What few opportunities came his way, therefore, he exploited to the utmost. From his own resources, he paid for information concerning a projected Russian waterway which would further canalize Poland's trade.[9] On another occasion, he reported the details of an attempt by an Englishman to sell congreve rockets to the Russians, presumably for use against the Turks.[10] In 1828, Chatfield acquired a copy of the highly secret *"Conduiten Liste,"* which outlined the techniques of assuring loyalty in the Prussian civil service.[11] Of course, the Foreign Office was pleased to receive these important bits of information and complimented Chatfield for his zeal. But it could not, for obvious reasons of economy, provide every politically conscious and ambitious consul in its employ with the special funds he requested for these purposes. When no promotion rewarded his efforts, young Chatfield's discontent mounted; he despaired of ever being emancipated from the Baltic port.

Furthermore, life at Memel was galling to this ex-Life Guard, who had reveled in the society of his native and beloved London. Accustomed to the cultural activities and niceties of the City, he found little to do at this particular Prussian port with its eight to nine thousand unenlightened souls and its coarse, petty, and disrespectful authorities.[12] Only once, and quite by accident, could he recall a social function comparable to those he had enjoyed in London, and that was in July, 1829, when the Empress of Russia and her brother the Crown Prince of Prussia stopped at Memel on their way to St. Petersburg. In the excitement, the municipal authorities forgot to invite the British consul to the ceremonies honoring the royal visitors — an omission which offended him but which

---

7. From Bidwell, February 20, 1828; to Earl of Aberdeen, No. 13, December 31, 1828, F.O. 64/155; to Aberdeen, No. 24, December 31, 1829, F.O. 64/160.
8. To Aberdeen, No. 15, September 12, 1829, F.O. 64/160; to Bidwell, pvt., January 24, 1831, F.O. 64/176.
9. To Shee, No. 13, March 16, 1831, F.O. 64/176.
10. To Shee, No. 15, April 1, 1831, F.O. 64/176.
11. To Shee, p.encl. "Conduiten Lists" (1828), October 18, 1833, F.O. 64/192.
12. To Aberdeen, No. 15, September 12, 1829, F.O. 64/160.

he attributed more to their "gross ignorance of the ordinary observances of etiquette and politeness, than to any intention to convey a premeditated slight to my character." At Chatfield's suggestion, however, the Russian consul made up for the error; and then the proud Englishman announced: "I had the honour of being presented to the Empress by the Prince of Volkonsky and of conversing with Her for some minutes. I also had the honour to be introduced to and to be most graciously addressed by His Royal Highness the Crown Prince." That afternoon, and because of his acquaintance with some ladies in the retinue: "I had the honour to remain with the Royal Party in the Garden, and witnessed the affable charming manner in which the Empress received several of the wives of the principal Burghers, and of certain of the Lithuanian peasantry, who approached properly dressed in their peculiar and rude costume, singing, first on horseback and then on foot, apparently much to the entertainment of Her Majesty." On the morning of her departure, the honored Chatfield "attended at Her Majesty's residence at the hour she chose to continue Her journey to St. Petersburgh, when she condescended to bid adieu in the most gracious manner."[13]

The royal visit to Memel was unquestionably the highlight of an otherwise drab four years in the North. When the consul traveled to Berlin in the spring of 1830 to seek medical advice, the royal family of Prussia again greeted him with condescension, much more than he had a right to expect, he wrote many years later.[14] He only regretted that because of a disfigured face he was obliged "to go into the country to avoid accepting several invitations I had been favoured with by the Court."[15] And Chatfield's acceptance by the royal family opened up many doors to him, especially among the military and key officials in the Prussian government. He renewed these acquaintances at Aix la Chapelle in the summer of 1830, and they in turn introduced him to other notables of Europe. Young Frederick was thoroughly at ease with, and enjoyed the company of, these people who really counted. No wonder the thought of returning to an uninspiring and painful existence at Memel for another cold winter was more than this Londoner could bear. Only a miracle could save him from that fate.

—◆—

Considering the airs and inclinations of the British consul, one might easily assume that he was the scion of one of England's leading

13. To Aberdeen, No. 13, July 21, 1829, F.O. 64/160.
14. To Bidwell, No. 6, September 13, 1830, F.O. 64/165; to Earl Granville, No. 12, March 20, 1852, F.O. 15/77.
15. To Bidwell, pvt./conf., August 15, 1830, F.O. 64/165.

families. Certainly, his commission in the Life Guards would seem to indicate this. Such was not the case however, and therein lies the mainspring of this man's driving ambition for recognition and status. The Chatfield family, at least in the early nineteenth century, belonged to the rising middle class of Georgian England. If Frederick Chatfield were alive today, he certainly would challenge this classification by pointing to the pedigree of the Chatfields of Ditchling and Cuckfield in Sussex County, leaving us with the impression that this old English family belonged to the gentry. Under extreme pressure, he might admit to the term "lesser gentry," but it is doubtful that he would go lower. Yet the fact is that his great grandfather and his grandfather were both yeoman farmers. The latter moved from Cuckfield around the middle of the eighteenth century to Croydon, in Surrey County, where he busied himself as a distiller.[16]

On the other hand, Chatfield could well boast of his father's career in the Honorable East India Company's Maritime Service. From a fourth officer in 1771, Allen Chatfield rose to the rank of captain by the end of the century. His marriage, in 1786, to the daughter of Charles Thomas Coggan of the East India House certainly did not hinder his career in the service and may have added immeasurably to his personal fortunes.[17] The close connection with the East India Company, moreover, facilitated Allen Chatfield's appointment by Parliament to the five-man commission empowered to study and handle the Dutch claims which resulted from the renewal of hostilities with Holland in 1795. Due to the ingenuity of the claims commissioners, this assignment — much to the surprise of the English government — proved to be a lucrative one which lasted fourteen years. It was during that period that the Chatfield family made its appearance felt in London society.[18] The best proof of this contention can be found today in the Public Library and Museum of Brighton, England. Shortly before his death in 1872, Frederick Chatfield donated two paintings to that institution: one, a magnificent work by Aert de Gelder (1645-1727) entitled "The Marriage Contract;" and the other, a portrait of Mary Chatfield by the celebrated painter of London's society,

---

16. John Comber, *Sussex Genealogies* (Cambridge, 1932), pp. 90-119 (Comber, *Sussex*); also, Henry Cheal, *The History of Ditchling in the County of Sussex* (Lewes, 1901), p. 158.

17. Comber, *Sussex*, p. 113.

18. After considerable discussion and investigation, the House of Commons passed a resolution on May 1, 1809, which censured the conduct of the five commissioners for having rewarded themselves too liberally at public expense. See, *Annual Register*, Vol. LI (1809), pp. 90-98, 496-508, and HPD, XIV, 291-326.

John Opie.[19] The portrait of Frederick's mother, which has been exhibited in many countries, attests to the social prominence and affluence of a distiller's son in the London of the 1790's and early 1800's.

Though biographical facts about Frederick Chatfield during these early years are hard to come by, certain inferences can be drawn from those that do exist. He had two older brothers: Charles, the senior partner of the law firm Chatfield, Wingate, and Hart at 16 Austin Friars in London, and Allen Thomas, who followed in his father's footsteps as an officer in the H.E.I.C.M.S. Then, at the turn of the century, Mary Chatfield, in her mid-thirties, bore four children in rapid succession: Alfred (early 1800), Frederick (February 6, 1801), Cecil (late 1801), and Emily (in 1803). By 1812, both Alfred and Cecil had died, leaving Frederick the youngest son of elderly parents. In her sorrow and to compensate for her losses, Mary Chatfield understandably smothered her two youngest with more affection and attention than was good for them. The evidence indicates that Frederick and his baby sister Emily led a pampered existence at 42 Welbeck Street in the Parish of St. Marylebone, London.[20] The close attachment between mother and son also helps to explain why Frederick, among the brothers, inherited her portrait, why he took such pride in exhibiting it, and where he acquired that deep religious feeling which permeates his correspondence. As we shall see, many of his personal characteristics may have been shaped by an elderly and over-protective mother.

As for Frederick Chatfield's formal education, the record is cloudy. From his excellent command of military science and certain allusions in his correspondence, it would appear that he attended either the military college of the East India Company at Croydon or the Royal Military Academy at Woolwich, both near London.[21] In either case, Chatfield received a sound general education, which his curious mind improved upon throughout the remainder of his life by reading extensively on many subjects. In November, 1818, he began a three-year stint in the Life Guards, first as a cornet and then a sublieutenant, serving "under the late Lord Cathcart, until circumstances arising from the heavy expense of the Regiment caused me to retire."[22] On the day he left the

19. Ada Earland, *John Opie and His Circle* (London, 1911), p. 269.
20. Comber, *Sussex*, p. 114, which mistakenly gives Frederick's birth year as 1800 and does not mention Alfred at all. In the *Wimbledon Parish Register*, Alfred's death is listed in 1805 and Cecil's in 1811; also see Allen Chatfield's will in Somerset House, dated April 12, 1824, and probated on October 12, 1831.
21. To John Backhouse, June 30, 1833, F.O. 15/13; Samuel Lewis, *Topographical Dictionary of England* (5th ed., 4 vols., London, 1842), IV, 623-627.
22. To Granville, March 20, 1852, F.O. 15/77.

Guards, he purchased a lieutenant's commission in the 20th Foot Regiment and immediately went on half-pay status.[23]

To have placed Frederick in the "expensive cavalry regiment" with the sons of England's leading families must have strained the financial resources of the elderly Chatfields. It could reveal their social aspirations but more likely those of their young son, who, by his own admission, had very little conception of the value of the pound sterling. "I ran into several extravagances," a wiser Chatfield wrote many years later, "incurring debts which I gratefully acknowledge, that the liberality of my good parents long before their death, mainly relieved me from; and experience having taught me the misery of being in debt, I have since carefully adapted my expenditure to my means, and I am consequently free from such perplexities, either at home or abroad."[24] From Paris, on June 29, 1823, young Frederick wrote hopefully to a creditor, a baker by the name of Sassford who served his parents' home, "You will oblige me by not mentioning the subject to my family."[25] The subject in question was a loan of sixty pounds, which he had incurred a few months before leaving the Guards, and which, by the time it came to the notice of the Foreign Office in 1845, had more than doubled. Learning that young Chatfield was in Paris and perhaps fearing that he did not intend to pay the loan, the anxious baker complained to the parents; and Mrs. Chatfield, writing from her summer home in Brighton, was "extremely surprised and concerned that Mr. Frederic has any engagements unsettled with Mr. Sassford."[26]

In short, Frederick Chatfield, before he embarked upon his career, had been a pampered, socially ambitious, and financially irresponsible son of elderly parents. But father Chatfield apparently drew the line to the young bachelor in 1826 and told him that it was high time he gave serious consideration to a career. It was perhaps Lord Cathcart, his superior in the Guards, who recommended him to the attention of the Foreign Office, aided also by his own father's contacts in government.

<hr>

That was the background of Lieutenant Frederick Chatfield who impressed high Prussian officials in Aix la Chapelle with his military knowledge and his familiarity with London's high society. As we shall

---

23. Comber, *Sussex,* pp. 113-114; Edward Hertslet, ed., *Foreign Office List* (London, 1872), p. 73.
24. To Aberdeen, No. 3, January 28, 1846, F.O. 15/42.
25. To Silvester Sassford, June 19, 1823, F.O. 15/41.
26. Alfred Daniell to Chatfield, Wingate, and Hart, p. encl., June 2, 1846, F.O. 15/43.

see, he had an uncanny ability for making friends among the military, an attribute which would stand him well in his future career. Not only high Prussian officials but also Dutch and Belgian dignitaries took a liking to the young Englishman, namely, Count d'Aubremé, a Belgian who had served as Dutch Minister of War, and Count Liedekirk, who had been Vice Chamberlain at the same court.[27] At Aix la Chapelle, Lieutenant Chatfield and his distinguished friends discussed European politics, the possible consequences of the "July Monarchy" in France, and the latest gossip from the royal courts of Europe, which he relayed to the Foreign Office as if to convince his superiors that he was no ordinary run-of-the-mill consular appointee.[28]

But as the month of August, 1830, reached its midpoint, the young man pondered the recent circular of July 5 in which Lord Aberdeen had informed that consuls on leave for private purposes were only eligible to receive one-half their pay. This, he thought, was an unreasonable imposition almost amounting "to a sentence," especially for an officer whose health had broken down in the line of duty. He pleaded with John Bidwell to present the facts of his case to Lord Aberdeen, so that an exception might be made.[29]

Actually, the consul was grasping for straws to stay at Aix la Chapelle, and he perhaps suspected this. If the Foreign Office could be nagged into making an exception of his case, his strategy would then be to plead for an extension of his leave — anything, so that he would not have to go back to the miserable port of Memel for another winter.[30] But what would he do if Aberdeen's decision were unfavorable? Would he actually return to Memel, or should he give up his career in the foreign service? If he did so, what would his parents say and what else could he do? These were some of the questions and thoughts tormenting young Chatfield as the month of August waned.

It is one of those quirks of history that a disfigured face brought *this* Englishman to Aix la Chapelle at one of the key moments in Europe's colorful annals. A disfigured face on some other Englishman might not have had any meaning at all.

---

27. To Bidwell, No. 7, November 18, 1830, F.O. 64/165; to Bidwell, pvt., January 16, 1831, F.O. 64/176.
28. To Bidwell, No. 10, October 7, 1830, F.O. 64/165.
29. To Bidwell, pvt./conf., August 15, 1830, F.O. 64/165.
30. To Bidwell, October 10, 1830, F.O. 64/165.

CHAPTER ONE

The Upstart Spy

This claim is utterly inadmissible. Mr. C. was thanked for what was supposed to be Zeal for the service that prompted him to communicate what he conceived to be important information. . . . But when Mr. C. converts this request into a command and founds upon his compliance a claim to pecuniary remuneration I can only say that if it be consistent with Mr. C.'s feelings to make such a demand it is not consistent with my duty to support it.[1]
—Sir George Shee, February 1, 1831

The people of Aix la Chapelle scurried into the streets to hear the electrifying news from Belgium in the final days of August, 1830. Speculation was rampant as to the significance of the recent riots and demonstrations in Brussels and elsewhere, and interpretations differed according to one's political leanings, hopes, or fears. Some chose to regard the uprisings as the first stage of Belgian independence from Holland; others questioned whether the economic and political grievances of the Belgians were serious enough for such a step. Prince Auguste of Prussia, who had been in Brussels when the trouble started, told Frederick Chatfield that it was just the action of a "drunken disorganised mob" rather than "a revolution headed by persons instigated by the hope of gaining some specific object."[2]

On Monday morning, August 30, young Frederick recorded his first impressions of the Belgian uprisings, relying heavily upon his royal source. Though Prince Auguste preferred to think that there was no genuine revolution in progress, perhaps from fear of the consequences, the facts in Chatfield's dispatch seem to indicate otherwise. At Vervier, a large manufacturing town near the Prussian border, great destruction of property had taken place; the chief families had escaped with their lives, leaving their homes to be pillaged by the rabble. The ominous news, from the Prussian point of view, was that the working people of Eussen, on Prussia's side of the border, had marched to the aid of their associates at Vervier, "and upon their arrival as if by magic every one appeared decorated with a Tricolor Cockade in the french or the National Colour." Was France again determined to reach the Rhine, her "natural frontiers," by promoting social upheaval? Was she thus capitalizing upon wide-

---

1. Marginal note by George Shee, February 1, 1831, in Chatfield to Bidwell, pvt., January 24, 1831, F.O. 64/176.
2. To Bidwell, August 30, 1830, F.O. 64/165.

9

spread unemployment and discontent among the Belgians, as well as among the Rhenish subjects of Prussia, many of whom still cherished their former connections with France? No one could say as yet, but Prussian officials were apprehensive that the contagion might spread into their territory.

It would seem that Prussian fears were justified, for at six o'clock on Monday afternoon the English informant added a postscript to his first dispatch in which he announced the riots that had just taken place in Aix la Chapelle. Incited by agents from Vervier and Eussen, the "common people" of Aix la Chapelle poured through the streets crying for work, destroying the property of "persons supposed to be obnoxious to their interests," and trying to force the prison.[3] Frightened by this challenge from the workers, the principal burghers took up arms in defense of the government; and after a few well-aimed shots at the ringleaders, the masses dispersed. More than one hundred and fifty persons were arrested for their part in the melee, while the burgher force continued to patrol the city and remained armed until the arrival of troops from Coblentz.[4] There was no question now what Prussia's strategy would be; she would amass an army of observation on the frontier to prevent the revolution from spilling over into the Rhenish Provinces. She would not, however, interfere openly in "the affairs of the Netherlands." Young Chatfield had learned this in a twenty-minute conversation with Prince William, brother of the King of Prussia.[5]

———◆◆◆———

As the British consul sent home the eye-witness reports of the disturbances in the vicinity of Aix la Chapelle, he sensed immediately that here was his chance to play a significant political role. Through his contacts with the Prussian Court, and especially the military, he could inform London of Prussian policy, troop movements, and the attitudes of the Rhenish people toward the Belgian revolution. And he thoroughly enjoyed his self-appointed task: "I write slovenly and bad on purpose," he told Bidwell with boyish glee at this God-sent opportunity for cloak-and-dagger work.[6] Not satisfied with hearsay reports on military movements, the British spy went on a personal inspection tour of the cities along the Rhine in late September and early October, 1830; he reported his findings to the Foreign Office. One important conclusion of this tour was

---

3. *Ibid.*
4. To Bidwell, Nos. 3-4, September 1, 6, 1830, F.O. 64/165.
5. To Bidwell, No. 6, September 13, 1830, F.O. 64/165.
6. To Bidwell, No. 7, sec., September 8, 1830, F.O. 64/165.

that the Rhineland, though it had grievances toward Prussia, was not yet ready or ripe for revolution.[7]

During the month of October and the first half of November, the unofficial observer continued to send military intelligence to the Foreign Office in which he emphasized more and more Belgian events near the Prussian border, especially the attack upon Maestricht.[8] Again, dissatisfied with the passive role of reporting hearsay evidence, Chatfield, in the company of an ex-minister of Prussia, embarked upon his second tour, this time to Brussels where the revolutionary congress was about to meet. On the way he noted conditions at Liege, the hunger of the common people there, typical village scenes with a decorated tree of liberty and a speaker "haranguing the curious ones," the "spirit of restlessness" at Louvain, and all facts which might conceivably have military importance. On November 18, he arrived in Brussels and remained there for ten days — a key period in the nationhood of Belgium. Through friends of his in the Belgian congress, young Chatfield was able to attend the sessions of the 18th, when the delegates voted unanimously to declare "The Belgian nation independent."[9] The unnoticed Englishman sat quietly through many of the sessions of this important congress, taking special notes on the extemporaneous remarks which he claimed were usually distorted in the journals or were not included in the proceedings. Undoubtedly, it was the remarks attributed to Van de Weyer and de Celles, men with whom the Foreign Office would have to deal in the complicated Belgian question, that first attracted attention to Chatfield's dispatches and prompted Foreign Secretary Palmerston to encourage further reports from the young consul.

As Chatfield described the momentous events which marked the birth of the Belgian nation, his choice of adjectives and quotations revealed an unsympathetic observer. Especially disturbing to him was the strong sentiment in the congress for union with France. "It is then that we would plant the three-coloured Flag, symbol of liberty, upon all the thrones that have believed themselves able to parcel off the people like herds," he paraphrased an impassioned orator. "Let Crowned heads reflect upon this," the speaker continued, "it is not our fate which will be decided but theirs."[10] When Mr. Rodenbach presented his "injudicious and outrageous" motion for the perpetual exclusion of the Orange dynasty, Van de Weyer and de Celles got up and spoke strongly in favor of "Exclu-

7. To Bidwell, No. 10, October 7, 1830, F.O. 64/165.
8. Dispatches for October 10, 14, and November 1, 1830, F.O. 64/165.
9. To Bidwell, November 18-19, 1830, F.O. 64/165.
10. *Ibid.,* in portion written on Friday, November 19, 1830.

sion." They railed against European intervention in Belgian affairs, and Van de Weyer's words on this were: "I assert notwithstanding all intervention has been disavowed by the Great Powers, that a secret, concealed, underhanded (*secrete, sourde, sous-main*) intervention exists."[11] It was "out of the question," the revolutionary continued, to consider the Prince of Orange for the Belgian throne. At this point, Chatfield noted disdainfully that Van de Weyer "indulged in some unbecoming remarks" about the royal family of Holland. Belgians should choose their own prince, he exhorted the congress with emotion, for was it proper for the world to believe the erroneous idea "that amongst a Nation of Belgians, no one could be found capable and worthy of being chosen to the chief authority?" De Celles' remarks were even more objectionable since he spoke undisguisedly in behalf of union with France. Chatfield warned that he had submitted these observations "to save a surprise, for if it be correct that Mr. de Celles has substantial grounds for serving France in particular, it is clear that in his quality of member of the diplomatic commission no communication can be made, that will not speedily find its way toward France into French Councils." The consul concluded with these words: "The inclinations towards France in the Congress, and the acknowledged imitation of its institutions in the framing of their own merits the deepest attention."[12]

Upon returning to Aix la Chapelle at the end of November, 1830, the self-appointed observer continued his evaluation of the political scene in Belgium. In his opinion, an articulate minority, by appealing to the emotions and the patriotism of the Belgians, had made it impossible to return to the former connection with Holland. Thus moderates, who preferred the candidacy of the Prince of Orange for the Belgian throne, were helpless against the swelling tide for independence. They admitted to Chatfield that rather than support independence, which would not bring them one fourth the commercial protection they had enjoyed under Holland, they would choose the lesser of two evils — union with France, even though it was distasteful to them. "I do not wish to appear an alarmist," Chatfield cautioned on November 30, "but I have good reason to believe notwithstanding any assurances that France may please to give to the contrary, that she is not displeased at the disposition which Belgium is reduced to manifest in her favour." Unless the moderates and their candidate, the Prince of Orange, received support from some quarter, Belgium would become French:

11. To Bidwell, November 30, 1830, F.O. 64/165.
12. *Ibid.*

If such an event occurs, I conceive it my duty frankly to state my opinion, humble as it is, that it would be hailed as a signal to the Prussian Provinces to rise; within the past few week's the sentiments of the people here and in the vicinity of Coblentz, have undergone a material change. I do not speak merely of the lower classes but mean the generality of the substantial Bourgeois — those that formerly belonged to France begin seriously to contemplate the possibility of a change, they direct their views to the country, and do not always care to dissemble their sentiments. No one refuses to do justice to the benevolent intentions of the King, nor to the Prudence and sagacity which characterise for the most part his measures, but they allege, that in their actual state without a guarantee for the future, they hold no security against oppression and misrule by a succeeding sovereign.[13]

The analysis of the 30th, based upon two months of intensive research and intelligence work in the field, revealed Chatfield's capacity and techniques as a political analyst. In effect, he was suggesting this policy to Lord Palmerston: France and French influence had to be stopped at all costs by supporting the candidacy of the Prince of Orange and the moderates' position in Belgian politics. This group came closer to representing the wishes of the majority, or more exactly, what Frederick Chatfield felt the majority of Belgians *should* want since it also served the best interests of England.

How much Lord Palmerston was directly influenced by his secret correspondent, it is difficult to say. Palmerston did not abandon the candidacy of Leopold of Saxe-Coburg until January, 1831, and then, for a brief period, supported the Prince of Orange. One thing is definitely certain; Chatfield's recommendation preceded that of Lord Ponsomby from Brussels in December and January. Conceivably Ponsomby's support of the same course of action, and for identical reasons, may have convinced Palmerston that Chatfield's suggestion was meritorious.[14]

Once he persuaded himself that England should interfere in Belgian affairs to stop France, Chatfield's subsequent dispatches hammered away at the need for intervention. One way to prove this was to stress the weakness of the provisional government of Belgium, which thus made it susceptible to French influence. In his dispatches he pointed out the government's inability to collect taxes because Belgians had no confidence in it as well as the lack of "national enthusiasm" in Belgium despite all efforts to convince the world to the contrary.[15] Incident after incident

---

13. *Ibid.*
14. For a discussion of the January decision, see Charles Webster, *The Foreign Policy of Palmerston: 1830–1841* (2 vols., London, 1951), I, 122–123.
15. To Shee, No. 13, March 16, 1831, F.O. 64/176.

proved these generalizations and underscored the urgency of intervention.[16] From the "least violent of the public provincial prints," Chatfield extracted quotations reflecting Belgian discontent with Louis Philippe's refusal to permit his son to occupy the throne of Belgium; they attributed this to the intrigues of England and Holland, both determined to prevent France from realizing her "natural frontiers — the Rhine." "These observations it is true," a worried Chatfield added, "emanate from persons not in power, but should any thing occur to bring the Republican Party into office, they may perhaps be regarded as the creed upon which they would act."[17]

From this last quotation as well as his strong Dutch leanings, it might be assumed that Chatfield's politics were extremely conservative. With regard to the threat of social revolution in the Rhenish Provinces, he remarked once: "I sincerely hope that every possible precaution will be adopted by the Prussian Government to prevent the possibility of disaffection breaking out in the ranks, for in the actual posture of affairs, it would grieve those who wish well to established governments, and who dread anarchy and democracy, to see troubles commence in this country."[18] Yet the assumption concerning his political outlook is more apparent than real. Chatfield was no more conservative or reactionary than Lord Palmerston, who was also accused of being a disguised Tory, an insincere liberal, or a hypocrite for some of the stands he would take. Both men — it must be remembered — were ENGLISHMEN, whose alignment on a particular issue would depend upon how it would affect the interests of their country. It was this policy of "expediency" which made Palmerston so controversial. The same might be said about the unknown Frederick Chatfield.

An expanded France, pretending to be the champion of the new liberalism astir throughout Europe, constituted a real danger for England; and in this respect, Great Britain had much in common with the autocratic powers of Europe. This was the message that young Chatfield was sending home to Lord Palmerston in the reports concerning the revolutionary ferment in the Rhenish Provinces of Prussia. He kept the Foreign Office informed of public opinion in the cities of the Rhineland, the size and nature of the troop movements, and especially the great danger of defection among the conscriptees of the Rhenish Landwehr.[19] Prussia

---

16. To Bidwell, December 9, 27, 1830, F.O. 64/165; to Shee, No. 11, February 27, 1831, F.O. 64/176.
17. *Ibid.*
18. *Ibid.*
19. To Bidwell, November 30, December 9, 27, 1830, F.O. 64/165; to Shee, No. 12, March 3, 1831, F.O. 64/176.

was indeed worried: on her western flank there were the Belgian uprisings; and on her eastern flank, the Polish rebellion erupted in late November, 1830, and soon spread to the northern Russian-Polish provinces of
Lithuania and Samogitia. It almost seemed that the wild-eyed orator in
the Belgian Congress, whom Chatfield quoted in an earlier dispatch, had
spoken prophetically. Perhaps — and this was the suggestion emerging
from Chatfield's analysis — England might take advantage of the autocrats' distress to shackle France, save the Belgian situation from getting
out of hand, and at the same time prepare the ground for England's
leadership as the savior of Europe and the champion of a safe liberalism.
But, Chatfield hinted in March, 1831, the British government had to act
swiftly for "there is every reason to believe, that as soon as the Polish
movement is quelled, the Russians, Prussians, and Austrians will decide
upon interfering to settle the confusion which exists in Belgium so much
to the prejudice of all Europe."[20]

As Lord Palmerston read the lengthy and well-documented dispatches from his secret correspondent in western Prussia, he must have
been impressed with the knowledge, the insights, and the grasp of the
overall picture which they reflected. And there was little that escaped
the attention of that aggressive observer. On another trip through Belgium, for example, young Frederick conversed with a certain general
whose services, he later reported to the Foreign Office, could be bought
by England if she chose to use him.[21] With regard to Liege's resistance
to Leopold's candidacy — at that time England's choice for the Belgian
throne — the indefatigable Chatfield wrote a twenty-four page memorandum on the economic bases for that opposition.[22]

———◆·◆———

Although he undoubtedly impressed the Foreign Office with his
ability to acquire and interpret intelligence, Chatfield's superiors were
less pleased with some of his personal characteristics, namely, his arrogance, conceit, and aggressiveness. In this too he resembled Lord Palmerston but with a significant difference. His subordinate position did
not lend itself to such luxuries of individuality.

The news received from the Foreign Office in January, 1831, was
music to the consul's ears. Viscount Palmerston, who only recently had
replaced Lord Aberdeen as secretary of state for foreign affairs, enjoyed

---

20. To Shee, No. 13, March 16, 1831, F.O. 64/176.
21. Reference was to General Van Halen; see, to Shee, April 14, 1831, and
    April 17, 1831, F.O. 64/176.
22. To Shee, No. 28, May 26, 1831, with mem. enclosed, F.O. 64/176.

perusing Chatfield's dispatches and urged him to continue forwarding important political information to London. Moreover, on January 4, he received instructions to send his reports directly to Sir George Shee, the under secretary of state and Palmerston's close friend. And on the 6th, John Bidwell wrote privately to Chatfield intimating that he might expect to receive full pay for his work, despite Lord Aberdeen's refusal to make him an exception to the half-pay dictum for consuls on leave. These were all gratifying indications that the new master in the Foreign Office was one who recognized talent and would not resort to the cheeseparing policies which had disappointed the young consul in previous years. Could he not infer from Palmerston's approval of December 23 that his work was considered "on service" and that therefore he was eligible to draw his full salary? If this was true, it followed that he would not have to return to that dreadful post at Memel. The facts seemed to indicate the validity of this inference, at least to young Frederick; and so, without waiting for a formal confirmation from the Foreign Office, he drew his salary for the last quarter of 1830.[23]

Once again on the pay roll thanks to his own initiative, Chatfield's next step was to convince his superiors of the propriety of his actions in this matter. On January 24, 1831, the over-confident agent wrote to Bidwell explaining how he had arrived at the "inference." Moreover, to assure himself that the Foreign Office would keep him at Aix la Chapelle, he added rather shamelessly: "Unless I felt certain of being able at the present moment even in an unofficial character to render more service here, than I could hope to do at Memel, I should be reluctant to propose remaining where I am, but the geographical situation of Memel as I have often had cause to regret, totally prevents a superintendence of anything beyond the mere mercantile interests of traders resorting to the Port." Besides, "without intending to arrogate praise to myself," the regulations which he had enacted at Memel for the protection of British subjects "are so clearly understood, that but little caution is now requisite to maintain their due observance."[24] When Sir George Shee read this request on February 1, he scribbled his sharp reaction in the margins of the letter — the self-evident quotation which introduces this chapter. Mr. C. had to be taught a lesson in humility; the honorable baronet would not be dictated to by a subordinate, no matter how valuable or brilliant he might be.

Unmindful of Shee's response to his request, young Frederick sought an interview with him in mid-March, 1831, when he returned

---

23. To Bidwell, pvt., April 17, 1831, F.O. 64/176.
24. To Bidwell, pvt., January 24, 1831, F.O. 64/176.

to London because of illness in the family. Unfortunately, no record remains of this meeting between Sir George and the unofficial English spy; but it is safe to say that some unpleasant truths were cited to Mr. C., who suffered his first encounter with a Palmerstonian Foreign Office. It apparently did not differ from its predecessors. The best Sir George could do for him was to refer his request for full salary to Lord Palmerston himself, but at the same time he assured the consul that it would be forwarded without his blessings. Chatfield's lengthy and "unconnected" letter of March 16 tells a graphic story of the verbal lashing he had received at the interview with Sir George. With unaccustomed humility — in some sections, at least — the young man pleaded his case before "Old Pam." He explained his perhaps mistaken "inference" of Palmerston's remarks of December 23, but he humbly beseeched His Lordship to keep in mind his outstanding work at Memel, ferreting out valuable political information at his own expense, etc. As he wrote, the young consul regained confidence in himself and began to discuss the general political situation in Europe, urging this or that action and pointing out how important it was for England to have a capable observer on the Belgian-Prussian border. Throughout the hodgepodge, he sprinkled pleas not to deduct his salary.[25]

Though Sir George had visibly shaken him, Frederick Chatfield was not the type of person who could be kept down for long. A perennial optimist, he dared hope that Lord Palmerston might overrule George Shee. With stubbornness and resiliency of character, especially when he was convinced his cause was just, he bounced back at his superiors by devoting himself wholeheartedly to his espionage work as if nothing had happened. He seemed possessed, almost vindictively, with the desire to prove his superiors wrong and ungrateful for having rejected his just claims. Back in Aix la Chapelle, he wrote privately to John Bidwell and applied pressure upon him to influence Palmerston's verdict:

> I am so situated in regard to my family, that I cannot possibly solicit their intervention to relieve the embarrassment a deduction will occasion me; my father's advanced age (upwards of 82) precludes the possibility of naming money matters to him, and although I am sure to be placed some day in a situation beyond the reach of temporary annoyances, or inconvenience, and with power to reciprocate favours conferred by friends — I frankly confess that at this moment, I shall suffer great embarrassment by losing half my allowance.

Then, he subtly reminded Bidwell, "I did not, nor shall not, without

---

25. To Shee, No. 13, March 16, 1831, F.O. 64/176.

your concurrence allude in any way to the private letter you wrote me on January 6th last."[26] That was the letter in which John Bidwell had hinted — prematurely as it turned out — that Chatfield might expect to collect his full salary.

On April 19, Lord Palmerston passed judgment on the consul's salary request. In his opinion, there was "no substantial reason" for making Mr. Chatfield an exception to the half-pay ruling.[27] When this indifferent verdict reached Aix la Chapelle, Mary Chatfield's pampered son exploded, overwhelmed with anger. Unable to contain himself any longer, he felt that he had to write to Bidwell and that he had to tell Shee and Palmerston what ingrates they were. In no mood to blame himself for having acted impetuously in drawing his salary, his distraught mind sought out a scapegoat — John Bidwell: "Under the circumstances of my case, I cannot but feel this resolution to be the most harsh towards me; and but a poor return for the expense and inconvenience I have proved that I have incurred, by a zealous wish to spare no effort towards furthering the service of my office." And all this trouble and inconvenience, he hinted viciously, stemmed from "the non fulfillment of promises." So that the barb could not fail to hit its mark, the angry consul added, "It is with no slight pain that I find myself compelled to seek favour in respect to money matters, which I am little in the habit of doing, and should not do now, if I had known last January as much as at present."[28]

With venom still in his pen, Lieutenant Chatfield pointed it at his superiors on April 29; Lord Palmerston picked up his weapon on May 15. "I do think," the arrogant underling noted, "that the letters I have received fairly admit the inference, that it was *intended** my absence should be considered on service." Palmerston underlined the word "intended," placed an asterisk beside it, and then commented laconically: "Evidently by him but not by me." Then the furious consul expressed an opinion concerning the department's economy measures and how they worked hardships upon deserving men who hated to be placed on the level of begging for money. "But I must here take leave to observe," he blustered, *that it is much beyond my humble means to continue to make the sacrifices I have, and which I believe few individuals similarly placed think of practising,* now that I find such very

---

26. To Bidwell, pvt./conf., April 14, 1831, F.O. 64/176.
27. From Bidwell, No. 1, April 19, 1831, F.O. 64/176.
28. To Bidwell, pvt., April 28, 1831, F.O. 64/176.

rigid and scrupulous economy brought to bear upon myself." After underlining the major portion of this threat, Palmerston sallied with the question: "Who ever desired him to do so?"[29]

It would be interesting to know what impressions Lord Palmerston formed of the young consul as he read the fiery dispatch. The spirit and style of the prose was strikingly similar to his; the man obviously had talent of the type needed in his department; but the young upstart had to learn his place at the bottom rung of the diplomatic ladder. When he learned some humility, there would be time enough to consider his promotion.

Contrary to what one might expect, Chatfield did not abandon his espionage work nor did he return immediately to Memel. In fact, the lengthy economic memorandum on Liege was written almost a month after dispatching the angry note to London. Nor was his confidence shaken by the unfavorable decision. Quite the contrary, on May 19, the nervy consul made another proposal to the Foreign Office. For some time, he wrote, rumors had circulated throughout Europe that a Congress of Plenipotentiaries would meet at Aix la Chapelle to discuss the Belgian question. Prince Nicholas Esterhazy had virtually confirmed these reports when he passed through Aix la Chapelle on the 18th. In the belief that this intelligence was correct, Frederick Chatfield desired Lord Palmerston to know that he would willingly assist "the personage selected to represent His Majesty upon this occasion, in any character, consistent with the office I now hold, which it may please His Lordship to appoint." Among his qualifications, he listed: "my long acquaintance with the whole court at Cologne," the consideration "I enjoy with the military and civil authorities here, and the local knowledge I possess."[30] Nothing came of this brazen request, for Lord Palmerston would not hear of a meeting place other than in England. But how long could such ambition be kept down?

———◄●►———

The amazing Mr. Chatfield, however, was as much a realist as he was a perennial optimist. He had understood Shee correctly in the March interview and had anticipated Palmerston's rejection. The angry outburst, in short, was not due to surprise but to his own stubbornness and conceit. Before departing from London, young Frederick had begun preparations for his return to Memel. Since the Board of Trade was the main obstacle to his recommendations concerning the direct registration

---

29. To Shee, No. 21, April 29, 1831, F.O. 64/176.
30. To Shee, No. 26, pvt./sep., May 19, 1831, F.O. 64/176.

of British shipmasters, he personally interviewed Lord Auckland and apparently impressed him so with his arguments that Chatfield was asked to draw up a memorandum on the subject.[31] At the same time, the consul badgered the Foreign Office to secure the cooperation of Prussian authorities on this measure.[32] He also suggested that the jurisdiction of the Memel consulate be extended to Tilsit, on the new post road from St. Petersburg to Berlin, and that he be allowed to appoint a vice consul there.[33] If the Foreign Office wanted him to return to Memel, it should help to make the position respectable.

Actually, the idea of returning to the Baltic post was no longer abhorent to young Chatfield. Not only could he collect his full salary there, but, more importantly, the Memel consulate now lent itself to the political role which he loved so much. The Polish uprisings had spread to the nearby provinces of Samogitia and Lithuania and, as if this were not enough, a cholera epidemic had started in Russia and was threatening to cross over into Prussia. With events such as these transpiring in the vicinity of Memel, how could he miss keeping his name before his superiors? It occurred to him, furthermore, that he need not wait for Lord Auckland's decision on the British shipmasters or upon the slow channel of communications from London to Berlin — the cholera epidemic was a godsend for his campaign to enhance the prestige of the Memel consulate. On May 30, 1831, just before leaving Aix la Chapelle, he cleverly suggested that all British masters coming from Memel be required "to produce a certificate under my hand of the state of health at Memel and in Prussian Lithuania . . . at the time of their departure."[34] When he reached Berlin on June 12, he discussed this measure with a Prussian minister who assured him that his country would cooperate in its enforcement.[35] Before receiving formal approval from the Foreign Office, therefore, Chatfield had already subjected English shipmasters to his authority. By putting his suggestion on a patriotic basis — to prevent the spread of cholera to England — the consul succeeded where logic and reason had failed.[36] He had learned an important lesson in dealing with the Palmerstonian Foreign Office, one which he did not forget.

On the afternoon of June 20, a Russian steamboat docked at the port of Memel, bearing no less a personage than Field Marshal Ivan

31. To Shee, No. 15, April 1, 1831, p. encl.s, F.O. 64/176.
32. *Ibid.*
33. To Shee, No. 13, March 16, 1831, F.O. 64/176.
34. To Bidwell, No. 29, May 30, 1831, F.O. 64/176.
35. To Shee, No. 30, June 12, 1831; to Palmerston, No. 47, July 19, 1831, F.O. 64/176.
36. To Bidwell, No. 32, June 26, 1831, F.O. 64/176.

Paskevich, the celebrated conqueror of Persia and the new commander of the Russian army in Poland. With customary ease, Frederick Chatfield struck up a friendship with the famous Paskevich by informing him that in Berlin he had been told that Prussian authorities would permit the flow of supplies via the Vistula to the Russian forces in Poland.[37] In return, the grateful field marshal took the consul into his confidence, discussed the errors of his predecessor in Poland, and announced his plans for ending the insurrection. As Chatfield thought about the information he had given the Russian leader, however, it occurred to him that it was a serious mistake to permit Russian goods to pass through Prussian territory. Much of Paskevich's equipment, he noted, had been in Persia, where it was believed the cholera germ had originated, and through infected portions of southern Russia.[38] If Russians were to be made exceptions to the cholera regulations, he reasoned, the sanitary cordon all along the Prussian frontier and the burdensome regulations on the movement of persons near the infected areas were all useless. "At this moment," Chatfield wrote on July 5, "the whole of the Samogitian frontier on the Russian side is infested with the cholera, and it is remarkable that wherever the filthy, illfed, neglected Russian soldier passes the disease is left behind."[39]

It distressed the English consul to think that for political reasons Prussia might gamble with the health of her subjects and — what was even worse — that of all Europe. No wonder the epidemic spilled over the border in July, 1831, and in early August hit the port of Memel, where people died by the scores. As one of Chatfield's servants came down with the disease, the young Englishman wondered apprehensively when it would strike him. In the meantime, he kept the Foreign Office informed of the epidemic's course with detailed statistics on deaths, the effectiveness of various medical measures, and all information concerning the nature of the malady. Again, the Foreign Office had an able observer in the field, whose dispatches were extracted and circulated to other departments of government in London. So important did they consider Chatfield's reports on the cholera and the political events occurring in the area that in July he was instructed to write directly to Lord Palmerston.[40]

By August 27, 1831, the cholera crisis was beginning to subside in eastern Prussia, and young Frederick — always disposed to interpret in

---

37. To Shee, No. 31, June 22, 1831, F.O. 64/176.
38. To Shee, No. 32, June 25, 1831, F.O. 64/176.
39. To Shee, No. 38, July 5, 1831, F.O. 64/176.
40. To Bidwell, June 4, 1832, F.O. 65/202.

grandiose lines the events he had the fortune to witness — offered Lord
Palmerston a "humble" analysis of the disease and how best to protect
oneself from it. "The surest preservatives," he told Palmerston, "are
contained within ourselves, and may be found in our 'morale.' I am convinced that the state of mind has great power either to accelerate the
reception of the disorder, or to aid in rejecting it entirely." The experience at a small place like Memel had confirmed this conclusion:

> no death has yet occurred which may not be traced either to in-
> temperance and incaution, or to a nervous dread of taking the
> disease — a readiness to consider a prognostick, every trifling twinge
> or imaginary pain, which at any other time would not be cared for;
> in consequence to remain at home in bed taking medicines unneces-
> sarily, awaiting a real attack; and to change of a sudden previous
> habits are alone sufficient to superinduce an attack, and have al-
> ready been the means of largely adding to the number of victims.

His own survival demonstrated the validity of this analysis since
"the very indisposition for which it became advisable I should drink the
waters of Aix la Chapelle last season proves that the internal organization of my body peculiarly predisposes me to the cholera morbus, which
shews itself in a derangement of the functions of the lower stomach."
The best defense against the dreaded disease, therefore, was self disci-
pline, mental control, exercise, and common sense observance of cleanli-
ness.[41] Whatever the merits of this medical interpretation, few doctors
today would disagree with Chatfield's suggestions as, at least, the minimum standards for control of the disease. It may have been mere coincidence that the consul's life was spared on two occasions — in 1831 and
in 1837, while serving in Central America — but Chatfield, at any rate
attributed it to his own diagnosis of the disease.

In addition to the cholera intelligence, Lord Palmerston received
valuable reports from Memel on the progress of the Polish insurrection
in Samogitia and Lithuania. Judging from the nature of the military
information sent to London by the ex-Life Guard, Prussian and Russian
military men were not very security conscious, or else they had been
convinced by the sly English Lieutenant that he was sympathetic to their
cause — an impression which he tried to cultivate. Paskevich told him
that General Diebitsch's mistakes in Samogitia and Lithuania had pro-
longed the war by keeping five of Russia's best corps and ablest generals in the north, thus weakening the effort in Poland proper. He would
not repeat his predecessor's error. At whatever the cost, Paskevich was

---

41. To Palmerston, No. 70, August 27, 1831, F.O. 64/176.

determined to wipe out the Poles once and for all.[42] From General Man-
derstierna, Chatfield learned of the surprising strength and courage of
the Polish army, how Polish peasants had facilitated General Dembin-
ski's maneuvers in the midst of overwhelming Russian forces, and about
the low morale of Russian generals, who realized that they had little to
gain by defeating the puny adversary and much to lose if they were defeated.[43] It was clear to young Chatfield, however, that with Prussian support and the determined leadership of Field Marshal Paskevich the
Polish revolution was doomed to failure.

The effects of Paskevich's strategy in the north were not long in
manifesting themselves. In early July, 1831, a demoralized Polish force
appeared on the Prussian border, severely beaten and without ammunition and supplies. For months and with the support of the peasantry in
the northern provinces, generals Chlapowski and Geilgud had successfully disrupted the enemy's rear and had prevented the flow of supplies
overland to the Russian forces in Poland. But the situation changed
abruptly with the recent reverses in the field. The only hope left was to
seek asylum in Prussia and somehow or another get the men back to
Poland for the final battle. On July 12, 1831, the Polish generals were
on the border, alarmed at the bitterness of their troops and debating
whether or not to cross the line into Prussia. When the British consul
heard of their presence only a few miles from Memel, he hurriedly
mounted his horse and rode off to witness the historical spectacle.

"I have to regret," he noted with excitement, "that my feeble powers
of writing will not allow me to do justice to the remarkable scene which
in part passed under my own eyes." Despite this unaccustomed modesty,
young Chatfield successfully captured the spirit of the moment, the
desperation of the Polish forces, and the anxiety of the small Prussian
force — forty Landwehr lancers and one officer, "who were called upon
to take charge of upwards of four thousand highly excited and infuriated
men." Only half of the troops had crossed the narrow footpath, which
marked the boundary between Prussia and Russia, and none of them
was willing to obey General Geilgud's orders to put down their arms.
Angry and mutinous voices shouted disrespectful epithets and accused
Geilgud of betraying them to the Russians and of deliberately planning
the defeats of the last few days. Why should they obey his orders? They
would listen only to General Chlapowski and providing the Prussians
guaranteed that they would not be turned over to the hated Russians.
The situation was tense and foreboding. Chlapowski appealed to the men

---

42. To Shee, No. 46, July 16, 1831, F.O. 64/176.
43. To Shee, No. 32, June 25, 1831, F.O. 64/176.

and some listened; the Prussians gave vague assurances; but that was not enough. The clamor for blood heightened; and on July 13, General Geilgud was brutally murdered by his men.[44] This act of desperation, this deed of bitterness, recorded graphically what everyone there sensed in his heart: the Polish Revolution was nearing its end. Prussia would never allow these Poles to join their army at Warsaw.

As Frederick Chatfield watched the negotiations between Chlapowski and the Prussians drag on to their logical conclusion — the internment of the Polish prisoners — he could appreciate that Prussia's best interests lay in cooperation with Russia. The Poles with their wild ideas and revolutionary nature, if permitted to form a nation, would not only block Russia in Europe but also prove to be a dangerous neighbor for Prussia. Despite his personal admiration for such men as General Chlapowski, the young Englishman believed that the Poles were not ready for independence.[45] His sense of justice and humanity, however, cried out against the Prussian treatment of the Poles and the obvious partiality shown to the Russians. He noted disdainfully how the authorities, at the bidding of the Russians, had tried to confiscate notes of the Polish National Bank in General Chlapowski's possession. On the other hand, a satisfied consul explained how the general had foiled his enemies by refusing to sign the notes, so that they were only worthless pieces of paper.[46] And as Chatfield reported the details of these negotiations to Lord Palmerston, he wondered what Prussia's policy would be in the postwar period. Would she turn over these prisoners to a wrathful Russia, or would she win the praise of the civilized world by pursuing an enlightened policy toward them? Young Frederick naively hoped that the latter would be the case, even though his reports indicated otherwise.

Chatfield's increasing sympathy for the Poles and the wishful thoughts concerning Prussia's future policy reflected a mind groping for a solution to the problems of Europe — a mind torn by a desire to preserve a society he loved and yet painfully aware that it had notable weaknesses, underscored by the recent uprisings. As the Polish revolution ended, he breathed a sigh of relief that the radical solution of uprooting the old order had failed, for he believed that the "Liberalism" of the radicals was visionary and anarchical in its consequences. It assumed that the old order was entirely bad, and this Chatfield could not accept, at least not for England. On the other hand, he found it difficult

---

44. To Shee, No. 46, July 16, 1831, F.O. 64/176.
45. To Palmerston, Nos. 66, 73, 82, August 20, September 2, 13, 1831, F.O. 64/176.
46. To Palmerston, No. 58, August 6, 1831, F.O. 64/176.

to condone the extremist position on the right, predicated on the assumption that there was nothing wrong with the old order and that it should be maintained unaltered and by brute force if need be. It was abundantly clear to the British consul that Russia, at least, would follow the latter course; unfortunately, she might succeed in persuading her Prussian ally to do likewise.[47] But this solution, he reasoned, was as productive of evil as the radical's program, for he could not conceive of a system of repression which would absolutely eradicate the challenge to the old order. Even if such a system were possible, it would be inhumane and hardly a credit to the civilization of nineteenth-century Europe.

Like Palmerston and other Englishmen of his day, who countenanced the Reform Bill of 1832, Frederick Chatfield believed that the wisest policy was to grant limited concessions to the challengers of the old system in order to preserve the way of life he loved. Undoubtedly, the obstacles were much greater on the Continent than in England, but he was convinced that essentially the same approach should be followed. Commenting on a widely-held hope of the radicals, Chatfield wrote: "Civilization and humanity could not but gain by a change in the Russian system, yet it is preferable that the people should be endebted for an amelioration of their position to wise and moderate acts of legislation rather than to the passing of the country through the ordeal of anarchy and Revolution — by some the shortest path is considered the best."[48] With regard to the Poles, "the most merciful if not in the end the most politic course" for Russia to follow would be to grant a general pardon because, the consul reasoned: "Recourse to vindictive measures by wantonly bereaving hundreds of families of parents and friends would tend to exasperate the excitement, which every method should be adopted to allay." "There is small doubt," he concluded, "that the excessive dread of the consequences in the event of the Russians recovering their full power in Poland, had materially contributed to encourage the extraordinary resistance we have witnessed."[49]

Russia, however, was in no mood to take into account the enlightened views of the British consul at Memel, and as he realized this his dislike for the Russians increased. On October 8, 1831, he reported to Palmerston the ruthless measures that had been taken in Samogitia, where even the "humble, half civilized peasants" were placed under suspicion. When they naively expressed the hope that England and France would help to achieve liberty for their province, they were flogged and

47. To Palmerston, Nos. 82, 86, September 13, 24, 1831, F.O. 64/176.
48. To Palmerston, No. 106, November 18, 1831, F.O. 64/176.
49. To Palmerston, No. 86, September 24, 1831, F.O. 64/176.

cautioned to keep their mouths shut. Such actions were uncalled for and "inflame needlessly that rancorous feeling which prevails in the country against musovite oppression." With a little imagination and some reforms calculated to show these peasants that Russia was indeed their mother, she could have gained their unquestioned allegiance. Instead, Russia's policy was one of brute force, of "revengeful excesses," to maintain the status quo — a closed, obscurantist, and exclusivistic society. Rumor had it, moreover, that special commissions were studying the possibility of a mass-removal policy for Poland, calling for the confiscation of estates, the internment of the "most implicated families," and their replacement by loyal Russian families — a devilishly cruel plan to which "the generality of Russians will have but one objection, namely that the sentence is too lenient." [50] On November 18, Chatfield wrote to Lord Palmerston that Russia had begun to implement the removal policy. determined to snuff out "the flame" in Poland. [51]

Clearly, Frederick Chatfield doubted that Mother Russia would lead the way to a peaceful and enlightened world; and he had strong reservations that Prussia could restrain or influence her stubborn ally on the "Polish Question." The only alternative — and young Frederick reached this conclusion very early — was the benevolent intervention and leadership of Great Britain. On August 20, this Palmerstonian consul wrote as follows:

> It does not bely [sic] to me to treat of the immense difficulty that the settlement of the Polish question in any lasting form presents, but I would certainly recommend (should the Russians succeed, and the contrary can scarcely be conceived) that as a *boon* to the Poles, the power of trading with foreign countries across its own borders should be insisted upon; it would be of infinite advantage to *British Industry* and it is a point upon which every Polish proprietor would stand. Prussia for her own sake would hardly be disposed to raise her transit duties, and Russia ought to be prevented throwing difficulties in the way of a free navigation of the inland canals and navigable streams. [52]

Actually, Chatfield first suggested this to Bidwell on July 7, and then directly to Lord Palmerston on July 19, when he indicated the type of reciprocal trade program that might work. [53]

This daring policy suggestion was both imaginative and naive. It

---

50. To Palmerston, No. 95, October 8, 1831, F.O. 64/176.
51. To Palmerston, No. 106, November 18, 1831, F.O. 64/176.
52. To Palmerston, No. 66, August 20, 1831, F.O. 64/176.
53. To Bidwell, No. 42, July 7, 1831; to Palmerston, No. 48, July 19, 1831, F.O. 64/176.

was naive in assuming that Russia would cooperate. In many dispatches from Memel, Chatfield himself pointed out Russia's unwillingness to make concessions to her ally Prussia; there was no reason to expect that she would do otherwise for England. Chatfield knew this quite well, but what he really hoped for was that Great Britain would take a strong line toward Russia by forcing her to make these concessions and thus be enlightened despite herself. He also assumed, perhaps incorrectly, that the Poles' major grievance was economic rather than political. That his suggestion might in the long run backfire on Russia and lead to a successful movement for Polish independence did not seem to perturb Mr. Chatfield. In fact, he perhaps secretly counted on this, knowing that his country would stand to benefit from it. These were the ideas and the suggestions of a young Englishman who soon would be chosen as the first British consul to Warsaw.

The tone of Chatfield's letters on the salary question changed markedly when he returned to Memel. At Bidwell's suggestion, he adopted a new approach, applying for an allowance to compensate him for the deductions that had been made in his salary.[54] He no longer blamed Bidwell and the Foreign Office but rather his personal enemy Thomas Fonblanque, the British consul at Königsburg. Major Fonblanque, on the other hand, had wasted no love upon the "inexperienced subaltern," whose appointment to the Memel consulate had considerably reduced the jurisdiction of his own post. When he learned of Chatfield's secret service work at Aix la Chapelle, he complained to the Foreign Office that he should have been chosen for that assignment.[55] On this point, Chatfield commented as follows:

> It is not the first time his inveterate itch for writing has turned to my inconvenience. The grounds of this suspicion are the following: On returning through Berlin one of his nearest friends observed to me that he understood, at first, that my absence from Memel was on service; I asked, suspecting the drift of this remark, whether Fonblanque had told him so, he said no, but that he had written to Fonblanque on the subject, who after receiving a letter from London in answer to some enquiries he had made assured him that such was not the case. From this I infer that he has introduced my

---

54. To Bidwell, pvt., May 29, 1831; to Palmerston, No. 50, July 24, 1831, F.O. 64/176.
55. Thomas Fonblanque to Palmerston, sec., March 20, 1831; *idem* to *idem*, March 28, 1831; Fonblanque to John Backhouse, April 8, June 4, 1831, F.O. 64/177.

name in his public letters; *and that to get rid of his importunities, my fair claims have been sacrificed.* I have no doubt something of this sort has happened, and should I not be deceived I hope some favour will be shown in consideration of the disappointment I have endured and that a recompense will be accorded to me in such a way, as would not be known publickly.[56]

Apparently, Chatfield's inference was well founded. It does not seem likely that the cautious Bidwell could have made the mistake of hinting that the consul might receive remuneration for his work without some assurance from George Shee or Lord Palmerston.

Several questions suggest themselves in connection with the new consulate established at Warsaw. Was this the recompense which Chatfield hoped for, and was he in any way responsible for the establishment of the new post, as he boasted many years later?[57] Though Chatfield answered these questions in the affirmative, it is doubtful that he was correct in either case. There was talk of opening the Warsaw post in early 1831. In fact, Thomas Fonblanque had applied for the position when he wrote to the Foreign Office concerning his rival's activities at Aix la Chapelle. Nor is it probable that Lord Palmerston would choose the consul at Memel for the position just to pay off an old debt, however gratifying this thought might be to Chatfield's ego.

On many occasions, Lord Palmerston averred that the position at Warsaw was commercial and not political in nature. The fact is, however, that there was not enough trade there to justify the appointment of a British consul, unless Palmerston hoped to follow through on Chatfield's suggestions of August 20 to open up Poland's trade. But again, it is doubtful that Palmerston seriously considered adopting the strong line against Russia which was implicit in that recommendation. The only other justification for a commercial agent was to protect the twenty to thirty English families in Warsaw, who might have suffered property losses during the Polish uprisings.

Notwithstanding Palmerston's denials, the political motive figured strongly in the creation of the Warsaw post. In Chatfield's instructions of January 5, 1832, he was told "to furnish His Majesty's Ambassador at St. Petersburg and His Majesty's Minister at Berlin with every information upon matters of political interest which may come to your knowledge, and attend to such instructions as either of them may at any time transmit to you."[58] Ordinarily, these words would fail to carry

---

56. To Bidwell, pvt., October 31, 1831, F.O. 64/176.
57. To Granville, No. 12, March 20, 1852, F.O. 15/77.
58. From Palmerston, No. 1, January 5, 1832, which includes Chatfield's commission of December 31, 1831, F.O. 65/202.

conviction for they could be interpreted as standard instructions to any consul, who in those days served in both a commercial and political capacity. In this case, however, the context is important. Lord Palmerston was well aware of Great Britain's innocuous representation at the royal courts in question: Chad, the English minister at Berlin, was an avowed Tory who sympathized with the Prussian system and Lord Heytesbury was entirely too cautious and willing to please the Russians. Realizing the need for an able and imaginative representative in St. Petersburg, Lord Palmerston shocked the Russian world in April, 1831, with the news that he planned to send Stratford Canning to the Russian capital. Understandably, this report worried Russia. She could not afford to have a man of Canning's ability at her court, snooping, meddling, and reporting every action there to London. The celebrated Prince and Princess Lieven — the toast of London and personal friends of Lord Palmerston — hastened to convince him that Canning's appointment would be a mistake.[59] At this juncture, Palmerston desisted but cleverly held the Canning appointment over Russia's head in order to get her cooperation in Belgian affairs. This was a smart move, but it also had its disadvantages. With no Stratford Canning in St. Petersburg, how could Palmerston know whether the Russians were actually adhering to the Treaty of Vienna, which guaranteed a constitutional government for Poland? It perhaps occurred to Palmerston that he might be able to have his cake and eat it too. By withdrawing Canning's appointment, he could get Russian cooperation in Belgium; and by appointing an unknown Canning to Warsaw, he could get correct political intelligence as well.

Be that as it may, there was no doubt in Mr. Chatfield's mind that his new appointment was political. Elated beyond words that the Foreign Office had finally recognized him, he promised gratefully to dedicate himself to his new position with "zeal and assiduity" in order to justify the faith which Lord Palmerston and Sir George Shee had shown in him. Never one to sell himself short, however, he had some comments to make about the Warsaw post. To begin with, the salary of six hundred pounds was hardly sufficient for Great Britain's representative at the Polish capital. "Such close economy, he told Sir George, would prevent him from "distributing small presents where they may appear useful." Of course, in making these observations, "I have no view but the public service." In other words, Chatfield concluded, "I am requesting to have my hands unfettered for the sake of being enabled to work with more

59. Webster, *Palmerston,* I, pp. 68, 183-184, 196, 320-322.

power and facility." Either the salary should be raised or the Foreign Office should provide him with a substantial expense account. Moreover, since the Warsaw position was clearly political and the representatives of other nations there had higher titles, he suggested that his rank be raised to that of consul-general.[60]

There is reason to believe that this new display of over-confidence did not set well in London. Sir George Shee was slightly miffed when he answered that he was in no way responsible for the Warsaw appointment: "You are indebted for it entirely to Lord Palmerston to whom therefore your thanks should be addressed."[61] When Palmerston read Chatfield's request for more money and a higher title, he made no comments; he merely refused it, except for a minor commitment on postage charges.[62] But when Chatfield proposed to Bidwell that he would like to return to London for a few weeks to discuss minor points in his instructions, Viscount Palmerston took up his pen and wrote in the margins: "Mr. Chatfield is always ready enough to quit his Post. It does not appear necessary for him to come to London. His employment is commercial and not diplomatic."[63]

---

60. To Palmerston, No. 112, December 12, 1831; to Shee, pvt., December 13, 1831, F.O. 64/176.
61. From Shee, pvt., December 27, 1831, F.O. 64/176.
62. From Backhouse, No. 2, January 5, 1832, F.O. 65/202.
63. Note by Lord Palmerston, February 7, 1832, in Chatfield to Bidwell, January 24, 1832, F.O. 65/202.

CHAPTER TWO

Consul and Minister

Exaggeration does not at any time characterise my correspondence.[1]
—Chatfield, May 25, 1832

You appear to have mistaken the nature of your appointment.[1] . . .
You are the British Consul, and not the British Minister at Warsaw.[2]
—John Backhouse, June 20, 1832

As the young consul read His Majesty's commission of December 31, 1831, it thrilled him to be singled out as "Our trusty and well beloved Frederick Chatfield, Esquire," and all because of Lord Palmerston's "most flattering and kind recommendation of me." Aware of the delicate nature of his assignment, he promised to be neutral in the momentous political events that would soon unfold before his eyes. Undoubtedly this would be a difficult task, since one party would receive him well and the other "with distrust," but by watching his language and conduct he felt sure he could get useful information from both sides. As for Palmerston's instructions concerning the liaison with Heytesbury and Chad, the aggressive Chatfield, already determined to play an independent role, presumed that "it will not be necessary to keep up as active a correspondence with the Russian capital, as I shall not fail having the honour to do with Your Lordship." And considering the "inquisitorial nature of a Russian Post Office," he thought it advisable to communicate with London through private channels rather than official ones.[3] There was no question in *his* mind about the nature of the Warsaw assignment. Even before his arrival there, he had stopped at Königsberg presumably to take leave of his Prussian friends but actually to observe the disposition and numbers of the military units along the route to Warsaw. No one asked him to do this, but then he was not the type of agent who had to be asked. As for the promise of neutrality, his reports already contained stories of Russian atrocities.[4]

———◄•►———

A weary Englishman made his way through the streets of Warsaw

---

1. To Palmerston, No. 56, May 24, 1832, F.O. 65/202.
2. From Backhouse, No. 9, June 20, 1832, F.O. 65/202.
3. From Palmerston, No. 1, January 5, 1832; to Palmerston, No. 4, February 20, 1832, F.O. 65/202.
4. To Palmerston, No. 2, February 20, 1832, F.O. 64/185; to Palmerston, Nos. 5, 6, February 24, 28, 1832, F.O. 65/202.

on the morning of February 27, 1832, observing the ravages of the late war and wondering what his reception would be like at the Palace de Brühl. One can well imagine the look of stupefaction in Count Witt's eyes when he was told at eleven o'clock that morning that there was a foreigner downstairs who requested an audience with the military governor general and who claimed to be the British consul to Warsaw. This could not be, Witt must have thought to himself; there was *no* trade between England and Poland. The man downstairs was obviously an English spy, sent there by Lord Palmerston; and St. Petersburg had to be informed immediately. Despite these apprehensions, the urbane Count Witt welcomed Frederick Chatfield to Warsaw, made some nervous remarks about how the Russians were trying to assuage the ill will of the Poles, and graciously invited him to attend a carnival ball three nights hence, as if to prove to the Englishman that life in Warsaw was as jolly and as gay as before. But young Frederick was not deceived by this reception; he sensed that he was under suspicion and that the Russians would watch his every move. He wrote to Palmerston on March 1: "I close my letters so carefully, that I conceive it next to impossible to open them without completely destroying the envelope." If the Russians were tampering with his mail, he wished to be notified so that he might take other precautions. In the meantime, he would try to disarm Russian suspicions by living quietly and modestly until the authorities at St. Petersburg had confirmed his exequatur.[5]

Life in Warsaw with its one hundred and twenty thousand souls— thirty thousand less than before the war — was just about as Chatfield had imagined it, a vanquished city in fact and in spirit:

> The capital has quite the aspect of a place occupied by a victorious enemy. The few families of distinction which remain, seldom show themselves in public places of resort, and most of them assume deep mourning. In conversation they recur to the harsh, and in many instances savage treatment adopted towards families and children of individuals who took a prominent part in the late transactions — treatment which they regard as affording a poor promise of what is in reserve for themselves, as a nation. They await in considerable anxiety the promulgation of the decree, which is to regulate their future destinies, and which the field marshal Paskewitsch who is hourly expected to arrive from St. Petersburgh, will it is supposed bring with him.
>
> The streets are crowded with Russian officers and soldiers — cossacks and Baskirs — officers of the late Polish army who are distinguishable by a mixed civil and military costume, with a vast

---

5. To Palmerston, No. 7, March 1, 1832, F.O. 65/202.

number of discharged and wounded men, who have no other means of subsistence, but by demanding alms. At every moment individuals notoriously inimical to each other may be seen saluting as friends, and an instant after they have shaken hands, if either be asked who his friend is, he will probably reply that he really does not know — 'mais c'est un Polonais, ou c'est un Russe' as the case may be. Persons also who by the merest chance saved themselves from the popular fury during the revolution are again here, saluting, and being saluted by some who perhaps regret their escape.[6]

There was both a sense of emptiness and a feeling of apprehension tugging at the heartstrings of the defeated Poles. Count Witt, a well-intentioned general and a member of what Chatfield called the "European" faction in Russian politics, was pursuing a firm but conciliatory policy toward the residents of Warsaw. But what would happen to them when the "Asiatics" took over, men like Paskevich whose avowed solution to the Polish problem was complete and absolute suppression? Under "Asiatic" rule, the impending ordinances and constitutional reforms would be so much paper, strictly for European consumption. The fact would be a ruthless suppression of all vestiges of Polish nationality, the Treaty of Vienna notwithstanding. Warsaw and her people, therefore, were without hope; and nowhere was this more evident than at the carnival ball of March 1, 1832, "one of the completest failures I ever had the fortune to witness," observed young Chatfield. The "rank and fashion" of Warsaw did not attend, or was not invited; and except for a few members of the bourgeoisie and an English lieutenant, bedecked in the regimentals of the 20th Foot, the guests "were in some shape dependent on Russian favour."[7]

At first, the exaggerated fears and close supervision of the Russian authorities at Warsaw apparently amused Mr. Chatfield. He seemed to relish the cat-and-mouse game which, of course, further inflated an already oversized ego. But as days passed without receiving the confirmation of his exequatur, he became apprehensive that Warsaw officials might successfully pass on their fears to St. Petersburg.[8] Lord Heytesbury, to whom he wrote on this subject, mildly reprimanded him for his suspicions and assured him that Count Nesselrode had promised to forward the confirmation to Warsaw within a few days. In a fatherly and condescending tone, which must have galled the young consul, Lord Heytesbury explained to him that his position in Warsaw for the first month would be a delicate one, but that if he were careful, if he re-

---

6. To Palmerston, No. 8, sep., March 3, 1832, F.O. 65/202.
7. *Ibid.*
8. To Shee, March 12, 1832, F.O. 65/202.

ported just the facts and refrained from commenting upon them, then everything would work out smoothly — advice which Palmerston thought was sound. The underling Chatfield, however, was less convinced; he informed Palmerston that he had replied to Heytesbury in the same tone, "conceiving his observations were in part meant for the edification of the letter readers in the Post Office."[9]

In the meantime, the unofficial Chatfield rented a home in Warsaw and hired servants as if to convince the Russians that he, at least, had no doubts concerning the eventual confirmation of his credentials. On March 10, the redoubtable Paskevich, now Prince of Warsaw, assumed command at the Polish capital. Young Frederick wasted no time in renewing his acquaintance with the field marshal, and by deliberately stressing his predilection for things military he was invited to numerous reviews which permitted him to acquire the priceless information that he sent home to London on the Russian army.[10] As a newcomer, and especially as one under suspicion, Chatfield realized that it would take time to become familiar with events in Warsaw and that if he pushed too fast "the object may be defeated." He hinted, not too subtly, that the Foreign Office could expedite the process by providing him with a special expense account to open up reliable sources of information.[11]

By the end of March, Mr. Chatfield received official recognition as British consul to Warsaw. In his non-political capacity, he performed efficiently and expeditiously in presenting the claims of British subjects who had suffered losses during the recent hostilities.[12] Furthermore, from a deep religious conviction that Englishmen living abroad should have decent places of worship and burial, he contributed generously out of his own pocket to the support of an English church in Warsaw. In fact, it was at his suggestion that the Foreign Office initiated the practice of donating twenty pounds annually for that purpose.[13]

As a political agent, the consul proceeded cautiously in the months of March and April and, according to him, he won the confidence of a highly-placed Russian official within a "fortnight" after his arrival.[14] For obvious security reasons, the informant's name did not appear in Chat-

9. To Palmerston, No. 14, March 13, 1832, p. encl; to Palmerston, No. 16, March 20, 1832; from Shee, No. 3, April 6, 1832, F.O. 65/202.
10. To Palmerston, Nos. 16-17, March 20, 1832, F.O. 65/202.
11. To Shee, March 12, 1832, F.O. 65/202.
12. To Bidwell, No. 86, August 27, 1832; to Palmerston, No. 90, September 10, 1832; to Shee, October 20, 1832, F.O. 65/202.
13. To Palmerston, No. 21, March 24, 1832, F.O. 65/202; F.O. to Colonel Barnett, October 31, 1833, F.O. 65/210.
14. To Shee, October 20, 1832, F.O. 65/202.

field's dispatches; but it is clear from the type of information which he gave the Englishmen that he was a "European" and a military official, high enough in rank to know of policy decisions and decrees before they were actually implemented. Was it mere coincidence that the "fortnight" mentioned by Chatfield was on or about March 10 when Count Witt was relegated to a subordinate position under Paskevich and that Count Witt received deferential treatment in the consul's analyses of the Polish situation?[15] The evidence suggests that either Witt or one of his close associates was supplying the British consul with information.

While there was still hope that the "Europeans" might regain the ascendancy in Warsaw, or at least mitigate the harshness of the "Asiatic" program, Chatfield reported political events with some degree of objectivity, at least by comparison to a later period. Although Paskevich still kept him high on the list of *"extremement espionné,"* Chatfield could appreciate Russia's problem in controlling a hostile Poland.[16] Her authority had to be maintained, and there was a real need to check the Poles' "anarchical views and failings of character and principles." Nonetheless, he objected to the means employed by the Russians and felt that the Poles deserved better treatment.[17]

In the final weeks of April, 1832, a log jam of frustration was piling up in Chatfield's mind as it became evident to him that the vindictive faction had undisputed control of Russian policy toward the Poles. To offset the obnoxious "letter readers" at the Post Office, who were beginning to annoy him noticeably, he asked Palmerston for a cipher.[18] He also tried sending dispatches by private messenger to Berlin, hoping that they would be forwarded to London without any trouble. But to compound his annoyance, he learned that Prussians were equally avid readers of his dispatches in order to collect the fifty-ducat reward for any letter bearing upon Russian affairs.[19] Whereas the Russians spared no expense to learn what the British consul was doing and writing, Chatfield lacked the means to escape their strict censorship.[20] Instead, the niggardly Foreign Office, in a letter of April 6, had announced Palmerston's wish "that you bear in mind that your character is purely commercial" and had reprimanded him for spending over twenty-five pounds in forwarding a special report to London. To add insult to injury, he was told "that there was nothing in the despatch in question of sufficient importance in

---

15. To Palmerston, No. 58, May 26, 1832, F.O. 65/202.
16. To Palmerston, No. 35, sec., April 16, 1832, F.O. 65/202.
17. To Palmerston, No. 34, April 14, 1832, F.O. 65/202.
18. To Palmerston, No. 33, April 13, 1832, F.O. 65/202.
19. To Palmerston, No. 35, sec., April 16, 1832, F.O. 65/202.
20. To Palmerston, No. 43, April 24, 1832, F.O. 65/202.

His Lordship's opinion, to require the incurring of the before-mentioned expense."[21] These words cut the British consul to the quick; and as he nursed the rebuke in the first week of May, a daring idea struck him. He was about to relieve the log jam.

———

Frederick Chatfield decided that the time had come for England to take a stand on principle: she should intervene in Polish affairs against the inhumanity of the Russians. Although aware that his actions might cost him his career in the foreign service, he was determined to proceed with the scheme. After all, justice was on his side and so was the English press, upset by reports of Russian brutality in Poland. Since the Russians took such great interest in his letters, Chatfield planned to satiate their curiosity, disheveling some eyebrows in the process. An incensed Russian government would surely demand his immediate recall, and Lord Palmerston would then be faced with a black or white alternative: to appease the barbarian or to champion the cause of humanity and civilization.

To make this grand plan work, the propagandist in Warsaw would have to appeal to every sentiment, prejudice, and motive to which Foreign Secretary Palmerston might respond. Certainly, young Frederick reasoned, "Old Pam" would not reject England's destiny as the leader of constitutionalism in Europe. If he did so, he would betray himself as an appeaser of the autocrats. And what about Poland as a new market for English manufactures? By minor sacrifices in the Canadian timber trade, Poland some day might become as useful "as a Colony to England."[22] The aggressive Chatfield also considered it in order to make an appeal to His Lordship's vanity:

> In future, the whole turn of Russian politics as regards peace or war in Europe will rest upon Poland — and it is this opinion which urges me to impress on attention at home, the policy of encouraging this Post. And I hope the remark will not be deemed intrusive, if I observe, that the resolution to accredit an individual to Poland, instantly an opening offered, is regarded as no slight token of Your Lordship's foresight and penetration.[23]

This was a daring campaign by a clever agent, but it remained to be seen whether or not he had chosen the right moment to put "Old Pam" on the spot.

---

21. From Shee, No. 3, April 6, 1832, F.O. 65/202.
22. To Palmerston, No. 65, June 16, 1832, F.O. 65/202.
23. To Palmerston, No. 66, June 17, 1832, F.O. 65/202.

Although the outline of his anti-Russian campaign was visible in the dispatch of May 5, the consul's program of denigration began in earnest on May 19, 1832. "The sole aim and tendency of every measure adopted by the government," Chatfield explained, "is the enfeebling, harassing, and impoverishment of Poland, beyond the power of recovery, without any regard to the manner of effecting it." Lieutenant Chatfield, ex-Life Guard, sounded the call to arms:

> It is inhumanly calculated, that after the disappearance or absorption of two generations, the whole country will arrive at that state of barbarism, which the rulers of the present day shortsightedly conceive most fitted to its welfare, or rather to the maintenance of their own despotic power.
>
> The measures of the government all lean to this point, no efforts are spared to attain it, by preventing the dissemination of European ideas, and by plunging the people, their ideas and habits, into the lowest depths of Asiatic incivilization. . . .
>
> It is clearly to the interests of Europe, that for the preservation of its freedom a firm barrier should be opposed to the too rapid approach, and the near establishment of so restless and dangerous a neighbour as Russia. Without quitting her frontier, her armies are now stationed in great force, within a shorter distance of the chief cities of Germany, than was ever known before — a point well deserving the most serious consideration.[24]

Chatfield's assertion that exaggeration did not creep into his correspondence appears almost ludicrous, as one studies the adjectives and clauses sprinkled throughout his dispatches: "In utter contempt of every principle of honour and good faith," "their own nefarious purposes," "unexampled rapacity," "gross injustice and arbitrary character," "oppressive nature and cowardice of the measure," "vindictive oppression," "detestable scheme," " the abominable law of recruiting," "this execrable measure" — all of which betrayed his prejudices as well as his program of action.

Who could remain insensible to the human appeals of this master propagandist, this British Quixote in Warsaw? For those whose hearts might bleed for the plight of children, he would tell how "A few days ago the majority of a school of boys was arrested in the middle of the day, as they left their desks," or he would impassionately describe the grief of parents who had lost their "children of tender years."[25] If Prussia encouraged her faithless ally to violate the amnesty promise, "she must eternally share the disgrace and dishonour of the transaction. But

---

24. To Palmerston, No. 51, May 19, 1832, F.O. 65/202.
25. Dispatches 51 (May 19) and 52 (May 20).

who will interfere in behalf of the poor children and their parents?"[26] For those who believed in the freedom of the individual, he would describe the mercenary and merciless espionage activities in Warsaw, the arbitrary arrests, and the "midnight" raids "by parties of the police escorted by Cossacks," forcing the flower of Polish manhood to wither away in the Russian army for fifteen years, "a period which is equivalent to a sentence of death, especially as they will be removed to the distant governments of Kasan and Siberia."[27] Respect for the property rights of an individual? There was no such thing in a Russian Warsaw, where property was confiscated on the slightest pretext.[28] And if one believed in religious freedom and the separation of church and state, young Frederick would inform of a decree, shown to him confidentially by his informant, to make schismatics of Polish Catholics and to tie them indissolubly to the Russian government.[29]

If Lord Palmerston were really sincere in his efforts to guarantee constitutional government for Russian Poland, as reports had it, Frederick Chatfield would then demonstrate the hypocrisy of recent ordinances which could easily be set aside by an ukase.[30] One need not expect constitutionalism from the Russians; on the contrary, Chatfield averred that Russia and her ally Prussia were bent upon extending autocracy within their borders and would squelch any attempts in favor of representative government.[31] Chatfield assured Palmerston that Russia's policy was to make Poland politically and economically "a desert." "One third of the commercial wealth of Warsaw," he noted, "has already left, and every encouragement is given to merchants and tradespeople to retire into Russia. The government goes so far as to remit debts due to itself, and to pay or arrange such as may be due to the national bank by individuals willing to transfer their business to other parts of the Empire."[32]

The "Asiatics" would stop at nothing to destroy every reminder of Polish nationalism. With brazenness, they stole the "national possessions" including Polish paintings, history books, documents, and artifacts —

---

26. No. 58 (May 26).
27. Nos. 51 (May 19), 52 (May 20), 71 (June 26).
28. No. 45 (May 5).
29. No. 61 (June 1).
30. Nos. 42 (April 23), 54 (May 22), and 56 (May 24). Also see "Correspondence between Great Britain and France respecting the affairs of Poland," July, 1831, and "Correspondence between Great Britain and Russia respecting the affairs of Poland," 1831, 1832, in British Foreign State Papers, vol. 37, (1848–1849), pp. 1413-1444.
31. To Palmerston, Nos. 75, 80, July 12, 24, 1832, F.O. 65/202.
32. No. 62 (June 4).

all of which were transported to the victor's capital in St. Petersburg. If the color of barriers in the streets of Warsaw were once white and red, the Russians now changed them to black and white. No detail escaped the eye of the vindictive Asiatics. To "denationalize" Poland, they altered the curriculum of the few schools which were allowed to remain open so that only safe and unimaginative courses would be offered. And to convince "Messieurs les Polonais" that they erred in challenging the Empire, a hand-picked delegation of Poles — some bribed, others threatened — proceeded to St. Petersburg to apologize for their error and to thank the Emperor for the benevolent rule of Mother Russia. While the "national deputation" scraped at the feet of Nicolas I, the "spoils" from Warsaw would be brought into the court, thus underscoring the degradation and humiliation of the vanquished Poles.[33] "The question as to the expediency of striving to obliterate all national evidence," the young Englishman observed, "need not be mooted here; but it maybe very well doubted, if the precipitancy and coarseness with which this object is being pursued, will not lastingly disgust those, who are unaccustomed to view with indifference, the principles of good faith set aside, or a violation of the commonest rules of justice."[34] "The conduct of the Russian government upon this occasion," Mr. Chatfield analyzed, "can only be likened to that of a child, which breaks in pieces, in its pettish anger, an object that it has not the ingenuity to mend."[35]

As if determined to obtain the correct Russian reaction, Mr. Chatfield spared no one in his "smear" campaign, not even Emperor Nicolas I. All his remarks concerning Nicolas led to only one conclusion: the Emperor was a treacherous and vindictive Asiatic. "I will not dwell longer upon the subject," he remarked wearily: "I am fatigued with contemplating the sad events passing around, the results of perhaps one of the most remarkable breeches of public faith ever committed by a Sovereign towards his people."[36] His judgment "warped by passion and revenge" and his vanity shaken by the Polish Revolution, Nicolas I was the willing instrument of the Asiatics.[37] "Heaven only knows," sighed Mr. Chatfield, "the real measure of wretchedness experienced by the unhappy natives of Poland, and the Russian Polish Provinces, and few until now ever imagined that the present Emperor possessed such a large share of the hereditary character of his ancestors."[38]

---

33. No. 45 (May 5).
34. *Ibid.*
35. No. 57 (May 24).
36. No. 56 (May 24).
37. No. 58 (May 26).
38. No. 59 (May 27).

While the exposé was in progress, the British agent complained of the inadequacy of his salary at a place destined to become increasingly more important, especially if Palmerston followed his lead. In asking for such a raise, Chatfield realized: "I incur the risk of being suspected (erroneously) of covetous or sordid motives." Yet it was his duty to the public service to speak up: "As the first individual whom the British Government has accredited to Poland, in the quality of consul, it may be proper I shall describe the precise nature of the office, which indisputably possesses far higher attributes, than the humble title it bears may seem to indicate." Since it was evident to him that his primary function was political, it followed that he had to maintain a certain position in society — and Warsaw was far more expensive than London — equal to and certainly not below that of other foreign envoys. After all, he was the representative of the most powerful and richest country in the world, and it would be disgraceful for him, as well as his country, to be relegated to an inferior condition. He recommended, therefore, that the salary be increased to one thousand pounds, plus a substantial contingency fund for buying confidential information. Such special allowances, the consul argued, were indispensable in cities like Warsaw "where there are so many spies employed by the Police." [39]

Foreign Office reaction to this request, as well as to the fiery crusade against Russia, was annoyingly consistent and not calculated to relieve the consul's frustration. On April 6, the Foreign Office reminded him that his function was commercial. On June 12, both Lord Palmerston and William IV endorsed a dispatch cautioning Mr. Chatfield "to adapt the tone and style of your dispatches to the character of official correspondence." [40] The real blow to Chatfield's ego came in the dispatch of June 20 which repeated the "commercial" chant, refused his salary request, and cuttingly reminded him that he was the "British Consul" at Warsaw, not the "British Minister." With characteristic impatience and arrogance, the angry consul fired back an answer: "I am perfectly aware it does not become me to contend with Your Lordship in opinion, farther than I conceive in my humble judgment a sense of duty to the publick service may allow." The allowance turned out to be considerable, as he stubbornly repeated and expanded upon his earlier arguments. Trying to control himself, as he recalled the slur that he was a consul and not a minister, he wrote: "I do not ask for the means of living expensively, but simply for the power to maintain a footing of equality with those I am residing amongst, a competency regulated by the wants

---

39. No. 60 (May 27).
40. From F.O., No. 5, June 12, 1832, F.O. 65/202.

and usages of the place." "Under the circumstances," the headstrong consul concluded, "Your Lordship will perhaps allow me to recommend my application to reconsideration."[41] In addition, the brazen consul noted in the postscript that Palmerston's last two letters, admonishing him for partisanship, had given "much satisfaction here" to the letter readers in the Post Office.

Although it was small consolation to Mr. Chatfield, the Russians took their cue admirably well and reacted in predictable fashion. Count Nesselrode dashed off a message to the Lievens in London on May 26, 1832, in which he demanded the immediate recall of the meddlesome Chatfield, who "exploits every opportunity to attach himself to those men who by their disposition are known to be hostile to Russia," encouraging them with the hope that England will not be an "impassive spectator." At such a critical moment, when Russia was trying to prevent the recurrence of anarchy, how could England condone Chatfield's actions? "What would the English Government do," he asked, "if some Russian consular agent took it upon himself to foment a spirit of insubordination in England, to exploit the troublesome elements that might exist there, or to incite a hostile disposition toward the present administration?" Under these conditions, Great Britain would have the "incontestable right" to demand the recall of such an agent, just as Russia now insisted upon the recall of Mr. Chatfield "from a post where he has violated the confidence of his own country and has betrayed ours."[42] On the jacket of the request for recall, there is a note that the decision to dismiss Chatfield was reached on June 24. Yet Lieven received the letter on the 7th and did not submit a formal request until the 29th. These interesting facts suggest that the Lievens personally contacted Palmerston on this matter shortly after receiving Nesselrode's letter. If the decision was arrived at on June 24, why did Lord Palmerston wait until August 31 to write the formal letter of recall to Frederick Chatfield?

It is difficult to escape the conclusion that Lord Palmerston was pursuing a policy of appeasement with regard to Russia during most of the year 1832, at least until October. Since the spring of the year, there were accusations that he was a tool of the Russians, unwilling to stand up to them on the "Polish Question." In June, when the English press and politicians in the House of Commons made derogatory remarks about the Emperor of Russia, which incensed Nicolas I, some noted that

---

41. To Palmerston, No. 74, July 3, 1832, F.O. 65/202.
42. Prince Lieven to Palmerston, June 29, 1832, which includes Nesselrode to Lieven, May 26, 1832, F.O. 65/204.

Palmerston remained silent and did not bother to correct the remarks about the Tsar. This silence, one authority contends, "marked the beginning of Palmerston's public defense of the Liberal Movement."[43] There seems to be little basis for this interpretation if we keep in mind what Chatfield was writing to Palmerston as well as the latter's remarks on June 28 in the House of Commons when Cutler Fergusson introduced his controversial motion that Great Britain solemnly protest against "the extinction of the political existence and nationality of Poland."[44] The *Times* hoped that Palmerston would favor the motion, but he did not.[45] This was certainly a peculiar way of defending the Liberal Movement.

It could be argued, as many did, that Fergusson's motion was a needless provocation which might have precipitated war with Russia; but Lord Palmerston's objection to it had a different basis. It was not so much fear of Russia but rather the hope that by yielding to Russia on the "Polish Question" she would then give her wholehearted support to Palmerston's Belgian diplomacy. His policy was one of expediency and of putting first things first. If it meant he had to appease Russia by sacrificing the Poles and Frederick Chatfield, then this had to be done in order to achieve the greater end. Significantly, the Durham mission, whose objective was to seek Russia's cooperation in Belgian affairs, was sent to St. Petersburg in June, 1832. Considering the public agitation on Polish matters, it was also understandable that Palmerston should wait a few months before recalling the British consul at Warsaw. To have announced it in June would have been a foolhardy move, to say the least.

And so, on August 31, Lord Palmerston recalled a British agent who in many respects anticipated some of the stands for which he later became famous:

> The object of His Majesty's Government in sending a British Consul to Warsaw, has been so often and so distinctly stated to you, that it is needless for me to remind you, that the character with which you were invested was purely that of a Commercial agent, appointed to watch over the interests and property of British subjects. To these duties was indeed superadded, that, which equally belongs to every British Consul abroad — the Duty, namely, of reporting such local occurrences of a political nature as it may be interesting to His Majesty's government to know, — of pointing out, where necessary, the results to which such occurrences may be expected to lead, — of directing attention to such facts, as may

---

43. Webster, *Palmerston,* I, 191.
44. HPD, XIII, 1115-1150.
45. *Times* (London), June 28, 29, 1832.

be particularly deserving of notice. But you have at the same time been enjoined to observe the greatest circumspection in conduct and language, and carefully to avoid all acts or expressions which might be construed as in any way identifying you with local feelings and opinions.

Representations, however, have been made to His Majesty's Government, from which it appears that you have not acted with that prudence and discretion which are so peculiarly necessary in the Post in which you have been placed; and the tone of many of your dispatches which I have more than once had occasion to animadvert upon, has tended to confirm the unfavourable impressions which the representations alluded to were calculated to convey.

His Majesty's Government, though willing to believe that you have been led away, as much by overzeal in the execution of your Duties, as by misconception of the nature of them, yet feel that such a line of conduct must of necessity defeat the object which the government had in view by the appointment of a British Consul to Warsaw; and, even if established international usages, allowed them to hesitate in complying with the request of the Russian government for your removal from Warsaw, the considerations above mentioned would induce them to do so.[46]

Although the perennial optimist in Warsaw was disappointed that his crusade had died on the vine, he assured himself that Palmerston's words were not intended for him but for the "letter readers," who would promptly forward a copy to St. Petersburg. When he acknowledged Palmerston's letter on September 20, he mentioned subtly that the recall had come through the regular mails, as if to say that he was aware of being sacrificed to the Russians.[47] And though he did not know what Palmerston hoped to gain by this move, he was sure that it did not reflect discredit upon him. Convinced of this, he wrote two documents on September 17, three days after receiving the recall letter. The first one, a letter to Sir George Shee, suggested his appointment to a vacancy in Bordeaux, France. It was only fair that the sacrificial victim should pick his next position.[48] The second document, a venture into creative writing, was a lengthy memorandum describing the consul's farewell interview with the great Paskevich at one o'clock on the afternoon of the 17th.[49] The purpose of this clever treatise, probably only a figment of his imagination, was to justify his career at Warsaw and, at the same time,

46. From Palmerston, No. 10, August 31, 1832, F.O. 65/202.
47. To Palmerston, No. 92, September 20, 1832, F.O. 65/202.
48. To Shee, pvt./conf., September 17, 1832, F.O. 65/202.
49. "Particulars of an Interview with the Fieldmarshal Prince of Warsaw, Count Jean Paskevitch d'Erivan," September 17, 1832, in No. 92, September 20, 1832, F.O. 65/202.

to point out to Lord Palmerston the futility of appeasing the Russians. At this stage in their development, it would seem that Frederick Chatfield was more "Palmerstonian" than Lord Palmerston himself.

"Since your Lordship's despatch came through the Post office," young Frederick commented in the preface, it was understandable that the Prince of Warsaw should know the purpose of Chatfield's visit and had actually prepared himself for it. The field marshal received the consul "in his closet quite alone," and Frederick came directly to the point. He announced his departure for London in the next few days. Paskevich feigned surprise and then nervously asked if the consul expected to return to Warsaw in the near future. Chatfield said no. After another moment of silence, Paskevich asked what arrangements had been made for a successor: "I answered, that I was in possession of no details having simply received an order to proceed to England."

Another nervous pause, and then the Russian blurted out that he had never been convinced that there was enough business in Poland to justify a full-time English consul. "To this uncourteous speech," the indignant consul replied "that the commercial intercourse betwixt England and Poland was far from being as inconsiderable as he supposed, and that when greater confidence in the stability of public affairs in the country prevailed, it was probable the foreign trade would take a new impulse, and become more widely extended." Since the description of the farewell visit was for Palmerston's benefit, Chatfield recorded that part of the alleged conversation in which he told the field marshal how successful he had been in presenting British claims to the authorities in Warsaw. And as a devoted servant of His Majesty's Government, he also took advantage of the opportunity "to recommend to the Marshal's protection, the case of an Englishman who had received some time before a promise of the payment of his claims, etc. etc. The Marshal said the matter should be attended to etc. etc. etc." So far so good; in a few pages Palmerston could see that the Russians had never thought much of his idea to place a British agent in Warsaw and that this particular consul had done a wonderful job along "commercial" lines in a place where there was not much commerce. The Polish market, however, did have possibilities.

Then the conversation took a different turn. "The Prince," Chatfield noted, "in a hurried manner and with a degree of excitement in his tone which surprised me, and without being in any way invited to the subject by me, asked if I had read the inscription upon the statue of King Sigismund — near the palace wherein he is designated King of Poland, and Tsar of Muscovy." The fact that the Russians tolerated such a statue was ample proof of their "leniency and modernization" toward the Poles and this despite "the extraordinary provocation given to the government to act with severity." At this point, "he requested me to examine an oil painting which was standing on a chair opposite the door by which I entered, and evidently placed so as to attract my notice. It represented, as he said, a scene that occurred some centuries ago, in which six or seven Russian Boyards appear prostrate before a King of Poland, whose horse is trampling under foot the muscovite colours." This picture, said Paskevich, shaking with emotion, was taken from the museum of a private society in Warsaw, where it had been kept "for the exclusive exhibition to the Poles, and made use of to excite their animosity and passions." Here was convincing proof of the insubordination of "Messieurs les Polonais," proof of "what ancient date their hatred is towards the Russians," proof of "how unwilling they are to suffer it to decline, or wear out."

Since the excited Prince of Warsaw has made such an issue of the picture — the justification for the suppression of the Poles — young Frederick walked over to it, studied it for a moment, and then remarked that "the subject was certainly founded on an historical fact of antiquity." As he looked at the picture more closely, he commented that he did not think much of it as a work of art. Paskevich hurriedly concurred: "Non ce n'est rien cela." It was the intention of the work that made it important. At this point in the narrative, author Chatfield turned to the reader, Lord Palmerston, and in a series of footnotes completely demolished the field marshal's *pièce de resistance*. This picture was a fabrication, painted by the Russians themselves, and deliberately planted there to convince the British consul that Russia's harshness toward the Poles was justified. The reader had no alternative but to conclude that Russians were liars and that the British consul was right in standing up to them.

Then, the clever Chatfield went back to the narrative. When the Prince of Warsaw detected some doubt in the Englishman's eyes, he called his attention to a piece of paper in the left hand corner of the picture with the number 42 on it. The point was obvious; this picture was but one of a large collection of drawings upon similar subjects — all of which demonstrated conclusively the treachery of "Messieurs les Polonais" and their hatred of the Russians. Chatfield thought about this for a moment, wrinkled up his nose, and then, "presumed to express a doubt of the possibility of keeping such a collection, and especially for such a purpose from the knowledge of the Russian authorities previous to the revolution, who possessed every facility, if not by direct, at least by indirect means, to acquire information of the circumstance, delicately hinting at the inquisitorial character of the Police, established by the late Grand Duke Constantine." Into the trap stepped the Prince: "The Marshal exclaimed 'Oh they did not know how to act, they bestowed their attention upon wrong points,' leaving it of course to my inference, that his own system of Police is more perfectly organized."

Author Chatfield had not yet exhausted his arsenal; there was still the final scene. Here we see the famous Paskevich, indomitable on the battlefield, overwhelmed in a clash of words with a brilliant Englishman. His only choice now was to retreat to the defense mechanism, common among all Russians, of comparing Poland to Ireland. He insinuated that England had used force to keep the Irish down. Lieutenant Chatfield immediately charged into the breach:

> I observed that the only force which the English government displayed or used in Ireland, was directed to ensure the welfare of the people, and the proper observance of the laws of the country, that obedience to the constituted order of things was all the Government desired, and that an intemperate use or an unconstitutional stretch of Power was utterly unknown in the country, that Ireland derived its best advantages from the salutary regulations of England, whose Government was influenced in all its legislative measures towards her, by an anxious solicitude to assist a full development of her resources.

When the vanquished Marshal presumably admitted the truth of these assertions, the triumphant Chatfield withdrew from the castle. A few days later, he left Warsaw, returning to London in mid-October, 1832. Though the veracity of the account may be questioned, Chatfield's motives in writing it were obvious.

❧

Back in London, Frederick Chatfield began to wonder if he had misjudged the letter of recall: that it was not an act of appeasement after all, and that perhaps his career in the service was in serious jeopardy. His letters to Sir George Shee reflected a mounting concern for his future, though he was still adamant that the circumstances had justified his actions. But the tone of his letters contrasted noticeably with the arrogance and self confidence of his Warsaw dispatches. He now requested "most humbly to solicit that my earnest desire for employment may be brought under Viscount Palmerston's consideration." He no longer insisted on this or that appointment but "thankfully" would accept "any appointment which His Lordship may be pleased to bestow upon me."[50] And the longer the Foreign Office delayed in answering his request, the more worried he became. On November 3, he wrote to

---

50. To Shee, October 20, 1832, F.O. 65/202.

George Shee: "Perhaps, Sir, Lord Palmerston would be disposed to consider my anxiety for employment with greater favour, if His Lordship were assured that I never make any communication respecting Polish affairs to my private acquaintances in this country, that I do not even give an opinion as to the correctness of the statements of the newspapers."[51] Frederick Chatfield was finally beginning to realize the consequences of his impetuous actions in Warsaw, how they had conformed to the clamor in the press, and that Palmerston, with a mind of his own, was not going to permit the foreign policy of his country to be dictated by the passing whims and fancies of the journalists and Mr. Chatfield.

The month of October, 1832, was one of decision and awakening for the British foreign secretary, furious at himself for having appeased the Russians or thinking that he could bargain with them for anything. They had interpreted his actions as a sign of weakness, and consequently the Durham mission failed to get a clear-cut commitment from Russia on intervention against Holland. Apparently that young chap in Warsaw had been right all along; the Russians could understand only one thing— brute force. Lord Palmerston therefore revived the threat of sending Stratford Canning to St. Petersburg; significantly, his relations with the Lievens began to break down when he learned of the failure of the Durham mission to St. Petersburg.[52] With or without the help of the autocrats, France and England would now force the stubborn Dutch king to comply with the Treaty of November 18, 1831, establishing the independence of Belgium. According to the strategy of intervention, a French expeditionary force would proceed overland to attack the citadel at Antwerp, while the British navy blockaded the Scheldt and enforced a strict embargo of Dutch ships. Reports circulated, however, that Prussia would not tolerate the coercion of Holland; and there was uneasiness concerning the movements of the Prussian army, which appeared to confirm the suspicion that the Anglo-French intervention might have serious consequences.[53] Though still determined to go ahead with his plans, Lord Palmerston first took the precaution of consulting an expert on Prussian military matters, none other than the discredited British consul from Warsaw.

Unfortunately, no minutes were kept of Frederick Chatfield's first meeting with Lord Palmerston, though it can be reconstructed by inference from subsequent letters. There is reason to believe that both men

51. To Shee, November 3, 1832, F.O. 65/202.
52. Webster, *Palmerston,* I, 167-174, 181, 191, 196-198, 321-327.
53. *Ibid.,* pp. 168-174.

were equally impressed with each other and that the advice given to the younger man stayed with him for many years. Undoubtedly Foreign Secretary Palmerston told Mr. Chatfield that he still had a great deal to learn about diplomacy and the ways of diplomacy, despite his correct evaluation of the Russians. Then the master proceeded to explain the intervention strategy and discussed the widely-held opinion of military observers that Prussia might resist the move, thus precipitating a general European war. What did he think of this possibility? One can well imagine how flattered and honored Frederick Chatfield must have been when Viscount Palmerston asked him this question. He thought about it for awhile and then stated his humble opinion, based upon observation and experience. The Prussians were obviously against the move, they would attempt to frustrate it by amassing their forces in a threatening pose along their western border, but they *would not* and *could not* go on the offensive. Chatfield explained why he thought this would be so, apparently to Lord Palmerston's satisfaction. Since a great deal was at stake and to be sure that he was not in error, Chatfield offered to go on a secret reconnaissance mission through western Prussia to verify his conclusions. Lord Palmerston agreed.[54] The nature and organization of Chatfield's dispatches from Prussia indicate that he was there to test conclusions which he had discussed before leaving London in early November, 1832.

The English spy wrote his first dispatch from Brussels on November 12; and on the following day he proceeded to Antwerp, where he reported on Belgian attitudes toward the impending occupation of the Citadel.[55] After returning to Brussels, he traveled eastward to Aix la Chapelle and Cologne; then, northward along the Rhine to Dusseldorf and Munster; and from thence, to Hanover. He continued to Leipzig, the easternmost point of his trip, and then proceeded westward through Frankfurt A.M., Mainz, Coblentz, Cologne, and Juliers, finally returning to Aix la Chapelle by the end of December, 1832. In early January, 1833, Chatfield was back in London for a second interview with Lord Palmerston. The French forces, in the meantime, entered the town of Antwerp on November 19; the English supported the move with a strict embargo; and the Citadel surrendered on December 22. The Prussian army, contrary to expectations or fears, did not move across the border.

---

54. To Palmerston, No. 11, December 10, 1832, F.O. 30/47, in which Chatfield recalled: "In my last interview with Your Lordship I had the honour of submitting the advantage which I conceived would accrue to the object of my journey, by making a circuit through the chief stations, and I am now satisfied of the correctness of my view."
55. To Palmerston, Nos. 1, 2, November 12, 14, 1832, F.O. 30/47.

Chatfield's main argument, supporting the conclusion that Prussia would do nothing about the impending action at Antwerp, was the nature of the Prussian army. He explained that Prussia had one of the largest and most formidable military establishments in Europe with commissioned and noncommissioned officers whose ability and devotion to service were exceptional. As a means of national defense, at the minimum of expense, the Prussian system was nearly faultless. But, as an offensive army, it had notable weaknesses, mainly stemming from the fact that, except for the officer corps, it was primarily an army of draftees. Furthermore, the allegiance of these soldiers to Prussia was an acquired one, and their service was performed in their native provinces with rare exceptions. To these weaknesses, the shrewd observer added the constant turnover of personnel and the poor morale of the soldiers, who resented the discrimination practiced in the conscription process and the real hardships imposed upon their families as a result of their service. To prove this latter point, Chatfield cited the trouble Prussia had experienced with the Landwehr in provinces adjacent to Poland. The Prussian system, he concluded, was an excellent defense instrument "as long as each individual perceives a distinct personal interest endangered; but the question arises, whether in offensive wars" one can depend upon it or "whether it will not be essential to convince the country that the petty interests of individuals are closely identified with the schemes of the government." As for the Anglo-French intervention, Prussia would find it difficult to convince her subjects that they should quit their homes, expose their lives and property "in a doubtful contest, whose issue if even successful, can add little perceptible good to their position."[56]

Chatfield wrote the above analysis on November 23, three days after his arrival in Aix la Chapelle — hardly time enough to gain such an insight into the Prussian system. His subsequent dispatches merely buttressed this conclusion, which he obviously had discussed with Lord Palmerston earlier in the month of November. And this was not just the opinion of the "movement party" at Munster, Chatfield assured Palmerston. It was also expressed to him by "individuals confidentially employed in the service of the government." And it was no coincidence, Chatfield wrote on December 9, that the Rhenish Provinces chose the present opportunity to demand constitutional reforms from Prussia — the price she would have to pay for their cooperation.[57]

The weakness of the military system, Chatfield explained, was

56. No. 3 (November 23).
57. No. 9 (December 9).

symptomatic of the "want of nationality" in the component parts of Prussia. Her subjects — Poles, Swedes, Saxons, Rhinelanders, or French — had an "acquired allegiance" rather than an innate one; and there were those, "the designing and mischievous," who exploited the differences and grievances of her subjects, propagating the notion that a change could not possibly be worse and might be better. And there was notable discontent throughout Prussia. The mercantile classes, "an unquestionable power in Prussia," were dissatisfied with the tight-money situation, which they attributed to a government that did not understand their interests and that had made concessions to Russians at the expense of native industry. They also resented keenly the discrimination in the military service favoring the nobility.[58] In effect, Chatfield was saying that Prussia's subjects had a patriotism of the pocket-book variety; and there were many indications that this patriotism, if it can be called that, had not reached the point where Prussia could count upon their loyalty to achieve her diplomatic objectives.

A final argument, which Chatfield developed in support of his conclusion, was the ineptitude of Lieutenant General Müfling, whom he had the pleasure of meeting at a "soiree." What he heard at this social function convinced him that "as long as he remains at the head of the Prussian Army of Observation no idea will be seriously entertained of venturing upon a hostile movement." Though he was unquestionably an able strategist, it was common opinion among his officers and men that he lacked the ability to make rapid decisions in a military situation. "Another reason why his continuance with the army may be viewed with a political interest," the astute observer continued, "is his unpopularity with the troops."[59] Both officers and men resented his cold, haughty deportment and his indifference to the promotion and claims of anyone else besides himself. This monomaniac could not lead the Prussian forces on the offensive nor inspire confidence in his leadership. It followed, therefore, that Prussia, despite her desire to do so, would not resist the Anglo-French action.

The documentation on the secret mission to Prussia should warm the hearts of military historians, not only for its quantity but its facts, insights, and analyses. Once again, Frederick Chatfield proved himself as a researcher and as an agent who could suggest sound policy. After his second interview with Lord Palmerston, the hard-working spy followed up his mission with further reports from contacts in the area. In no way did they detract from his earlier conclusions, and, of course,

58. No. 14 (December 20).
59. No. 21 (December 31).

he took great pride in watching events bear out his interpretation.[60] As late as January, 1834, Chatfield continued as an unofficial observer of political events in Prussia and Poland, submitting dispatches and documents to his superiors in the Foreign Office and discussing them with Lord Palmerston.[61]

The Foreign Office was especially pleased with Chatfield's performance in Prussia, and for once he had no complaints to make about the expense money which was granted to him for the mission. On the contrary, he gratefully thanked Lord Palmerston "for the favour and generosity shewn to me, and which are particularly agreeable to my feelings, as implying, that my humble services meet Your Lordship's high approval."[62] Understandably, the perennial optimist now presumed that the success of his Prussian mission had more than offset the Warsaw fiasco, especially since Palmerston was finally getting around to a tough policy toward Russia. With greater humility than usual, Chatfield suggested his next appointment in a dispatch of February 25, 1833:

> With great deference, indeed with some hesitation after the reiterated marks of favour which I have had the honour to receive at Your Lordship's hands, I beg permission to submit to Your Lordship's consideration, an humble request to be again employed in His Majesty's Service, in any capacity which Your Lordship may be pleased to determine.
>
> Though well aware that it does not become me to intimate a choice, still I may possibly assist Your Lordship's decision, if I venture to mention, having heard that the appointment of Resident at the United States of Central America, or Guatemala, remains open, and to add, that it would be agreeable to me to undertake the duties of that Post.[63]

Lord Palmerston made a note of this request, and a few months later chose Frederick Chatfield to be the next British consul to the United States of Central America.[64]

After seven years of brilliant service, Frederick Chatfield's dream of a promotion from the consular to the foreign service was about to

---

60. To Palmerston, Nos. 3, 4, January 23, 24, 1833; to Shee, pvt., January 24, 1833, F.O. 30/47.
61. To Bidwell, March 2, 1833, F.O. 65/210; to Backhouse, January 11, 1834, F.O. 64/198, which included the minutes of a recent interview with Lord Palmerston.
62. To Palmerston, No. 5, January 31, 1833, F.O. 30/47.
63. To Palmerston, February 25, 1833, F.O. 65/210.
64. From Backhouse, March 14, 1833, F.O. 65/210; from Backhouse, June 10, 1833, F.O. 15/13.

materialize. No longer would he have to put up with the chant that his primary function was commercial and not political; he would be *the* British representative in all of Central America with perhaps a staff of assistants and vice consuls to compile statistics which he would then interpret for the Foreign Office. And it thrilled him to think that among the candidates for this post, which included colonels, Lord Palmerston recommended him, a mere lieutenant, for a position which commanded a salary of 1,200 pounds, or twice his Warsaw salary. This was a genuine reward for his conscientious work. Here was the golden opportunity to climb the diplomatic ladder to recognition and status.

Why should Chatfield be so elated when his rank was merely that of consul? The reason was clear to anyone who understood the consular service as well as he did. He was going to Central America as a minister plenipotentiary to conclude a Treaty of Commerce and Amity with that Republic. If the treaty were ratified, whoever negotiated it would automatically be eligible for a promotion in rank to at least that of chargé d'affaires, perhaps even minister as in the case of Mexico. No wonder he was overwhelmed with joy when he learned Palmerston's decision. No wonder his letter of acceptance oozed with a gratitude and humility, never seen before or since in his correspondence with the Foreign Office.[65] As Columbus before him, the amazing Mr. Chatfield was about to blaze a path in the New World, where his career undoubtedly would bear the fruits he longed to taste.

---

65. To Palmerston, June 12, 1833; to Backhouse, June 12, 1833, F.O. 15/13.

CHAPTER THREE

Minister Plenipotentiary

I will not presume to offer any further observations upon the above questions, nor upon the answers which have suggested themselves to me upon the perusal of them. My principal object has been to draw Your Lordship's attention to the several points which appeared to me of the greatest importance in the consideration of the Question of Honduras. . . and if my researches upon the subject shall prove of the least utility, it will afford me matter of sincere gratification.[1]

—Chatfield, February 3, 1834

Unavoidable delays in completing the draft of the Central American treaty kept Frederick Chatfield in England another nine months after his appointment in June, 1833. The Colonial Office was determined to secure in the treaty the Republic's explicit recognition of England's rights to British Honduras — a point adamantly insisted upon by the residents of Belize, the capital of the British establishment on the northern coast of Guatemala.[2] Although a harbinger of future difficulties, the lengthy delay had its advantages as far as the consul was concerned; inadvertently it afforded him the luxury of a valuable training period. During those months, he made considerable headway in mastering the fundamentals of the Spanish language; he profited from the insights of fellow countrymen who had been in Central America or had interests at stake there; and perhaps more importantly, considering his talents for research, it gave him a splendid opportunity to study and digest the extensive documentation and literature on Central America in the Foreign Office archives. When Mr. Chatfield wrote the words which introduce this chapter, he was already one of the best informed men in England on the history and affairs of Central America. In that key dispatch of February 3, 1834, he not only asked Lord Palmerston for instructions on seven questions which involved policy decisions concerning the thorny territorial problem of British Honduras but he also proceeded to answer them in convincing fashion. And many of the arguments and suggestions in that dispatch were eventually adopted by the British Foreign Office.[3]

As Chatfield perused the treaty draft and the series of special instruc-

---

1. To Palmerston, February 3, 1834, F.O. 15/14.
2. Mem., F.O., September, 1833; F.O. to Board of Trade, November 12, 1833; C.O. to F.O., September 28, 1833, F.O. 15/13: C.O. to F.O., March 11, 1834, F.O. 15/15.
3. To Palmerston, February 3, 1834, F.O. 15/14; Mem., C.O., January 20, 1835, F.O. 15/17.

tions of March 19, 1834, it pleased him to learn that he was given substantial discretionary authority in the impending negotiations. Moreover, Lord Palmerston had accepted his suggestion that Spain, and not Central America, should be consulted in the event that the territorial question could not be avoided. In complete agreement with the intent of the Foreign Office to negotiate a strictly commercial treaty, the consul noticed however that Palmerston, with some inconsistency, had yielded to the Colonial Office and to the Judge Advocate on an important point of terminology. Throughout the treaty, the phrase "His Britannick Majesty's Dominions" was replaced by the provocative expression "the territories, dominions, or places in the possession and occupation of His Britannick Majesty." In Chatfield's opinion, this apparently harmless substitution threatened to raise the "Question of Honduras" and would thus jeopardize the success of the treaty mission. Lord Palmerston's assurance that the new phrasing would actually preclude any further discussion of boundaries did not console Chatfield, for there was nothing in the documentation which he had read to support such an assertion.[4]

Historically, the "Question of Honduras" represented a clash of rival interpretations of international law, which dated back to the famous discovery of Christopher Columbus. There is, moreover, a striking parallel between Spain's legal position vis-à-vis her challengers in the colonial centuries and that of the American nations in the course of the nineteenth century. When the United States of Central America, the former Captaincy General of Guatemala, declared its independence from Spain on September 15, 1821, it inherited the problem of Belize. Simply stated, the question then was whether Great Britain had a right to claim sovereignty to any portion of continental Middle America and its adjacent islands. Initially, the controversy arose over the status of British Honduras proper, usually referred to as Belize by contemporaries; then, it extended to the Bay Islands in the Gulf of Honduras, especially the strategically-located island of Ruatán; and eventually came to involve England's right to exert a protectorate over the Mosquito Shore, which today comprises the Atlantic coast of part of Honduras, all of Nicaragua, and a portion of Costa Rica. The problem in the nineteenth century, in other words, covered more territory than that which is involved in the present dispute between England and Guatemala.

After the effective discovery of the New World, Spain — and the

---

4. From Palmerston, No. 4, March 19, 1834, plus draft of treaty; from *idem*, No. 5, March 19, 1834; to Palmerston, No. 3, July 5, 1834, F.O. 15/14.

same holds true for her Iberian sister's claim to eastern South America—based her legal title to lands overseas upon the right of conquest and upon her willingness to assume the obligations of spreading the gospel among the heathen natives, a euphemism for a papal grant. But when reports of fabulous discoveries were broadcast throughout Europe, non-Iberians and non-Catholics immediately challenged the validity of the religious rationalization for preempting the New World. They argued that Spain and Portugal could lay claim only to those islands which they held effectively. By the same token, the challengers reasoned, anything they could grab and hold from the Iberians was legally theirs — the right of effective occupation, so graphically described in European diplomacy by the dictum "No peace beyond the line." Without the resources and manpower to garrison the far-flung reaches of her Empire, Spain inevitably and reluctantly yielded to her adversaries' point of view, concentrating her defense efforts upon the approaches to the two heartlands of Mexico and Peru. By the Treaty of Madrid, in 1670, she acknowledged England's sovereignty to Jamaica and to the British colonies in North America; and shortly thereafter, other European powers won similar concessions on the fringes of the Spanish Empire.

From Jamaica as a base, English woodcutters with gangs of Negro slaves visited the eastern coast of Central America, traded with the Mosquito tribes, and persuaded those Indians to allow them to cut mahogany and logwood. Periodically, Spanish squadrons would clean out the pesky interlopers from the Mosquito Shore and nearby islands, only to have them return with alarming regularity. With the help of the Mosquitos, also known as Sambos from their affinity to Jamaican slaves, Englishmen plied their woodcutting trade virtually unmolested. And in the eighteenth century, as England's power increased with the size of her navy, Spain was compelled to make further concessions, legalizing the woodcutting activities of English subjects. By the Treaty of 1783, and a further convention of 1786, the King of Spain authorized Englishmen to cut wood on the mainland of Central America in a shallow coastal area between the rivers Hondo in the north and the Sibun in the south, providing Great Britain also agreed to prevent her subjects from frequenting the Bay Islands and the Mosquito Shore. This woodcutting concession involved no relinquishment of sovereignty and explicitly forbade settlement and the cultivation of lands within the limits of the grant. Such was the legal origin of what became British Honduras.

However nicely diplomats in Europe might work out the details of the Belize concession, their contemporaries in the area — both Spanish and English — considered the treaties meaningless stopgaps, dictated by the exigencies of the moment and the temporary advantage that one nation might have over the other. A state of war still existed, as far as they were concerned, and they acted accordingly. English wood-cutters, guided by a psychology of abundance which prompted them to strip an area hurriedly of the choicest woods, expanded considerably beyond the original limits of the Belize grant. And whenever possible Spanish colonials — oftentimes rivals for the same wood — armed expeditions to repel the Belizean advance. In the north, for example, a Yucatán force attacked the British in 1796, causing them to abandon the lower bank of the Hondo River. But in the west and in the south, on the frontiers of the Captaincy General of Guatemala, the wood cutters' advance proceeded steadily in the face of little resistance. By September 15, 1821, Englishmen had extended their activities to the Sarstoon River in the south and to this side of Garbutt's Fall in the west — an area from three to five times the original concession of the 1780's. Since possession was nine-tenths of the law, according to the old adage, and no one had dislodged them from the lands beyond the limits, Belizeans argued vehemently that they were theirs to keep. In their own unsophisticated way, they were utilizing the old right of effective occu-pation, just as England had done in the Treaty of Madrid more than a century and a half earlier.

In place of Spain's religious premise for claiming title to the New World, the American nations, having won their independence from tyrannical European mothers in the eighteenth and nineteenth centuries, substituted the political ideal of representative government, or what Professor Arthur Preston Whitaker has called the "Western Hemisphere Idea."[5] According to the *mystique* of New World liberals, the Americas would and should be reserved for the glorious experiment in democracy, receptive to humanitarian ideas from whatever the source yet cautiously vigilant against the cancer of Old World governmental institutions. The famous message of President James Monroe, for example, was merely the United States' version of a territorial sentiment which was commonly shared by her American sisters to the south. In theory, Hispanic Ameri-cans preferred — and still do — an absolute application of the territorial formula which would compel European nations to give up their colonies in the Western Hemisphere; whereas the United States with the Monroe Doctrine actually came closer to the position forced upon Spain in 1670, recognizing the existing colonies of European nations but expressly for-bidding any further colonization. Needless to say, this "American sys-tem," as Frederick Chatfield called it, did not impress the non-American

5. Arthur Preston Whitaker, *The Western Hemisphere Idea: Its Rise and Decline* (Ithaca, 1954).

powers any more than Spain's peculiar version of international law had convinced the non-Iberians in the colonial centuries.

With regard to Belize, Central Americans also argued that their nation had "derivatory" rights, since at one time the area of the wood-cutting concession formed part of the Captaincy General of Guatemala. They explained, moreover, that according to Spain's theory of empire the New World holdings were considered the personal property of the Spanish king; they were, in other words, not really colonies in the strict sense of the word but *reinos,* or kingdoms, which shared a common monarch with say the Kingdom of Castile. With the deposition of the king by right of revolution, his lands reverted not to the Spanish nation but to the people, which in the former Kingdom of Guatemala meant the new governmental unit which replaced the king, the United States of Central America. England, therefore, would now have to acknowledge the Republic as the new grantor of the woodcutting concession made in the 1780's. Incidentally, this was good Hapsburg law with a dash of John Locke, though the right to depose a monarch was also implicit in the Spanish system.[6]

The rugged English woodcutters at Belize, however, were not lawyers; and they found it difficult, as well as inconvenient, to understand the niceties of Spanish legal theory. The cultured alumni of the University of San Carlos in Guatemala City could spin elaborate arguments to their hearts' content; but Belizeans aimed to keep what they had, leaving to others the task of articulating their positive sentiments in comparable legal verbiage. Frederick Chatfield performed this function in the above-mentioned dispatch of February 3, 1834, which embellished upon the old right of effective occupation. Arguing cleverly that Great Britain had always considered Belize a colony in fact, if not in theory, he cited numerous documents and examples to prove his contention. These possessory, or "prescriptive," rights, furthermore, allowed England to claim title not only to the original grant of the 1780's but also to the lands occupied before September 15, 1821. It likewise followed that England did not have to consult anyone on the question of sovereignty; if she felt compelled to do so, then Spain alone had any right to treat the subject. Under no conditions should England discuss the matter with Central America, a third party who had nothing to do with the eighteenth-century treaties.[7] Since Chatfield's arguments completely denied the validity of the Central

---

6. For a good study of Hapsburg law, see John H. Parry, *The Spanish Theory of Empire in the Sixteenth Century* (Cambridge, 1940).

7. To Palmerston, February 3, 1834, F.O. 15/14.

American position, they obviously would win very few supporters in Guatemala City.

———◆•◆———

Despite his very clear-cut ideas on the "Question of Honduras," Frederick Chatfield — the realist and the diplomat — fully appreciated the historical context in which he would have to negotiate the commercial treaty, as well as the importance of avoiding the territorial issue. He felt sure that the provocative terminology of the treaty draft would not aid his cause. Let us now consider briefly the historical basis for this apprehension.

The attitudes engendered by the economic nature of the British establishment — however erroneous they may have been in fact — exacerbated the hostility of rival nationalities and further heightened the tension over the territorial issue. The Belizean woodcutter, for example, believed that he needed room for expansion and that the mahogany supply within the original limits of the eighteenth-century treaties had long since been exhausted. And since he was not willing to abandon his wasteful practices in favor of conservation techniques, feeling that they would merely add to his costs and thus put him at a disadvantage with competitors, these beliefs were economic realities to him. In this frame of mind, he understandably would resist any attempt to force him back within the old limits; conversely, to meet the fierce competition of rivals, he would champion further expansion southward to forests along the Guatemalan coast, the Bay Islands in the Gulf of Honduras, and the Mosquito Shore.[8] In applying pressure upon Belize, interestingly, Central Americans started from the same assumptions.

The first wave of irritation between English Belize and the Central American Republic resulted from the promulgation of a law in 1823, emancipating the Negroes of Central America — the first nation in the world to do so, boasted her patriots. Ironically, the Belizean reaction to this humanitarian decree could not have been more militant, as woodcutters charged emotionally that the law was vindictively and deliberately conceived to force the evacuation of Belize. Without gangs of slaves to cut down trees, they could not remain in business for long; and emancipation in the nearby Republic would contribute to their financial ruin by encouraging Negroes to flee from their masters. In a population of five thousand, the two or three hundred whites likewise feared the racial implications or consequences of the law, so much so that they even pleaded with the Colonial Office to change the complexion of the royal

---

8. Thomas Miller to Lord Aberdeen, February 2, 1835, p. encl.s and mem. by Colonel Francis Cockburn, F.O. 15/17.

force at Belize from colored to white. At the same time, a militant commission of Belizean magistrates traveled to Guatemala City to demand the immediate return of fugitive slaves and to threaten strong action if the Republic refused to comply.[9]

Although the fugitive slave issue involved only a few Negroes, its psychological impact was tremendous since it aroused nationalistic feeling in Central America to a fever pitch and thus focused the spotlight upon the territorial question for the first time in the national period. A cherished principle of human rights was at stake; so was the prestige of the young nation which could not afford to yield to the dictation of a British commission that peremptorily demanded either the repeal of one of its laws or adequate compensation for human property.[10] The situation went from bad to worse and was never really settled, despite rumors — perhaps politically inspired — that the federal government under President Manuel José Arce had been willing to compromise on this vital issue. More important historically, as a harbinger of things to come, was the action taken by the Belizean magistrates in 1828. Over the objections of the superintendent of Belize, they imposed a retaliatory duty of five percent on all Central American goods passing through their port. From the Guatemalan point of view, this was an outrageous duty levied by Englishmen upon their hosts, who tolerated their presence on the northern coast. The Republic's agent in London, moreover, failed to receive a satisfactory answer, or apology, from the British government.[11]

The anglophobia, resulting from Belizean acts, might have been checked, or mitigated somewhat, if the British Foreign Office had made it perfectly clear that Belizeans were acting unofficially. All indications, however, pointed to the powerful influence of Belize interests in London. The Central American commissioner in London, for example, found it virtually impossible to negotiate a commercial treaty with the Foreign Office because of obstacles arising from the territorial question. Even the great Canning, wrote Marcial Zebadúa, was not insensible to the loss of English property, however human or mobile. Yet convinced that Central America needed British recognition, Commissioner Zebadúa

---

9. See documents in F.O. 15/14, folios 157-163, 179-238, 274-276; F.O. 15/6, folios 70-77, 96-100; F.O. 15/7, folios 284-319; F.O. 15/8, folios 91-97; F.O. 15/9, folios 16-26, 35-38, 78-95.
10. Marshall Bennett to Edward Codd, June 14, 1826; Codd to Horton, July 21, 1826, which includes a "Report of the Senate of Guatemala," May 27, 1826, F.O. 15/9.
11. Consulado Nacional de Guatemala to Ministro de Estado y Negocios Eclesiásticos, April 24, 1828, A.G.N.G./CLCA, leg. 170, exp. 03620; Marcial Zebadúa to *idem,* December 6, 1828, A.G.N.G./CLCA, leg. 170, exp. 03625.

recommended the subordination of the human principle, though admirable and worthy, to the greater ends: "our stability and our independence."[12] When the liberals returned to power in 1829, after three years of bitter civil war against the Arce government, they were incensed at Zebadúa's suggestion to compromise principle, all of which seemed to confirm the prevailing rumor that President Arce and the hated conservatives of Guatemala had come to terms with Belize. As a result, Zebadúa was recalled from London in 1830, allegedly because the federal government could no longer bear the financial burden of his diplomatic mission.[13]

Actually, Zebadúa's letter of recall marked the beginning of the liberals' disillusion with the British government. In the first flush of independence, grateful to England for her role in the political emancipation of the Americas, they counted heavily upon her enlightened leadership and example, never linking the actions of ignorant Belizeans with the official policy of Great Britain. But now Zebadúa's suggestion concerning the fugitive slaves implied that their earlier enthusiasm and confidence had been misplaced. And so long as the Foreign Office danced to the tune of Belize, the Central American Republic could expect little from Great Britain. The nation's leaders drew the same inference from an incident which occurred in May, 1830, when the acting superintendent of Belize removed some settlers from the island of Ruatán.[14] Though the Republic finally accepted the English explanation for this first Ruatán incident, more and more Central Americans began to realize that they needed a counterpoise to command respect from Belize.

Another irritant in the relations between the British establishment and the neighboring republic stemmed from the nature of Belize as the major entrepôt for English manufactures in the Central American market. A simple matter of geography and established facilities made it possible for the port of Belize to be the first to capitalize upon the free trade policies of the Republic. By 1824, for example, there were already at least four commission houses at Belize handling the bulk of the trade with Central America. In this traffic, the British merchant acted primarily as a wholesaler, selling his goods to Central Americans who traveled the lengthy route from Guatemala City to the northern coast. The Central American retailer paid for the manufactures with specie or such staples

---

12. Zebadúa to Ministro de Estado y del Despacho de Relaciones, December 1, 1828, A.G.N.G./CLCA, leg. 170, exp. 03625.
13. Zebadúa to Palmerston, September 27, 1831, p. encl. of June 18, 1830 by Julián Ibarra, F.O. 15/11.
14. Charles Dashwood to John Backhouse, November 3, 1830, p. encl.s, F.O. 15/10.

as cochineal and indigo which could bear the expensive freight charges to the northern port. In the first few years, the Belize trade flourished; British manufactures flooded the new market, and the production of indigo and cochineal increased by leaps and bounds.[15] Rather than an irritant, it would seem that the trade through Belize would eventually form a harmonious bond between the port and the market.

Instead, the characteristics and conditions of the traffic, coupled with the resentment in Central America over the territorial issue, produced disharmony and grievances — alleged and real — that the parasitic British houses at Belize were usurping the fruits of Central American labor with their monopoly of imports. There was, of course, a great deal of economic nonsense and exaggeration in these charges against the Belizeans, who were blamed irrationally for every economic ill. Yet one cannot deny the political significance of these grievances in straining relations between Englishmen and Central Americans.

A few examples should suffice to illustrate the potential for mischief. Native craftsmen, unemployed or depressed by the innovations in the economy, were easily persuaded that foreigners were responsible for their plight. Longing for the old non-commercial way of life, they clamored for protection against the unrestricted introduction of British manufactures and blamed the liberals for their free trade measures. To them free trade meant the sacrifice of native interests to those of the outsider. To make matters even worse, the foreigner in question was a heretic, an Englishman who was usurping the nation's territory. And joining the clamor against the British establishment were the merchants, or retailers of the Republic, especially in Guatemala. Spanish merchants, who in the good old days had been the middlemen in the trade with Spain, were, of course, resentful of the new order which subjected them to the control of British importers, who were now enjoying their former privilege of arbitrarily setting prices at whatever levels the traffic would bear. Understandably, they blamed the Belizean houses for the high prices and blandly overlooked their own markup in the sale of the manufactured product. In their case much of the resentment was due to the loss of power and the emergence of competitors among the Central Americans themselves. As the native entrepreneurs prospered, they too shed their initial gratitude to the Belizean houses and developed a similar phobia toward the middleman. At the first opportunity, of course, both groups of merchants mentioned above would try to break the connection with Belize by trading directly with business firms in Europe. But this took time and especially money.

---

15. Dashwood to Backhouse, March 3, 1831, F.O. 15/11.

The Central American consumer and the producer of raw materials — for all practical purposes, one and the same person — likewise placed their complaints at the doorstep of the foreign importer. Unwilling to deny themselves the luxury of British manufactures, they rushed to the stores to buy the coveted goods, paying hard cash or indebting themselves to local merchants. Eventually the day of reckoning arrived; they developed the taste for these new products without the corresponding ability to pay for them, mainly because of the nature of the Belizean traffic. The distance and expense in forwarding exports to Belize dictated a specialization in the cultivation of indigo and cochineal, for bulkier low-priced materials, grown near the Pacific coast where Central America's population was concentrated, could not participate in that trade. And as Central Americans produced more and more indigo and cochineal, the surplus situation either created opportunities for abuse on the part of the Belizean buyer or depressed prices in the English market, thus reducing the producer's margin of profit. His transportation costs, however, remained fixed. The Central American grower, of course, blamed the foreigner. Four or five Belizeans — the complaint ran — were arbitrarily fixing the price of their exports at levels which had nothing to do with the going price in the London market. It followed, therefore, that Belizeans were deliberately conspiring to produce an unfavorable balance of trade for Central America, were draining the nation of its specie, and were determined to make all Central Americans their economic vassals. To be sure, Belizeans were not entirely guiltless of the charges raised against them; and whenever abuses occurred, they were magnified to substantiate Central America's grievances.[16]

Though many Central American liberals correctly understood the political inspiration underlying these accusations, they nevertheless believed that there was a potential for monopolistic abuse in the Belizean trade and that it might thwart the economic development of their country. Whenever political conditions permitted, therefore, these liberal leaders tried to round out their nation's economy with measures that promised a more competitive situation. They encouraged, for example, the establishment of rival English houses in Guatemala City which might use Belize as a mere transit point or which would import their goods via Cape Horn to the Pacific coast of Central America. In this latter case, they hoped to provide an outlet for bulkier exports which were excluded from the Belize trade. Another pet project of this period was the estab-

16. Antonio Larrazábal to Secretario de Estado y del Despacho de Relaciones, November 27, 1830, A.G.N.G./CM, leg. 3484, exp. 79644; "Exposición," Mariano Gálvez, April 30, 1830, B.N.G./HS, 1830, p. 7.

lishment of a Guatemalan port at Santo Tomás on the Gulf of Honduras, as a rival entrepôt to Belize. Others suggested the possibility of dredging the mouth of the River Dulce, so that ocean-going vessels might enter Lake Izabal, also known as the Gulf of Dulce, and thus utilize the established facilities at the port of Izabal.[17] And still others favored the popular and perennial scheme of cutting an interoceanic canal through the state of Nicaragua — a project which would open up all of Central America to the world's commerce.

Considering the aggravation of the territorial question, these economic proposals undoubtedly had political implications as well. After the Ruatán incident of mid-1830, there were those who urged closing Atlantic customhouses to Belizean imports, a rather drastic proposal which illustrated the intensity of feeling in Central America.[18] Without a substitute channel for Central American exports, however, the proposed measure might have done more harm to native interests than to Belize. Instead, and following the cue of the Belizeans themselves, the federal congress, in December, 1830, levied a discriminatory tariff of five percent upon all imports from Belize. This duty remained on the books for many years to come.

As might be expected, Belizeans complained vociferously to authorities in London; but without a commercial treaty with Central America, England could do nothing about the discriminatory levy. Moreover, Belize's residents wasted no love upon the various projects to undermine the importance of their harbor, especially the possibility of a rival port at Santo Tomás. If Guatemalans succeeded in establishing a port there, they perhaps would also occupy Ruatán Island in strength — a move which could bring about the economic ruin of British Honduras, Belizeans feared. From Ruatán, Guatemalans could protect Santo Tomás, control Belize, and frustrate any ambitions the Belizeans might have of expanding their woodcutting activities to the south. Understandably, they strongly urged British authorities to occupy that strategic island in the Gulf of Honduras.[19]

Also, the agents of other foreign powers in Central America were not remiss in capitalizing upon anti-British feeling. According to Chatfield, John Verveer, the Dutch envoy, was personally responsible for encouraging the five percent discriminatory tariff against Belize.[20] Ex-

---

17. Zebadúa to Ministro de Estado y del Despacho de Relaciones, December 6, 1828, A.G.N.G./CLCA, leg. 170, exp. 03625.
18. Larrazábal, *loc.cit.*
19. Henry Cooke to Lord Howick, August 13, 1831, October 12, 1831, F.O. 15/11. Also see documents cited in footnote 8.
20. To Francis Cockburn, October 10, 1834, F.O. 252/15.

ploiting the opportunity, Verveer also negotiated a contract with the federal government giving Holland the right to construct the Nicaraguan canal. Moreover, there were reports that he promised secretly to have his country assume the foreign debt owed to British creditors, thus relieving Central America from any financial connection with the English.[21] When Dutch support failed to materialize, because of the Belgian uprisings, a so-called "French" party gained the upper hand in the Central American congress. This faction demanded the recall of Marcial Zebadúa from London, deliberately sought the protection of France against England, and favored commercial concessions to the French in order to harm Belize. Rather than Zebadúa, who was considered pro-British, the francophiles secured the appointment of Próspero Herrera, who was also in London, and empowered him to negotiate a commercial treaty with the Parisian government.[22]

The reports of an impending treaty with France and the Belizean complaints of a discriminatory tariff reawakened interest in an English treaty with the young American nation.[23] As a matter of fact, before Zebadúa's letter of recall reached London, the Central American envoy had approached Lord Aberdeen on the possibility of resuming the treaty negotiations which were canceled during Canning's incumbency. He was strongly supported in this action by John Irving, the senior partner of the Reid-Irving House in London.[24] For some time, the British bondholders, who took over the Central American loan from the bankrupt House of Barclay, and the Reid-Irving firm, which assumed responsibility for some of the dividend payments on the loan and the expenses of Zebadúa's mission in England, had pressured Lord Aberdeen to protect their investments in Central America. Although Aberdeen steadfastly refused to intervene officially in behalf of what he called speculators, he was nevertheless amenable to Zebadúa's overtures in September, 1830, providing the latter could prove that a stable government existed in Central America.[25] Two months later, when Palmerston headed the Foreign Office, the negotiations with the Central American agent began in earnest. Zebadúa's recall, however, dictated a shift in the scene of negotia-

21. Charles Dashwood to John Backhouse, October 3, 1830, F.O. 15/10.

22. Próspero Herrera to Count Sebastiani, September 15, 1832, A.A.E.P./CPAC, vol. 2.

23. Mem., John Backhouse, August 31, 1831, F.O. 15/11.

24. Zebadúa to Secretario de Estado, March 1, 16, 1830, A.G.N.G./CLCA, leg. 170, exp. 03629.

25. Zebadúa to Aberdeen, September 6, 1830; *idem* to Palmerston, December 27, 1830, F.O. 15/10; Aberdeen to Dashwood, October 13, 1829; *idem* to Reid-Irving Company, October 23, 1829, F.O. 15/8.

tions from London to the federal capital of Central America; and it became Frederick Chatfield's responsibility to bring those negotiations to a successful conclusion.

In formulating the draft of the commercial treaty, Lord Palmerston benefited from the advice of both Marcial Zebadúa and John Irving. The latter seemed particularly interested in the Parisian negotiations and had forwarded a copy of the French Treaty to the Foreign Office.[26] His close cooperation with the British foreign secretary was also suggested in the following note by Palmerston on December 12, 1833: "Irving told me Zebadua was to be President."[27] On another occasion, the shrewd financier observed privately to Lord Palmerston:

> I have written to Mr. Zebadua to give Mr. Chatfield a cordial and friendly reception, which I have no doubt he will do; but the confidence and influence which he may enjoy, will much depend upon himself as to his decorum and deportment, not only towards those in authority, but the People at large. All assumption of superiority, or what is generally called "taking airs," would shock their pride and prejudices, and would not go down at all.[28]

Conceivably, Marcial Zebadúa may have reached some understanding with Lord Palmerston before his departure from London in late 1831. Unquestionably piqued at his recall and the appointment of Herrera for the French assignment, he perhaps gave his promise to lead the opposition in the Central American Senate against the French treaty.[29] There is little doubt that he was largely responsible for the defeat of that treaty in the spring of 1833, thanks also to the support of free trade senators who objected to the special concessions offered to French traders.[30] Zebadúa and Palmerston, moreover, discussed the territorial question and agreed that they should try to avoid it, concentrating solely upon a commercial treaty. At a later date, Zebadúa told Chatfield that Lord Palmerston had also hinted at the possibility of a territorial settlement according to the limits of the eighteenth-century treaties with Spain — an assertion which has not been confirmed by other

26. Mem., John Backhouse, April 17, 1831, F.O. 15/11; to Palmerston, September 17, 1833, and John Irving to Palmerston, pvt., September 17, 1833, F. O. 15/13.
27. Note, Palmerston, December 12, 1833, to encl. "Manifestación pública . . ." by Marcial Zebadúa, December 31, 1832, in Chatfield's dispatch to Backhouse, November 8, 1833, F.O. 15/13.
28. Irving to Palmerston, pvt., September 17, 1833, F.O. 15/13.
29. "Manifestación pública," *op. cit.*, p. 29; this printed article can also be seen in B.N.G./F, 1832.
30. William Hall to John Bidwell, Nos. 8 (June 20) and 14 (November 1, 1833), F.O. 15/13; Clairambault to Duc de Broglie, No. 7, July 18, 1833, A.A.E.P./CPAC, vol. 2.

evidence.[31] At any rate, Frederick Chatfield received oral instructions to contact the former Central American commissioner upon arriving in Guatemala City.

With these background facts in mind, Chatfield's reservations concerning the terminology of the treaty appeared justified. In late March, 1834, the minister plenipotentiary received his sailing orders and boarded H.M.S. *Belvidera* at Portsmouth for the long voyage to Jamaica in the West Indies. From there, he booked passage on the surveying vessel *Thunder* for the last leg of his trip to Belize, arriving at that port in the final week of May, 1834.[32] A fortnight in the pleasant company of the Cockburns — the Superintendent of British Honduras and his charming wife — helped the weary traveler to recover from the long sea voyage and softened his adjustment to the pressing climate of the tropics. Those two weeks in Belize, incidentally, marked the beginning of a very close relationship between "My dear Consul" and "My dear Colonel," the best friend Chatfield would ever have among the superintendents of that establishment during his long career in Central America. Colonel Francis Cockburn listened attentively to the comments and plans of the junior officer, promising his full support with but one reservation: he had special instructions, dated October, 1829, to resist any encroachment upon the lands claimed by the British subjects at Belize. He hoped, however, that this situation would never arise.[33]

On the Belizean schooner sailing toward the mouth of the River Dulce, where Chatfield had arranged to meet Commander Owen of the *Thunder,* the consul wondered how he would be received by Guatemalan officials at Fort San Felipe, almost midway between the Atlantic coast and Lake Izabal, and how they would react to the news that Owen's mission was to survey the lake. Considering the reported anglophobia of Central Americans, he was pleasantly disarmed when the fort authorities welcomed the scientific expedition and offered to assist it in every possible way. This was Chatfield's first encounter with Central Americans, and he was favorably impressed. Perhaps, the perennial optimist thought to himself, Belizeans were prone to overstate the case against Central America, as well as the resentment that existed there against the English. One of the consul's first official acts in Guatemala City was to thank Governor Mariano Gálvez for the cooperation of his state in furthering the worthwhile project of Commander Owen. He assured him

31. To Palmerston, No. 28, December 17, 1834, F.O. 15/14.
32. To Palmerston, No. 10, August 18, 1834, F.O. 15/14.
33. From Cockburn, September 13, 1834, F.O. 252/8; to Palmerston, No. 1, June 25, 1834, F.O. 15/14.

that published copies of the survey would be forwarded to the state capital in due time.[34]

After a tedious seven-day trek on muleback from the port of Izabal, the British consul, on the morning of June 23, 1834, looked down upon the beautiful valley which surrounds the city of Guatemala. The road from the coast, if one can call it that, presented "extraordinary difficulties" in climbing from sea level to an altitude of five thousand feet. But the scenery was awe-inspiring. This was indeed "one of the most splendid, and by nature fertile countries perhaps on the globe," remarked the English consul, whose visions of empire were stirred by the remarkable work of mother nature in Central America.[35] With British capital, with British "know how," and under British direction, Chatfield was confident that the destiny of this bountiful land would be realized. And he would be the pioneer blazing the path for his countrymen. As Frederick Chatfield stood on the rim of that valley, he was exhilarated by the thought that some day Englishmen would remember his role in linking the fate of this rich country to that of England. This dream of empire — a product of sincere patriotism and personal ambition, indistinguishable motives in his own mind — became an obsession with this Englishman, and only by taking it into account can we hope to understand his subsequent actions.

Despite the blessings of nature, Central America's political life was hectic — in fact, it was again in the throes of revolution when Chatfield entered Guatemala City. Only recently, the governor of El Salvador had pronounced against the Union, presumably because the federal congress, which had just terminated its sessions at Sonsonate in the same state, had voted to move the federal capital to San Salvador. Although immediately suppressed, the rebellion was symptomatic of the political unrest in the country since the outbreak of civil war in 1826. The states, led by the liberals, had defeated President Arce and the *serviles* of Guatemala in 1829; but the vanquished conservatives, from their exile in Mexico, had kept the nation distracted and penniless with threats and actual attempts at invasion. When these failed, they turned to subversion and infiltration of liberal ranks, creating dissension between the states and the Republic. A case in point was the recent pronouncement of Governor San Martín, inspired by those who ardently desired the downfall of the Republic — a liberal experiment which threatened the old way of life with all its special privileges and prerogatives.

If there had been more unity and genuine faith in the Republic

---

34. To Palmerston, No. 10, August 18, 1834, F.O. 15/14.
35. To John Backhouse, pvt., June 26, 1834, F.O. 15/14.

among the liberals themselves, the subversive tactics of the *serviles* would have been less effective. But liberals, being what they are, were hopelessly divided on many important issues, and especially on the vital question of constitutional reforms concerning the power structure of the Republic. The leaders of small states complained of the overwhelming influence of Guatemala in the federal government, and Guatemalans were equally adamant that the principle of proportional representation should not be sacrificed. When Chatfield appeared upon the scene, the Republic was at the ebb of its power; the states had assumed many of its prerogatives, and were acting as virtually autonomous units. Only the lower house had met at Sonsonate, and the Senate had not held sessions since 1833, when the federal capital was located in Guatemala City. To make matters even worse, President Francisco Morazán completed his first term of office on June 16, leaving the federal government in the hands of Vice President José Gregorio Salazar.[36] With federal elections scheduled for the fall of 1834, later postponed to January of the following year, there would be the inevitable fierce struggle for power among the numerous presidential aspirants while a weak caretaker government tried vainly to keep the lid on the pot.

Given the unstable political milieu, the British minister plenipotentiary was in a quandary as to how to proceed with his mission. William Hall, an English merchant and the acting vice-consul for many years, briefed him on the political situation and mentioned that Marcial Zebadúa, the first minister and secretary of state in the last congress, had returned recently to Guatemala City. Though presumably he left Sonsonate for reasons of health, the truth of the matter, Hall informed, was that he was forced to resign his cabinet post because of his faction's unpopularity in the recent congress.[37] The question in Chatfield's mind was whether he should feign ignorance of Zebadúa's resignation and commence negotiations on the treaty, or whether he should proceed immediately to San Salvador to present his credentials to the Salazar government. In line with Palmerston's instructions, and convinced that he had nothing to lose by adopting the former course, Mr. Chatfield contacted the ex-minister on the day after Zebadúa's arrival in Guatemala City.[38]

With elections in the wind, the British consul realized, perhaps at Zebadúa's indication, that it would be almost impossible to negotiate an English treaty exclusively commercial in nature. Aspiring politicos

---

36. "Ynforme," Miguel Alvarez, January 24, 1835, F.O. 254/4.
37. To Palmerston, Nos. 7 (August 7) and 8 (August 11, 1834), F.O. 15/14.
38. No. 1 (June 25).

would inevitably vie with each other in proclaiming their patriotism on the question of Belize, making it an important political issue in the campaign. And the candidates of the so-called "French" party, which was still smarting from the defeat of its treaty in the 1833 sessions, would have a distinct advantage over the "English" party unless Chatfield took positive steps to strengthen Zebadúa's hand in the political struggle ahead. Chatfield was prepared to do this, which accounts for his decision to meet with the discredited minister in a series of interviews from June 24 to July 6. At these meetings the two men were actually discussing political strategy, while the letters to the Foreign Office which described the interviews explained the obstacles to Chatfield's treaty mission and suggested what further concessions Palmerston should be prepared to make in support of the "English" party.[39]

To convince Lord Palmerston, the English agent resorted to the ingenious technique of presenting Zebadúa's objections or suggestions to the treaty followed by Chatfield's rebuttals.[40] The clue to the latter's purpose in reporting these discussions was Zebadúa's objection to the terminology of the treaty, which would needlessly embarrass his party by raising the territorial question. Although sharing his colleague's sentiments on this point, Chatfield tried lamely to defend the phraseology of the treaty. In November, the consul repeated the request for a change in the terminology without pretending that it was anyone else's opinion.[41]

The ex-minister offered two clever suggestions, clearly intended to strengthen the position of his faction in the event the territorial question intruded itself: first, he favored a time limit of ten years for the English treaty; and, secondly, he urged Great Britain to consider a clause abandoning any claims she might pretend to have to the Bay Islands and to the Mosquito Shore. With a time limit, Zebadúa and his supporters might possibly succeed in negotiating a strictly commercial treaty, for they could then argue that the recognition of a powerful European nation would put Central America on her economic and political feet for the first time, postponing the troublesome territorial question for a future date when the Republic would be in a better bargaining position. Hardly consonant with his shrewd ability as a political analyst, Chatfield pretended that he did not understand the intent of this proposal, as if he were deliberately employing a negative approach to get Lord Palmerston to take the initiative on it. The second suggestion was also meaningful in the light of Palmerston's willingness to accept a territorial settlement

---

39. No. 7 (August 7), p. encl.s.
40. No. 3 (July 5).
41. No. 23 (November 13).

according to the lands occupied on September 15, 1821.[42] A self-denial clause to the Bay Islands and the Mosquito Shore would produce, in effect, a settlement similar in scope to the eighteenth-century treaties with Spain; and again the "English" party might reasonably expect to get a compromise of this sort through the federal senate.

Another suggestion, intended more to enlighten Palmerston on a troublesome point which would surely be raised by the anglophobes, concerned the inclusion of a paragraph in the treaty similar to article fourteen of the Mexican treaty (1826). That article had defined the northern border of British Honduras as the Hondo River, just as in the treaties of the 1780's. Central Americans could thus argue convincingly that if England had been willing to accept the northern limit of Belize, according to the Spanish treaties, she could not — with any semblance of justice — deny Central America the western and southern limits indicated in the same treaties. The issue, of course, might be averted if Palmerston were to implement Zebadúa's constructive suggestions; but in any case the Foreign Office should prepare a convincing, as well as a consistent, explanation for refusing Central American desires on this point. Chatfield reminded Palmerston that he had formulated such an explanation in his February dispatch and hoped that the Foreign Office would find it acceptable. In essence, the consul supported the old right of effective occupation. Since Englishmen had not expanded beyond the Hondo, the same northern limit of the Spanish treaties could be used in the Mexican treaty. But in Central America's case, the eighteeenth-century limits were not valid for the simple reason that British settlers had effectively occupied lands considerably beyond them. Although this was an exasperating answer from the Central American point of view, it followed logically from Chatfield's assumptions on the "Question of Honduras."

While awaiting Palmerston's reaction to the suggestions, Zebadúa and Chatfield planned to influence public opinion for a commercial treaty with Great Britain. In a covering letter to senators, accompanying the Spanish translation of the treaty, Chatfield stressed the Republic's need for English recognition and the fairness of the British treaty as compared with the special concessions sought by France in her proposed convention. To reject such an equitable treaty, he threatened mildly, "might lead to the impression that the political existence of the Republick is not sufficiently established to deserve admission to the rank of an independent nation."[43] This remark is meaningful in the light of the

---

42. F.O. to C.O., February 19, 1834, F.O. 15/15.
43. To Palmerston, No. 3, July 5, 1834; to Backhouse, pvt., June 26, 1834, F.O. 15/14.

Zèbadúa-Aberdeen negotiations in London, for it underscored the close
cooperation of the two men who were outlining political strategy in
Guatemala City.

Aware of Zebadúa's unpopularity in the last congress, however,
Chatfield realized that he needed a broader base of support for the English treaty in order to assure its ratification. Utilizing a letter of introduction from the Cockburns, he wrote to Colonel John Galindo on July
5, hoping — it would seem — to establish an important military contact
with the federal government at San Salvador. The reply, received on the
24th, looked promising as the colonel, an Irishman by birth, discussed
political affairs and appointments. Since Galindo mentioned Zebadúa's
dismissal from office, Chatfield knew that he could no longer continue
the pretext of dealing with him.[44] On July 25, moreover, he talked with
General Carlos Salazar, the vice president's brother, who informed him
that Zebadúa had misled him into thinking that he was authorized to
negotiate a treaty for the federal government. Without any discredit to
himself, and according to plan, Chatfield protested his good faith in
dealing with Zebadúa and focused the blame on his erstwhile colleague.
He described the political triumph exultingly to Lord Palmerston.[45]
Henceforth, the consul would have to deal directly with the federal
authorities. He chose, however, to remain in Guatemala City where he
awaited the outcome of the presidential elections and hoped to ingratiate
himself with the leading contenders.

In early August, 1834, Frederick Chatfield had an opportunity to
meet ex-president Francisco Morazán, who — rumor had it — would
probably be reelected if he cared to run again. Interestingly, at this time,
the Englishman's opinion of Central America's great military hero was
"unfavourable." Although a brave and successful general, the consul
observed, "he is not known to possess much energy and decision of character, and in an administrative capacity he is considered deficient."[46]
This was the consul's way of saying that if Morazán were elected for a
second term he might not, or would be reluctant to, accept the strong
executive powers which many politicians were proposing as a basic and
needed reform to the Constitution of 1824. Furthermore, Chatfield had
reason to believe that the general might not cooperate in negotiating a
strictly commercial treaty and that he would probably insist upon a
settlement of the Belize question.

44. To Galindo, July 5, 26, 1834, F.O. 252/9; from Galindo, July 15, 1834,
   F.O. 252/6.
45. To Palmerston, No. 7, August 7, 1834, F.O. 15/14.
46. To Palmerston, No. 8, August 11, 1834, F.O. 15/14.

On the morning of the 16th, General Morazán called at the consul's home in Guatemala City to find out what his instructions were on the territorial issue. Chatfield began his account of the interview with these words:

> Notwithstanding I am honoured by Your Lordship's instructions to to decline entering into a discussion with the government of this country as to the rights of Great Britain within the settlement of Honduras, still the subject is one so much dwelt upon here, that it would be injudicious to object altogether to entertain it, and as long as my observations do not partake of an act of negotiation, but are confined to an explanation that our tenure of Honduras depends upon circumstances with which this Government has neither a right nor an interest to interfere, and that Central America can in no sort pretend to decide upon the rights of Great Britain within the limits which she actually occupied at the period when the independence of Guatemala was declared, I conceive that by consenting to touch upon it, I am securing an effective mode of avoiding present and future difficulty, in the conclusion of the Treaty now in progress, or in the conclusion of any subsequent arrangement respecting boundaries, which England and Central America may find it convenient to enter into.[47]

England's position on the "Question of Honduras," as explained to General Morazán, was the one Chatfield formulated in the dispatch of February 3, 1834, mentioned earlier in this chapter. Of course, Morazán objected to the Englishman's assumptions and at one point in the discussion dropped the hint that his government might seek the recognition of the former mother country, thus settling the question once and for all in Central America's favor. Upset by this remark, Chatfield countered with the threat that such action would only "tend to hasten any discussion which Great Britain and Spain mutually, may find it convenient to hold upon the subject."[48] Not that he was ready to use this weapon yet but he wanted Central Americans to know that it was a possibility if they pushed him too far. In a more positive vein, the British consul suggested that perhaps England might be willing to settle the boundary question according to the lands occupied on September 15, 1821.

More importantly, Mr. Chatfield outlined for the first time what might be called his "Doctrine of Mutuality" in which he stressed the community of interests that existed between Belize and Central America. He emphasized, for example, the defense value of the British establishment as a bulwark against Mexican aggression from the north and

---

47. No. 9 (August 16).
48. *Ibid.*

Colombian territorial designs in the south, the importance of English Belize as a valuable outlet for Central American exports to Europe, and the greater security of British shipping against the depredations of pirates. As we shall see, Frederick Chatfield — the statesman — utilized this constructive approach to advantage among the liberal leaders of Central America for many years to come. When Morazán finally accepted it, he was no longer the incompetent administrator whom Chatfield had described in early August, 1834.

After his interview with the ex-president, Chatfield realized that his chances for a promotion to the diplomatic rank of chargé d'affairs were in jeopardy.[49] Though perhaps unavoidable, his explanations of the British position on Belize were certain to increase the difficulty of negotiating a purely commercial treaty. It seemed that the only course open to him now was to appeal to rational minds with the "Doctrine of Mutuality"; and, indeed, there were signs during the month of August that this approach might be effective. In Guatemala Governor Mariano Gálvez, a likely candidate for the presidency, awarded valuable concessions to Englishmen, announcing what Chatfield hoped would be a new era of harmony in the relations between Central America and Great Britain. Because of this optimism, it never occurred to him that his own countrymen, in pursuing selfish ends, might deliberately try to embarrass the consul's treaty mission. Perhaps this optimism was more a reflection of his faith in the liberality of Governor Mariano Gálvez, for there was no question that he favored the Guatemalan's candidacy for the presidency of the republic. Gálvez was an able administrator.

—◆—

"Business is business" perhaps best describes the philosophy of Marshall Bennett, a rugged nineteenth-century individualist with many "irons in the fire," to quote Mr. Chatfield. According to the consul, Mr. Bennett found himself in the comical position of using "his best influence to get grants of territory made around Belize, which in Belize as a Magistrate, he votes to be an unwarrantable encroachment on the part of the very persons he a few weeks before urged to make the cession."[50] This "sad old rascal" — one of the printable epithets applied to him at Belize — will weave in and out of our story for many chapters to come.[51] In 1826, he was the petulant and outspoken leader of the Belizean commission which demanded the return of fugitive slaves; and a few

49. No. 13 (September 1).
50. To Cockburn, pvt., October 31, 1834, F.O. 252/15.
51. From Major Anderson, November 14, 1836, F.O. 252/8.

years later, he favored strong British consuls in Central America in order to protect the rights of Englishmen.[52] And when the enterprising Bennett found that he could not beat them, he joined them. He received all types of concessions from liberal state governments — mines, houses, land, plantations, etc.

In early 1834, Mr. B. and his Spanish colleague Carlos Antonio Meany were negotiating for an extensive land grant in the Guatemalan departments of Chiquimula and Vera Paz. Eyeing the choice woods along Lake Izabal, Mr. Bennett apparently was determined to corner the wood supply for himself and thus compel his erstwhile cohorts at Belize either to work for him or through him. The Gálvez government, on the other hand, was primarily interested in colonizing the lands in question. It hoped that the wood and other resources would serve as incentives for private capital to finance the colonization of the Guatemalan north — equivalent to the West in the history of the United States. When Chatfield arrived in Central America, Mr. Bennett was mulling over a scheme whereby he could get the desired woods and still meet the requirements for colonization.

Along came Thomas Gould to solve Mr. Bennett's problem. Mr. Gould was the agent for a London association called the "Eastern Coast of Central America Commercial and Agricultural Company," facetiously described later by a Belizean editor as the "Grand Company, with a long name on a h–ll of a long, long, brass plate on the door of their office."[53] In December, 1833, when Chatfield first met Gould in London, he suspected, along with the *Morning Herald,* that the directors of this new company were brazen speculators who had purchased the worthless stock of the old "Poyais Company" of the 1820's, hoping to revive its value. Since the so-called "Eastern" coast obviously referred to the Mosquito Shore, Chatfield notified the directors at Number 7, Tokenhouse Yard, that the sovereignty to the land in question was seriously disputed between Colombia and Central America, not to mention the even more tenable claim of the King of the Mosquitos. Having discouraged the company in strong terms, it surprised Chatfield to learn that Gould was a fellow passenger on the *Belvidera.*[54]

With open arms Mr. Bennett greeted Mr. Gould in Belize and persuaded him that a land grant on the "northern" coast of Guatemala would better suit the purposes of the London company. Off the two went to Guatemala City, where in the early part of August, 1834, they closeted

---

52. Bennett to Ellice, September 16, 1829, F.O. 15/8.
53. *Belize Advertiser* (Belize), No. 53, September 28, 1839.
54. To Palmerston, No. 12, August 23, 1834, F.O. 15/14.

themselves with state authorities. While doing so, they consciously avoided Mr. Chatfield, his advice and influence. Though offended by the secretive ways of his countrymen, not to mention the slight to his official character, the British consul rejoiced at the outcome of their negotiations. On August 19, the enlightened Guatemalan governor signed two contracts which gave Englishmen extensive rights to portions of Chiquimula and practically the entire department of Vera Paz, adjacent to British Honduras.[55]

So that the Foreign Office and Colonel Cockburn might understand his reasons for favoring the land grants, Chatfield described these concessions enthusiastically in dispatch number twelve of August 23, which, in duplicate, was forwarded immediately by special messenger from Guatemala City to the port of Izabal. According to the consul the Eastern Company's grant in the department of Vera Paz, covering an area approximately one hundred and twenty miles in length and seventy miles in width, abounded in minerals and woods, was ideal for cattle and sheep raising, and had a potential for producing a variety of commodities — vegetables, tobacco, coffee, cocoa, sugar, cotton, drugs, indigo, cochineal, wheat, etc. "Added to these advantages of production," the glowing description continued, "the extensive inland navigable waters it possesses, and its proximity, for foreign trade, to the Gulf of Dulce, render it a most valuable possession."[56] Bennett's grant, Chatfield added, was even more promising in the short term since it depended "for success on fewer contingencies." In the Vera Paz grant to the Eastern Company, Guatemala reserved for herself a strip of land eight leagues in depth, or about thirty-two English miles, along the northern shores of Lake Izabal. With minor exceptions, Messrs. Bennett and Meany were granted the first five leagues of the governmental strip, which were especially rich in mahogany. Upon delivery of one thousand English Tower-Proof muskets —and a deadline within a year's time was set for this — they could begin to exploit the resources on their grant. If they met certain colonization requirements, the lands would be theirs at the end of twenty years.

When Belizeans learned of these land grants, they were understandably concerned as well as envious of their competitor's good fortune. Even more disturbing were the rumors that Mr. B. had still another iron in the fire, which Chatfield had only hinted at in the dispatch of August 23. For another thousand rifles, he was going to receive a second

---

55. No. 15, p. encl.s, September 17, 1834, F.O. 15/14; also see *Brief Statement . . . Eastern Coast of Central America Commercial and Agricultural Company* (2d. ed., London, 1840), pp. 21-31.
56. To Palmerston, No. 12, August 23, 1834, F.O. 15/14.

land grant on the Gulf of Honduras, officially awarded to him in January, 1835.[57] And, of course, this second grant also abounded "in the choiciest description of Timber, particularly mahogany and Brazilwood." "But," Chatfield explained on September 17, "its principal advantage is the possession of the Port of Santo Tomas del Castillo, with a most spacious and safe anchorage, and capable under proper management of forming a formidable rival to the Port of Belize. This contingency however is far distant, even should the country receive such a new and powerful impulse as the colonisation of the interior of it, on the extended scale at present contemplated."[58] There was no doubt in Belizean minds as to Bennett's intentions; and the possibility that the "sad old rascal" might also finance a rival entrepôt at Santo Tomás did not lessen their worries.

But Frederick Chatfield did not share the apprehensions of his countrymen at Belize. Since Englishmen would always be Englishmen, the land grants, he felt, would inevitably bind Central America to the benevolent influence of Great Britain, perhaps even to her Empire. In the dispatch of August 23, Chatfield noted, for example, that Bennett's grant would "of course eventually form a part of the possessions of the British in Belize."[59] At the time, in fact, the consul was actually more worried about the possibility that the recipients would not follow through with their contracts, especially the Eastern Company. Suspecting that the directors of the company might use their grant solely for stock market purposes, he forwarded the dispatches of August 23 (original and duplicate) in all haste, hoping that they would reach London before Mr. Gould's return. Once having read Chatfield's arguments in behalf of the land grants, the Foreign Office presumably would then compel the directors of the Eastern Company to discharge their obligations faithfully, or else enlist responsible parties to implement the colonization program in Guatemala. Those, at least, were Mr. Chatfield's expectations; but Bennett and Gould, suspecting that their consul was unfavorably disposed toward their grants, had other plans. After a lengthy and painstaking investigation. Chatfield learned that the two gentlemen in question, who happened to be aboard the ship which carried the letters from Izabal to Belize, had criminally intercepted them. Thus, Colonel Francis Cockburn, who was supposed to read them before he sent them on to London, was deprived of the consul's wisdom concerning the land grant.[60] As we shall see, this was merely Chatfield's ration-

57. No. 15 (September 17).
58. *Ibid.*
59. No. 12 (August 23).
60. No. 16 (October 10); to Cockburn, pvt., Octover 10, 13, 1834, F.O. 252/15; to Backhouse, pvt., October 13, 1834, F.O. 15/14.

alization for a later incident which strained relations between Belize and Guatemala. It reflected his annoyance with the intrigues of fellow Englishmen.

There is still another British subject who must be accounted for in the story of land grants in the Guatemalan north; namely, the handsome, swashbuckling Irishman, Chatfield's political informant at the federal capital. Colonel John Galindo, whose rank was earned in the Central American army, had gained a considerable reputation for himself on the frontiers of the Republic, having been assigned to the task of regulating them. He had served, for example, as the commandant of the Petén district in the northeastern corner of Vera Paz, south of Mexican Yucatán and west of British Belize. On March 24, 1834, Governor Gálvez awarded Colonel Galindo a land grant in the Petén. The same area was assigned to the Eastern Company in the August contract, although later a declaration was appended to the company's contract, stipulating that the Petén would become its property only in the event Galindo failed to meet the prerequisites of his grant.[61] So that there could be no doubt on this point, Chatfield wrote to Mr. Gould on September 30 and recommended that the directors of the company secure the cooperation and utilize the knowledge and experience of Colonel John Galindo, "an officer of merit in the service of the federal government." [62] In a letter of the same date to Colonel Cockburn, it was evident that the British consul regarded Galindo's grant in the same light as the others, that is, from an imperial point of view.[63]

The Guatemalan governor followed the limits of the eighteenth-century treaties in assigning the three English grants which bordered on the British establishment. In effect, he threw the "advocacy" of Central America's claims to the area into the hands of other Englishmen, hoping — it would seem — to pit countrymen against countrymen and thus weaken Belizean influence in London.[64] Though he found this thought annoying, Chatfield was not unduly disturbed by the Guatemalan strategy, perhaps from a conviction that Governor Gálvez, at least, was guided by more noble motives. Besides, there was no doubt in his mind that Central Americans were deceiving themselves by thinking that Englishmen, in the long run, would ever lend themselves to the objectives of another nation. Much could be said in behalf of the consul's

---

61. To Palmerston, No. 15, September 17, 1834, F.O. 15/14.
62. To Thomas Gould, September 30, 1834, F.O. 252/9.
63. To Cockburn, September 30, 1834, F.O. 252/15.
64. To Palmerston, No. 12, August 23, 1834, F.O. 15/14.

assumption and confidence; but since other factors impinged, the question has only academic interest.

The Belizean reaction to the land grants was more important historically. Fellow Englishmen or not, the realists at Belize were in no mood to permit anyone to occupy lands east of Garbutt's fall, where Galindo might challenge them, or between the Sibun and Sarstoon rivers, where Mr. Bennett and the Eastern Company had claims by virtue of the recent grants. There was no mistaking this ugly mood. On September 11, when letters from Colonel Galindo reached Belize indicating that he was about to occupy his Petén grant, the explosion occurred. Under no circumstances would they allow the dashing Irishman to carry out his plans. Colonel Cockburn, without the imperial advice of "My dear Consul," was equally adamant: he wrote immediately to his brother, who commanded the British naval forces in the West Indies, and requested ships to aid him in deterring Central American aggression.[65]

The first news of the militant reaction at Belize reached Guatemala City on September 30. Like wild fire, the report spread that a certain Mr. Young, a Belizean magistrate on his way to Guatemala City as the representative of Colonel Cockburn, had reached the port of Izabal and there threatened wildly that Belizeans were ready to take the law into their own hands if Galindo dared to move into the Petén. "You can have no conception of the irritation which prevails here against our possession of Honduras," Chatfield wrote to Cockburn, because of Young's "silly observations" and the "great deal of nonsense" he was uttering at Izabal.[66] Chatfield tried, as best he could, to correct the situation by explaining to Gálvez and others that Young was not authorized to make such remarks and by deliberately avoiding the garrulous envoy when he arrived in Guatemala City on October 9.[67] But the damage was already done. As in the case of the fugitive slaves, Belizean militancy again placed the territorial question beyond the reach of rational minds.

During the hectic month of October, 1834, another rival British interest began to show its hand; in fact, Colonel Cockburn and most Belizeans attributed the Galindo move to the commercial firm of Skinner-Klee in Guatemala City, the agents of the Reid-Irving House in London.[68] Chatfield disagreed with the accusation at the time, apparently because of Charles Rudolph Klee's cooperation in submitting a lengthy

---

65. From Cockburn, p. encl.s, September 13, 1834; from *idem,* November 22, 1834, F.O. 252/8.
66. To Cockburn, pvt., October 13, 1834; to *idem,* October 31, 1834, F.O. 252/15.
67. To Cockburn, October 31, 1834, F.O. 252/15.
68. From Cockburn, September 15, 1834, F.O. 252/8.

report on the trade potential of Central America and the feasibility of an English "coasting trade" on both the Atlantic and Pacific.[69] Grateful therefore to the Hanoverian Klee and since he had also made the acquaintance of George Ure Skinner, the absent Scottish partner, in London, the consul seriously doubted the imputations from Belize. Yet it turned out that Klee did support an appeal to the Guatemalan government by the Spanish house of Carlos Murphy and Juan Matheu for a two percent rebate on import duties at the Pacific port of Istapa, where a shipload of British manufactures had recently arrived on consignment from the Plock and Logan Company in London. Governor Gálvez granted the rebate on October 10, though it was postdated to August 30 so as to apply to the Murphy-Matheu shipment. A reasonable bounty, lasting two years with a drop to one percent in the second year, it resembled the federal concession of two percent on exports, intended to stimulate national shipping.[70] But suspicious Belizean importers, who considered the state rebate the first step in a deliberate campaign to force them out of business, accused British interests in Guatemala City of selfishly inciting a discriminatory program against Belize. Their suspicions materialized in November, 1834, when heated Guatemalan nationalists clamored for an additional twenty percent federal duty on Belizean imports, as well as other measures against British shipping on the Atlantic.[71] By that time, even Chatfield's eyes opened.

Disappointed at the turn of events which virtually assured the failure of his treaty mission, Mr. Chatfield searched for explanations and countermeasures to the formidable opposition that confronted him. For the first time, he was visibly annoyed with his own countrymen for their contribution to the surge of anglophobia. During the month of October, he realized how Galindo had duped him into thinking that he would champion British influence in Central America. He now regarded him as a selfish, vainglorious, and unpatriotic scoundrel who — sin of all sins — was willing to "denationalize" himself and to discredit his mother country. And he was not the only one whose conduct was unbecoming. Bennett and Gould betrayed a criminal streak in waylaying his dispatches; Belizeans with their foolhardy statements and militancy seemed determined to live up to Guatemalan apprehensions, thus undermining Chatfield's "Doctrine of Mutuality"; and British shipmasters, off the coast of Costa Rica, further blackened the English name with "their

---

69. To Cockburn, pvt., October 10, 1834, F.O. 252/15; from Charles Rudolph Klee, October 5, 1834, F.O. 252/6.
70. To Duke of Wellington, cons. No. 7, p. encl.s, June 1, 1835, F.O. 15/16.
71. Belizean merchants to Wellington, p. encl.s, February 21, 1835, F.O. 15/7.

dishonest and unenglish procedure," acting like pirates and treating Central Americans as if they were savage peoples. The Foreign Office had to do something about this, Chatfield complained to Lord Palmerston.[72] Even his good friend Colonel Cockburn — with or without the dispatches of August 23, which incidentally did not mention Galindo's grant — failed to consult him before sending Mr. Young to Guatemala City. Chatfield's allegation that the superintendent would have acted otherwise if Bennett and Gould had not intercepted dispatch number twelve only underscored his disappointment with "My dear Colonel" for not waiting to hear from him first.[73]

The British consul was not idle in meeting the October crisis. On the 13th, he suggested to the Foreign Office that the time had come for England to approach Spain on the question of sovereignty to British Honduras, a threat which he had made in the August interview with General Morazán and which the English government actually implemented in January of the following year.[74] In the meantime, he wrote to Vice President Salazar suggesting the appointment of a two-man commission to negotiate a commercial treaty with him in Guatemala City. For this purpose, he recommended the names of "two of the cleverest people in Central America to be pitted against me, here": Governor Mariano Gálvez, a prominent contender for the presidency; and José Francisco Barrundia, the ideologist of Central America liberalism and formerly provisional president of the Republic.[75] "The advantage of meeting such Persons in business," Chatfield explained, "is that they are more open to conviction and plain sense than individuals whose ideas are less enlightened; besides, there is less likelihood of an Act of theirs being rejected by the Congress or the Senate."[76] These two liberal lights, Chatfield reasoned to himself, could fully appreciate his "Doctrine of Mutuality" and the dire consequences for Central America if the ultra-nationalists had their way on the question of Belize. The threat of referring the boundary issue to Spain, therefore, gave Chatfield a weapon which he could hold over the commissioners' heads, or, more likely, a persuader which could be used effectively at the next congress to

72. To Palmerston, Nos. 17 (October 13) and 19 (October 22, 1834), F.O. 15/14.
73. See documents cited in footnote 60.
74. To Backhouse, pvt., October 13, 1834, F.O. 15/14; to Cockburn, pvt., October 13, 1834, F.O. 252/15.
75. To Cockburn, pvt., October 10, 1834, F.O. 252/15.
76. To Backhouse, pvt., October 13, 1834, F.O. 15/14.

assure the ratification of the English commercial treaty. Apparently, the two great liberal leaders of Guatemala gave Chatfield reason to believe that they sincerely hoped to avoid a disastrous rupture with Great Britain.

Perhaps Chatfield's strategy might have been successful if his Irish rival in San Salvador had not been so convincing. Riding the crest of the nationalistic wave, the resourceful colonel threw off his mask in the month of October to meet the challenge of Frederick Chatfield and the Belizeans. He convinced the federal authorities at San Salvador that the Republic, whose prestige had declined dangerously in past months, would perish if it failed to take a firm stand on Belize. They should not be deceived by the English trickster in Guatemala City who only recently suggested the appointment of a treaty commission to meet with him; the federal government should insist upon a territorial settlement as the *sine qua non* of any negotiations Chatfield might hold with Gálvez and Barrundia. Agents like Chatfield and Cockburn, the colonel pointed out, were tailoring a policy of their own to meet the selfish interests of Englishmen at Belize; and this policy did not accord with the enlightened attitude of the British Foreign Office.[77] If allowed to run roughshod over Central America, Chatfield and company would fasten upon her the iron-clad monopoly of Belizean importers and would not rest until Belize were declared a British colony, thus usurping Guatemalan sovereignty to her northern frontier, violating the territorial integrity of the Republic, and challenging the glorious territorial formula of the Americas.

The solution was an obvious one: Central America should take her case before the bar of enlightened world opinion by sending a diplomatic mission to the United States and to Europe. To prove his loyalty, allegiance, and true love for his adopted country, the gallant Irish colonel offered his services. He would personally defy the Belizeans by occupying the Petén with settlers from North America, or from Holland, or from any country whose sons and daughters would venture to come to the land of promise and opportunity, astride the great canal linking the East and the West. In the United States, he would try to interest the government, or private investors, to undertake the great canal project, which would free Central America from the economic tyranny of the British at Belize; he would also convince the State Department that the Belizeans were violating the message of President James Monroe; and thus the North American sister would use her influence in London to secure a territorial settlement according to the eighteenth-century Spanish treaties. And in Europe, Galindo promised to seek the mediation and support

---

77. To Palmerston, Nos. 23 (November 13) and 28 (December 17, 1834), F.O. 15/14.

of other European powers for the same end, so that the British Foreign Office, pressured from all sides, would look favorably upon a settlement of the territorial issue. While in Europe, moreover, he would recruit teachers for the introduction of the Lancastrian system of education into Central America.[78] With such potent and irresistible arguments, Galindo understandably gained the advantage over Chatfield, who by October 31 was already aware that the colonel might be sent to Europe to discuss Belize with Lord Palmerston. "You and I," he told Colonel Cockburn, "are regarded as quite impracticable on the subject."[79]

To complicate matters for the English consul, the Belizean agitation, coming as it did during the campaign for state elections in Guatemala, fostered a vindictive program to force the evacuation of British Belize by an appeal to the xenophobia of the Guatemalan electorate. Here was an explosive issue upon which political opposites could either join or vie with each other, depending upon the advantage they hoped to achieve. And Governor Mariano Gálvez, Chatfield realized, was on the proverbial spot as he ran for reelection, which he needed in order to improve his chances for the presidency of the Republic. Thus, on October 10, Gálvez had awarded the two percent rebate to Pacific traders — a wise political move which could be interpreted, on the one hand, as anti-Belize and yet pro-English on the other, since it helped British interests trading via the Horn. Appreciating Gálvez' predicament and hoping to strengthen his hand for the presidency, Chatfield had to overlook the vindictive implications of the two percent rebate. To have done otherwise would have embarrassed Governor Gálvez and his liberal faction at a time when the conservative opposition was trying to discredit him for the English grants in the Guatemalan north. Chatfield was aware that in mid-October the Guatemalan *serviles,* capitalizing upon the Belize issue, were conspiring to overthrow Gálvez and to lead an attack upon the hated foreigner. The uprising broke out on October 31. Fortunately, it was quickly suppressed by the Gálvez government, thanks in part to Chatfield's cooperation. He publicized the fact that there were British ships on both coasts ready to protect the lives and property of English subjects.[80]

---

78. In addition to Chatfield's dispatches on the subject, this analysis of the Galindo mission is based upon documentation in MDCIA, III, and also in F.O. 15, volumes 17 and 18. For the specific reference to the recruitment of teachers, see E. C. J. Lewin to Palmerston, January 20, 1836, F.O. 15/18. Also see the excellent article by William J. Griffith, "Juan Galindo, Central American Chauvinist," *Hispanic American Historical Review,* Vol. XL (February, 1960), 25-52.
79. To Cockburn, October 31, 1834, F.O. 252/15.
80. To Cockburn, November 1, 1834, F.O. 252/15; to Palmerston, Nos. 20-22, November 7-12, 1834, F.O. 15/14.

Despite his efforts and because of the political context, Chatfield was powerless to prevent the formation of a well-organized campaign against Belize during the months of November and December, 1834. The Guatemalan vindictives — of all political hues — outlined discriminatory measures which they hoped would be passed at the next federal congress, scheduled for early January. The basic assumption of the campaign was that British Belize was entirely dependent upon Central America for survival and thus vulnerable to economic sanctions. At the next congress, therefore, Guatemalans would ask for an additional twenty percent federal tariff against Belize with a further threat that if it did not force Belizeans back to the limits of the eighteenth-century treaties all intercourse would be stopped; they would urge the establishment of a rival port at Santo Tomás; they would seek concessions favoring British shipping coming around the Horn; and they would advocate opening up the Republic's ports to Spanish shipping, thus gaining the former mother country's favor in the territorial dispute. Belizean merchants and woodcutters, the vindictives asserted, would have only two choices when confronted with this energetic opposition: either abandon the northern outpost or annex themselves to Central America in order to share in the concessions being made to other Englishmen.[81] That, in short, was the essence of the Guatemalan crusade against Belize, to which we must also add the plan to send Colonel Galindo abroad.

In anticipation of the vindictives' program, Chatfield suggested that Great Britain refer to Spain on the question of sovereignty to Belize, hoping, as pointed out above, that this action would directly facilitate the ratification of an English commercial treaty. But he also justified the suggestion on the ground that Spanish recognition of the English title would permit the superintendent of Belize to issue land grants for purposes of cultivation.[82] The justification, incidentally, merely echoed a strong Belizean sentiment for colonial status with all the economic benefits that would accrue from the imperial connection. Chatfield, on the other hand, regarded the right of cultivation in terms of the vindictive programs outlined above; and on October 31, he first hinted at the most appropriate countermeasure to thwart Galindo and the hate-Belize crusade.[83]

81. To Palmerston, No. 28, December 17, 1834, F.O. 15/14; Miguel Alvarez to Mariano Gálvez, March 2, 1835, and the correspondence of Guatemalan officials concerning the subject of that letter, A.G.N.G./CMRE, leg. 164, exp. 0341.
82. To Backhouse, pvt., October 13, F.O. 15/14; to Cockburn, pvt., October 13, 1834, F.O. 252/15.
83. To Cockburn, October 31, 1834, F.O. 252/15.

The best deterrent, Chatfield reiterated frequently in the months of November and December, was to encourage the colonization of the Eastern Company's grant in the department of Vera Paz. "It is worth reflecting," he warned Palmerston, "what embarrassment might arise should any people but the English prepare to avail themselves of the Project."[84] He was especially worried about the rumor that Colonel Galindo intended to occupy his grant in the Petén with foreign colonists and presumably with the support of their mother country. To counter this action, Chatfield proposed that the Foreign Office encourage the Eastern Company to follow through on their contract, *compelling* the directors to establish their first settlement in the Petén district, adjacent to British Belize. Although he proceeded to extol the natural attributes of the Petén to prove his point, Chatfield's objective was unmistakably political or imperial in nature.[85] The Petén was a potential granary for the British establishment; and if occupied by Englishmen, bound by cultural and economic ties with the residents of Belize, no campaign of attrition by vindictive Central Americans could ever force the evacuation of the British outpost on the northern coast of Guatemala. With Englishmen growing all manner of exports in the hinterland, the manufacturing traffic via the Atlantic would continue; and Belizeans would be able to control the return cargoes, relieving themselves of their dependency upon Central American exports. Although Chatfield denied the "fallacious" assumptions of the anti-Belize crusade, his brilliantly conceived Petén suggestion started from the same premises.[86]

Apparently because the implications of his proposal were so clearly imperialistic, the British Foreign Office chose to ignore it. Nevertheless, it remained one of Chatfield's principal objectives in Central America for many years, conditioning, as we shall see, his attitude toward the colonization efforts of the Eastern Company. The only immediate result of the Petén suggestion was that it prompted Lord Palmerston to frustrate Galindo's recruitment of colonists in Holland.[87]

Chatfield's counter strategy notwithstanding, the federal government under Vice President Salazar was swayed by Colonel Galindo's advice. On November 10, the Gálvez-Barrundia commission received authorization to negotiate with Frederick Chatfield, providing the latter agreed to treat the territorial question. This proviso, as Galindo had

---

84. To Palmerston, No. 23, November 13, 1834, F.O. 15/14.
85. To Palmerston, Nos. 21 (November 7) and 28 (December 17, 1834), F.O. 15/14.
86. Nos. 21-23 (November 7-13).
87. From John Bidwell, No. 7, May 13, 1836, F.O. 15/18.

expected, undermined Chatfield's strategy in naming the treaty commissioners in Guatemala City. When the consul replied that he could not meet the condition stipulated, the federal government politely informed him that it had no choice but to send an envoy directly to London.[88] During the month of December, Salazar appointed John Galindo to represent the Republic, and the necessary preparations were made for his immediate departure. Determined to achieve a diplomatic victory on the territorial question, the Salazar government wrote letters to the various governmental heads whom Galindo would meet on his mission. The acting secretary of state, Miguel Alvarez, sketched the territorial question in a letter to the United States government, requesting its support in defense of the American territorial formula and reminding the State Department that Belizeans had violated the Monroe message of 1823.[89] In another letter to the French government, Alvarez explained Galindo's mission and urged France to exert her influence in London to assure its success. Underscoring the role of the "French Party" in the decision to send Galindo abroad, he hinted that France might reasonably be expected to gain some preference for her support.[90]

Galindo's victory came as no surprise to Frederick Chatfield considering the agitation over Belize and the fierce competition of political groups in proclaiming their patriotism. As might be expected, a deep resentment rankled in his mind toward those who had done most to thwart his treaty mission: first, his meddling countrymen — Galindo, Bennett, and Klee; next, the *serviles,* whom he despised for the religious and economic prejudices which they fomented against foreigners; and finally, the French or non-English type of liberal who would not listen to his "Doctrine of Mutuality," perhaps from vile, political ambitions.[91] Because of them, the obnoxious John Galindo would now be sent over his head to Lord Palmerston in London, announcing the failure of his treaty mission. Because of them, his ambition of a promotion to diplomatic rank was in serious jeopardy. But he was not beaten yet; he had plans for a counteroffensive; and he was determined to teach his enemies a lesson. They would learn to respect His Britannic Majesty's consul in Central America.

In fighting back at his enemies, the English agent continued to work with "enlightened" Guatemalan liberals such as Governor Gálvez. A

---

88. To Palmerston, No. 29, p. encl.s, December 29, 1834, F.O. 15/14.

89. Miguel Alvarez to John Forsyth, December 30, 1834, MDCIA, III, 85.

90. Alvarez to Ministre des Affaires Etrangères, December 30, 1834, A.A.E.P./ CPAC, vol. 2.

91. To Palmerston, No. 22, November 12, 1834, F.O. 15/14.

Gálvez victory in the state elections would strengthen his bid for the presidency; and with Gálvez as president, Chatfield felt sure he could stop the Galindo mission. On November 12, interestingly, when he already knew that the treaty commissioners could not negotiate with him, Chatfield praised Governor Mariano Gálvez; and on the following day, he asked Lord Palmerston to consider possible concessions in order to secure a commercial treaty with Central America. For obvious reasons, he asked for permission to change the terminology of the treaty. More importantly, he requested the inclusion of an additional article "that for a period of six years British ships in the ports of Central America shall continue to pay the same amount of tonnage duties as are now payable, and which exceed those paid by national vessels 6 d. a ton." Chatfield reasoned:

> This concession would be very grateful to the federal government, as preserving an advantage to every state in the Republick, and it would likewise benefit Belize in consequence of this charge pressing only upon ships frequenting the Ports of the South Sea, where already several special privileges are conceded for the encouragement and profit of those persons who preferably trade by the Pacifick to prejudice Honduras.[92]

The article, in other words, could help in undermining the vindictive program proposed by Guatemalans, who were directly concerned with the Belize question, by appealing to the pecuniary interest of the four remaining states of the Union. Moreover, the proposal left no doubt that Chatfield blamed the Skinner-Klee house for the anti-Belize program and that he was prepared to make them regret it. The question is: Did Gálvez ask for these concessions, or was this a case of Chatfield anticipating a Gálvez victory at the next federal congress? The evidence is conflicting. On the one hand, the consul hinted that certain parties in Guatemala City had approached him on the subject of reciprocal trade arrangements, though no mention was made of their names.[93] Yet the events described in the next chapter suggest that it was solely the consul's idea.

As for the meddlesome Irishman, Chatfield had already outlined his offense in early November. At all costs, he would try to prevent the colonel's departure by an appeal to public opinion. He would point out the Irishman's opportunism in volunteering for the diplomatic mission, how much Central America's prestige would suffer in Europe by sending a foreigner to represent her, and the unconstitutionality of Galindo's

---

92. No. 23 (November 13).
93. No. 15 (September 17).

appointment since the Senate had not ratified it. If, despite this appeal, Galindo proceeded on his mission, Chatfield would then alert the British representative in Washington, D.C., urging him to discredit Galindo in the eyes of the State Department. In the meantime, he would persuade Palmerston not to receive a British subject as the representative of a foreign nation and he would also prepare Belize for a counteroffensive against the vindictive program that would certainly be introduced in the January sessions of the Central American congress.[94]

——•••——

Insurmountable obstacles prevented the successful conclusion of Frederick Chatfield's treaty mission during the first six months of his career in Central America. Undoubtedly, his explanation of the British position on the "Question of Honduras" contributed to the failure of his diplomatic mission as minister plenipotentiary; but, considering the political events described, it is questionable that an official silence could have changed the outcome. Although faced with a formidable task, he nevertheless approached it with the calmness and shrewdness of a statesman, a result perhaps of his first interview with Lord Palmerston after the Warsaw fiasco. And despite his failure, it still remained to be seen how effective his countermeasures would be.

---

94. Nos. 23 (November 13), 28 (December 17), and 29 (December 29).

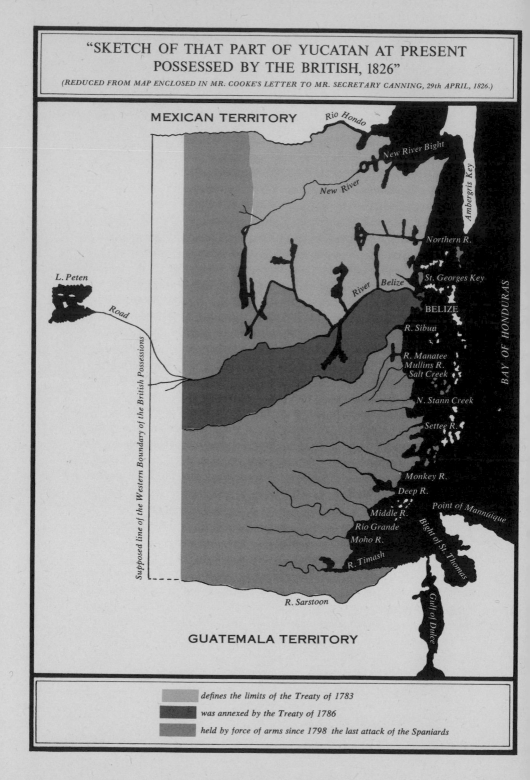

"SKETCH OF THAT PART OF YUCATAN AT PRESENT POSSESSED BY THE BRITISH, 1826"

(REDUCED FROM MAP ENCLOSED IN MR. COOKE'S LETTER TO MR. SECRETARY CANNING, 29th APRIL, 1826.)

MEXICAN TERRITORY

Rio Hondo

New River Bight

New River

Ambergris Key

Northern R.

L. Peten

St. Georges Key

River *Belize*

Road

BELIZE

R. Sibun

BAY OF HONDURAS

R. Manatee
Mullins R.
Salt Creek

N. Stann Creek

Supposed line of the Western Boundary of the British Possessions

Settee R.

Monkey R.

Deep R.

Point of Mannuique

Middle R.
Rio Grande
Moho R.

Bight of St. Thomas

R. Timash

Gulf of Dulce

R. Sarstoon

GUATEMALA TERRITORY

> *defines the limits of the Treaty of 1783*
>
> *was annexed by the Treaty of 1786*
>
> *held by force of arms since 1798 the last attack of the Spaniards*

British Honduras, 1826

CHAPTER FOUR

Reciprocal Annoyance

Although in the conflict this government may lose an eye, yet it will have the gratification of pulling out both the eyes of Belize.[1]
— A Guatemalan, January 30, 1836

The Belize legislative body must take an enlarged view of the subject, and although at a present sacrifice, not hesitate to pass such regulations of reciprocal annoyance as will best serve to replace matters upon a proper level.[2]
— Chatfield, December 17, 1834

After a difficult and wearisome trip from Guatemala City to the Pacific coast, the British consul rode into San Salvador on January 18, 1835, nine days after the opening session of the special federal congress. He hurried to the scene of this important gathering, which many expected would pave the way for the vaunted reforms of the Constitution of 1824, in hopes of correcting the erroneous impressions which his Irish rival had propagated and of frustrating, if possible, the colonel's departure from Central America.[3] Fortunately, as far as English interests were concerned, the nature of the special congress and its limited objectives, which included the election of a president and the establishment of the federal district, prevented the introduction of the anti-Belizean program. Moreover, sensing a strong feeling against Great Britain, fanned by an active Guatemalan delegation, Mr. Chatfield prudently chose to remain silent while he outlined in his mind the best defense against the reports of Belize's detractors.[4]

To further their campaign against the British establishment, Guatemalan delegates were assuring federal authorities that Belizeans were anxious to annex themselves to the Republic rather than suffer "that distress which an interdiction of the trade between this country and Belize will occasion"— a rumor which the consul attributed to the merchants Klee and Murphy. But Chatfield seriously doubted that members of this special congress, or for that matter those of the regular congress scheduled for two or three months hence, would sanction the "visionary

---

1. As quoted in, to Palmerston, No. 2, January 30, 1836, F.O. 15/18.
2. To Palmerston, No. 28, December 17, 1834, F.O. 15/14.
3. To Palmerston, No. 2, January 10, 1835; to Backhouse, pvt., February 1, 1835, F.O. 15/16.
4. To Wellington, cons. No. 7, June 1, 1835, F.O. 15/16.

schemes" of a few selfish merchants in Guatemala City who aspired to a monopoly of the country's trade. If they should succeed, however, he would certainly capitalize upon the suspicion and envy that existed in Central America against the large state of Guatemala. He would see to it, in other words, that the oppressive regulation was brought to bear "in equal force upon the ports of the States of Honduras and Costa Rica, where it will encounter a determined opposition."[5] At a time when constitutional reforms and measures for effective union were the order of the day, England's representative in Central America would stress the fact that the proposed legislation against Belize, though presented in nationalistic guise, was actually conceived to further the special interests of Guatemalan merchants. As we shall see, conditions were ripe for this shrewd political strategem, only one of many tactics employed by Chatfield to defend his countrymen.

——◆◆◆——

During the sessions of the special federal congress, the English consul experienced a change of heart with regard to Governor Mariano Gálvez, whom he had referred to on many occasions as an enlightened liberal guided in every respect by reasonable principles of action. It will be recalled that Chatfield had counted heavily upon a Gálvez reelection in Guatemala and that without qualification had hoped that he would also win the presidency of the Republic. As it turned out, the governor won the state elections handily; but at San Salvador the situation was different. For the second time, the presidential vote went instead to General Francisco Morazán. Suddenly and without adequate explanation, Chatfield reached the conclusion that Gálvez had been the prime mover of the campaign against Belize since its inception. Accordingly, he now described the erstwhile champion as a "shrewd, pettifogging, corrupt lawyer," who controlled the actions of the incompetent Vice President Salazar.[6]

In no mood to do justice to his former friend, Chatfield interpreted Gálvez' actions cynically as those of an unscrupulous political opportunist. To be sure, the Guatemalan governor was a shrewd political tactician, who had presidential aspirations; but Chatfield erred in denying that Gálvez was sincerely concerned about the territorial integrity of his state and nation — just as anyone might make the same mistake in questioning the consul's own devotion to the British cause by attributing it solely to personal ambition. It might be argued, in fact, that the two

5. To Backhouse, pvt., February 1, 1835, F.O. 15/16.
6. *Ibid.*

men were very much alike, which perhaps helps to explain their initial attraction to each other and their subsequent enmity. Both men were equally capable, shrewd, devoted, stubborn, and ambitious. If Chatfield had been a Guatemalan, he would have reacted in the same manner as Gálvez to reports that Belizean magistrates had officially proclaimed the territorial limits of their establishment and that Colonel Cockburn had encouraged the settlement of lands between the Sibun and the Sarstoon by some two thousand Honduran Caribs, who had fought with the conservative invasionary forces of 1831–1832. As an Englishman, Chatfield could easily overlook these reports; but a Guatemalan, and especially the leading public servant of the state, could not callously ignore such matters without committing political suicide or betraying his patriotic convictions. Governor Gálvez, therefore, complained to the federal government about the alleged encouragement of Carib settlements in the disputed zone; and on January 30, 1835, Secretary of State Miguel Alvarez assured him that an official protest would be lodged with the British government.[7] Apparently, the Carib issue, which does not appear in the British documentation, was the turning point in the relations between the English consul and the Guatemalan governor. It should be noted that Chatfield did not raise an accusing finger at Gálvez until February 1, 1835.[8]

The decision to play a passive role at the special federal congress was also expedient while Chatfield was awaiting replies from London and Belize to letters he had written in December of the past year. Convinced that Belize could defend itself against the proposed economic restrictions, he recommended a program of "reciprocal annoyance" which included the levying of a special tax on Bennett's wood, as well as "countervailing restrictions" upon Central American exports using the English port. These retaliatory measures, Chatfield assured the Foreign Office, would disprove the "fallacious" assumption that Belize was entirely dependent upon Central America and thus vulnerable to economic sanctions. To punish the vindictives and to advance the "Doctrine of Mutuality," his strategy was simply to prove the opposite thesis: that Central America needed and was dependent upon Belize.[9]

In the meantime, Colonel Cockburn had not been idle in protecting the interests of the British establishment and whenever possible he had

---

7. Gálvez to Alvarez, January 19, 1835, and Alvarez de Gálvez, January 30, 1835, A.G.N.G./CMRE, leg. 164, exp. 03417. Also see, John Galindo to John Forsyth, June 1, 1835, MDCIA, III, 88.
8. To Backhouse, pvt., February 1, 1835, F.O. 15/16.
9. To Palmerston, No. 28, December 17, 1834, F.O. 15/14; from Cockburn, January 9, 1835, F.O. 252/8.

done his best to implement Chatfield's recommendations. For example, when in October, 1834, the consul suggested the advantages of consulting with Spain on the question of sovereignty, the superintendent hurriedly dispatched his secretary Thomas Miller to lobby for the Spanish negotiations in London. The documentation on the Miller mission to Europe leaves no doubt that Belizean alarm was primarily the result of Marshall Bennett's woodcutting activities and grants to the south of Belize. Among other things, Thomas Miller had instructions to ask for colonial status which would give English settlers at Belize the right to cultivate lands, thus diversifying their economy and relieving them from a sole dependence upon the wood trade; to seek permission to tax wood that had been cut in areas beyond the limits of the British establishment; and to encourage the occupation, or purchase, of the Bay Islands, "the very key to our possessions in the Bay of Honduras."[10] In short, the Miller mission, which resulted from Chatfield's suggestion of October, 1834, was Colonel Cockburn's answer to John Galindo's tour abroad.

Of more immediate importance, the December letters from Guatemala City led to the calling of a special meeting of Belizean magistrates on January 8, 1835, in which they resolved to levy retaliatory duties if the Central American congress dared to legislate discriminatory measures against Belize. Perhaps intentionally, no mention was made of the type of duty that would be imposed; but considering the opposition voiced by Mr. Gentle and Mr. Walsh, both of whom were buying wood from Marshall Bennett, the reference was obviously to a levy upon wood. At any rate, the important thing at this time was the threat of retaliation; and Colonel Cockburn wasted no time in forwarding a copy of the minutes to Frederick Chatfield, urging him to circulate it to advantage at the federal capital. The document arrived in San Salvador on February 11.[11]

Upon receiving assurance of Belizean support, the English consul decided that the time was ripe to launch an offensive; and on February 14, the day before the adjournment of the special congress, he wrote the equivalent of an ultimatum to the federal government. In a letter to the secretary of state, Chatfield argued that the Guatemalan bounty of two percent, granted in October, 1834, to merchants importing through Istapa on the Pacific, was unconstitutional. Since it was an obvious case of usurping the federal government's prerogatives, Guatemala should be compelled either to repeal the bounty or to apply it equally to all her ports. And if this action were not taken by April 1, Chatfield threatened,

---

10. Thomas Miller to Aberdeen, p. encl.s and mem., February 2, 1835, F.O. 15/17.
11. From Cockburn, January 9, 1835, F.O. 252/8.

British Belize would retaliate with an equivalent duty on all Guatemalan products going through its port.[12]

What prompted this reversal of strategy? By the consul's own admission, the move was intended to force the federal government to resume negotiations with him on the English commercial treaty without the *sine qua non* of a territorial settlement. The threat of Belizean retaliation, coupled with the report that British ships were daily expected at Belize in response to Colonel Cockburn's request for naval support, would presumably make Governor Gálvez realize the serious consequences that might attend the vindictive program against Belize. This in turn would lead him to urge Vice President Salazar, still in charge of the federal government during the absence of General Morazán, to renew treaty negotiations. With one stroke, therefore, Chatfield would force Gálvez to retreat, would punish Klee for the rumors he had spread about Belize by denying him the two percent bounty on a ship which had just arrived in the port of Istapa, and would prevent the departure of Colonel Galindo, since now there would be no further reason for his mission.[13] This, at least, was the house the consul had built. Interestingly, only Cockburn was kept informed of this maneuver, though Chatfield referred to it fleetingly in a dispatch to the Foreign Office some three months later. He never sent a copy of the ultimatum to London, however.[14]

Although the evidence is far from conclusive, a more likely explanation for the power move is that it was suggested to Chatfield by someone who wished to discredit Gálvez, thus weakening any influence the governor might hope to wield over President Morazán. In this case, it would be public opinion, fearing a rupture with Great Britain especially at a critical period in the history of the Republic, which would undermine the vindictives' anti-Belize campaign. Conceivably, judging from Chatfield's remarks, Secretary of State Alvarez may have recommended this action. By mid-March, 1835, federal authorities had agreed to Chatfield's conditions on the renewal of the treaty negotiations without waiting for Gálvez' reply on the Istapa bounty. Then, suddenly, Vice President Salazar withdrew his promise on the ground that he had received a letter from Morazán which announced his impending arrival at the federal capital. Salazar argued that the matter should therefore be left to President Morazán.[15]

---

12. To Miguel Alvarez, February 14, 1835, F.O. 252/5.
13. To Wellington, cons. No. 7, June 1, 1835, F.O. 15/16.
14. *Ibid.;* to Cockburn, April 4, 1835, F.O. 252/15.
15. To Backhouse, pvt., March 16, 1835; to Wellington, No. 5, p. encl.s, March 31, 1835, F.O. 15/16.

. With the deadline of April 1 fast approaching, the English consul wrote to Miguel Alvarez on March 28 asking him what the position of the Morazán government would be on the treaty and the Istapa bounty. At the same time he enclosed a copy of a letter he had received on the 27th from Belize in which a British naval officer wondered naively — undoubtedly for Chatfield's benefit and use — whether blockade tactics would be justified in the event the federal congress chose to pass discriminatory measures against the English port. The hint was not wasted; Alvarez promptly replied that the treaty would be brought to Morazán's attention soon after his arrival in San Salvador and that the Istapa bounty issue, clearly unconstitutional in his opinion, would be presented to the federal congress.[16]

Surprisingly, the British consul hurriedly accepted these vague promises as a satisfactory answer to the ultimatum of February 14, persuading himself at the same time that the resort to naval action was no longer necessary. The de-emphasis of physical force — at least, at the governmental level — confirms the interpretation that Chatfield's threats were inspired by internal political considerations, namely, to raise the spectre of an imminent rupture with Great Britain in order to weaken Governor Gálvez' control over the federal government. If Chatfield had been working alone on this strategy, it is reasonable to assume that he would have continued with the negative threat of naval action; instead, he pursued an indirect approach of persuasion which implied close cooperation with an anti-*Galvecista* element in the federal government. He was "sanguine enough to hope" that "after a few explanations" President Morazán would abandon his mistaken ideas concerning Belize and would authorize Alvarez to conclude a commercial treaty with him. "I certainly am desirous it should be done," Chatfield explained to Colonel Cockburn, "for I think among other advantages it will be a means of removing those sources of irritation and misunderstanding which have existed between this territory and Belize."[17]

Preparing himself for the inevitable fight with the *Galvecistas* who would certainly oppose any attempt to negotiate a British commercial treaty at the next federal congress, Chatfield wrote some letters in early April, 1835, to London and Belize which recommended measures intended to undermine Gálvez' power and to encourage the negotiation and ratification of the treaty. Since Belizeans stood to gain handsomely

16. *Ibid.;* to Cockburn, April 4, 1835, F.O. 252/15.
17. To Cockburn, sec., April 4, 1835, F.O. 252/15 and also F.O. 15/16.

from his efforts, he felt that it was only right that they should give him their unstinted support. First, they had to destroy the "impression," circulated by Klee and Murphy in order to weaken the recent ultimatum, that out of self interest Belize would not dare tax Guatemalan products. It was imperative, therefore, that they enact a retaliatory levy of two percent on wood and on cochineal. On his part, Chatfield would further embarrass the Guatemalan government by promising rebates of the Belizean tax to anyone who would sign affidavits stating that he had suffered from the fiscal acts of the Gálvez government. Measures such as these, Chatfield assured Cockburn, "will occasion a sufficient outcry in Mr. Galves' ears." In the postscript, he noted shrewdly that Carlos Meany, Bennett's partner, would be the first to complain of a wood tax.[18] And secondly, since a commercial treaty with Central America would relieve Belize of the discriminatory five percent federal tariff, Belizeans should willingly provide the means to assure its ratification — one thousand to one thousand five hundred pounds sterling would probably be sufficient.[19] In a similar request to the Foreign Office, Chatfield explained that in matters of this kind bribery was the customary procedure in the young republics of America. A case in point, according to the consul, was the United States treaty of 1826 which cost John Williams, the American envoy, five thousand dollars to ratify.[20] To which Lord Palmerston commented on August 17: "I should not object to a moderate charge of this nature, if by its means the object in view could be accomplished."[21]

If Chatfield expected Governor Gálvez to cower before the ultimatum, he was sorely mistaken. It merely convinced the governor that Belize and the meddling English agent had to be taught a lesson. In no uncertain terms, the Guatemalan government questioned the consul's interpretation of articles 69 and 178 of the federal constitution and cited historical examples and arguments in defense of the state's right to levy duties for the welfare of its people. And as for Chatfield's threat of retaliation, the Gálvez administration recommended that the federal government should assist the British consul in carrying it out, thus ruining the Belizean trade "which is so harmful to us."[22] Clearly, Messrs. Klee and Murphy had convinced Gálvez that the ultimatum was a bluff which

---

18. To Cockburn, April 4, 1835, F.O. 252/15.
19. To Cockburn, sec., April 4, 1835, F.O. 252/15 and F.O. 15/16.
20. To Backhouse, pvt./conf., April 6, 1835, F.O. 15/16.
21. *Ibid.*
22. Miguel Alvarez to Mariano Gálvez, March 2, 1835, A.G.N.G./CMRE, leg. 164, exp. 0341, which includes Chatfield's ultimatum and is followed by the Guatemalan analyses of April 30 and May 22.

Belizeans themselves would not back — a correct evaluation of their position, incidentally.[23]

Contrary to expectations, President Morazán delayed his arrival in San Salvador for a month after the opening session of the federal congress and thus placed the responsibility for the executive's message of April 22 on the shoulders of Vice President Salazar. As the opening date drew near, Chatfield consulted with Miguel Alvarez concerning the executive's recommendations, hoping that the message would contain nothing to inflame minds against the British establishment. The secretary of state — perhaps from a desire to discredit Salazar and Gálvez as Chatfield suspected — assured him that there was nothing provocative in the executive's statement to congress. Yet nothing could have been further from the truth. The Salazar speech of the 22nd bristled with resentment against Belize and contained a perfect exposition of the *Galvecista* program.[24] In vain, Chatfield tried to prevent its publication and dissemination. It appeared on May 8, 1835. The battle for control of the federal congress had started.

The Salazar speech of April 22 emphasized the importance and advantage of developing the Pacific coast trade so as to destroy the "monopoly of the establishment on the northern coast." Rather than repeal the Guatemalan bounty of two percent, the vice president recommended generalizing it to all Central American ports on the Pacific. In effect, such a measure would extend to importers the federal bounty which already existed for exporters and national shipping interests on the Pacific. These steps were necessary to correct the territorial aggression of Belize, and the vice president promised that he would suggest other actions in the future. The executive's message also contained other references which alarmed the English consul, especially the remarks concerning the importance of reconsidering a commercial treaty with France and of reviving the Dutch canal project and loan — all of which would tend to minimize British influence in Central America. Moreover, Salazar announced the impending departure of Colonel Galindo, now that financial arrangements had been made for his mission.[25]

Despite the vice president's recommendations, the federal congress of 1835, as the earlier special congress, failed to legislate the discriminatory program against Belize. In fact, because of its "friendliness" to the interests of Great Britain, according to Chatfield, it was nicknamed

---

23. To Cockburn, April 4, 1835, F.O. 252/15.
24. To Wellington, No. 6, May 22, 1835, F.O. 15/16.
25. *Ibid.,* p. encl. *Gaceta del Gobierno Federal* (San Salvador), No. 6, May 8, 1835.

"El congreso británico."[26] Chatfield's victory was all the more remarkable since it was achieved without the use of the navy and without any economic sanctions. At a public meeting on March 4, 1835, Belizeans merely passed a new tax schedule on wood, falling heavily upon the product of foreigners and especially aimed at the harmful competition of Mr. Bennett and his Spanish partner on the coast of Guatemala and Honduras.[27] As far as other Central American exports were concerned, however, Belizeans refused to comply with the consul's suggestions.[28]

Chatfield's success in "The Britannic Congress" of 1835, by no means as complete as he would have desired, was primarily the result of fortuitous circumstances in the political development of Central America, as well as his own ability and willingness to work within that framework. He sensed, for example, that responsible liberal leaders, anxious to establish the Republic upon a firm foundation, were determined to achieve this great national objective at all costs, thus ending the interminable chaos of the past. Refusing to divert their energies along any other channels, they questioned the motives and the consequences of the course of action which Governor Gálvez was suggesting to them. They knew what England was prepared to do; there was some basis to doubt the motives of Guatemalan merchants and perhaps even those of the Guatemalan governor; and they reasoned that it was pointless, if not suicidal, to implement the vindictives' program without first awaiting the results of Colonel Galindo's mission to the United States and to Europe. Furthermore, they feared that the agitation over Belize would serve to increase the political importance of the *serviles* in the federal government, a trend which was noted by Chatfield and the French representative in Central America.[29] In fact, it might be argued that Governor Gálvez himself and many of his genuine supporters were partially convinced by these arguments and thus withheld some of the support which seemed implicit in Salazar's fiery speech. Be that as it may, Chatfield definitely allied himself with the unionists, or constitutional reformers, who were receptive to his "Doctrine of Mutuality."

On May 23 there appeared in San Salvador a nine-page pamphlet written anonymously by "An Enquirer into the Truth" and addressed "To the Public." According to Frederick Chatfield, he paid for, circulated,

---

26. To Cockburn, ext., August 8, 1835, F.O. 252/15.
27. To Cockburn, June 30, 1835, F.O. 252/15; to Palmerston, No. 16, June 1, 1836, containing Chatfield's comments upon the proceedings of March 14.
28. To Cockburn, June 30, 1835, F.O. 252/15.
29. Clairambault to Ministre des Affaires Etrangères, No. 42, July 1, 1835, A.A.E.P./CPAC, vol. 2.

and presumably wrote this article which was largely responsible for the defeat of the *Galvecistas*. "An influential member of congress," Chatfield explained, was so impressed with the arguments it contained "that he has consented to own himself their author, a consent which necessarily implies a full concurrence in the subject matter of the paper, from which I anticipate the best result, thinking it will cause many persons to alter their erroneous opinions respecting Belize."[30]

His hints concerning the authorship notwithstanding, it is abundantly clear that Mr. Chatfield did not write this article; at best he may have only suggested its general arguments. The "influential member of congress," it would seem, was the real author of the treatise. And judging from the style, as well as the power and conviction of the words in the text, it most likely was written by José Francisco Barrundia, the second member of the treaty commission which the consul had recommended in the previous year. In a later dispatch, Chatfield described Barrundia as "an ultra democrat in principle, sincere in his opinions, and honest in his political conduct," "the only person, who from his position and character could with impunity criticize and impugn the proceedings of the Chief of State of Guatemala," and "who by parenthesis writes with a grace and facility, to which I cannot do justice in a translation."[31] With Barrundia questioning Gálvez' motives, presaging the disastrous split of 1837, the vindictive program against Belize was doomed to failure, at least during the congressional sessions of 1835.

Since Chatfield and the Barrundia-type of liberal were to be allies for the next few years, we should consider the main arguments in the aforementioned pamphlet for the insight it provides into the unionist mind. Central America's translator of Milton's *Paradise Lost,* with a neo-classical style that was the envy of contemporaries, began the treatise by exhorting his countrymen to appreciate the historical importance of the present congress in the establishment of effective union, the dream of all genuine patriots and liberals. This dream, however, might easily be sabotaged if Central Americans did not abandon the "pernicious system" of legislation for special interests. Laws, the great Barrundia continued, should be solidly based upon a concern for the general welfare; otherwise, "it is a chimera to expect the fulfillment of those benefits, which the wisdom of our institutions attempts to secure."

As an example of his point, the author referred to the recently

---

30. To Wellington, cons. No. 7, June 1, 1835, F.O. 15/16.
31. To Palmerston, No. 28, September 20, 1837, F.O. 15/19. For a commendable study of this liberal, see David Vela, *Barrundia ante el espejo de su tiempo* (2 vols., Guatemala City, 1956–1957).

published state document in which the executive extolled the great benefits of promoting the commerce of the Pacific and raised the charge of
monopoly against the port of Belize. The burden of proof, it seemed to
the author of the treatise, should be upon those who made such
assertions and recommendations to the general government of Central
America:

> Bearing in mind that trade, if duly protected by law and then left
> to its own natural operations, will always find its proper level and
> that merchants carry on their business according to the greatest
> advantage to their individual interests, it seems the height of admin-
> istrative blindness to persist in sacrificing the public revenue for no
> visible equivalent whatsoever.
>
> We continually hear it said that we should avoid all communi-
> cation with Belize, but no valid proof is offered to substantiate this.
> We are told frequently that Belize monopolizes Central America's
> commerce, the import as well as the export trade. The truth is that
> the slightest knowledge of the navigation of our coasts, with refer-
> ence to the geographical location of Belize, will convince the most
> biased person that the communication between this establishment
> and the northern ports of the States of Nicaragua and Costa Rica
> is virtually impossible, and that therefore its trade, generally speak-
> ing, is restricted to the port of Izabal. It is not Belize where the will
> prevails to establish monopolies but rather in the center of our own
> country. The real monopolists are those who insist upon diverting
> our commercial relations from their ancient and natural channels
> and who try to deceive the public with regard to the nature of the
> traffic through the port of Izabal, pretending that as a result of it
> the country is at the mercy of a few individuals who reside in a
> foreign establishment. Are these people telling the truth? To whom
> belongs the commodities which are introduced into the Republic
> via Belize? Are they not the property of persons in Europe, who
> have consigned them to agents in this country, or that of persons
> living here, for whose convenience they are disembarked there in
> transit? As for the charge that the prices of our exports to Europe
> are subject to the whim of Belize's settlers (where factories do not
> exist, nor the capacity to use the principal commodities of our
> trade), we judge that it does not deserve our refutation.[32]

To demolish Salazar's assertion that the promotion of the Pacific
route would be of advantage to the nation, the "Enquirer" demanded
proof in the form of lower prices which, as yet, were not the case. What
assurance would the public have of lower prices once Belizean competition were removed? In comparing the two routes, the author pointed

---

32. To Wellington, cons. No. 7, June 1, 1835, with enclosure "Al público,"
    May 23, 1835, F.O. 15/16. I translated this portion.

out that freight charges per ton coming around the Horn averaged from 35 to 37 dollars, whereas via the Atlantic to Izabal, 10 to 12 dollars — a difference of 25 dollars. This difference, the author scored convincingly, went to foreign shipping interests on the Pacific route, while on the Atlantic route it remained within the country in the form of wages to carriers, etc.

In conclusion, Barrundia stressed that his purpose in writing these words was to remind the legislature not to exceed its jurisdiction by meddling in economic affairs in behalf of special interests: "Let our merchants compete with each other for supremacy in commercial matters, while the government fulfills its obligation to everyone impartially, by a just vigilance of its interests insofar as the public welfare is concerned." Moreover, he continued, the policy of inflicting higher duties on northern ports than on southern ports, being manifestly unfair to those states with ports on the Atlantic, might compromise the dignity of the Republic by provoking "a collision, or an act of disobedience," not to mention the damage it would inflict upon the nation's treaty obligations to Colombia and the United States. Barrundia's final words, much more forceful in the original, were translated as follows by Frederick Chatfield:

> Topics of a diplomatick nature we avoid touching; we therefore abstain from saying anything respecting the encroachments of the inhabitants of Belize, though the subject be so much pressed upon our notice; but we strongly suspect that the wrongs we are said to sustain by that settlement, are not so grievous as the publick is entreated to believe; for what reason we do not enquire. Be this as it may, now that we possess the means of consolidating our political power, let us not waste our strength in unprofitable disputes, but rather let us sacrifice upon the altar of our country's good, the dissensions which have hitherto perplexed our course, and by a sincere union help to establish to the best of our ability upon a firm foundation, the prosperity and happiness of the Central American Republick.[33]

Though the consul gloated to his friend at Belize that the pamphlet had made the "Istapa party in Guatemala very wrathful," he was not satisfied with the limited victory in the congressional sessions of 1835.[34] The federal tariff of five percent was still on the books; the Guatemalan bounty had not been repealed; and Colonel Galindo had left on his mission. At the first favorable opportunity, the "wrathful" merchants in Guatemala City would certainly revive their efforts against Belize; and Galindo's activities abroad, no matter what their outcome

---

33. *Ibid.*, Chatfield's translation.
34. To Cockburn, July 11, 1835, F.O. 252/15.

might be, were bound to embarrass Chatfield's position during the next congress. To prevent this, it was all the more imperative for him to negotiate a commercial treaty with the federal authorities and to contrive effective measures of "reciprocal annoyance." But on June 10, Chatfield received instructions from the Duke of Wellington, who had replaced Palmerston in the Foreign Office, to abandon his treaty mission pending negotiations with Spain on the question of sovereignty to British Honduras.[35] The English consul, however, chose to ignore Wellington's orders in the belief that the Foreign Office would reverse its decision once it learned that there was a strong likelihood of negotiating a treaty. Besides, he perhaps reasoned, such an announcement was not politically expedient, for it would have played into the hands of the *Galvecistas*. Again the consul revived the proposal he had made in November, 1834: that British shipping should pay higher duties for a period of six years — a concession intended to thwart the Klee-Murphy interests and to improve the financial situation of the federal government.[36] According to Chatfield, in expectation of this favorable article, the national congress not only rejected Salazar's recommendation for a two percent federal bounty on imports but also repealed the existing rebate on exports. As a result, he boasted, Belizean shipping was placed "on a footing of equality" with national shipping.[37]

Apparently the prospect of the favorable commercial article turned many congressmen against the Galindo mission. For example, a federal bill was passed prohibiting foreigners from occupying high military positions in the Republic. Though it is not clear how much Chatfield influenced the law, he definitely favored it since it applied to adventurers like Galindo.[38] He admitted, however, that he had encouraged members of congress to publish papers respecting Galindo's "ridiculous mission so that when he returns he will find his merits pretty correctly appreciated."[39] Moreover, according to the British consul, the favorable trade article also prompted General Morazán to hold out the possibility that Galindo would be recalled. On July 11, 1835, Chatfield urged Superintendent Cockburn to forward Morazán's letter of recall to London with all haste and at the same time asked him to keep a sharp lookout for Galindo's letters from Europe, *"letting me know of such arrivals."*[40] The

35. To Wellington, June 20, 1835, F.O. 15/16; on June 10, 1835, Chatfield received word not to continue with the treaty mission.
36. To Wellington, No. 9, June 30, 1835, F.O. 15/16.
37. To Palmerston, No. 16, August 11, 1835, F.O. 15/16.
38. *Ibid*.
39. To Cockburn, ext., August 8, 1835, F.O. 252/15.
40. To Cockburn, July 11, 1835, F.O. 252/15.

aggressive consul, it would seem, learned a valuable lesson from the "letter readers" in Warsaw.

—•••—

On July 20, two days before the adjournment of congress, the English agent left the federal capital and returned to Guatemala City where he anxiously awaited news of Galindo's mission. Until March, 1836, when the next congress met, he remained in the Guatemalan capital where he observed his rival's actions and made preparations for the impending struggle over the British treaty and the discriminatory program against Belize. As usual, there was no lack of suggestions pouring from the imaginative mind of the British consul, determined to protect what he considered to be the best interests of Great Britain. "I seek no exclusive advantages for Belize," he explained to Cockburn, "but I am desirous that these people should admit the utility of the settlement to themselves."[41] His main objective, therefore, was to educate the Central American public on the merits of the "Doctrine of Mutuality."

The doctrine, however, was a two-sided coin; and Chatfield was convinced that Belizeans were largely responsible for the resentment that existed in Central America against them. "In candour," he wrote to his friend at Belize, "it must be confessed, that the mode of conducting itself towards Central America has principally contributed to acquire for the settlement, the names Parasites, Monopolists, and such like, so liberally given." Belizeans had failed to develop constructively the trade opportunities which attended Central Ameican independence, "acting under the mistaken idea, that the good fortune which a casualty had placed in their way would not diminish, and that Central America, from circumstances, must be tributary to the settlement in matters of trade." Thus they neglected to establish branch houses in the Republic for the supply of retailers; and even worse, they incurred the ill will of Central American consumers by charging extravagant prices for poor quality goods. Understandably, this shortsightedness encouraged "persons of greater discernment," once the opportunity arose, to establish direct connections with houses in England, thus eliminating the Belizean middleman. As a result, a trade which might have flourished if Belizean merchants had been more enlightened was reduced "to one of mere agency."[42] Belize became a mere transit point rather than an entrepôt. And would Belizeans ever change their ways? Mr. Chatfield wrote disconsolately: "It is a remark-

---

41. To Cockburn, ext., August 8, 1835, F.O. 252/15.
42. To Wellington, cons. No. 7, June 1, 1835, F.O. 15/16.

able circumstance and forms an exception to the just title which belongs to the English to be considered the most intelligent and enterprising nation in the world that a British settlement should have passively allowed the advantages to which the proximity of Central America invited it to escape its possession."[43]

What angered Chatfield most was Belizean unwillingness to help themselves. Except for the tax schedule on woods, they refused to levy duties on other Central American exports. They refused, in effect, to sacrifice a paltry agency fee of two dollars per bundle on commodities passing through their port. Thus they prevented their consul in Guatemala City from reciprocally annoying the advocates of discriminatory duties. A disappointed English agent wrote to Cockburn on June 30, 1835:

> I regret the magistrates' shortsightedness. I shall always be of the opinion that Belize has the power within itself to command Central America in commercial matters, but then it must be by shewing some degree of independence in its intercourse and not by alleging an indifference which its acts contradict. . . . It should be noticed that no impediments are placed in the way of a commerce *from* this country *to* Belize, a proof of the utility of the settlement to Central American trade. . . . I must reiterate my conviction of the Policy of retaliatory duties. I am certain that the necessity of retaining them would not last three months, and if they had been imposed just before the cochineal crop was ready for shipment, the congress being in session would have enabled me to stipulate for the abolition of the five per cent duty so much complained of, which I am satisfied Belize might long since have got rid of, if it had taken the law into its own hands. My sole object is to get matters placed on a proper footing, and to bring about a more friendly understanding between parties who are mutually useful to each other.[44]

In promoting the "Doctrine of Mutuality," Chatfield therefore had to educate his own countrymen as well. In August, 1835, when he learned that there was a "scheme a foot" to improve the road between Gualán and Izabal, shortening the distance and "avoiding the really formidable mountain of Mico," the British consul strongly urged Belizeans to buy shares in the road company and to provide an engineer for this worthwhile project, which would reduce transportation costs to the whole Atlantic coast. "High freights," he explained, "are the chief cause why Istapa is able to compete with Isabal," and "any means therefore by which the communications by the North coast can be facilitated

---

43. To Charles Evans, May 6, 1836, F.O. 252/9.
44. To Cockburn, June 30, 1835, F.O. 252/15.

should be warmly encouraged in Belize." As if to shame his countrymen, he remarked: "Indeed, I have often wondered that more enterprise had not been shewn in Belize in these respects, for the settlement has very much within itself the power to govern the commercial transactions of this part of the Republick." Even Klee and Murphy had purchased two shares in the company, he added with an exclamation mark.[45]

Unwilling to believe that Belizeans could persist in refusing to follow his lead, Chatfield outlined another scheme on August 8 which he thought might be palatable to them. At any rate, he felt that they had to show "a little moral strength," if they expected to rid themselves of the Istapa duty and the federal tariff, "equal to a discriminatory duty of seven per cent against the settlement." This is what he proposed:

> The object being to favour, and not to hamper the trade between the two countries, it occurs to me that the imposition of a duty by the government of Belize might be managed as to occasion little real inconvenience to trade. Suppose a meeting were to pass a resolution to the effect, that viewing with concern the unfriendly disposition of the Government of the Republic of Central America towards the commerce of the settlement, as demonstrated by the continuance of a discriminatory duty of 5% on goods imported from it, purchased therein, and by the tacit sanction given by the federal government to the levy of a higher rate of duty on the importation of goods in the Port on the North Coast of that State of Guatemala, than that payable in the port on the South coast of the same State, and considering that the Vice President of the Republic in his speech to Congress on the opening of its ordinary session for the present year, urged the necessity of imposing additional restrictions on the trade carried on between British Honduras and Central America the meeting is of the opinion that in order to secure the settlement from the operation of enactments evidently levelled against its trade by the Government of the Central American Republic, a countervailing duty of ——— should be placed on all goods imported into the settlement from Central America, during such period as discriminatory duties continue to be levied in Central America, in the design to prejudice the commerce of Belize. . . . In order however to avoid the inconvenience which the sudden enforcement of this Resolution might occasion to the trade of the inhabitants of Central America, with whom the settlement desires to maintain an intercourse of the most perfect reciprocal utility, it is resolved that the aforesaid duty shall not come into operation until 6 months after the passing of this Act.[46]

Chatfield had a twofold objective in attaching the six-month clause. First, it would let "this government understand that other governments

---

45. To Cockburn, August 15, 1835, F.O. 252/15.
46. To Cockburn, ext., August 8, 1835, F.O. 252/15.

deem it fair to give notice of changes in commercial regulations, and not to bring them into practice as soon as they pass the legislature, without regard to previous engagements which individuals in trade have made." In short, he aimed to teach the young nation a lesson in international relations. And secondly — by far, the most important reason for the clause — the resolution would go into effect sometime after the middle of March, 1836, while congress was in session. "This space," Chatfield noted, "will afford me an opportunity to get the subject properly understood by the publick, and so perhaps to produce measures which shall prevent altogether the need of carrying the threatened rule into effect." To make the scheme work, the consul insisted that Belizeans could not back down on their threat: "no casual person should suppose there will be a hesitation to execute the law if passed, for it would be speedily known here, and the Government would then be more strongly than ever confirmed in its error, as to the inability of Belize to defend its commercial interest by retaliatory measures."[47]

During the fall of 1835, two of Chatfield's suggestions had undisguised imperialistic overtones. On September 12, for example, he suggested to Lord Palmerston, who had returned to his post in the Foreign Office, that Great Britain should purchase certain sections of Mr. Bennett's grants through a third party, thus securing "the future absolute command of the passage of the river Dulce" and "a perpetual right to land in a situation which would prevent Saint Thomas ever becoming a rival port of Belize."[48] That is why he had taken an unusual interest in securing the federal government's confirmation of the Guatemalan grants to Bennett and to the Eastern Company. Secondly, when Chatfield learned that the Eastern Company had sent a Mr. Fletcher to establish the first settlement in its Vera Paz grant, he was determined that the location should be in the Petén, for reasons we have discussed in the last chapter. "I will take upon myself the responsibility of saying," he told Cockburn, "that there is no spot on the shores of the Rio Dulce, the Gulf, or the River Polochic, suited to the reception of new settlers from Europe."[49]

In proposing these various measures — none of which were ever put into effect, incidentally — Chatfield reflected concern over the possibility of a Galindo victory in Europe, as well as the counteractions he expected from the Istapa party in Guatemala City. And on December 19, 1835, it appeared that his apprehensions might materialize; his Irish rival, he

---

47. *Ibid.*
48. To Palmerston, No. 17, September 12, 1835, F.O. 15/16.
49. To Cockburn, ext., August 8, 1835, F.O. 252/15.

learned, was making arrangements to bring Dutch colonists to the Petén.[50] On the same day, he complained to Palmerston that the Skinner-Klee house had pointed out to Governor Gálvez the oppressive nature of the South Sea duty, a two percent ad valorem tax "on goods and merchandise imported from the South side of this Republic into England." And Mr. Klee was also urging the governor to correct the injustice by enacting local regulations, "meaning, I suspect, restrictive duties against Belize, as shall place British commerce on the north and south sides of the Republic, on what they consider an equal footing." Chatfield was likewise distressed by the report that the Skinner-Klee house and the Plock-Logan company in London were considering a petition to Parliament for the repeal of the South Sea duty.[51] Incidentally, the duty was dropped early in 1836, much to the consul's displeasure.

Despite the consul's threats and incessant maneuvers, Colonel Galindo left Belize for the United States in late April, 1835, perhaps with the financial support of Charles Klee. At Chatfield's suggestion, the British representative in Washington, Charles Vaughn, tried his best to discredit Galindo in the United States. Apparently, he was successful.[52] Yet, on Christmas Day, 1835, Governor Gálvez received the welcome news that Galindo "had succeeded beyond his hopes" in talks with the British government, that the Foreign Office was disposed to accept a territorial settlement according to the limits of the eighteenth-century treaties, and that the directors of the Eastern Company were being favored by the London government.[53] While the governor's elation knew no bounds, Chatfield despaired. He did not know, of course, that the report from London was but a figment of the Irishman's imagination. Aware that the federal government had also received letters from the colonel, the worried consul penned a hurried note to a contact in San Salvador and urged him to learn their substance.

By the end of January, 1836, Chatfield had received conflicting reports about Galindo's mission. On the one hand, Robert Parker, a British merchant at the federal capital, wrote these discouraging words which confirmed what the consul had already heard in Guatemala City:

---

50. To Palmerston, No. 30, December 19, 1835, F.O. 15/16.
51. To Palmerston, No. 31, December 19, 1835, F.O. 15/16.
52. Charles R. Vaughn to Palmerston, July 4, 1835, enclosed in, from Cockburn, October 20, 1835, F.O. 252/8.
53. To Palmerston, No. 32, December 29, 1835, F.O. 15/16.

The folks here are all alive with the Colonel's communications. In the first place he writes that Mr. Miller was sent from Belize to Madrid to purchase the land in dispute, and that he had failed in his mission. Secondly, that the English government are ready to appoint Commissioners to define the boundaries. Thirdly, that he should be invested with a higher character, to carry this business successfully through to the interest of Central America. He mentions a long string of M.P.'s, who are all deeply interested in seeing justice done to this country. With this flattering account of the Colonel's they say here, that it is as they always said, the English had Belize on a lease, and that now they will either have to leave, or to join Central America. I am told that General Morazan does not mean to invest the Colonel with any character but continues his recal [sic].[54]

It worried Chatfield to think that members of Parliament might support the Central American version of the territorial question, perhaps because of representations made by the directors of the Eastern Company and other interested parties. Angrily he blamed John O'Reilly, the first British consul to Central America, for agreeing openly with the *"reino,"* or kingdom, thesis of the Central Americans and especially for inculcating his fellow Irishman, who in a less prosperous period had lived in O'Reilly's house, with the same notion. Undoubtedly basing himself upon Cockburn's reports about the activities of Thomas Miller, Chatfield also suspected that the United States government was not so indifferent to the Galindo mission as Charles Vaughn had indicated; and the same was true of the French government. According to Chatfield's sources, the French and American agents in Madrid had actively worked against Miller's mission. Furthermore, the consul feared that Spain, in order to win special consideration in Central America's trade, would perhaps cooperate with her former colony on the territorial question.[55]

The French consul's actions in Central America appeared to confirm Chatfield's suspicion that France was capitalizing upon England's embarrassment in order to renegotiate the old commercial treaty: "It seems that he is endeavouring to have it believed, that His Majesty's Government broke off the negotiation of the commercial Treaty which I had proposed to this government, on account of the difficulty of securing by it all that is wanted for Belize, and that the project of forming a colony in the vicinity of that establishment is secretly favoured in order to get by underhand means, that which cannot be obtained by upright ones." He would certainly combat "this notable insinuation," Chatfield

54. To Palmerston, No. 2, January 30, 1836, F.O. 15/18.
55. *Ibid.*

promised Lord Palmerston: "I have already adopted measures to destroy so groundless a suspicion, in the minds of the very few persons, I hope, who are capable of doubting the integrity of the British government."[56] The British consul was obviously upset by the discouraging news of Galindo's success and Miller's failure.

On the other hand, Colonel Galindo had also reported that Lord Palmerston was throwing all manner of obstacles in the path of a territorial settlement. For example, Palmerston told him that only England and Spain could legitimately treat the question of sovereignty to British Honduras — Chatfield's old argument. The British foreign secretary, moreover, insinuated that his government would not discuss the question of limits while Central America's boundary with Mexico remained unsettled. This was "distasteful" information to Central Americans, Chatfield noted, "for it is construed into a desire on the part of Great Britain, to increase the embarrassed state of the relations of these two sister Republicks, which are already much embroiled."[57]

Palmerston's unfavorable reaction to the Galindo mission, Chatfield realized, had increased Governor Gálvez' influence with the federal government, especially since the governor had sent military aid to quell a recent insurrection in the State of El Salvador. "The conductor of the federal government," as Chatfield now graphically described the improved position of his Guatemalan opponent, would certainly propose and perhaps succeed in legislating the discriminatory program against Belize. More than a pamphlet, appealing to unionist sentiment, would be necessary to defeat the *Galvecistas* at the 1836 federal congress. The situation, in Chatfield's opinion, now called for a display of force: "I beg leave to recommend that a communication should be transmitted from the Admiralty to the officer Commanding His Majesty's naval forces in the Pacific whose aid under such circumstances I should wish to secure."[58] But Lord Palmerston thought otherwise. Chatfield's "violent measures" were unnecessary, he shrewdly analyzed, for vested interests in Central America were too strong to permit the implementation of the vindictives' program.[59]

Sensing that the proper opportunity was at hand, Governor Mariano Gálvez delivered a "flaming" speech to his state legislature in which he recommended the strong anti-Belize program which Guatemalans should insist upon at the next federal congress, scheduled to meet in March,

56. To Palmerston, No. 3, January 30, 1836, F.O. 15/18.
57. To Palmerston, No. 2, January 30, 1836, F.O. 15/18.
58. *Ibid.*
59. From Palmerston, No. 11, August 31, 1836, F.O. 15/18.

1836.[60] With regard to the usurpers at Belize, the governor exclaimed: "We have been entirely too patient and forbearing." The times called for action: Guatemalans should deny their commerce to an establishment "which lives and grows from our sacrifice." Alluding to the position taken by the Barrundia liberals in the previous congress, Governor Gálvez remarked emotionally: "I appeal to all those who love the integrity of our territory and who are affected by the national honor and not a mistaken zeal, perhaps suggested by the usurpers themselves."[61] And the governor was not to be denied. On April 18, 1836, a Guatemalan delegate arose from his seat in the national congress to present a petition urging action on the following three measures: first, a twenty percent additional tariff upon Belizean imports, or products coming through the port of Belize; second, the establishment of Santo Tomás as the major port of entry on the Atlantic, relegating Izabal to a minor capacity; and third, the sanction of direct trade with Spanish ports.[62] As with Salazar's message in the previous year, the vindictives had fired the first salvo. The difference was that they fired it from an improved position, for this time unionists could no longer argue that the federal government should await the outcome of Galindo's mission to Europe.

In meeting the *Galvecistas'* challenge, Frederick Chatfield had to rely almost exclusively upon his own resources and imagination. Timid Belizeans — an evaluation shared by both Chatfield and Cockburn — turned down the scheme which the consul had proposed in August, 1835, and thus denied him a political weapon which he hoped to use effectively upon the federal body. Furthermore a disgusted Cockburn had not even bothered to relay Chatfield's recommendation on the Gualán-Izabal road company, knowing that the tight-fisted merchants would refuse even that positive move. Of course, the English consul was furious when he learned of Belize's refusal to support him. In an angry letter of May 6, he reminded Belizean merchants that they were certainly a peculiar brand of Englishmen not to recognize their opportunities.[63] To which a contrite spokesman for the merchants replied:

> Our not being intelligent or enterprising as other British merchants is, no doubt, to be regretted; we only profess to be simple and honest people who are rather bound to follow the direction of others in England than our own inclinations, nor do we think that they would approve of our risking their property in that country. This

60. From Cockburn, March 5, 1836, F.O. 252/8.
61. "Mensaje," Mariano Gálvez, February (?), 1836, F.O. 254/5.
62. "Proposición," April 18, 1836, in No. 14, to Palmerston, May 6, 1836, F.O. 15/18.
63. To Charles Evans, May 6, 1836, F.O. 252/9.

much I venture to surmise that whenever they think Central America is in such a state of security as, prudently, to warrant their employing their capital there they will do so without hesitation and not think an instant of Great Britain's losing a very valuable depot.[64]

Until their consul in Guatemala City obtained a commercial treaty for them, in other words, Belizeans would not budge. They were simply unwilling to make any sacrifices toward that end. What made Chatfield's task so frustrating was that rivals in Guatemala City knew this.

Except for Lord Palmerston's stand against the Galindo mission in the early months of 1836, the London government likewise did little to aid its representative in Central America, apparently ignorant of, or indifferent to, his strategy and objectives. In fact, the British government, unwittingly it would seem, undermined Chatfield's position in Guatemala. It refused to purchase Bennett's lands, as Chatfield had suggested in September.[65] Parliament also repealed the South Sea duty, an action which helped the consul's rivals — Klee and Murphy. But, more importantly, the Board of Trade rejected the Belizean wood tax schedule on grounds of principle: that Belizean magistrates had no right to levy such taxes and had usurped Parliament's taxing power. Chatfield was beside himself; but the Board of Trade categorically refused to listen to his political arguments and justifications for the tax on non-Belizean woods from the Bay of Honduras.[66] In short, the only action which Belizeans were willing to take in support of their consul in Guatemala City was repealed by the English government, leading to some very interesting consequences which we shall describe in the next chapter. Trying to salvage something from this setback, Chatfield was at least able to argue that the repeal of the wood tax was proof of Great Britain's good intentions with regard to Central America — an argument which Belizeans themselves had urged him to spread.[67]

Chatfield's immediate reaction to the Guatemalan petition of April 18 was to threaten that Great Britain would not remain passive to the proposed measures, especially the discriminatory tariff of twenty percent. To convince his adversaries — and in the process support his unionist allies — he undoubtedly displayed some of the letters which he had exchanged with naval officers on the Atlantic and Pacific, indicating that

64. From Edward Theil, pvt., June 10, 1836, F.O. 252/6.
65. From Bidwell, No. 2, January 12, 1836; from Palmerston, No. 11, August 31, 1836, F.O. 15/18.
66. Office of the Committee of the Privy Council for Trade to Fox Strangeways, September 2, 1836; to Palmerston, Nos. 15 (May 27) and 16 (June 1, 1836), F.O. 15/18; to Major Anderson, June 17, 1836, F.O. 252/15.
67. From Edward Theil, pvt., June 10, 24, 1836, F.O. 252/6.

he could reasonably expect their assistance if the situation warranted it.[68] He also threatened Gálvez, Klee, and Murphy that if they persisted with their program he would personally see to it that the repeal of the South Sea duty would not be applicable to Central America "until the country has concluded a Treaty with England, and has abated its efforts to injure British trade by Belize" — another threat, incidentally, which the British government would not back, though Chatfield did not know it at the time.[69] According to the consul, President Morazán was still against the *Galvecista* program; and Chatfield's threats, implicit in a letter written to Miguel Alvarez on April 22, were intended to strengthen the president's position. He later boasted that the letter to the secretary of state had forced the withdrawal of the Guatemalan petition; but actually what he meant was that the bill was referred to the executive for his recommendations.[70]

Even though the failure of Galindo's mission weakened the unionist position, the economic arguments against Belizean discrimination, which the pamphlet of the previous year had highlighted, still carried conviction in the federal congress of 1836. This was evident in the executive report presented to the federal congress on May 27 by Bernardo Escobar. Speaking for the president, Minister Escobar favored the Santo Tomás plank of the Guatemalan petition and suggested merely that perhaps a larger bounty would be necessary to encourage the construction of warehouse facilities at the new port. The executive, furthermore, strongly supported the measure to open up Central American ports to Spanish shipping since it accorded with the principle of free trade. But the first proposal — the discriminatory tariff — was detrimental to the Republic's interest. In justification of the executive's negative, Escobar pointed out that the tariff would eliminate Belizean competition and thus permit local capitalists to form "a genuine monopoly" and to fix prices at will. Moreover, it would do harm to the little merchant, who did not have the resources to trade directly with Europe, forcing him either to give up his business or to resort to smuggling. In this latter case, the federal government would suffer a loss of revenues.[71] These were powerful argu-

---

68. In F.O. 252/8, see letters to naval officers dated March 30, June 23, October 8, 1835; and January 16, 1836.

69. To Palmerston, No. 12, April 22, 1836; Privy Council for Trade to Backhouse, August 25, 1836; from Bidwell, November 1, 1836, F.O. 15/18.

70. To Palmerston, No. 14, May 6, 1836, F.O. 15/18.

71. J. Bernardo Escobar to Secretarios del Congreso General, May 27, 1836, F.O. 254/7.

ments; and despite their more favorable situation, *Galvecistas* could not overcome them.

<hr/>

The defeat of the negative plank of the petition, for it should be noted that the two positive ones passed, underscored an important characteristic in the Chatfield-Gálvez rivalry. Neither one could command the full support of his constituents, so to speak, for a retaliatory measure. From his office in London, Lord Palmerston had astutely and correctly analyzed the situation in Central America; there were too many vested interests to permit the passage of a discriminatory tariff against Belize.[72] As a result, both Gálvez and Chatfield realized that they had to proceed indirectly in achieving their objectives. In Chatfield's case, the most effective weapon was the natural alliance with the unionist liberal; and anything he could do, therefore, to strengthen the cause of union, or the establishment of an effective Central American Republic, would undoubtedly — he convinced himself — eventually serve the best interests of Great Britain. As far as Gálvez was concerned, he could not generate sufficient nationalistic feeling for the issue of territorial integrity under prevailing conditions. While his motives, or those of the Guatemalan merchants, could be questioned, Governor Gálvez would have trouble convincing the four remaining states of the union — and their representative, the national government — that Great Britain constituted a real danger to Central America. At least, that was the situation during the federal congress of 1836; and Gálvez had to content himself with legislation on the two positive planks of the April petition.

Although Chatfield happily reported the defeat of the discriminatory tariff, he was perfectly aware that the *Galvecistas* had made considerable headway, especially with regard to the Spanish trade law. As for the Santo Tomás proposal, he knew that it could not succeed without adequate financial support. Although he did not disapprove of the free-trade principle which prompted liberals to support the Spanish measure, he was well aware of its political implications, which might prove embarrassing to Great Britain. He knew, for example, that Gálvez and his liberals would capitalize upon the measure in order to gain the support of the former mother country on the Belize question. Furthermore, if the *serviles* ever came back into power, the trade connection with Spain might serve as the entering wedge for reestablishing the old colonial pattern and would eventually lead to restrictive policies against other foreign shipping. Equally perturbing to Chatfield was the rumor

<hr/>

72. From Palmerston, No. 11, August 31, 1836, F.O. 15/18.

that the federal congress would reconsider the French treaty in the 1837 sessions.[73] And on June 3, 1836, the rumor was given substance by the arrival of a new French consul-general, Auguste Mahelin, with specific instructions to conclude a commercial treaty with Central America.[74] To protect British subjects from discriminatory abuses, considering the arrangements that might be made with Spain or France, a commercial treaty was still indispensable.[75]

As demonstrated time and time again, Mr. Chatfield could be alarmingly deliberate once his mind was made up. "A principal aim since my arrival in Central America," he explained to Lord Palmerston, "has been to render the Republick dependent in apparent trifles upon the British settlement, in a view gradually to connect it by interest to that Establishment, which I conceive to be the surest method of destroying the present prejudice."[76] During the congressional sessions, therefore, he lobbied with considerable success in behalf of an effective postal communication system between Belize and the Republic. And on May 27, 1836, the federal congress authorized the president to work out an arrangement with the British consul, leaving the final approval for the project to the next congress. On August 9, Chatfield presented his "Project of a Post Office Regulation between Belize and Central America," containing nine articles which detailed the manner in which the mail would be handled.[77] Satisfied with the proposal, President Morazán issued a decree establishing the postal system and recommended it to the attention of the states. It would seem that Chatfield's "Doctrine of Mutuality" was bearing fruit. But his erstwhile enemy in Guatemala City, suspecting the consul's motives in promoting the postal reform, defeated the project. His government voted against the measure on the ground that in the future it might be used as proof of Belizean recognition.[78] In this case, it was the governor who annoyed the consul.

By far, Frederick Chatfield's most constructive effort in behalf of Central America union — a deliberate policy for reasons mentioned above — was the impetus and support he gave to basic financial reforms in the Republic. Some words of background are in order for the proper comprehension of this important topic.

---

73. To Palmerston, No. 21, June 11, 1836, F.O. 15/18.
74. To Palmerston, No. 19, June 8, 1836, F.O. 15/18.
75. No. 20, also dated June 8, 1836.
76. No. 17 (June 4).
77. To Major Anderson, August 15, 19, 1836, F.O. 252/15; to Palmerston, No. 32, November 18, 1836, F.O. 15/18.
78. Alvarez to Gálvez, November 24, 1836; Guatemala to Alvarez, December 21, 1836, A.G.N.G./CMRE, leg. 165, exp. 03439.

Despite auspicious beginnings, the financial history of the United States of Central America degenerated into an "impenetrable chaos" — to use the words of Governor Mariano Gálvez, who as a former minister of the Treasury could speak with competence on this subject. In 1824, English financial houses, capitalizing upon the optimism as well as gullibility of British investors with regard to the young American republics, literally fought each other for the privilege of lending money to the Republic. John Baily, who represented the House of Barclay and Herring, emerged the victor with a contract in which his firm agreed to float a loan of 1,421,000 pounds sterling, which at the exchange rate of about five to one totaled roughly seven million dollars, or pesos. With this money, the young American nation planned to establish its credit, to purchase ships for its defense, and to subsidize the education of a limited number of its youths — the future leaders of the country — in the enlightened institutions of the English nation. That, at least, was what the leaders of the Republic hoped for when their envoy Marcial Zebadúa sailed for London in 1826.

Almost immediately Zebadúa realized that the financial house was up to no good, avoiding him mysteriously and refusing to answer his pertinent questions about the loan except in general and vague terms.[79] Then came the awful truth; the House of Barclay and Herring went bankrupt, saddling the Republic with the full responsibility for the Central American bonds, which, of course, depreciated to a fraction of their original value. To make a long and obscure story short and meaningful, in 1828, Marcial Zebadúa placed an advertisement in the *Times,* recognizing bonds totaling 163,000 pounds and requesting the bondholders to submit their certificates for his signature. Of this amount of indebtedness, the Republic presumably received 70,000 pounds, though the amount accounted for in Guatemala City was only 65,663 pounds — the discrepancy, so it was claimed, had been pocketed by John Baily and the House of Aycinena in Guatemala City. What made the situation even less palatable to the liberals, who regained power in 1829, was that the amount received by the Republic had been used, or squandered, by the "intrusive government" of President Arce and the *serviles,* the Marquis of Aycinena and company. The liberals, however, dutifully recognized the foreign debt.[80]

---

79. Zebadúa to Secretario de Estado, June 5, August 21, 1826, A.G.N.G./CLCA, leg. 170, exp. 03602-03603; document by Juan Francisco Sosa, November 12, 1825, A.G.N.G./CLCA, leg. 169, exp. 03592. For an excellent analysis, see Robert S. Smith, "Financing the Central American Federation, 1821–1838," *Hispanic American Historical Review,* Vol. XLIII (November, 1963), pp. 483-510.
80. To Palmerston, Nos. 23 (July 1) and 24 (July 22, 1836), F.O. 15/18.

In the meantime, the Reid-Irving firm had replaced the defunct House of Barclay as the Republic's agent in London and had paid the expenses of Zebadúa's diplomatic mission in England as well as the dividend payments up to 1828.[81] The Central American Republic therefore had obligations toward the Bondholders' Association and to the Reid-Irving Company; and these two interests, it will be recalled, had asked Lord Aberdeen to intervene officially in their behalf, which the foreign secretary had refused to do on the ground that the British government could not be employed to protect the interests of speculators. The risk, in other words, was solely theirs. When the bondholders repeated their request to the Foreign Office, in early 1836, Lord Palmerston concurred with the opinion of his predecessor. Nevertheless, in a letter of February 28, Palmerston urged Chatfield to present the bondholders' memorial to the Central American government and to do what he could for them without threatening official action from the British government.[82] By this time, with eight years of arrears in interest payments, the foreign debt totaled 241,684 pounds sterling, or 1,208,420 dollars.

The federal government, however, was in no position to make a payment to the bondholders. In fact, it could barely command enough revenue to meet ordinary administrative expenses. And this had been the story since the recognition of the foreign debt by the liberals. From 1831 to 1832, the invasions by conservative expeditionary forces prevented the accumulation of a surplus to meet those obligations; and from that time until early in 1835, the weak central government was unable to restrain the states from usurping the customs revenues. Even the important tobacco revenue was taken away from it and subsequently abolished by the states.[83] Indeed, financial reforms were overdue; and Frederick Chatfield, whatever his motives may have been, deserves considerable credit for the role he played in initiating them during the federal congress of 1836.

Ironically, the two inveterate rivals were in accord on the subject of financial reforms. As a matter of fact, on May 20, 1836, Chatfield congratulated Governor Gálvez for an editorial that appeared in a Guatemalan periodical, *El Seminario,* recommending action on the federal

81. Zebadúa to Secretario de Estado, October 5, 1826, A.G.N.G./CLCA, leg. 170, exp. 03605; Reid-Irving Company to Zebadúa, November 24, 1826, *ibid.* exp. 03606; Alexander Reade to Palmerston, p. encl., November 4, 1836, F.O. 15/18.

82. From Palmerston, No. 4, February 28, 1836, F.O. 15/18.

83. To Palmerston, No. 23, July 1, 1836, F.O. 15/18; to Palmerston, No. 9, p. encl., March 18, 1837, F.O. 15/19.

debt. After requesting eight copies of the publication, which the British consul planned to circulate in neighboring republics as proof of Central America's disposition to settle with her creditors, Chatfield also asked a special favor of the Guatemalan governor. He hoped that Gálvez would publish an article of his commenting upon the recent editorials in the London *Times* on the subject of the foreign debts owed by Hispanic nations. Incidentally, Gálvez complied by inserting Chatfield's article in a July issue of the *Seminario* along with his own recollections of the House of Barclay and Herring loan.[84]

The Central American bondholders, interestingly, renewed their request for the official intervention of the Foreign Office. They did this because of optimistic reports in England concerning the flourishing state of the Central American economy and the stability of governmental institutions there. They reasoned that in the light of such reports the Central American Republic was not acting in good faith, for they had not received a single dollar even toward the payment of interest. The irony of the situation was that the favorable picture of Central America resulted from the promotional efforts of Colonel Galindo and especially the directors of the Eastern Company, who for some time had been actively pressuring the Foreign Office to recognize their land grant in Vera Paz at the expense of British Belize. In supporting financial reform, therefore, Governor Gálvez desired to substantiate the directors' assertions concerning the great opportunities that existed in Central America. He felt, of course, that this would certainly help Guatemala's cause in the territorial controversy over Belize. On the other hand, Chatfield's interest in a debt settlement, as one might expect, was to bind the Republic more closely to the interests of British nationals. When he received Palmerston's dispatch of February 28, containing the bondholders' memorial, Chatfield immediately asked for an interview with Secretary of State Miguel Alvarez.[85]

The long interview of May 25, 1836, laid the basis for even a stronger alliance between Frederick Chatfield and the federal government; and conceivably it may have also influenced the Escobar report upon the Guatemalan petition two days later. At the interview, the two men talked about the erroneous impressions which the British public was receiving concerning the alleged prosperity and stability of Central America, as well as the problem that those reports posed for the Repub-

---

84. To Gálvez, May 20, 1836, F.O. 252/13; to Palmerston, No. 25, August 5, 1836, F.O. 15/18.
85. To Palmerston, No. 23, July 1, 1836, F.O. 15/18; "Mensaje," Mariano Gálvez, February (?), 1836, F.O. 254/5.

lic. To save face, the federal government had to make some gesture toward the settlement of the foreign debt, though Chatfield was abundantly aware of the fact that it lacked the financial resources to do so. At this point, the consul recommended certain measures to help the federal government out of its predicament and at the same time pave the way for desperately needed financial reforms. He suggested, for example, that the Republic revive the old tobacco monopoly, assigning one-half of that important revenue source for the liquidation of the foreign debt. In addition, he recommended improvements in the collection of customs, he noted the qualifications and type of customs official the government should insist upon, and he urged the acceptance of the principle that lower customs and tariffs would not only decrease smuggling but also increase the amount of revenues collected. Another recommendation was the assignment of a Guatemalan consul to Belize.

To expedite these needed reforms, the British consul then volunteered to draw up a tentative law of customs and a new tariff schedule to serve as a model for any law which the government might wish to frame in the near future. Alvarez thanked Chatfield for his suggestions, accepted his offer of a model customs and tariff law, and promised that he would discuss these matters with the president. On June 5, Chatfield submitted his model; and on the following evening, he met with Morazán and Alvarez to discuss his proposed law of customs and clarify some of its points.[86] Apparently, Chatfield's constructive suggestions and labor in behalf of the financial structure of the Republic deeply impressed President Morazán. On August 8, he wrote confidentially to Chatfield, thanking him for his interest in the "prosperity of my country."[87] The alliance between Frederick Chatfield and the federal government was now firmly established.

During the final weeks of the congressional sessions of 1836, Mr. Chatfield displayed a rare talent for democratic politics as he maneuvered to convince congressmen of the need for a debt settlement and financial reforms. On June 8, the bondholders' memorial was presented to the federal congress, and while it was being discussed he continued to meet with federal officials. In another interview with President Morazán, on June 12, the British consul suggested to him "the advantage of moving Congress to authorize the government during the congressional recess to arrange the claims of the bondholders with me as their repre-

---

86. To Palmerston, No. 23, July 1, 1836, F.O. 15/18; from Alvarez, June 5, 1836, and to Alvarez, June 6, 1836, F.O. 252/5; to Anderson, August 15, 1836, F.O. 252/15.

87. From Morazán, conf., August 8, 1836, F.O. 252/5.

sentative in this country, adding that this arrangement would not pledge the government to any distinct course, while it would confer upon it the ability to treat the subject at the earliest favourable opportunity." Morazán agreed. In describing this interview to Palmerston, the consul made no mention of any attractive offer which might have influenced the president's decision.

With Morazán's approval, Chatfield then "prevailed on a deputy to bring the motion forward in Congress on June 13th."[88] Two days later, the executive recommended favorable action on the motion. And on June 20, the day before adjournment, the legislators gave their approval. During the recess of congress, the executive was given extraordinary powers to amend the organic law of finance, to alter the tobacco law, to frame a new law of customs and tariff schedule, and to arrange for the liquidation and payment of the foreign debt. All acts resulting from this congressional decree, of course, were subject to the final approval of the next congress.[89]

Unquestionably, the authorization of June 20 was a remarkable feat of political strength by the unionist element in the federal congress of 1836. Without basic financial reforms, the idea of effective Central American union was ridiculous — a realization which had influenced the thinking of congressmen. The significance of the measure was the decision of congress to put the cause of Central American nationalism to its true test: that of the pocketbook. And support for the measure came from all sides. Anti-unionists felt that it would hasten the dissolution of the hated Republic and give an impetus to the states' rights movement, leading eventually to the independence of each of the five states. Unionists, like Morazán and Barrundia, on the other hand, believed that the time for decision was at hand. The Republic could no longer flounder aimlessly along undefined lines. And Chatfield, for his own reasons, encouraged this latter group.

At the interview with General Morazán on June 12, 1836, the British consul had made an attractive offer, or possible concession, if the federal government were willing to settle with him on the foreign debt. He would use his influence with the bondholders to scale the debt down by reducing the interest rate from six to four percent, apparently on a retroactive basis judging from the correspondence on this proposal. Chatfield maintained, in his letter of July 1 to Lord Palmerston, that he had made no hint of such a concession to the federal authorities; he merely wanted to know how Palmerston and the bondholders felt about

88. To Palmerston, No. 23, July 1, 1836, F.O. 15/18.
89. Decree, June 20, 1836, in No. 26, to Palmerston, April 4, 1838, F.O. 15/20.

it.[90] Yet certain remarks and allusions in the correspondence with Miguel Alvarez, as well as in President Morazán's speech to congress of March 15, 1837, indicate that they had been approached on this matter and were awaiting the bondholders' response to Chatfield's suggestion.[91]

There is other evidence to substantiate the close cooperation between Chatfield and the Morazán government on the foreign debt. On August 5, for example, he also asked the bondholders to provide him with a copy of the accounts current of the original financial house, adding that it would facilitate the settlement of their debt. "If I discovered debts in it due by individuals in this country to the House of Barclay and Company," he explained, "I should use my discretion as to acquainting the government with them, in order to assist it to make a payment to the Bondholders."[92] Though the request was rejected on the ground that it would link the defunct house with the present bondholders, Chatfield's motive in making it was political, intended to relieve the federal government from the pressure and criticism of liberals who resented the entire debt transaction. If his request had been granted, Chatfield would have compelled certain Spanish merchants in Guatemala City, who perhaps were involved in the Baily-Aycinena discrepancy of the amounts received from the House of Barclay, to make the first installment in the liquidation of the foreign debt. This would have been a smart political move, undermining liberal criticism of the debt especially from the Gálvez camp, and striking at the hated *serviles,* many of whom were pretending to be ardent supporters of the Guatemalan governor.[93] Irregardless of the outcome, the request underscored an intimate contact with the federal government as well as Chatfield's support of the *Morazanistas.*

Interestingly, Lord Palmerston was beginning to change his mind on government intervention in behalf of financial interests. On August 15, in contrast to the dispatch of February 28, he instructed Chatfield to caution the federal government that Great Britain might conceivably intervene to secure a settlement for the bondholders. Matters now took an ironic twist. Whereas formerly Palmerston had continually restrained the aggressive consul, now the underling recommended patience to the master in London. He assured him that President Morazán considered the debt a "sacred" obligation. The Republic, he told Palmerston and

---

90. To Palmerston, No. 23, July 1, 1836, F.O. 15/18.

91. To Palmerston, Nos. 9 (March 18) and 13 (May 2, 1837), F.O. 15/19; "Mensaje," Francisco Morazán, March 15, 1837, F.O. 254/5.

92. To Palmerston, No. 25, August 5, 1836, F.O. 15/18.

93. To Palmerston, No. 24, July 22, 1836, F.O. 15/18; to Gálvez, July 22, 1836, F.O. 252/13.

the bondholders, was sincerely trying to establish its financial under-pinnings. Besides, he was certain that His Lordship would see the picture in its proper perspective once he read the contents of the July 1 dispatch, the one in which Chatfield hinted at a possible reduction in interest rates.[94]

———•◦•———

By June, 1836, Frederick Chatfield had hit upon the best means of reciprocally annoying Belize's enemies: the "Doctrine of Mutuality" and the strengthening of Central American union. As we have seen, his most significant contribution was the impetus he gave to financial reform in Central America, leading to the promulgation of the Federal Tariff of February 27, 1837, and the new Law of Customs, both of which were not fully enforced until January, 1838. And, as expected, these measures in turn aided British interests. The five percent discriminatory tariff against Belize, for example, was dropped.[95] Moreover, on April 11, 1837, the federal congress sanctioned the arrangement which Morazán and Chatfield had reached on the foreign debt, assigning one-half of the tobacco revenues for its liquidation.[96] Indeed, these were concrete results of Chatfield's cooperation with the federal government, which extended to other projects as well. In late 1836 and early 1837, when the federal government was thinking seriously of appointing a surveyor for the Atlantic approach to a Nicaraguan canal, Chatfield encouraged British naval officers to assist in surveying the Pacific approach for an inter-oceanic passageway.[97]

In two federal congresses, Mr. Chatfield gained invaluable political experience. Considering the refusals from London and Belize, he certainly realized that he would have to rely upon his own resources and imagination to protect British interests in Central America. Fortunately, political conditions in the Republic had worked in his favor during the two congressional sessions, but how long could he count on this situation continuing without a commercial treaty to fix and regulate the relations between Central America and Great Britain? And what stresses could his alliance with the *Morazanistas* bear? Ironically, in mid-1836, just when the alliance was strongest, there were already danger signals on the horizon.

---

94. To Palmerston, No. 34, November 25, 1836, F.O. 15/18.
95. To Palmerston, No. 15, June 19, 1837, F.O. 15/19; to Palmerston, No. 26, April 4, 1838, F.O. 15/20.
96. To Palmerston, No. 15, June 19, 1837, F.O. 15/19.
97. To Palmerston, No. 7, March 3, 1837, F.O. 15/19.

CHAPTER FIVE

Rude and Uncivilised

The government will I suspect find itself some day in trouble by the foolish manner in which it starts claims to places that do not belong to it.[1]
                                                    —Chatfield, January 2, 1837

A residence in this Republick requires the patient relinquishment of the ordinary enjoyments of civilised life, while the political state of it, places life and property in constant jeopardy; this is more particularly applicable to me, in consequence of the prevailing error that every person in the country who is not a Central American must be an Englishman, an error which goes to concentrate upon the English the whole weight of that antipathy which is commonly entertained against foreigners in rude and uncivilised countries.[2]
                                                    —Chatfield, June 26, 1837

As rumors of a cholera epidemic at Belize charged the atmosphere of the federal capital in late August, 1836, Frederick Chatfield recalled vividly the hectic experience at Memel a few years earlier. Though he fully appreciated the fear which was generated throughout Central America by these unconfirmed reports, he nonetheless believed that Governor Mariano Gálvez had acted precipitously in banning all intercourse with the British establishment. Federal authorities also shared this view and "wisely" favored a short quarantine of eight days. But in Guatemala City, Chatfield's erstwhile rival would not hear of this; and the federal government dared not stand in opposition. Just how long these "violent measures" would continue, Chatfield hesitated to predict; he suspected, however, that because of revenue losses and the inconvenience to traders "alarm and prejudice" would yield "to interest."[3] This suspicion proved to be an accurate one. The quarantine was lifted prematurely in December; and by the spring of 1837 the dreaded sickness had skipped across to the Pacific coast leaving a trail of death and panic.[4]

Hard hit by the scourge as well as other calamities, the Indians were almost hysterical. Malevolent tongues exacerbated their anxiety by attributing the epidemic to two sources: first, the English colonists of the

---

1. To Major Anderson, pvt., January 2, 1837, F.O. 252/15.
2. To Palmerston, No. 17, June 26, 1837, F.O. 15/19.
3. To Palmerston, No. 29, October 21, 1836, F.O. 15/18.
4. "Memoria," Carlos Salazar, Guatemala, 1837, pp. 14-15; "Mensaje," Mariano Gálvez, March, 1837, F.O. 254/5, also in *El Editor: Periódico de los Tribunales* (Guatemala), No. 4, March 4, 1837, B.N.G./V, leg. 836.

Eastern Company who had recently arrived in Vera Paz; and secondly, the *liberales* of the government who presumably were conspiring — among other things — to decimate the Indians, to take their lands away from them, and to turn them over to the English heretic. Understandably, therefore, the Indians were terrified by the *cordones* which the Gálvez government placed around the areas infected with cholera; and they were sure that government doctors were poisoning the water in their streams as part of the scheme to turn over their lands to foreigners. The situation had dangerous political and social implications, not least of which was the danger to the lives and property of foreigners.[5]

The cholera struck with fury at San Salvador in April, 1837, and carried away nearly ten percent of its fifteen thousand inhabitants. Given these conditions, the federal congress promptly adjourned its sessions, and its members sought the safety of the countryside. Nor was the British consulate spared. On the contrary, all its servants died of cholera — an unfortunate occurrence which gave substance to the widespread belief that the English were responsible for the epidemic. Unable to induce "Persons to enter my service," Chatfield lamented, he had no alternative but to close his doors and go out into the country for several weeks. Thanks to "Providence" and "the rigid abstemiousness of my habits," Chatfield survived the ordeal. Other less sophisticated minds attributed his survival to an alliance with the Devil.[6]

Yet the grim reaper had cut a swath dangerously close to Frederick Chatfield on April 22, 1837, at an Indian village near the federal capital. But for the "miraculous interposition" of the Almighty, Chatfield tells us, he barely "escaped being hewn to pieces;" he was spared "the horror and ignominy of dying under the indian knife."[7] This traumatic experience at the village of Zugapango left an indelible imprint upon the consul's mind; it conditioned his attitude toward Indians in general and especially toward those persons who would incite them to action for base, political motives.

In need of exercise and diversion, the former cavalry officer mounted his horse daily for a ride into the neighboring countryside. Every afternoon he followed the same routine, hoping that the Indians would consider him a familiar sight and thus allow him eventually to ride unarmed. From the plaza, he would take one of the short streets which

---

5. From William Hall, June 16, 23, 1837, and April 7, 1837, F.O. 252/18; Frederick Crowe, *The Gospel in Central America* (London, 1850), pp. 140-141.
6. To Palmerston, No. 16, June 26, 1837, F.O. 15/19.
7. To Palmerston, No. 17, June 26, 1837, F.O. 15/19.

led to the Indian section — a series of huts scattered over a large area of broken ground. Then he followed one of the narrow mule paths, "bordered by high hedges of rank foliage," which penetrated the tropical wilderness of the surrounding countryside. At a certain point in the interior, he would dismount and rest for awhile. Occasionally, he would walk over to a nearby stream while mulling over in his mind the next dispatch to Lord Palmerston. Later, he would remount for the trip back to San Salvador. Ordinarily this daily ride would have raised no suspicions; but during the cholera crisis, and considering the Indian's agitated state of mind, it was fraught with danger, to say the least. The Indians began to ask themselves questions. What was this "foreigner" doing? Why did he always stop near the same stream, the one which provided water for the village of Zugapango? They could see only one explanation.

On the afternoon of April 27, 1837, the Indians lay in ambush near the foreigner's turning point in the interior. As usual, the rider came up the path; and just as he stopped to dismount, the Indians leaped from their hiding places and greeted him with blood-curdling yells which were enough to paralyze the likes of Frederick Chatfield. Momentarily speechless and unable to resist, he allowed himself to be shoved and jerked by the screaming mob in the direction of Zugapango. "Here is the man who poisons the river," shrieked the ringleaders as they approached the village. The British consul protested his innocence in vain. But the sea of ugly faces was not in a rational mood. What saved him at this time was the Indians' fear that his body and clothes wreaked with cholera.

Regaining his composure as he entered the village of Zugapango, Chatfield guided the mob imperceptibly toward the church in hopes of enlisting the aid of the local priest. The *padre* was not around! Then he led them toward the *cabildo,* or government house, in the expectation that the aldermen might be able to calm the Indians. But little encouragement came from that quarter. The *alcalde* and his assistants, "some of whom were drunk," only aggravated the situation. "Instead of affording me the protection and aid I so greatly needed," Chatfield recalled, "they seemed to partake of the popular delusion." They "continually passed their hands across my throat, saying that unless I spoke the truth respecting the poisoning of the waters, they would cut my head off." When the Indians learned that their captive was the leading Englishman in Central America, Chatfield was in real trouble.

For an hour and a half, the consul suffered the torments of his irate captors, thoroughly humiliated in the process. Looking for a vial of poison, they forced him to dismount and to empty his pockets several times. When they failed to find the incriminating evidence, they compelled him to take off his shoes. Just how Frederick Chatfield got out of this hair-raising predicament, we will perhaps never know. The Indians refused the bribe of a donation to the church. Chatfield explained that he conceived the "judicious action" of offering to drink the waters of the nearby streams, thus "happily persuading" the Indians to release him.[8] The popular rumor, however, was that the Indians, not Chatfield, had thought up this crude test of justice. According to a North American source, the consul was made to drink "the water of twelve different streams, in such a quantity that the poor man well nigh burst."[9] Be that as it may, the terrifying experience left its mark upon the British consul and its significance would soon be evident.

Despite what was clearly a flagrant insult to the British nation, Chatfield decided — wisely it would seem — not to interpret it as such, especially after conversing with General Morazán on the morning following the incident. He felt sorry for the Indians whose minds were so deranged by their inordinate fear of cholera. To soothe and console them, as well as all Central Americans, he translated into Spanish a short prayer from the English liturgy and offered it to the federal government for circulation.[10] A judicious and magnanimous gesture, it would go far to convince agitated minds in Central America that Englishmen were not insensitive to the suffering in their midst. At the same time, it undermined those malicious wags who were blaming the English for the crisis. But Auguste Mahelin, who resented the failure of the French treaty in the recently adjourned congress of 1837, was determined to make the Zugapango incident a big issue. He adamantly insisted upon justice and respect for members of the diplomatic corps in Central America. The federal government thus had no alternative but to prosecute the head officials of the nearby Indian village, who were brought to San Salvador to stand trial. The case against them, however, had to be dropped since the star witness refused to identify his attackers. He explained his action to Palmerston in these words:

> I verbally declined appearing from an opinion that after my conversation with the President I could not consistently do so, and that if I became a Publick prosecutor it must be as the Representative of His Majesty's Government in this country — a position which I considered it wisest to avoid appearing in.[11]

Chatfield's magnanimity at the time of the Zugapango incident, which reflected a continuation of the alliance with the federal govern-

---

8. *Ibid.*
9. James J. Jarves, *Scenes and Scenery* . . . 1837–1842 (London, 1844), p. 307.
10. To Morazán, April 24, p. encl., May 3, 1837, F.O. 252/5.
11. To Palmerston, No. 17, June 26, 1837, F.O. 15/19.

ment, is all the more remarkable in view of certain developments in the territorial dispute. As in a previous situation, his enterprising countrymen had contributed to the extension of the area of friction with Central Americans from Belize proper to the Bay Islands of the Gulf of Honduras and to the Mosquito Shore. This put an added strain on the working alliance between the British consul and the Republic for the simple reason that the boundary issue affected four states instead of one. Nicaragua, Honduras, and Costa Rica now were disposed to join with Guatemala in the common cause against the outside aggressor. Consequently, the federal government found it increasingly more difficult — if not impossible — to sidestep the territorial question in favor of union and stability.

— • —

As he perused the *Jamaica Despatch and New Courant* of May 12, 1836, the consul's neck stiffened upon reading an article which described the latest project of "Don Juan" Galindo, that "deceptious scoundrel" and "Arch-Villain." [12] With "a stroke of the pen," the ubiquitous colonel had proclaimed Central America's right to the southern reaches of the Mosquito Shore and had sent an expedition to occupy Boca del Toro, a little island off the mainland of modern Costa Rica which contained a population of about seven hundred souls, most of them English subjects from Jamaica. [13] Acting upon orders "to regularize" the frontiers of Central America, John Galindo empowered his father Philemon to establish the governmental district of "Morazán," which was to be placed under the jurisdiction of Costa Rica. The San José government, of course, welcomed the senior Galindo's visit to Boca del Toro with great enthusiasm. [14] But there were other claimants to "Buckatoro," who were less enthusiastic about the sudden turn of events. The government of New Granada (Colombia) regarded the expedition as an act of aggression; and, as Chatfield predicted, a New Granadian expeditionary unit forcibly relieved Philemon Galindo of his administrative duties by the end of the year. [15] New Granada and Central America, in other words, resumed a dispute which had been postponed by their treaty of 1825.

A third contender for the Boca del Toro was the Mosquito Nation,

12. To Palmerston, No. 22, p. encl.: *Jamaica Despatch and New Courant,* No. 1, 1192, May 12, 1836; June 17, 1836, F.O. 15/18.

13. To Palmerston, No. 27, September 13, 1836, F.O. 15/18.

14. *Ibid.,* p. encl.s; to Palmerston, No. 31, p. encl., October 28, 1836, F.O. 15/18.

15. To Palmerston, No. 37, December 26, 1836, F.O. 15/18; from George Stiessel, March 20, 1837, F.O. 252/6.

that ancient ally of Great Britain. The Galindo action, in effect, had raised the celebrated "Mosquito Question," which would preoccupy nations interested in Middle America for the next two and a half decades. And here, as elsewhere, Frederick Chatfield anticipated Great Britain's future policy toward the Mosquito Shore. On September 13, 1836, for example, he argued that because of the special historical relationship between England and the king of the Mosquito Indians the Shore was in effect a "mediatised district" — a protectorate, so to speak, of the British government.[16] For many reasons, which will be discussed subsequently, this concept was unacceptable to the British Foreign Office for some years to come.

Concurrently, the seeds of the "Mosquito Question" were being sown in the northern sector as well, in the vicinity of Trujillo, Honduras. The agitation there stemmed from the repeal of the Belizean wood tax by the Privy Council of Trade on the ground that it was a violation of Parliament's exclusive right to tax.[17] Authorities in London were singularly unimpressed with Chatfield's political arguments in behalf of the tax — the reciprocal-annoyance tactics described in the previous chapter. As a result, they unwittingly placed Marshall Bennett and his Guatemalan associates in a better competitive position with regard to the mahogany trade. Because of the tax repeal, Belizean cutters now were forced to expand beyond the limits of the British establishment. They simply lacked the wood resources of their competitors on the Guatemalan coasts, who flooded the port with their product. A surplus situation thus developed in which prices were forced downward to the detriment of the Belizean woodcutter. His labor costs remained higher, his supply of wood was limited, and he was still saddled with the responsibility for the tax burden of Belize — all of which dictated his expansion to new sources of supply in the Bay Islands and the Mosquito Shore in order to meet the competition of Marshall Bennett and the Guatemalan woodcutters.

Yet the foreign competitor still had the advantage of geographical proximity to the port of Belize which meant less delay and cheaper transportation costs. To offset this advantage, Belizean woodcutters petitioned the home government for permission to ship their wood directly from the new sources of supply, hoping at the same time to enjoy the preferential position of Belize in the English market.[18] Their expansion to the Mosquito

---

16. To Palmerston, No. 27, September 13, 1836, F.O. 15/18.
17. Office of the Committee of the Privy Council for Trade to Fox Strangeways, September 2, 1836; to Palmerston, No. 15, May 27, 1836, F.O. 15/18.
18. George Hyde to Palmerston, October 24, 1837, F.O. 15/19.

Shore commenced on a substantial scale in the latter part of 1836 when the House of Hyde and Forbes received grants from the King of the Mosquitos to cut wood along the banks of the Limón River, eight leagues to the east of Trujillo. Subsequently, King Robert Charles Frederick, whose alcoholism made him a pliable instrument of any adventurer, requested permission of the English Crown to ship wood directly to Great Britain under the same terms as Belize.[19]

The "old rascal" Marshall Bennett, as might be expected, could be counted upon to resist the intrusion of rival Belizean houses into territory whose wood supply had been subleased to him. More importantly the commandant of Trujillo was willing to use force in support of Bennett's claim, arguing that the territory in question belonged to the State of Honduras.[20]

That was the beginning of the "Mosquito Question" in the northern and southern extremities of the so-called Mosquito Shore; and it should be noted that now the two states of Honduras and Costa Rica had a vital interest in challenging British territorial designs upon Central America. Within a few months, Nicaragua also joined the mainstream of protest in behalf of Central America's territorial integrity. Moreover, the Bay Islands' dispute was also revived with the report that three English families had settled on Ruatán Island, the largest of the group. And Belizeans, it will be recalled, strongly favored the occupation of that island which they considered vital to the economic future of their port.[21]

Word of the Belizean operations on the Limón River reached San Salvador by early December, 1836. In the discussion which followed between Chatfield and President Morazán, the latter, though he held definite views on the "Mosquito Question," was nevertheless hopeful of avoiding a clash with Great Britain since it might harm the Republic and prevent its effective consolidation. Furthermore, the president's own interests were involved in the Limón operations; in 1834, he had received the original concession of wood-cutting rights to the Honduras coast and had then subleased this contract to Marshall Bennett. When he asked for Chatfield's advice on the matter, Morazán promised to step down from the presidency whenever the Mosquito issue became the subject of an official discussion between Great Britain and Central America.[22] The British consul shared Morazán's desire to postpone the issue, though

19. Robert Charles Frederick to King of England, May 8, 1837, F.O. 15/19.
20. From Macdonald, February 20, 1837, F.O. 252/8; also in No. 10, to Palmerston, p. encl.s, April 1, 1837, F.O. 15/19.
21. George Hyde to Palmerston, October 24, 1837, F.O. 15/19.
22. To Palmerston, No. 35, p. encl.s, December 16, 1836, F.O. 15/18.

he also presented the British view firmly albeit not belligerently. At this time, it seems that he wanted nothing to interfere with the treaty negotiations, especially since there was the likelihood that the French consul might successfully negotiate his treaty. Moreover, Chatfield was anxious to secure the passage of financial reforms in the 1837 federal congress. In short, the consul's alliance with the federal government was still in effect, even though it was undergoing its first serious strain. There can be no doubt, however, that Chatfield was visibly annoyed when he wrote the remarks which introduce this chapter.[23]

The spirit of compromise did not extend to British and Central American officials in the local area of conflict, however. Much of this was due to the nature of the new superintendent of Belize who took over his office in January, 1837. Irascible, haughty, and aggressive, Colonel Alexander Macdonald was destined to become Chatfield's serious rival for the mantle of leading British representative in Central America. And with or without the authority of his superiors in London, Macdonald set out to establish a British protectorate of the Mosquito Nation in fact as well as in theory. In no uncertain terms, he informed Mr. Bennett and the commandant of Trujillo that he would not tolerate any interference with the woodcutting activities of his constituents at the Limón.[24] To assure himself of support in England, the superintendent encouraged the King of the Mosquitos to request the protection of the British Crown against Central American aggression.[25] In the meantime, Macdonald backed up his words effectively without sparing the sensitivities of nearby Central American officials, for whom he had the utmost contempt. On one occasion, in early April, 1837, Macdonald remonstrated vigorously against the detainment of an Englishman, the captain of the schooner *Venus,* and demanded the payment of reparations.[26]

The merits of the case notwithstanding, the fact remains that a British official at Belize had prejudged the matter. To Hondurans, of course, this was a flagrant denial of their sovereign rights. Before long, the controversial Macdonald was accused of many more things, some of which were true and others not so. In either case he was fully capable of doing anything attributed to him. For example, reports circulated that he had begun the distribution of land grants in the disputed area between the Sibun and Sarstoon rivers and that he had occupied the

23. To Anderson, pvt., January 2, 1837, F.O. 252/15.
24. Macdonald to Lord Glenelg, February 12, 1837, F.O. 15/19.
25. Robert Charles Frederick to King of England, January 25, 1837, in No. 10, to Palmerston, April 1, 1837, F.O. 15/19; also in F.O. 252/8, from Macdonald, February 20, 1837.
26. Macdonald to Glenelg, May 1, 1837, F.O. 15/19.

islands of Ruatán and Bonacca. On the basis of letters which Macdonald sent to San Salvador, Chatfield knew that the superintendent could very well have carried out those measures. Macdonald had told him that if Morazán dared to remove the three English families from Ruatán he would not stand idly by.[27] The climax of Macdonald's aggressive maneuvers came on July 6, 1837, when he issued an ultimatum to the commandant of Trujillo ordering him to desist from any interference in the Limón and demanding immediate restoration of all confiscated wood. A refusal to comply, Macdonald threatened, would prompt him to call for naval action by the West Indian Squadron.[28]

In view of the foregoing, Chatfield's fabian policy with regard to the territorial issues became increasingly less tenable. Macdonald had aroused nationalistic sentiment in Central America to a fever pitch. At first, Chatfield was at a loss to explain the superintendent's actions and words. He suspected, however, that Macdonald had been carefully briefed in London before taking over his post. Perhaps his actions reflected recent policy decisions, Chatfield reasoned. For example, the remarks in the *Belize Herald* concerning land grants in the south seemed to indicate that Spain and Great Britain had arrived at some settlement on Belize, since the treaties of the 1780's clearly proscribed grants for cultivation.[29] Macdonald's protection of King Robert Charles Frederick, as well as his strong statements about the three families on Ruatán, also seemed to imply a series of significant policy decisions from London.

Chatfield urgently requested information on these various points since he, after all, would be called upon to defend the British stand in Central America. When he politely asked Colonel Macdonald for this information, the consul also reminded the superintendent that he should refrain from communicating directly with officials of nearby states, especially considering the delicate nature of the Belize problem.[30] He might have added, as he did in later years, that communication with Central American officials was the sole prerogative of the English consul; all other British officials should communicate with them through the consulate. To Chatfield's surprise and anger, Macdonald stubbornly refused to give him any information and continued to deal directly with the commandants at Trujillo and Omoa. The ultimatum of July 6, 1837,

---

27. From Macdonald, May 3, 1837, F.O. 252/8.
28. From Macdonald, July 6, 1837, F.O. 252/8.
29. To John Backhouse, pvt., March 17, 1837, F.O. 15/19; to Macdonald, April 21, 1837, F.O. 252/15.
30. To Macdonald, April 21, and pvt., March 31, 1837, F.O. 252/15.

was the last straw. Chatfield complained bitterly to the Foreign Office that he was being treated discourteously by the superintendent of Belize.[31]

The two strong-willed English rivals had begun their feud and struggle for personal power in Central America. Yet the fact remains that they were collaborators in formulating British policy in the area since their actions tended to complement each other. Both favored a protectorate of the Mosquito Shore; one announced it in September, 1836; and four months later, the other virtually implemented it. All they had to do now was to convince their respective offices in London— Colonial and Foreign. This would take time.

Thanks to the bellicose Macdonald, Guatemalan nationalists now had a sounding board throughout Central America. And they wasted no time in exploiting their opportunity. On June 1, 1837, *El Editor* in Guatemala City carried an article entitled "The Integrity of Our Territory." The author of the selection, as Chatfield suspected, was none other than Colonel Galindo who had just returned from Europe. In no uncertain terms, the Irishman scored New Granada's recent aggression at Boca del Toro, reminded Central Americans of Mexico's usurpation of Chiapas, and denounced English aggression — the alleged land grants at Belize and their woodcutting in Mosquitia. Emotionally, the editorialist advanced the just claims of Central America to the areas mentioned and strongly indicted those politicians, referring to the unionist faction, who had permitted the acts of aggression for the sake of internal peace: "Infamous peace! Peace which degrades the people! Peace which sooner or later will make us slaves of rapacious foreigners!" In his opinion, the time had come to apply economic pressure upon Belize in defense of the nation's territorial integrity — the only kind of action which Englishmen could understand.[32] As might be expected, the article in *El Editor* annoyed the British consul because of its inflamatory passages against foreigners, thus exposing them to attacks similar to the one he experienced at Zugapango. These violent charges in the Guatemalan press "which in some instances almost go so far as to impugn the British Honour and good faith," could not be left unchallenged.[33]

On the ground that such articles needlessly incited xenophobia, Chatfield demanded that the guilty newspaper in Guatemala City be

---

31. To Palmerston, Nos. 21 (July 26), and 26 (September 1, 1837), F.O. 15/19.
32. *El Editor* (Guatemala), June 1, 1837, A.G.N.G./LV.
33. To Palmerston, No. 21, July 26, 1837, F.O. 15/19.

curbed. The official protest was forwarded by Minister Alvarez to Governor Gálvez who, though he defended the "line of remark" in the offending article, promised to delete in the future, "paragraphs of a similar tendency." Slightly placated by this answer, Chatfield's patience with Gálvez was nonetheless wearing thin: "If he forfeits his promise I shall certainly notice the matter more formally, being indisposed to put up any longer with his rudeness."[34] Actually, the truce between the two rivals was short-lived. To counter the charges made in *El Editor,* Chatfield submitted an unsigned article defending Belize and the British position — a manuscript which the editor of that newspaper refused to publish until the author identified himself and paid for its publication.[35] Angered by the consul's efforts to defend Belize, Governor Gálvez felt that they in fact released him from his earlier promise. As a result, on July 20, another article appeared in *El Editor* bearing the title "The Robbery of the Republic's Territory by the English," in reference to the alleged occupation of the Bay Islands. War with England was inevitable, the writer asserted, if Englishmen continued "to rob our properties." To stop the aggression of European powers in the Western Hemisphere, he urged the calling of an inter-American conference:

> We form a small nation, but we belong to the political system of a Continent, which has already been outraged in various of its different sections, and which sooner or later will combine against the insolence of the power of foreigners. Let us excite the reunion of an American Diet . . . and in the meanwhile, let us strongly remonstrate with the government of the English metropolis. Let us prohibit our commercial relations with the settlement of Belize, and let us connect ourselves more closely with other markets.[36]

This was Chatfield's first encounter with what he called the "American System," an irritating notion which he fought tenaciously in his long Central American career. It had been implicit in Galindo's mission to the United States, but the selection in *El Editor* outlined it explicitly and in multilateral terms.

As Chatfield correctly suspected, the disgruntled Galindo was a prime mover in the resurgence of nationalism throughout Central America. The June 1 article was probably written by him; he wrote still others on August 31 and October 14 in which he condemned the rapac-

---

34. *Ibid.*
35. *El Editor* (Guatemala), Alcance al No. 15, July 20, 1837, B.N.G./V, leg. 836; also see No. 22, to Palmerston, August 1, 1837, F.O. 15/19.
36. *El Editor* (Guatemala), July 20, 1837, B.N.G./V, leg. 836. For Chatfield's translation, see enclosure to No. 22, to Palmerston, August 1, 1837, F. O. 15/19.

ity of his former countrymen. An outraged Chatfield noted Galindo's frequent disavowal of "the country of his birth," tantamount to heresy in the consul's mind.[37] On October 14, in a tract entitled "Honorable Nicaraguans," the fiery colonel beseeched the citizens of that state to put an end to their squabbles "whilst the foreign enemy is within our gates." Let us unite against the invaders: "Mosquitos, Zambos, and Englishmen."[38] Judging from the complaint which Galindo made to Palmerston, the annoyance was not all one-sided:

> I have to complain of Mr. Chatfield constantly and officially stating by speech and writing that I am a British subject, such pertinacity on his part cannot but be highly injurious to my career, and drives me into an extreme of opposition to counteract the effect of his uncalled for assertions.[39]

It would seem that Frederick Chatfield's countrymen were destined to obstruct, or embarrass, their consul's activities in Central America. In addition to Galindo, Bennett, Hyde, and Macdonald, he also had to contend with the ambitions of George Skinner and his German-born partner Charles Klee, both of whom were enmeshed deeply in Guatemalan politics. In 1837, Skinner set out to discredit the Eastern Company as a speculating venture, hopeful that the colonization contract would be annulled. And since the company had not met all of its obligations fully, Governor Gálvez seriously considered the annulment of the contract. What worried Chatfield was the prospect that a new English company — and it should be remembered that the Klee-Skinner house was closely associated with the Reid-Irving interests — might succeed in advancing Guatemala's territorial schemes. Such a company would indeed be formidable if it included the support of the Spanish house of John Matheu and Carlos Murphy, who in turn were agents for the House of Lloyds in Guatemala City. And the Lloyds, as Chatfield knew, had inquired about the colonization grant in Guatemala.[40]

Despite the provocations of his countrymen and the jingoistic press in Guatemala, the alliance between Chatfield and the federal government remained in effect as late as July 26, 1837. Still trying to negotiate a treaty with Central America, the consul asked Palmerston if the British

---

37. To Palmerston, Nos. 27 (September 20) and 38 (December 1, 1837), F.O. 15/19; *El Editor* (Guatemala), August 31, 1937, A.G.N.G./LV.

38. "Honrados Nicaragüenses," October 14, 1837, in No. 38 to Palmerston, December 1, 1837, F.O. 15/19.

39. John Galindo to Palmerston, April 30, 1838, F.O. 15/21.

40. To William Hall, pvt., September 1, 1837; from Hall, August 4, and September 8, 1837, p. encl., F.O. 252/18; to H. Roper (Lloyds), July 1, 1837, F.O. 252/9.

government would consent to a territorial settlement on Belize according
to the limits occupied in 1821, along with an English disclaimer to the
Bay Islands.[41] Nothing came of this suggestion, but it does illustrate
Chatfield's last minute effort to avoid a rupture on the territorial question.

The treaty negotiations with federal authorities, however, came to
an end when it was learned that Colonel Macdonald had issued his ultimatum of July 6 to the commandant of Trujillo. At this point, the federal
government could no longer ignore the territorial questions and still
expect to survive as the representative of Central America. Realizing
this, and honoring an earlier promise, President Morazán stepped down
from the presidency on August 11 while the minister of foreign affairs
debated the territorial questions with Frederick Chatfield.[42]

To carry conviction in these discussions and to help mold the
British position on the three-pronged territorial issue, Chatfield intensified his research efforts. His first move was to discredit Morazán, who
was pictured in the dispatches to Palmerston as a political opportunist
who was advancing the territorial question for his own pecuniary profit.
He "now discovered" that Morazán's grant of 1834, which he had earlier
believed extended from Omoa to Trujillo, actually included land beyond
Trujillo to the River Patook at latitude 16 North and longitude 84 West.
This was far beyond the disputed Limón River area. Moreover, Chatfield
learned that Morazán had petitioned the State of Nicaragua for a
similar concession from the Patook to San Juan del Norte, "thus claiming and exercising, without the smallest hesitation or enquiry on the part
of Central America, an act of full sovereignty over the whole of the
territory hitherto recognized as belonging to the Mosquito Nation."[43]
Morazán's request, however, was turned down by ambitious politicos in
Nicaragua who wanted to develop the wood resources on the Shore for
their own benefit. Rumor had it that they hoped to attract the support
of the United States by inviting North Americans to exploit the wood.[44]

In his conversations with Minister Alvarez, Chatfield recited the
long historical relationship between Great Britain and the Mosquito
Nation. As a result, he concluded that Central America had absolutely
no right to molest woodcutters from Belize who had received bona fide
grants from King Robert Charles Frederick. Alvarez, on the other hand,
doubted the existence of any such political body and remarked that it was

41. To Palmerston, No. 21, July 26, 1837, F.O. 15/19.
42. To Hall, August 11, 1837, F.O. 252/18.
43. To Palmerston, No. 24, August 19, 1837, F.O. 15/19.
44. *Ibid.;* for later reports on this, see No. 6, from John Foster, October 20,
    1837, F.O. 252/19, and from John Baily, December 15, 1837, F.O. 252/6.

a travesty of international law to dignify a band of uncivilized zambos with the status of a nation. At this point, Chatfield exploded "that their existence was certainly recognized by Great Britain, whom they are in alliance with, and in some respects *subject to.*"[45] In the heat of the discussion and without authorization — though he gambled that Macdonald had received specific instructions to this effect — Chatfield officially announced to Central America that the Mosquito Nation was a protectorate of Great Britain. He had gone out on a limb, so to speak, little suspecting that "Old Pam" would saw it off.

At this time the consul was also developing an extreme position on the Belize question, though he did not make it public in Central America. It would seem that the possibility of a new company (Skinner-Klee *et al.*) inheriting the colonization grant of the Eastern Company had prompted him to do further research on the "Belize Question." He presented the facts and conclusions of his latest findings to Palmerston in a dispatch of November 10, 1837. During the Spanish period, the consul argued, the effective frontier line of Central America, for various reasons, had been to the west of the Yucatán range. In short, Spaniards had not occupied effectively the lands to the east of Lake Petén in the northern section or the area near Cahabón, which had been the approximate colonizing site of the Eastern Company, in the southern portion of the frontier. The territory to the east of those two points, therefore, could be claimed by Great Britain. To settle for less, even the boundaries set down by Belizean officials in 1835, would be a gratuitous concession to the Guatemalans.[46]

As far as it is known, Lord Palmerston did not comment upon his underling's aggressive proposal, which was repeated several times in the next two years. Its real significance lies in the fact that it revealed Chatfield's concern for the colonizing aspirations of the Klee-Skinner interests in Guatemala City. The mention of the southern site of Cahabón suggests that he envisioned its incorporation or close cooperation with Belize, especially if settled by Englishmen, along the lines set forth earlier when he urged the Eastern Company to place its colony in the Petén. Significantly, when secession was rampant in Guatemala during the early months of 1838, he suggested that Macdonald encourage the secession of the Petén to Belize, a scheme strongly motivated as well by Chatfield's hatred of Colonel Galindo, who still maintained his rights to collect duties on the wood resources of that area.[47]

45. To Palmerston, No. 26, September 1, 1837, F.O. 15/19. Italics are mine.
46. To Palmerston, No. 35, November 10, 1837, F.O. 15/19.
47. To Macdonald, No. 1, conf., February 28, 1838, F.O. 252/15.

In the debate with Chatfield, Minister Alvarez riled his adversary with a refusal to consider any further negotiations on an English treaty. The inference, as far as the sensitive consul was concerned, was that the Republic wanted to be free to harass British subjects if it chose to do so. Apparently, the minister threatened to withhold the abolition of the five percent discriminatory duty on Belizean imports, which was called for by the Federal Tariff of 1837. In other words, Chatfield had cause to believe that the federal government would apply economic pressure on Belize for political purposes — the "Mosquito Question." This prospect made him furious: "To counteract the license with which the Central American government conceives itself at liberty to molest the trade of British subjects resident within its territory, I am inclined to take, and to recommend to Your Lordship's approval, a very decided line of procedure."[48]

It was in the context of the territorial discussions with Alvarez that Frederick Chatfield first outlined his special doctrine on forced loans. According to standing instructions of 1829, consuls were told that without a treaty British subjects in Central America were liable to military duty and to forced loans, as if they were natives of the country. Chatfield, however, had balked at these instructions, feeling that they were not applicable to "rude and uncivilised" countries. With or without a treaty, he was determined to insist upon the protection of his country-men.[49] On August 26, 1837, he announced to Palmerston that the states of the Republic had no right to levy forced loans according to such-and-such a clause in the Constitution of 1824. In fact, he argued, only under certain conditions did the federal government have this right. To begin with, the forced loan had to be general in its application, that is, it had to extend to the whole community before it could be legally demanded of a particular class. Foreigners, therefore, did not have to pay their quotas until there was proof that all natives had contributed — a condition which the consul admitted would be difficult to meet. This was the "very decided line of procedure" which Chatfield was prepared to take against the Republic:

> Should I be placed in a situation to contend with the general gov-
> ernment of the Republick for the protection of H.M.'s subjects,
> against exactions of this nature, I shall acquaint the government,
> that I will be responsible for the payment of the sums required,
> within a certain period, provided I am satisfied, at the termination
> of that period, that each native member of the community has duly

---

48. To Palmerston, No. 25, August 26, 1837, F.O. 15/19.
49. To Palmerston, Nos. 16 (February 24) and 39 (June 19, 1838), F.O. 15/20.

paid up his assessment; and I shall add an intimation, that any act of violence to obtain payment from the parties whom I have taken under my protection, will inevitably incur the heavy displeasures of H.M.'s Government.[50]

Though primarily a product of the troubled times, as well as Chatfield's sincere desire to protect the lives and property of his countrymen, the forced-loan doctrine also had political implications especially for the long run. Given the impoverished condition of the federal government, an outside control of its rights to raise funds could seriously hamper any plans to defend the territorial integrity of Central America. To be sure, this could discourage such action in defense of Central America; but it could by no means prevent it. The indirect consequences of the doctrine, however, had political meaning for the future. If the Republic, or any of the states, had been willing to deny itself the right to tax Englishmen, then the doctrine would merely protect British subjects as if they had the benefit of a treaty. This is perhaps all that Chatfield had in mind in 1837, when the treaty negotiations collapsed and there seemed little likelihood that the Treaty of 1826 with the United States would be renewed. In the past, it should be noted, English subjects had enjoyed the benefits of the American treaty.[51] But an astute political observer like Chatfield knew only too well that the governments in question would never abandon their right to levy forced loans or accept a modification of the attribute of sovereignty involved. Consequently, if they raised a loan for purposes which he considered objectionable, he could easily build up a case of abuse against them which would provoke British armed intervention.

Interestingly, he first outlined this technique in a dispatch of January 12, 1838, to his vice-consul in Guatemala City. On that occasion, he remarked that if the federal government forced a single Englishman to contribute one *cuartillo* against his will: "I would represent the circumstances in such a way to the Queen's Government, as should cause a demand for immediate restitution."[52] In London, Lord Palmerston rejected the procedure suggested by Chatfield and argued that governments had a right to levy forced loans providing they were not discriminatory. It was the proviso — which authorized the British consul to judge whether or not it was an impartial or discriminatory levy — that permitted Chatfield to maintain his position stubbornly despite the non-acceptance of his doctrine by the Foreign Office.[53]

50. To Palmerston, No. 25, August 26, 1837, F.O. 15/19.
51. *Ibid.*
52. To William Hall, January 12, 1838, F.O. 252/18.
53. From Palmerston, January 12, 1838, F.O. 15/20.

But these were long-range consequences of Chatfield's special doc-trine on forced loans. At the time, the maneuver — a clever one, it must be admitted — had a sobering effect upon General Morazán, though other federal officials like Alvarez were less impressed. Moreover, wor-ried about the internal threat to the Republic, Morazán did not feel that he could afford an open rupture with the British. And despite his own annoyance with the federal government, Chatfield likewise did not favor the dissolution of the former alliance. After all, the alternative to Mora-zán was hardly more attractive, especially in view of what happened to him at Zugapango. Therefore the alliance, though severely strained, managed to limp along for another year and a half.

—◆◆—

The Republic of Central America had led a fitful existence since its very inception; and, in early 1837, unionists hoped that the new tariff and other financial reforms would permit the stabilization and advancement of the nation. These sanguine expectations dissipated them-selves with the cholera crisis which unleashed the forces of anarchy throughout Central America. The epidemic brought in its wake social and racial unrest which in turn disrupted the country's economic life. World-wide economic troubles brought falling prices for exports and further aggravated the situation in Central America. There were other disruptive ingredients as well — the prospect of an effective general government which could collect duties, depriving the state regimes of this privilege; the ambitions of conservatives to unseat the liberals and their darling Republic; the political rivalry of cities within a state; and the partisan struggles of political opportunists. The cholera crisis of 1837, in effect, marked the beginning of the end for the Republic. From here on out, conservatives, states' righters, the "coloured classes," and the "Romish" elements all gained ground. The one "white" hope for a return to order, in the opinion of Europeans and the "respectable" people of Central America, was General Francisco Morazán.[54] And Frederick Chatfield shared this widely-held conviction.

At the time of the Zugapango incident, and even during the May uprising of Indians in El Salvador, Chatfield had not yet attached much importance to the use of Indians as political weapons. To be sure, he resented the anti-foreign slogans employed by the ringleaders of these disturbances but he felt that politically speaking the danger was only a potential one.[55] By July, 1837, however, the potential was fast material-

---

54. From John Foster, pvt., November 3, 1837, F.O. 252/19; from John A. Baily, Jr., March 16, 1838, F.O. 252/16.
55. To Palmerston, No. 17, June 26, 1837, F.O. 15/19.

izing in the large state of Guatemala because of a disastrous split in the liberals' ranks. A hitherto obscure Indian — Rafael Carrera — emerged from the political fires of that fateful year; and in due time he became the dictator of Guatemala, as well as the dominant figure in Central America for decades.

Anarchy and incipient secession were not strangers to Central American politics before 1837; but the final impetus toward the dissolution of the Republic resulted from the quarrel between Governor Mariano Gálvez and José Francisco Barrundia. For our purposes, there are specific incidents and trends in the complex Guatemalan picture which will serve to illustrate the major developments. The trouble began on January 1, 1837, with the introduction of Edward Livingston's penal codes, a well-intentioned experiment in judicial reform which subsequently was to be adopted by the remaining states of the union. The Gálvez legislature had also passed a law of financial reform (*ley de hacienda*), which called for a broader and more equitable tax base. With the cholera crisis, these reforms came under attack. Chatfield shrewdly analyzed the situation as follows:

> In the early part of last year [1837], the Code Livingstone (sic) was attempted to be put into practice throughout the state of Guatemala, and a body of judges and lawyers were despatched on a circuit through the principal towns and villages. To save expenses, some of these persons were commissioned to remain and make the valuations, upon which it was proposed to collect a property tax which a new financial law of the state decreed should form a branch of the annual publick income. The Indians, who of course could comprehend nothing of a jury system, and had never seen judges and lawyers visit them, except for the purpose of inflicting punishments, revolted against the intrusion, and their anger lost all bounds, when the person appointed to carry the vexatious and absurd financial law into operation, proceeded to take an inventory of their huts, and to assess the value of their patches of ground.[56]

Besides those listed above, there were other causes for the rebellion of more than thirty Indian villages in mid-1837. First, the Indians were fearful of the *cordones* placed around the areas infected by cholera.[57] Secondly, they strongly resented the awarding of public lands (*tierras baldías*) to special parties, lands which they had considered theirs since time immemorial though they did not have clear title to them.[58] And finally, disgruntled clergymen, as advisors to the Indians, were bent upon

---

56. To Palmerston, No. 9, February 5, 1838, F.O. 15/20.
57. From Hall, June 16, 1837, F.O. 252/18.
58. From Hall, June 30, 1837, F.O. 252/18.

discrediting all liberal reforms. "These persons," Chatfield explained, "sigh for a return to the slavish times which happily disappeared with the destruction of the monkish institutions in this country, and they hope to recover their former arbitrary dominion, by exciting a hatred against foreigners especially the English, who are invariably asserted to be beyond the pale of Christianity."[59]

Yet the Indian uprisings in Guatemala might have been quashed energetically, as they were in El Salvador, and their political significance minimized if the liberals of the state had remained united. In the opinion of many contemporaries, the Livingston codes were responsible for the rift among the liberals. In a general sense, this is a valid interpretation since the codes brought to a head a latent power struggle between the City of Guatemala and the outlying districts. If the judicial experiment had been implemented faithfully, it would have decentralized political power in the state.[60] When the supporters of Governor Gálvez realized this, they favored the weakening of the codes; the cholera crisis merely provided them with the opportunity and the excuse for such action. At this point — July, 1837 — José Franciso Barrundia raised his highly articulate voice in protest, especially since he was the champion of Edward Livingston's ideas in Central America. The "War over Principles" raged in the columns of *La Oposición;* and Barrundia told his ex-colleague many "hard truths," as Chatfield put it.[61] Gálvez replied in kind, and both sides marshaled their forces for the fall elections. With the support of the military, Governor Gálvez ruled with a strong hand as the situation went from bad to worse. To Chatfield's disgust, both political factions sought the support of "the man Carrera," thus raising him and his followers "to a degree of importance, as undeserved as it is disgraceful and dangerous to the country."[62] The vision of Zugapango was haunting the British consul as squabbling politicians placed in jeopardy English life and property.

In the midst of the Barrundia-Gálvez controversy, Frederick Chatfield developed his forced-loan doctrine. Unquestionably, his hostility toward Gálvez, because of the jingoistic articles in *El Editor,* encouraged him to resist a forced loan passed by the Guatemalan government on June 16. By the terms of the levy, William Hall, the vice-consul in Guatemala City, had to contribute five hundred dollars. At first, Chat-

59. To Palmerston, No. 12, February 16, 1838, F.O. 15/20.
60. Mario Rodríguez, *The Livingston Codes in the Guatemalan Crisis of 1837–1838* (New Orleans, 1955).
61. To William Hall, July 14, 1837, F.O. 252/18.
62. To Palmerston, No. 9, February 5, 1838, F.O. 15/20.

field refused to support Hall's petition for an exemption on the ground that he was a vice-consul; but when Hall revealed the discriminatory manner in which John Matheu had assigned the shares, he changed his mind. This was on July 28.[63] On August 26, the consul outlined his forced-loan doctrine to Lord Palmerston; and, on November 3, in antici-pation of the Guatemalan elections, he wrote to Hall:

> I am decided not to permit any English people to be molested in their property during the tumults which appear likely to occur; if it is alleged that we have no Treaty and have therefore no promise of protection, you can let it be known that I reply, that the English government by the same rule is not engaged to withhold all the means of retaliation which may be within their power.[64]

Then, on December 6, Chatfield complained officially to Minister Alvarez that Guatemala had no constitutional right to levy a forced loan.[65] Approximately two weeks later, in answer to the English protest which had been forwarded to Guatemala City, Gálvez insisted upon his government's right to raise forced loans and declared that the British consul had misinterpreted the Constitution of 1824.[66] When Minister Alvarez sided with the Guatemalans, in early January, 1838, Chatfield warned him that he would not permit a single Englishman to be taxed for partisan politics.[67] It should be evident from the above discussion that the British consul was primarily interested in protecting his country-men and their property.

Furthermore, Mr. Chatfield took steps to punish any person or group who contributed to the spread of anglophobia in Central America. This led him to develop another "most peculiar doctrine," according to the complaint of the Skinner-Klee house in Guatemala City. Chatfield flatly announced that he would withhold the protection of the British consulate from any firm whose senior partner was not English! Realizing that this novel doctrine, which was aimed at the German Carlos Klee, would be immediately challenged by interests in Guatemala City and London, the consul hastened to justify his action to Lord Palmerston: "Even if he were an Englishman, I should, under the circustances, feel considerable hesitation about interfering to relieve him, from the incon-

---

63. To Hall, July 28, 1837; from Hall, July 17, 1837, F.O. 252/18.
64. To Hall, pvt., November 3, 1837, F.O. 252/18.
65. To Miguel Alvarez, December 6, 1837, F.O. 252/5.
66. Alvarez to Mariano Gálvez, December 8, 1837; and Gálvez to Alvarez, December 19, 1837, A.G.N.G./CMRE, leg. 166, exp. 03466.
67. To Palmerston, No. 9, February 15, 1838, F.O. 15/20; to Hall, January 12, 1838, F.O. 252/18.

venient position into which his notorious partisanship has placed him."[68]
The consul simply could not forgive Carlos Klee for his contribution to
the rising clamor against the English as well as his part in the failure of
the earlier treaty mission. Lord Palmerston, however, demanded the
immediate abandonment of that strange doctrine; and his underling had
no choice but to obey.[69]

The political situation in Guatemala was fast approaching its inevitable climax by the end of 1837. Trade had long since come to a stand-
still, and banditry was rife. On December 29, William Hall evaluated the
scene with perception:

> The promises and inducements held out by this man Carrera are
> flattering to the prejudices and fanaticism of the greater part of the
> ignorant population of the country. He persuades all to join him,
> in order, as it is pretended, to bring about the restoration of the
> Arch-Bishop, and the friars, to destroy the foreigners, and to sub-
> vert the government, he being as he asserts supported and counte-
> nanced by Barrundia, the leader of the opposition party. . . . I have
> been assured, that the country is generally in his favour, and when
> to the above promises, so congenial to the religious and national
> prejudices of the lower classes, is added the hope of plunder, it is
> not surprizing, if numbers have joined him, and rendered him
> formidable. . . .
>
> If these bands of robbers are allowed to continue their career
> unmolested, increasing in numbers and audacity, every day, know-
> ing as they must do, the uncertain and divided state of parties in
> this capital, without any preparations for defence (the military
> being in an undisciplined and insubordinate state), it will not be
> altogether an impossibility, their putting their threats into execu-
> tion of attacking this place, and if such an attempt were to be
> made, it is with but too much reason to be feared, that they might
> be joined by the ill-disposed here, when a scene of pillage, confu-
> sion, and bloodshed would ensue, in which foreign and British
> lives, and interests would be the first to suffer.[70]

Almost a month later to the day, it all happened just as Hall had
said it would. A motley coalition of Governor Gálvez' enemies con-
verged upon Guatamala City. Liberals under Barrundia, and those from
Antigua, joined in an "unholy" alliance with "the man Carrera" and his
supporters. The Indians went on the rampage, and foreigners had to
conceal themselves from their wrath.[71] One observer compared Carrera

---

68. To Palmerston, No. 42, p. encl., December 27, 1837; from Klee-Skinner,
    December 22, 1837, F.O. 15/19.
69. From Palmerston, No. 4, July 4, 1838, F.O. 15/20.
70. From Hall, No. 8, December 29, 1837, F.O. 252/18.
71. From Hall, February 15, 1838, F.O. 252/18.

and his "hordes" with "Alaric when he invaded Rome — the sight was awful and horrible — to witness 4,000 barbarians rude, half-naked, drunk and elated, vociferating with all their might 'que viva la religión y mueran los estrangeros (Religion forever, Death to Foreigners.' "[72] Four days of plunder and finally Carrera was persuaded to lead his followers out of the city. He did so reluctantly but not before threatening to return if his demands were not met.

The monster had been created; and the opponents of Governor Gálvez began to realize the folly of their ways. Their ally Carrera was now insisting upon the reestablishment of the Church's prerogatives, the abandonment of the Livingston experiment, and the persecution of foreigners. As February progressed, the chieftain's supporters became "more insolent in their demands," and threatened a new attack upon the city. "British lives and property," William Hall wrote, "are therefore in the most imminent danger, and unless a Federal force be immediately sent, nothing can save this city from destruction." Morazán, Hall insisted, had to act promptly without waiting for an appeal from the Guatemalan government.[73] Fortunately, the appeal was made, and the federal authorities answered it with energy. By April 18, 1838, General Morazán was partially successful. Carrera and his "uncouth followers" were driven into the mountains, thus relieving the pressure on Guatemala City for the time being. Guatemalans were grateful, even those who had foolishly joined with the "barbarian" weeks earlier.[74]

Chatfield's worst fears about Rafael Carrera materialized during the tragic events of early 1838. The situation still remained dangerous since Morazán had not completely eliminated the menace to security. "Property is no where safe," Chatfield told Palmerston, "and towns are kept in constant alarm by bands of marauders who scour the country at discretion."[75] To bring order on a permanent basis, the federal government had to strengthen itself, a suggestion which the consul had made frequently as the Guatemalan situation worsened.[76] "Unless some decisive measures are adopted to reorganize the institutions of this Republick, on a sound basis," the consul wrote, "and honesty and justice are permitted to guide the course of the Government, complete anarchy will

---

72. To Palmerston, February 16, 1838, F.O. 15/20. Chatfield quotes his informant without revealing his name. It may have been John Baily, Jr. or Henry Savage.

73. From Hall, No. 2, February 16, 1838, F.O. 252/18.

74. To Palmerston, Nos. 22 (March 7) and 29 (April 18, 1838), F.O. 15/20.

75. No. 29 (April 18).

76. No. 12 (February 16).

ensue with the Indian and mulatto classes in the ascendant."[77] Undoubtedly Chatfield was thinking about his experience at Zugapango almost
a year earlier when he wrote those lines.

Faced with ominous prospects of a further breakdown in order,
Chatfield prepared himself for this eventuality. On April 18, 1838, he
asked Lord Palmerston to dispatch a British warship to the Pacific coast
for the month of September, when the annual indigo fairs would be held
in El Salvador and where considerable British property would be involved. In view of the elections scheduled for October and November,
the presence of an English ship was doubly imperative:

> As General Morazán cannot again be elected by law, there is every
> reason to expect, that a violent struggle will be made to force him
> into the Presidency; if the attempt should fail, some of the incapa-
> ble persons who are now at the head of affairs will succeed him,
> or else, the Servile, or old Spanish Party will come to power, and
> in any of these cases the country will have to undergo a series of
> tumults and disaster.[78]

Implicit in this remark, as well as in Chatfield's actions during the
course of 1838, was the hope that Morazán would assume dictatorial
powers until order was completely restored in Central America. In the
event Morazán refused to do this, however, Chatfield had to work out
means to defend the interests of his countrymen. The call for naval support and the forced-loan doctrine would be his principal weapons.
Another tactic would be to strengthen the federal government wherever
possible and especially by encouraging financial reforms at the federal
congress scheduled to convene on April 2.[79]

The task that lay before Chatfield was indeed formidable and discouraging. It is not surprising, therefore, that in mid-March, 1838, he
suffered a brief letdown. The Guatemalan scene did not appear promising; in Nicaragua, secessionists were gaining ground, and there were
constant rumors that they would try to attract the support of United
States on the "Mosquito Question"; Colonel Macdonald was annoyingly
uncooperative; and Minister Alvarez, in the absence of General Morazán, was listening more and more to the rascally Galindo. That ingrate,

---

77. No. 29 (April 18).
78. *Ibid.*
79. "Breves observaciones sobre el nuevo arancel y tarifa de aduanas," Guate-
    mala, February 28, 1838, in No. 26, to Palmerston, April 4, 1838, F.O.
    15/20.

Chatfield complained, had done more than anyone else to bring about "the unpopularity with which the English are viewed in Central America." Moreover, he had dared charge the Queen's Government with "rapacity, injustice, and oppression in their conduct towards this Republick." The embittered consul continued:

> His constant nonsensical assertion, that I am a dangerous man, and the greatest enemy Central America ever possessed, and that supported by the power of my government, I disregard the Laws of the country to force down those which suit British interests; moreover his recommendation, that every means should be taken to get me removed, added to the circumstances that one of the demands of the Chiefs of the present civil war is, that the English Heretics should be expelled from the country, render my position in the management of disputed questions unpleasant and difficult.[80]

And Colonel Galindo was by no means disinterested in the territorial questions, Chatfield pointed out. For example, there were positive indications that Galindo was negotiating for a contract on the Mosquito Shore, backed up — so it was claimed — by important financial interests in London, Paris, and New York.[81]

The real source of the consul's disappointment and frustration, however, was in England, not in Central America. The Foreign Office simply would not support him. He had just received a dispatch in which Palmerston refused to accept the protectorate idea implicit in Chatfield's "subject to" statement with regard to the Mosquito Nation. "Such an assertion," explained the master in London, "implies obligations on the part of this country, which could not properly or conveniently be assumed." "I have therefore to instruct you," Palmerston concluded, "not again to use that expression in your future communications with the Central American government."[82] Instead, the official line was that Great Britain recognized the Mosquito Nation and would not see "with indifference any attempt on the part of Central America to encroach upon Mosquito Territory."[83]

Palmerston's reprimand completely disheartened Mr. Chatfield who was only slightly consoled by the knowledge that Macdonald was acting without authorization. In due time, undoubtedly, he would receive similar rebukes on his forced-loan and the Carlos Klee doctrines. Four years of wasted effort!

---

80. To Palmerston, No. 27, April 6, 1838, F.O. 15/20.
81. No. 17 (February 26).
82. From Palmerston, No. 12, December 15, 1837, F.O. 15/19.
83. *Ibid.*

To compound the injury, the federal government had reopened an old wound. During Morazán's absence, the leaders of the government permitted the publication of an insulting article in *La Tijereta*, a local print. The writer of the article insinuated that consuls whose countries did not have a treaty with the Republic could not be recognized as political functionaries.[84] The English representative, therefore, should restrict himself to commercial functions. We can well imagine the roar that bellowed through the British consulate when those insolent words passed before Chatfield's eyes. He had heard the same chant in Warsaw, but he was not about to tolerate the same views from less worthy sources. The battle royal between the British consul and the federal authorities mushroomed to alarming proportions in the final days of March, 1838. As might be expected, Don Juan Galindo had a hand in the matter.

Tear-stained and trembling with fright, a fourteen-year-old English lad knocked at the door of the consulate on Wednesday evening, March 28. His master, the cruel Galindo, had just beaten him unmercifully, sobbed James Dearing, as the threw himself at the consul's feet and begged his protection. The boy undressed to give Chatfield "ocular proof" of the thrashing. Filled with compassion and anger, the consul scribbled a note to Galindo in which he announced the fact that young Dearing had requested the protection of the English flag and in which he ordered the immediate delivery of the boy's clothes and any wages due to him to the British consulate.

A few minutes after receiving the consul's note, the wild-eyed master delivered his reply in person — a torrent of abusive language. Chatfield was a meddler; he had no business tampering with his servants; the boy's mother had entrusted young James to him; and he had spent a considerable sum of money in bringing the lad to Central America. The consul stiffened and pointed out firmly that it was his responsibility to protect all British subjects in Central America and especially to prevent any attempt to enslave one of them. Young James was brought into the room; and, emboldened by the determined look in Chatfield's eyes, he "recapitulated in the presence of Galindo, the numerous instances of cruelty."[85] His mother had not intended for him to be Galindo's slave, only his servant. Cursing under his breath, the angry Irishman stomped out of the room. As he got to the street, he shouted that if the boy were not released by morning he would take the law into his own hands. In a report to Palmerston, Galindo maintained that Chatfield had grossly in-

---

84. *La Tijereta* (San Salvador), No. 3, March 30, 1838, in No. 27, to Palmerston, April 6, 1838, F.O. 15/20.
85. No. 27 (April 6).

sulted him that evening.[86] The consul, on the other hand, gave the impression that they had agreed to allow the boy to stay overnight in the consulate. In the morning young James would decide if he wanted to return to his master's house.[87]

On Thursday morning, the "Dearing Affair" blew up with the full force of a tempest in a teapot, partly because of the principle involved and also due to the long-standing animosity of the two main contenders. Young Dearing, knowing what he might expect if he returned home, did not change his mind on the following morning; and Galindo, who was gesticulating violently outside the British consulate, bellowed that his honor had been insulted and that he would demand justice. At ten o'clock that morning, Chatfield wrote a second note demanding the boy's clothes and pay.

In the meantime, the irate colonel stormed into the French consulate, where the personnel helped him write a note to the British consul challenging him to a duel. Captain de Conny, secretary of the French legation, delivered the note at noontime. "Very well," Chatfield replied upon reading the message, "there is no answer except to request that Mr. Galindo will send to me James Dearing's money and clothes." The consul, in short, refused to accept the challenge. "This suitable reply," he explained to Palmerston, "seems to have cooled the gallant Colonel's ardour, for I have heard no more upon the subject." On the other hand, Galindo explained to Palmerston: "Though this was not accepted, consideration for an agent of Her Brittanic Majesty prevented me from the common resource of posting."[88] Matters were getting completely out of hand.

Frederick Chatfield performed rather strangely on Thursday afternoon, almost as if he were deliberately trying to make a great issue of the affair. Knowing that he could not compel Galindo to deliver the boy's clothes and pay, since the colonel enjoyed military immunity, he allowed young Dearing to go back to his master's home. Certainly he must have realized that Galindo would never allow the boy to return. Was he therefore trying to build up a case of abduction, thus raising the principle of the inviolability of the British flag? It would seem so in the light of subsequent events.

The federal government was brought into the affair after Galindo seized the boy. When Chatfield insisted upon his return, Galindo turned young James over to Miguel Alvarez; and the latter refused to comply

---

86. John Galindo to Palmerston, April 30, 1838, F.O. 15/21.
87. To Palmerston, No. 27, April 6, 1838, F.O. 15/20.
88. Galindo to Palmerston, April 30, 1838, F.O. 15/21.

with a similar request from Chatfield, stating that it was now a matter for the federal authorities. The acting executive supported Alvarez; and on March 30, the objectionable article in *La Tijereta* appeared, causing the angry Chatfield to push the incident to its logical conclusion: an apology by the federal government for its refusal to accept "the inviolability of the British Flag."

Both sides realized that the situation had reached an impossible point and that some kind of a face-saving solution was necessary. At first, however, Chatfield was adamant. He issued an ultimatum demanding the boy's return by noon on April 2. When the federal authorities balked and failed to meet the deadline, Chatfield was aware that he had overstepped. Perhaps, he thought, Lord Palmerston, remembering his European experiences, might not support him in this case. Therefore, a compromise was reached on April 4 involving a very mild apology, if it can be called that, and the return of young James Dearing to the British consulate.[89]

Thus ended the "Dearing Affair" which threatened to wreck Chatfield's alliance with the federal government. It should be emphasized, however, that the incident reflected the consul's annoyance with Galindo and with certain federal officials. It did not alter his attitude toward General Morazán who was fighting Carrera in Guatemala at that time. Palmerston condoned Chatfield's actions, including the refusal to accept the challenge to a duel. In fact, the British foreign secretary failed to appreciate Galindo's remark that Chatfield was embarrassing him continually by insisting that he was an English subject: "I am not aware of any reason he can have for repudiating his country, or for thinking that Mr. Chatfield is doing him an injury by stating that he is a British subject."[90]

Imperceptibly the Foreign Office was coming around to a position in support of British agents in Central America.

---

89. To Palmerston, No. 27, April 6, 1838, F.O. 15/20.
90. Note by Palmerston, September 29, 1838, on Galindo's letter of April 30.

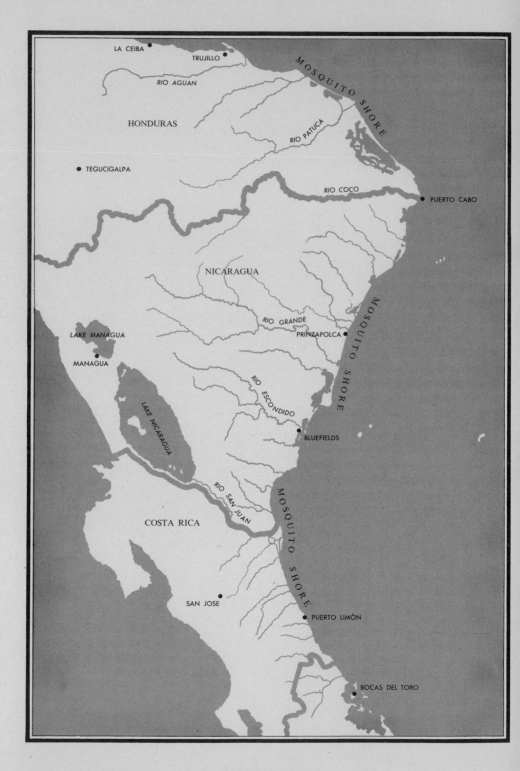

Mosquito Shore

CHAPTER SIX

Macbeth's Cauldron

I was just congratulating this unfortunate country on the New Tariff when my ears were din'd by the rumours from León that [were] worse than Macbeth's Cauldron.[1]

— John Foster, October 4, 1837

The rebellion of Carrera, which is a war of Barbarism against Civilisation, has since the departure of President Morazán from the state of Guatemala assumed fresh vigour. . . . It is a war for the destruction of Property, and for the concentration of all power in the country in the hands of the mulatto or coloured classes, to the exclusion of the European race.[2]

— Chatfield, August 16, 1838

Astirring in the Leonese cauldron was a scheme to declare Nicaragua's absolute sovereignty and independence at a grand fiesta scheduled for October 8, 1837. By no means was it a coincidence that John Foster, the British vice-consul in Nicaragua, should mention the Federal Tariff of February 27, 1837, in the same breath with rumors of secession. Indeed, an immediate cause for the disintegration of the Central American Republic derived from the reaction to financial reform. Part of the tariff went into effect in August, some of it in September, and all of it, plus the new law of customs, became the law of the land on January 10, 1838.[3]

The separatist movement gained momentum accordingly in Nicaragua, despite substantial resistance in Granada where "respectable" people favored the Morazán government.[4] With some justification, Granada feared that her rival's usurpation of federal revenues at the customhouses would perpetuate the governorship of José Núñez by allowing him to pay off the soldiery. And Leonese politicos, everyone knew, were a little too anxious to amass personal fortunes from the sale of wood and the negotiation of colonizing grants on the Mosquito Shore.[5] As the new financial program of the federal government materialized, however, Granadian views began to change. Perhaps much of this stemmed from

---

1. From John Foster, October 4, 1837, F.O. 252/19.
2. To Palmerston, No. 50, August 16, 1838, F.O. 15/20.
3. To Palmerston, No. 26, p. encl.s, April 4, 1838, F.O. 15/20.
4. From Foster, pvt., November 3, 1837, F.O. 252/19.
5. From John Baily, December 15, 1837, F.O. 252/6; from Foster, pvt., February 2, 1838, F.O. 252/19.

a renewed optimism in the prospects for an interoceanic canal — a plum which all Nicaraguans wanted exclusively for themselves. The State of Nicaragua, therefore, chose the path of secession on April 30, 1838, when it declared its provisional independence and announced that it would not return to the fold until drastic reforms were enacted in the federal pact of 1824.[6] In the meantime, federal customhouses and reve-nues became the property of the Nicaraguan state.

Nicaragua was not alone in her reluctance to accept financial re-forms, however liberal and well-conceived. It was a widespread sentiment throughout Central America. On December 8, 1837, the English vice-consul in Guatemala City predicted that the program would not be acceptable to Guatemalans.[7] Chatfield likewise noted the disruptive effect of the reforms in a letter to Palmerston:

> Looking at the geographical position of Nicaragua, Costa Rica, and Honduras, with ports upon both seas, they have reason for dis-regarding the federal government, whose existence is chiefly known to them by the abstraction from their coffers of the duties on the foreign import trade; in any other respect, the intervention of the federal government in the affairs of the states is unfelt; for except in the case of Guatemala it neither has the inclination nor the power to interfere in their domestic concerns.[8]

Yet the Republic could hardly expect to survive without a sound financial structure. The lack of revenues, as well as the state's unwilling-ness to contribute adequately to the federal coffers, was largely respon-sible for the Republic's inability to serve the states. And it was precisely to strengthen the union along these lines that the English consul had championed financial reforms, so essential for the protection and ad-vancement of British interests in Central America. In fact, as late as February 28, 1838, and despite strained relations with the federal gov-ernment, he offered constructive suggestions on the new tariff and law of customs in a twenty-five page treatise — a brilliant exposition of liberal economic philosophy. With these published remarks, the British consul hoped to influence the members of the eleventh federal congress which opened its sessions in early April.[9] That congress was the one that debated the all-important question of reforms to the Constitution of 1824. Since Frederick Chatfield later received blame for the dissolution

---

6. From Baily, May 8, June 15, and August 30, 1838, F.O. 252/6.
7. From William Hall, December 8, 1837, F.O. 252/18.
8. To Palmerston, No. 41, June 27, 1838, F.O. 15/20.
9. "Breves observaciones," February 28, 1838, in No. 26, to Palmerston, April 4, 1838, F.O. 15/20.

of the Republic, we should keep in mind his efforts in behalf of financial reform — a record which hardly bespeaks a negative influence upon the Central American Republic.

———◆•◆———

The secession crisis of 1838–1839 has generally been misunderstood or distorted, perhaps more from ignorance than intention. To analyze the causes for the failure of the Republic in any great detail is beyond the purview of this study. There are, however, certain trends and factors which must be noted for a proper understanding of the issues and interests at stake in the final year of the Republic's existence.

To begin with, the founding fathers of the Central American Republic had received their ideological inspiration from the Enlightenment and from the practical application of those ideas in the United States of America. In a spirit of optimism and of faith in man's ability to regenerate himself, they embarked upon an experiment in republicanism, or "Applied Enlightenment," fully conscious of the serious obstacles facing them. Some of these deterrents were: the ignorance of the masses in Central America; the racial tensions of a mixed society; the opposition of vested interests which had dominated this class-and-caste society for three centuries; a harsh topography which had always impeded effective communication, fostering an exaggerated feeling of municipalism and provincialism; and last, but not least, the lack of financial resources to implement a "new regime" for Central America.

Confronted with problems of this magnitude, one could argue convincingly that the whole experiment was futile and that anyone who insisted upon it was "starry-eyed." The implication of this defeatist attitude, which unfortunately has been all too standard an interpretation of the early liberal experiences throughout Latin America, is that governmental leaders were doctrinaire and unrealistic. This view deserves to be challenged for it is misleading, if not erroneous, and needs to be qualified considerably. In a recent work, Professor John Tate Lanning of Duke University has demonstrated that, prior to Independence, students at the University of San Carlos in Guatemala City had studied the ideas of the Enlightenment critically and that their approach was ecclectic as well as pragmatic.[10] Are we to assume that the alumni of San Carlos lost their heads with Independence? On the contrary, they approached the republican experiment realistically; and if they made mistakes, which they certainly did, we should not forget that this is in the nature of experimentation.

---

10. John Tate Lanning, *The Eighteenth-Century Enlightenment in the University of San Carlos de Guatemala* (Ithaca, 1956).

Perhaps the stereotype of the "starry-eyed" liberal has resulted from the confusion of theory with practice. The theory — the premises underlying the constitution and the laws — might easily be classified as unrealistic in view of existing conditions; but — and this is a crucial point — contemporaries regarded the theory as a set of goals, principles, and ideals toward which they should strive, not as a practical program which was to be implemented overnight. In short, as we shall see in the study of the 1838–1839 crisis, responsible liberals were willing to compromise; they faced up to their mistakes and adopted other solutions; they realized that the reform process had to be gradual if it were to be effective; and they earnestly strove to change conditions as well as to raise and educate the masses of the people so that eventually their nation might achieve the theoretical goals expressed so beautifully in their constitutions and laws. But when vested interests resisted even these modest advances, showing no willingness to compromise at all, the liberals then became uncompromising in return. At this point they were doctrinaire; but it is patently unjust, as well as erroneous, to assume that this had been their nature from the beginning. Such an assumption, moreover, leads to serious pitfalls: it obscures the intense ideological ferment and cleavage during the years of experiment and it overlooks the role which defenders of the *"Ancien Regime"* played in the breakdown of order in Central America, as well as their contribution to the failure of republicanism. In short, it is a question of adopting a wider and more reasonable perspective, one which will provide us with new insights into the political developments of the early national period.

The interpretation suggested here is not intended to absolve the liberals from all responsibility for the anarchic conditions which accompanied their governmental experiments. On the contrary, opportunism and partisanship among so-called liberal groups added to the difficulties of establishing stable governments in the various states of the Republic. And their disunity frequently strengthened the hands of the conservatives, allowing them to pursue divide-and-conquer tactics which eventually undermined the entire liberal program. A case in point was the Barrundia-Gálvez dispute of 1837–1838, which bred the future caudillo of Guatemala and thus hastened the final collapse of the Republic.

An important weakness of the 1824 Constitution, though an understandable one, was the assumption that *nacionalidad,* or national consciousness, was, or should be, full grown in Central America. At least this was a commendable ideal which had to be nurtured. Institutions based upon this premise, however, would inevitably tax the incipient nationalism of the average Central American, especially in times of duress. The constitution makers believed fervently in a government of the people, for the people, and by the people. As a result, the document which they drew up was far more nationalistic than the Constitution of the United States, its model. For example, Central Americans did not sidestep the constitutional issue which later contributed to civil war in the United States. According to their charter, the Republic could act directly upon the individual citizen on matters over which it had jurisdiction, rather than deal indirectly through the state governments. The general government, moreover, was solely responsible for substantive law; that is to say, it had the authority to draw up a uniform system of internal organization for all the states in the spheres of criminal, commercial, and civil law. These provisions, as well as others which enhanced the authority of the central government, made the Republic of Central America, at least in theory, less federalistic and more nationalistic than her North American counterpart. Much of the difference stems from the fact that in Central America the states were created *after,* and by provision in, the Constitution of 1824.

Since "the people" were sovereign, it followed that the legislative branch of the government should be the principal source of power in the new nation, while the executive and judiciary branches had limited jurisdiction and were subject to the control of the legislature. Judges, for example, did not have life tenure; the president's use of governmental revenues was strictly controlled, etc. In view of the colonial experience of strong executives who in turn controlled the judiciary, it is not surprising that Central Americans envisioned a new order in which congress, representing the people, should be the main source of power in order to prevent "tyranny." Unfortunately, the emphasis upon congressional rule led to such disastrous consequences as the Civil War of 1826–1829.[11]

By the same token, the spirit of *nacionalidad* meant the acceptance of the principle of proportional representation based upon universal suffrage. Although an enlightened principle, it opened up Pandora's box and encouraged demogoguery, partisan politics, and a vicious power struggle among the states with the smaller ones determined to prevent the control of Guatemala. Perhaps the problem would not have been so serious if the states had been more closely balanced. What is frequently overlooked, however, is that the founding fathers had anticipated this

11. For an excellent discussion of the 1824 Constitution, see the unpublished doctoral dissertation of Harold B. Fields, "The Central American Federation, 1826–1839: A Political Study" (Ph.D. University of Chicago, 1942), pp. 19-47. Also see the recent works by Thomas L. Karnes, *The Failure of Union: Central America, 1824–1960* (Chapel Hill, 1961) and Louis E. Bumgartner, *José del Valle of Central America* (Durham, 1963).

dangerous issue. In 1824, it was generally believed that two states would emerge from the area which later became Guatemala. The highlands, including the districts of Quezaltenango, Totonicapam, and Sololá, would form the State of Los Altos; and Guatemala proper would consist of the districts of Guatemala City, Vera Paz, Chiquimula, and Sacatepéquez. If these plans had not miscarried, the Republic of Central America might have consisted of six states, fairly evenly balanced with regard to population.

But both liberal and conservative interests in Guatemala City, who for centuries had dominated politics and trade alike in Central America, were against such a division of Guatemala. The *serviles*, who cooperated with President Manuel J. Arce in the civil war of the late twenties, left no doubt about their hostility to home rule in Los Altos. When the liberals regained power in 1829, Governor Mariano Gálvez likewise frustrated the highlands' dream of statehood. Then, in 1836, when the same Gálvez defeated a new law by which Los Altos could petition the federal government for admission to statehood, the highlanders seriously considered rebellion.[12] Understandably, they joined with José Francisco Barrundia in the Livingston dispute, not so much because they believed in judicial reforms but rather because the codes weakened Gálvez and would decentralize power in Guatemala.[13] When Gálvez fell in February, 1838, Los Altos seceded from Guatemala and immediately requested admission as the sixth state of Central America. The request was granted several months later. In view of this development, it would seem that there was now less reason for the other states to secede: one of their key reforms had been realized.

Implicit in the foregoing analysis was the growing power of the state governments, the theory of the constitution notwithstanding. A basic explanation for this was the anarchy of the 1820's and the aftermath of civil war. Given these conditions, the leaders of the Republic had to pursue a policy of expediency since they were in desperate need of help. Constitutional theory, therefore, went out the window; and the states organized themselves along historical lines with strong executives who controlled their respective legislatures. This anomaly in government complicated politics in Central America and further weakened the Republic's authority.[14] In the states, moreover, fierce partisan struggles occurred

---

12. Marcelo Molina, José M. Gálvez, J. Antonio Aguilar to Secretario . . . del Estado, Quezaltenango, February 7, 1838; "Acta de Segregación," February 2, 1838, Quezaltenango, B.N.G./HS, 1838.
13. Mario Rodríguez, *The Livingston Codes in the Guatemalan Crisis of 1837–1838* (New Orleans, 1955), pp. 24-25, 29.
14. *Paz I Orden* (San Salvador), No. 1, November 18, 1835, B.N.G./V, leg. 836.

among the politicians of the leading municipalities, each group desiring to capture control of the strong state machine for the benefit of their city. And regardless of the victor in these intra-state feuds, the state governments defied and usurped the prerogatives of the federal government. Thus was born the "states' rights" issue in Central America, one that had only been latent in 1824. The theory of the constitution had little, if anything, to do with this development. Circumstances of the times and the selfishness of state leaders, who lacked a national consciousness, were the real culprits in the story.

If we keep these various trends in mind, the secession crisis of 1838–1839 becomes meaningful. At the eleventh federal congress, which held sessions from April 5 to July 20, there were three basic questions underlying the clamor for reforms. First, should the reforms be total or partial? Secondly, should the states enact these reforms at a special convention, or should the reforms follow the procedure of amendments to the constitution? And thirdly, should the power of the union be extended or curtailed?[15]

The unionist position was ably presented in the *Noticioso Guatemalteco,* a newspaper in Guatemala City. The editorialist, using the initials F.M., acknowledged the mistakes made in 1824 and agreed that reforms were necessary to bring about "a more perfect union" in the North American sense. With perception F.M. discussed at great length the example of the United States and correctly diagnosed the compromise, or blending of principles, in the Constitution of 1787, making it partly nationalistic and partly federalistic. The merit and wisdom of the North American solution, the writer insisted, was borne out in Central America's experience.[16] Significantly, the *Noticioso Guatemalteco* announced that in future issues the *Federalist Papers* would appear in translation for the enlightenment of the readers and with the hope that they would help guide the reform movement in Central America.[17]

Unionists generally favored "partial reforms" by constitutional amendment as provided for by the 1824 document. In contrast to their earlier faith in the hegemony of the legislature, they now advocated reforms which would bring the executive and judiciary into balance with it. In short, they realized that their nationalistic assumptions of 1824 had been too advanced for the times and conditions in Central America; they were, therefore, returning to the practical solution embodied in the

---

15. *Noticioso Guatemalteco* (Guatemala), No. 5, March 2, 1838, B.N.G./V, leg. 836.
16. *Ibid.,* July 8, 1838.
17. *Ibid.,* July 26, 1838.

Constitution of the United States. Eventually, unionists also accepted the convention technique for the adoption of reforms — a point which must be stressed since states' righters tried to give the impression that the supporters of the federal government were against the calling of a convention. Quite the contrary, the real issue was who could control the convention in question and thus what type of government would replace the old republic.

Not without some irony, the example of the United States helped the opposition cause as well, thanks in large part to the efforts of a Guatemalan priest and conservative, Juan José Aycinena. Forced into exile in 1829, this recognized leader of the *serviles* returned to Guatemala during the Barrundia-Gálvez dispute and cleverly rebuilt his political fortunes. His success was phenomenal, as he capitalized upon the division in the liberal ranks. Adequate proof of this was his presence in San Salvador, representing his state in the federal congress. Without exaggeration, Father Aycinena was one of the most formidable opponents of liberalism in Central America; and there is no better example of his political acumen than the manner in which he undermined the Livingston Codes in Guatemala, while at the same time feeding the clamor for political amnesty in both liberal camps.[18]

Aycinena had spent much of his exile in the southern part of the United States, where he carefully observed political developments. The nullification crisis in South Carolina apparently made a deep impression upon him, for he mastered the arguments and assumptions of the states' rights doctrine. Shrewdly he introduced the states' rights position into the debates over reforms at the federal capital with enough conviction and subtlety to persuade even some unionists.[19] In the discussions, Father Aycinena argued that the United States of America was a "confederation" in which the states were sovereign and in which the general government could only act directly upon states as political units and indirectly upon the citizens of a state for specific purposes set forth in the federal pact. He proved his point by citing selections from various state constitutions. Then, in a clever discourse on semantics, he left his audience with the impression that the terms "confederation," "federation," and "league of states" were synonomous — all of them stood for a government of sovereign states associated, or joined together, for specific objectives.

The exposition built up to its logical conclusion. The Constitution

18. Rodríguez, *Codes,* pp. 21-22.
19. "Centro-Americanos," J. Basilio Porras, San Salvador, July 11, 1838, F.O. 254/2.

of 1824 had set up a unitary republic in Central America when it permitted the general government to act directly upon the individual and to limit the internal organization of the member states. Central Americans did not want that type of government; they wanted a "confederation," the astute cleric concluded. Reforms therefore should be "total," and the states should send delegations to a special convention which would draw up a pact establishing a true "Confederation of Central America."[20] The arguments were convincing, especially for those who had already decided upon the breakup of the Republic.

Nicaragua's provisional separation from the union on April 30, 1838, conditioned the discussion of reforms at San Salvador. Hopeful that she would reconsider her action, Congress voted a decree-amendment on May 30 which contained this significant clause: "The states are free to constitute themselves as they deem convenient, providing they maintain the republican, popular, and representative form [of government] and the division of powers."[21] To bring Nicaragua back into the union, in other words, the federal congress was willing to weaken the principle of substantive law.

But the May 30 decree fell short of achieving its objective; on the contrary, Nicaraguans and states' righters in general interpreted the measure as recognition of their absolute sovereignty and independence.[22] In passing the bill, unionists had intended no such thing. Instead they hoped — and Chatfield shared this feeling — that the decree in question would arrest secession in Central America, not promote it.[23] To discourage the opposite construction, Congress passed a new bill on June 9 which explained the intent of the May 30 decree: it was merely a move to free the states from all obstacles in bettering their internal organization, without relinquishing the "attributes which indisputably belong to the federal powers." According to the explanatory decree, states could not raise a military force, nor were they authorized to impose duties upon interstate or foreign trade without congressional approval.[24] Though this was a significant clarification of the May decree, Nicaragua persisted in her independent course. She was not willing to give up control of federal customhouses nor return federal monies, most of which had already been squandered by her politicos.

Disappointed with the June 9 decree since it represented a definite

20. "A los Estados," San Salvador, July 11, 1838, B.N.G./HS, 1838.
21. Decree, May 30, 1838, F.O. 254/1; also in B.N.G./HS, 1838.
22. From Baily, June 30, 1838, F.O. 252/6.
23. To Palmerston, No. 34, June 5, 1838, F.O. 15/20.
24. Decree, June 9, 1838, F.O. 254/1; also in B.N.G./HS, 1838.

victory for the unionists, Father Aycinena and his supporters intensified their efforts to reverse the decision in the next few weeks. By June 29, 1838, they were well on the road to success; on that date sixteen members of the special committee on reforms signed the majority report, drawn up by Aycinena. It contained three articles, presented by the committee as suggested amendments to the Constitution. Article one revealed the states' rights objective: "The federated states of Central America are and by right should be sovereign, free, and independent political bodies." Articles two and three paved the way for the establishment of a loose league of independent states.[25]

Fortunately, the minority report, signed by only three committeemen, reached the floor of congress at the same time. In no uncertain terms, the unionist minority scored the political revolution implicit in the three articles of the majority report. Sobered by the remarks of the minority group, Congress voted to extend its sessions to July 20 so as to have adequate time to consider the proposed amendments to the constitution, which needed a two-thirds vote to pass. This delay worked in favor of the unionists for it gave them time to explain to their fellow congressmen the serious consequences which would result from the passage of the three articles. In the meantime, unionists appealed to the federal authorities to bring General Morazán back from Guatemala, hoping that his presence, and any threats he might make about resigning the presidency, would help defeat Aycinena's project. By July 7, unionists felt that they were strong enough to permit a vote on the decree-amendments. And they were. The vote on article one ended in a tie; thus the core of the bill was defeated.[26]

Unquestionably the news that Morazán was on his way back to San Salvador saved the day for the unionists.[27] As we shall see, it is conceivable that Frederick Chatfield may have also influenced the vote on the 7th. Be that as it may, Congress wound up its sessions on July 20 after compiling an outstanding record of "partial" reforms — limited suffrage, tenure of office for the judiciary, a strengthened executive, etc.[28]

Unionists leaders understood the exact nature of their victory, hardly one to gloat over in view of the formidable states' rights challenge. Nicaragua was still out of the union; Aycinena had gotten sixteen

25. "A los Estados," *loc. cit.*
26. *Ibid.*
27. To Palmerston, No. 43, July 13, 1838, F.O. 15/20, in which Chatfield described a revolutionary plot that never materialized.
28. "Discurso . . . José Basilio Porras," July 20, 1838, in pamphlet dated July 25, 1838, San Salvador, F.O. 254/2. It contains an excellent review of the legislation passed by the eleventh congress.

signatures on his bill; and chances were that the reform amendments of 1838 would meet the same fate as those of 1835 — the states would refuse to ratify them. To prevent this outcome, and in recognition of the opposition's strength, unionists again resorted to compromise. In a decree of July 20, the federal government called for elections in November; and in another decree of the 18th, the government set down a new procedure for the ratification of reforms by the states in the event they refused to ratify the "partial" reforms passed by congress.

According to the decree of the 18th, all six states of the union, including the infant state of Los Altos, were asked to send delegations of five commissioners to the federal capital. After the initial meeting, the thirty delegates could move elsewhere to conduct their business if they desired. The commissioners were empowered to discuss reforms; if they felt it necessary, they could even draw up a new federal pact. Unionists, in other words, were disposed to accept the convention technique but not without some reservations. To prevent a political coup on the part of state delegations, they attached the following strings. If the state governments accepted the new pact framed by the commissioners, it would then be presented to the next federal congress, scheduled to meet on February 15, 1839. Since the fall elections would represent a recent mandate from the people, unionists believed that the federal congress should also vote on the pact. If it passed, the troublesome question about reforms would come to an end. If, on the other hand, the vote were negative, congress would then issue a call for a National Constituent Assembly to consider a new governmental system. The Senate sanctioned this decree on August 23. President Morazán signed it on August 25 and sent it forward to the states for their ratification.[29]

The July 18 decree was another illustration of the unionists' desire to compromise. That it outlined a circuitous procedure should not detract from the merits of the proposal; the safeguards were necessary in order to prevent a political revolution by the states' righters. But whereas unionists at least were willing to make concessions, the same was not true for the opposition who rejected the decree outright, thus raising doubts as to their sincerity and love for Central America. Since they adamantly refused to yield on this matter, they must be held accountable for the chaos that ensued. Moreover, as we shall see, this was not the last compromise offer which they turned down.

The troubled situation in the large state of Guatemala influenced the disobedience of state governments toward the federal authority.

---

29. Decrees, July 18, 20, 1838, and federal circular (Miguel Alvarez) to the States of Central America, August 25, 1838, F.O. 254/1.

Carrera and his followers had retreated into the mountains where stand-ard military tactics were ineffectual against his guerrilla methods.[30] The financial drain, moreover, was debilitating; and the federal government had used the tobacco revenues of El Salvador without any conclusive results. In July, 1838, General Morazán returned to San Salvador; no sooner had he left Guatemala, a revolution took place in which the *serviles* increased their power, along with clergymen who were secretly manipulating the "Barbarian."[31] On September 11, General Carlos Sala-zar in a daring pre-dawn attack surprised the Indian leader at Villanueva, only a few leagues from Guatemala City. He routed Carrera's forces, and wounded the caudillo. This might have been the end of Carrera, if Sala-zar had followed through with his victory. Unfortunately, he did not; and thus the wily chieftain escaped, healed his wounds, regrouped his forces, and soon went on the offensive once more.[32] It had to be done all over again. On October 10, 1838, General Morazán left the federal capi-tal at the head of a sizable expeditionary force. A great deal was at stake; this time he had to defeat Carrera once and for all. Otherwise, the Republic would disintegrate, for the wayward states would continue their defiance and eventually join with Carrera.[33]

Nicaragua categorically refused to accept the compromise decree of July 18.[34] In October and November, a war of broadsides raged between unionists and states' righters, each accusing the other of bad faith on the question of reforms. The broadsides merely underscored what everybody knew and could sense — the Republic was breaking up and civil war was on the horizon.[35] On November 5 and 15, Honduras and Costa Rica respectively announced their secession from the union. By the end of the year, it was a well-known secret that a combined force from Nicaragua and Honduras was preparing an invasion of El Salvador and an attack upon the federal capital. The "Allied States" of Nicaragua and Honduras signed a formal treaty on January 18, 1839, pledging themselves to offensive and defensive action against Morazán's tyranny. Once victory had been won, the allies would join together at a "con-vention" to form a true "Confederation of Central America." Costa Rica joined the two allies insofar as defensive action was concerned, but she

---

30. Charles G. DeWitt to John Forsyth, June 30, 1838, MDCIA, III, 150-151.
31. To Palmerston, Nos. 49-50, August 16, 1838, F.O. 15/20.
32. No. 57 (October 4).
33. *Ibid.;* and No. 59 (October 29).
34. "Al público," Miguel Alvarez, October 12, 1838, F.O. 254/2.
35. See the exchange between José Antonio Jiménez and José Antonio Alvarado, F.O. 254/2. One document bears the title "Al indecente, soez y sucio loco José Antonio Alvarado," November 10, 1838.

refused to participate in any aggressive move.[36] Retaliating weakly, the federal government issued a series of decrees, beginning on December 11, 1838, which placed an embargo upon the major ports of the three rebel states. Presumably this paper boycott would also avoid claims that might arise from the double payment of duties.[37]

Without any doubt, the Republic was nearing its end in late 1838. Three states had seceded, and the danger of defection was strong in Guatemala and even in El Salvador. Only Los Altos could be counted upon to remain loyal, for its very existence depended upon the Republic's survival. Moreover, already in evidence were the disastrous trends of future Central American history as unscrupulous caudillos swaggered to the fore in the rebellious states: Braulio Carrillo in Costa Rica, José Núñez in Nicaragua (although he soon fell), Francisco Ferrera in Honduras, and Rafael Carrera — the master of them all — in Guatemala.[38] Later in this chapter, we shall return to the tragic events of early 1839, the final gasp of the Republic leaving but a sentiment which has perdured to the present day.

—•••—

As order broke down, Frederick Chatfield feared for the lives and property of the thirty to forty English families who lived in the various states of Central America.[39] The anti-British slogans mouthed by the *Carreristas* did not relieve his anxiety; and perhaps because of what Carrera meant for the future of the area, the consul did not protest against the use of El Salvador's tobacco revenue, half of which was pledged to English creditors.[40] Carrera and his followers had to be stopped at all costs, and General Morazán appeared to be the only hope for victory over barbarism in Central America.

Although the British consul thought highly of Morazán, he had little use for the federal authorities who governed in his absence, unable to forgive them for the affront he suffered in the "Dearing Affair." Moreover, the federal government was aggravating the territorial questions with Great Britain by encouraging land-grant petitions in the disputed areas, as for example Don Juan Galindo's concession in Mosquitia.[41]

---

36. "Tratado . . . Honduras y Nicaragua," Comayagua, January 18, 1839, A.G.N.G./LV; Auguste Mahelin to Minister of Foreign Affairs, February 3, 1839, A.A.E.P./CPAC, vol. 3.
37. Decrees of December 11, 27, 1838, and March 27, 1839, F.O. 252/5.
38. "Revista compendiada . . . ," San Salvador, May 8, 1839, F.O. 254/2.
39. To Palmerston, No. 40, p. encl., June 23, 1838, F.O. 15/20, which lists 34 British subjects residing in Central America proper.
40. To Palmerston, No. 52, September 4, 1838, F.O. 15/20.
41. Nos. 17 (February 26) and 25 (March 14).

Those federal authorities also entertained the proposals of two gentlemen who had arrived from New Orleans earlier in the year. One of them, George G. Holdship, who represented the House of Soulette and Mural of New Orleans, hoped to capitalize upon the perennial Central American dream of an interoceanic canal through Nicaragua and offered the Republic a sizable loan in return for land grants and the control of certain revenues. Fearful that American interests would thus align themselves against the King of the Mosquitos, the British consul discouraged the canal negotiations with Holdship; and the latter therefore had to move to Nicaragua where he made similar overtures to the state government. He visibly annoyed Chatfield by insisting upon secrecy, so as to keep the negotiations from English ears.[42]

The second gentleman from New Orleans, José Antonio Mejía, was a Mexican general who had fought on the side of Texas and had been sent to Central America by the Texan government on a special mission which had ominous implications for Belize and the Bay Islands. In early May, 1838, Mejía petitioned the federal congress for a colonizing grant on the islands of Ruatán and Utilla. At about the same time, the resourceful Chatfield managed to see Mejía's special instructions, dated November 1, 1837, which outlined a fantastic alliance between Texas and the Central American Republic. The two states were to sign an offensive treaty which envisioned a scheme to revolutionize "the Mexican provinces of Chiapas and Yucatán." Not wanting to place "undue importance" upon Mejía's mission. Chatfield nevertheless alerted Colonel Macdonald at Belize since the project might affect "our possessions in Honduras."[43]

There were other indications that the Belize question might be revived, thanks to the entrepreneurial instincts of Chatfield's countrymen. The ubiquitous Galindo wanted a reconfirmation of his Petén grant, separating it from the concession made to the Eastern Company.[44] The "old rascal" Marshall Bennett was suspiciously interested in the renewal of the company's grant, perhaps only to enhance the value of his property at San Jerónimo.[45] The real serious development, however, was the appearance of Young Anderson, an agent for the Eastern Company, who

42. From John Baily, June 30, 1838, and from J. Moore, July 3, 1838, F.O. 252/6; to Palmerston, No. 45, p. encl.s, July 25, 1838, F.O. 15/20; to John Crawford, July 25, 1838, F.O. 252/10.
43. To Palmerston, No. 20, March 1, 1838, F.O. 15/20.
44. Brief Statement ... Eastern Coast of Central America Commercial and Agricultural Company (2d. ed., London, 1840), pp. 32-36; from Young Anderson, October 28, 1838, F.O. 252/6.
45. To Alexander Macdonald, No. 3, May 2, 1838, F.O. 252/15.

successfully obtained an extension of the original charter on October 15, 1838. By the terms of the new document, the company agreed to occupy the port of Santo Tomás with at least one hundred families.[46] With Santo Tomás in the hands of rival English interests, Belize appeared to be in trouble; and it should be noted that the federal congress of 1838 passed a two percent rebate on imports coming through Santo Tomás.[47] Chatfield had just cause for concern.

Since the Foreign Office refused to take an unequivocal stand on the territorial issues, or to support his various doctrines, Frederick Chatfield again had to meet the new challenges all by himself. When Los Altos seceded from Guatemala and it appeared that further disintegration of the state might occur, the consul urged Colonel Macdonald to encourage the secession of the Petén and its annexation to Belize.[48] In May, when it seemed that Young Anderson might succeed in Guatemala City, he urgently recommended that Macdonald take accurate measurements of Lake Petén and Cahabón in the hopes of committing the British government to the stand which he had outlined in November, 1837. He also asked Macdonald to discourage all Englishmen from participating in the Eastern Company's plan to occupy Santo Tomás.[49] Later, in a spirited correspondence with Young Anderson, the English consul berated the location of Santo Tomás while his correspondent did likewise for what he called the pestilential port of Belize.[50]

To defeat the various projects of Galindo, Holdship, and Mejía, Chatfield wrote two strongly-worded notes to Minister Miguel Alvarez on May 12, 1838, emphasizing that Great Britain would not tolerate any concessions in Mosquitia or on the Bay Islands. Alvarez turned these notes over to a "secret committee" of the federal congress where, according to Chatfield, they caused a "good deal of angry feeling against me." But, the consul continued, "this should be ascribed to the unwillingness of the Government to meet the question of the Mosquito Coast, and our rights at Honduras, dispassionately and rationally."[51]

Hopeful of capitalizing upon the resentment against Chatfield in

46. *Brief Statement,* pp. 37-56, which includes the new charter of October 15, 1838.
47. "Discurso," José Basilio Porras, July 25, 1838, F.O. 254/2.
48. To Palmerston, No. 14, p. encl., February 23, 1838, F.O. 15/20; to Macdonald, No. 1, conf., February 28, 1838, F.O. 252/15.
49. To Macdonald, Nos. 3 (May 2) and 5 (May 23, 1838), F.O. 252/15.
50. To Palmerston, No. 13, p. encl.s, March 5, 1839, F.O. 15/22; the correspondence between Young Anderson and Chatfield, beginning on October 28, 1838, can also be found in F.O. 252/6.
51. To Palmerston, No. 31, p. encl.s, May 19, 1838, F.O. 15/20; to Miguel Alvarez, Nos. 17-18, May 12, 1838, F.O. 252/5.

the federal congress, the French consul published an anonymous article on June 4, 1838, entitled "Concerning the Treaty between the Republic and France."[52] If the French treaty were negotiated, the writer pointed out, Central America could then depend upon a powerful ally in Europe, one who would support her claims against the English at Belize, the Mexicans in Chiapas, and the New Granadians at Boca del Toro. As one might expect, Chatfield reacted angrily to Mahelin's piece. It was bad enough, he told Palmerston, that "the English name is brought forward in an obnoxious manner" by Carrera and his ilk; but to have a colleague in the diplomatic corps join the chorus, was too much.[53] Monsieur Mahelin had to be taught a lesson.

The states' rights movement was hardly a source of consolation to Chatfield on the territorial questions and the wave of anglophobia rampant in Central America. To protect British interests in the states, he publicized his forced-loan views in an article entitled "The Essence of all Sound Policy is Justice." "Viator," alias Frederick Chatfield, cleverly rejected the arguments of Latin American jurists condoning forced loans.[54] What is interesting is that by the time of publication — in early June, 1838 — Chatfield had already received Palmerston's legalistic explanation of forced loans in which the master of the Foreign Office rejected the naked principle in the consul's doctrine.[55] But Chatfield stubbornly refused to accept "Old Pam's" verdict as final and decided instead "to keep to myself the knowledge, that under any circumstances these assessments can be made to include British subjects."[56] He simply would not deprive himself of a powerful weapon to protect British interests. He knew of Holdship's dealings with the Nicaraguan government and he suspected that the politicos at León would give the American everything he wanted. Moreover, he had also received information that French agents in Nicaragua were trying to get similar concessions.[57] The situation was going from bad to worse, and the consul needed an ally as well as the means to protect his country's interests. Perhaps if General Morazán were to return to San Salvador, Chatfield might be able to conclude a *modus vivendi* with the federal government, advantageous to both parties.

In the month of June, 1838 — it will be recalled — beleaguered

52. "Sobre el Tratado entre la República y la Francia," San Salvador, June 4, 1838, in No. 36, to Palmerston, June 14, 1838, F.O. 15/20.
53. To Palmerston, No. 37, June 15, 1838, F.O. 15/20.
54. "The Essence of all Sound Policy is Justice," Viator, San Salvador, June, 1838, in No. 39, to Palmerston, June 19, 1838, F.O. 15/20.
55. From Palmerston, No. 1, January 12, 1838, F.O. 15/20.
56. To Palmerston, No. 39, June 19, 1838, F.O. 15/20.
57. From John Baily, June 15, 30, 1838, F.O. 252/6.

unionists were likewise in need of help. On the 26th, news reached the federal capital of a Costa Rican coup. Braulio Carrillo had taken over the government on May 27 and one of his first acts was to send a note to Nicaragua, congratulating her on her secession from the Republic. Costa Rica, therefore, appeared to be on the verge of seceding; and there were rumors of dissident groups in Honduras and in Guatemala who were similarly disposed.[58] On the 29th, moreover, Father Aycinena's majority report came before congress. Unionists desperately needed an ally.

The specific details of Chatfield's rapprochement with the federal government in early July will perhaps never be known, although the main lines and consequences of their cooperation are crystal clear. With chagrin, Auguste Mahelin observed that Minister Alvarez had lost interest in supporting the French treaty from July 3 to July 6. Instead of defending it on the latter date, when it came before congress, Alvarez left the federal capital for Guatemala, presumably to arrange for a loan to pay the military. A strategy of delay subsequently killed the French treaty.[59] And Mahelin angrily blamed Chatfield for the outcome, charging that the British consul with funds supplied to him by Macdonald and the merchants of Belize had bribed certain congressmen to defeat the treaty.[60] The charge was hardly plausible in the light of Chatfield's experience with the closefisted merchants of Belize.

If his major motive was the defeat of Mahelin's treaty, then Chatfield's success left nothing to be desired. But what did he have to offer the unionists in return? The answer is contained in a letter of July 4, 1838, to Minister Alvarez, a dispatch intended for the states of Costa Rica and Nicaragua.[61] Noting the recent coup of Braulio Carillo, Chatfield surmised that Costa Rica would soon imitate the Nicaraguan example and would therefore confiscate federal revenues which included about 1,200 bales of tobacco. He reminded Alvarez that by the federal decrees of April 11 and 27, 1837, Central America had pledged half of the tobacco revenue for the liquidation of the debt to British bondholders. He strongly suspected, moreover, that the British government "would hesistate to agree that an alteration in the federal system of the republic should be considered a valid excuse for the nonfulfillment of engagements which were constitutionally approved by the Congress, the Senate, and the Executive, at a time when all the states were duly and

---

58. To Palmerston, No. 41, June 27, 1838, F.O. 15/20.
59. Auguste Mahelin to Minister of Foreign Affairs (Comte Molé), No. 55, July 12, 1838, A.A.E.P./CPAC, vol. 2.
60. Mahelin to Molé, No. 3, August 1, 1838, A.A.E.P./CPAC, vol. 2.
61. To the Central American Government, July 4, 1838, F.O. 252/5.

legally represented in the Legislature." It behooved the federal government, therefore, to act with energy in preventing "a misapplication of the proceeds of the tobacco duties which may have been or which are to be collected in the state of Costa Rica." The real objective of Chatfield's letter came out in the following selection, written in the third person:

> and he offers for the convenience of the National Government that the amount of this duty, which he conceives will this year be about 50,000 dollars shall be conveyed from the ports of Costa Rica in Her Majesty's ships of war (whose arrival may daily be expected) which it is intended to keep permanently stationed upon the south coast of Central America for the better protection of British interests in this part of the Republic.[62]

On July 11, after Alvarez returned from Guatemala, copies of this letter were duly sent to the Costa Rican and Nicaraguan governments.

Conceivably the consul's letter of July 4 may have contributed to the defeat of the states' righters three days later, especially if unionists took the pains to publicize its contents. The knowledge that British ships would prevent the takeover of federal revenues and the possibility that these sums might be made available to General Morazán unquestionably must have had a deterrent effect upon the states' rights movement.[63] Be that as it may, Costa Rica and Nicaragua clearly understood the implications of that letter as rumors circulated that General Morazán, at Chatfield's instigation, would soon arrive aboard British warships to collect the tobacco revenue.[64]

Of course, Chatfield had no authorization to use English ships in this capacity; in fact, he had no assurance that Lord Palmerston would grant the request for naval support which he had made in April. The consul was bluffing; but it is significant that the bluff favored the unionists. Moreover, Chatfield remained a supporter of unionism for several months and especially while Morazán was in San Salvador. This is all the more remarkable considering certain developments which threatened a rupture on the territorial questions. In a statesmanlike manner, the British consul seems to have toned down those incidents deliberately. Undoubtedly this was due in large part to the realization that the primary question in the latter part of 1838 was the survival of the Republic.

---

62. The July 4 dispatch and the answers to it by the governments of Nicaragua and Costa Rica are also enclosed in No. 52, to Palmerston, September 4, 1838, F.O. 15/20; also see, from Alvarez, September 3, 1838, F.O. 252/5.
63. To Palmerston, No. 43, July 13, 1838, F.O. 15/20.
64. From Baily, July 30, 1838, F.O. 252/6.

Let us now consider the major reasons for his pro-union stand, as well as additional evidence which confirms it.

One of the introductory quotations provides an excellent insight into Frederick Chatfield's views concerning the enemies of the Republic — the "Barbarism" of Rafael Carrera as opposed to the "Civilisation" of Morazán's world and the rule of the "coloured classes" in contrast to that of "the European race." As a devout Protestant, he detested the "romish" clergy, especially since they manipulated Carrera and taught his followers anti-English slogans. Equally strong was his hostility toward the *serviles* of Guatemala City, the old "Spanish Party" with all their "Spanish prejudices." If that group returned to power in Guatemala, the consul feared that they would resort to discriminatory trade policies against foreigners and would resist English institutions at every turn.

The documentation of 1838 demonstrates that the British consul was ideologically closer to the liberals, though he was thoroughly disgusted with the means they had employed since 1837.[65] Perhaps the main explanation for Chatfield's support of the Republic was his confidence in General Morazán. He was deeply convinced that the latter was the only white leader who could restore order to Central America. Yet Morazán's second term was scheduled to end in June, 1839; and the Constitution prohibited his reelection. Implicit in the political analyses which he sent to Lord Palmerston was the hope that Morazán would establish a dictatorship in Central America, at least until order was restored. His unrestrained admiration for Andrés Santa Cruz, the strong leader of the Peru-Bolivia Confederation, supports this interpretation.[66]

Now, let us consider other examples of Chatfield's unionism. The alliance with the federal government was especially evident in the case of the French consul. On August 1, 1838, Mahelin wrote angrily that he would no longer be diplomatic in his relations with a government so firmly under English influence.[67] Shortly thereafter, he resurrected an old claim against the Republic, dating back to 1827, and padded it to a preposterous figure, no matter which standards are used to judge it. On October 2, he issued an ultimatum to the federal authorities: pay the claim or suffer the consequences. Deeply insulted by Mahelin's note, President Morazán refused to acknowledge it; and before his departure

65. See, for example, Nos. 49-50 (August 16), 51 (August 21), and 57 (October 4, 1838), to Palmerston, F.O. 15/20.

66. Chatfield's correspondence with the British chargé in Lima, Peru (Belforde Hinton Wilson), 1838, F.O. 252/10.

67. Mahelin to Molé, No. 3, August 1, 1838, A.A.E.P./CPAC, vol. 2.

from San Salvador, on October 10, he instructed Alvarez to get Chatfield's advice on the matter, an assignment which the English consul accepted. Far from an impartial judge, the English ally decided that the claim was unjust and that Mahelin had behaved abominably in delivering the insulting ultimatum.[68] He recommended therefore that the federal government write a letter to the Ministry of Foreign Affairs in Paris, requesting Mahelin's recall. Such a note was sent to the French government on November 1, 1838, drafted by none other than Frederick Chatfield, Her Britannic Majesty's consul in Central America.[69] One could hardly ask for any closer cooperation!

George Holdship's secret negotiations with Nicaragua, a source of annoyance to Chatfield, likewise provoked a new doctrine which could be interpreted as pro-union. On July 25, 1838, having learned the terms of Holdship's contract with Nicaragua, Chatfield outlined the following course of action against it:

> I shall not lose sight of this business because now that Nicaragua is acting independently of the federation, its government must be called upon to pay off its proportion of the debt due to the British Publick, or to give proper security for it, before it can be permitted to incur new foreign engagements.[70]

Since he knew that Nicaragua could not pay one-sixth of the federal obligation to British creditors, Chatfield, in effect, was restricting the sovereignty of the seceded state. At a later date, this doctrine was used in a different context, applicable to all states which left the union.

The attempt to float a Belizean loan to support the campaign against Carrera also had a pro-union flavor, though other motives were involved as well. Chatfield recommended this action to Colonel Macdonald on August 22.[71] As collateral for the loan, the federal government was willing to permit a customs receivorship: Belizeans, in other words, could collect the revenue at the customhouses in return for an immediate advance of money. By encouraging the loan, Chatfield was actually implementing his old "Doctrine of Mutuality;" and it should be noted that such a loan would have undermined the Santo Tomás project, an important objective in the consul's eyes. When the loan failed to materialize, mainly because Guatemalan merchants supplied the needed funds, the consul found it difficult to disguise his disappointment, annoyed at

---

68. To Palmerston, No. 60, p. encl.s, November 5, 1838, F.O. 15/20.
69. Miguel Alvarez to Minister of Foreign Affairs (Molé), November 1, 1838, A.A.E.P./CPAC, vol. 2.
70. To Palmerston, No. 45, July 25, 1838, F.O. 15/20.
71. No. 51 (August 22); to Macdonald, No. 6, August 22, 1838, F.O. 252/15.

the cooperation of the Skinner-Klee house in floating the Guatemalan loan.[72] By then, he had also received Palmerston's stinging reprimand on the peculiar Klee doctrine.

There may have been another explanation for Chatfield's support of the proposed Belize loan. Three days before making the recommendation, he received some disturbing news from Guatemala City.[73] The state legislature, in response to the federal call for elections, had issued a special decree on August 5, 1838. According to article 43 of that decree, Guatemala invited the residents on the islands of the Bay of Honduras and those living between the Hondo and Sibun rivers to send delegates to the impending constituent assembly. In other words, Guatemala was encouraging Belizeans to participate in her government — an official proclamation, so to speak, of her sovereignty to the disputed area. In no uncertain terms, Chatfield demanded an immediate retraction of the offending article, as well as an apology.[74] Yet he chose not to force the issue in late 1838, considering it of little moment.[75] He thought differently about it in the following year, as we shall see. It is conceivable that he encouraged the Belizean loan in order to undermine the Guatemalan action. At any rate, his unwillingness to push the matter at this time merely confirmed his working alliance with the federal government.

Carrera's activities in Guatemala constantly worried the British consul, since they kept the country distracted, made normal peacetime pursuits impossible, and encouraged the defiance of Nicaragua and the states' righters in general. On October 4, Chatfield wrote a strongly pro-Morazán letter to Lord Palmerston in which he foresaw the significance of the general's return to Guatemala:

> He plays a heavy stake, and unless he acts with talent and energy, and can reestablish peace and order in the state, his reputation is gone, and with it the only chance of preserving the small share of civilisation existent in the Republick. I confess that I am not sanguine in believing that he will erect a firm superstructure on the present ruins . . . and it may be considered, that every dollar which the government expends without contributing to the permanent establishment of Peace, is equivalent to the like sum bestowed towards the accomplishment of the aim of Carrera and his abettors, for as soon as the resources of the government are utterly exhausted, the Priests and the coloured classes may take their own way.[76]

---

72. To Palmerston, Nos. 55 (October 1) and 56 (October 2, 1838), F.O. 15/20; to Skinner and Klee, September 25, 1838, F.O. 252/9.
73. From Henry Savage, August 4, 1838, F.O. 252/6, which Chatfield received on August 19.
74. To Miguel Alvarez, August 27, 1838, F.O. 252/5.
75. To Palmerston, No. 62, p. encl.s, November 21, 1838, F.O. 15/20.
76. No. 57 (October 4).

This quotation shows that Chatfield's views had not changed much during the following months — hardly the attitudes of a man who allegedly favored and contributed to the breakup of the Republic.

Perhaps the best evidence of Chatfield's cooperation with the federal government was the manner in which he handled an explosive report from Belize which reached him on October 2, two days before writing the sympathetic dispatch about Morazán. For purposes of description, we shall refer to the episode in question as the "Trujillo-Ruatán" incident. These were the facts of the case. On August 31, the commandant of Trujillo, when informed of a cholera epidemic at Belize, issued an order to the residents of Ruatán, banning all intercourse with the British establishment during the emergency. At the same time, the commandant announced that the Central American colors would be hoisted at Port Royal on September 1. Never at a loss for bellicose expressions, Colonel Macdonald reacted in predictable fashion. He would meet this "unprincipled aggression" with "all the power which I possess for resisting the injuries and revenging the insults practised upon British subjects." On October 6, Chatfield lodged an official protest with the federal government without forwarding a copy of Macdonald's peremptory note.[77] In other words, he deliberately minimized the episode and admitted as much to Macdonald: "Although my note upon the subject was not so explicitly worded as yours of the 10th ultimo to the Commandant of Trujillo, still enough was said in it for him to comprehend that the right of domain to the island claimed by Central America, was far from being recognized by us."[78]

Irony would have it that while Chatfield was displaying the restraint and talent of a statesman, Lord Palmerston experienced a metamorphosis in his attitudes toward Central America. The doctrines of his consul, as well as the belligerency of Colonel Macdonald, were beginning to find a sounding board in London. With regard to the stalemated negotiations with Spain, which the Duke of Wellington had initiated at Chatfield's suggestion, Palmerston favored their abandonment. There was no point in discussing England's title to that area with anyone. "Honduras is ours by the best of all Titles, that of the Sword," he told Lord Glenelg of the Colonial Office on September 14, 1838.[79] Suspecting that Wellington and Peel would oppose the grant of colony status to Belize, Palmerston urged indirect action toward that goal. When he learned of the Guatemalan decree (August 5, 1838), Palmerston reacted strongly; such

---

77. No. 58, p. encl.s (October 8).
78. To Macdonald, No. 8, October 8, 1838, F.O. 252/15.
79. Palmerston to Glenelg, September 14, 1838, F.O. 15/21.

an act of hostility, he told Chatfield, "will justify Proceedings of any kind."[80] His reaction to the "Trujillo-Ruatán" incident was no less bellicose; the Central American Republic should be cautioned to desist "from any measure which may lead to a collision between Great Britain and Central America."[81] Moreover, "Old Pam" followed up this warning with a recommendation to the Admiralty which led to the English occupation of Ruatán in April, 1839. He was learning fast, and Chatfield's days of frustration on the territorial questions were numbered. But, in late 1838, the British consul had no way of knowing that the Foreign Office was ready to follow; he could only remember a series of distressing reprimands and refusals to accept his suggestions and doctrines.

———◆◆◆———

Chatfield's position shifted imperceptibly in late October, 1838, as it became evident to him that the secessionist crisis was reaching the point of no return. If indeed the Republic was on the brink of dissolution, it behooved him to prepare for that eventuality. Several factors contributed to the change of emphasis. First, on October 25, Carrera and his bands, having successfully gotten around the rear of Morazán's column, attacked and pillaged the Salvadorean town of Santa Ana; and it was feared that he would strike at the federal capital next. The people of San Salvador prepared feverishly to resist the attack which fortunately did not take place.[82] The significance of Carrera's maneuver is that it encouraged the secession movement in Costa Rica and Honduras, both of which seceded a few weeks later; it suggested, in other words, that perhaps the invincible Morazán might not be able to cope with his challenger. In that case, the Republic was lost.

Another factor which emboldened secessionists throughout Central America was the absence of British ships on the Central American coasts, exposing Frederick Chatfield's bluff in the July 4 letter. As everyone knew, the logical time for the appearance of the navy would have been in September and subsequent months while the Salvadorean indigo fairs were in progress. Significantly, Chatfield expressed disappointment at the lack of naval support in the waning days of October.[83]

Regardless of his own personal leanings, Frederick Chatfield could not ignore these developments if British interests were to remain safe.

---

80. From Palmerston, No. 3, March 23, 1838, F.O. 15/22.
81. From Palmerston, No. 2, January 24, 1839, F.O. 15/22.
82. Auguste Mahelin to Minister of Foreign Affairs, No. 8, November 1, 1838, A.A.E.P./CPAC, vol. 2; to B. Wilson, October 31, 1838, F.O. 252/10; to Palmerston, No. 59, October 29, 1838, F.O. 15/20.
83. To Admiral Ross, October 29, 1838, F.O. 252/8.

Therefore, he wrote to the seceded states on December 24 and 26 reminding them that they were each responsible for one-sixth of the federal debt to British bondholders. Later, he also made it clear to the states of Honduras, Nicaragua, and Costa Rica that he would not tolerate forced loans upon British subjects. He insisted, moreover, that his notes to the various governments were not to be construed as recognition of their sovereign status; all that concerned him was the protection of British life and property.[84] And at this time Chatfield meant what he said — there was no political implication in announcing these two doctrines to the seceded states.

As for the federal government, the British consul adopted a different approach but with the same objective in mind — the protection of British interests. By mid-November, 1838, he outlined a proposal to loan the Republic money which it sorely needed — a scheme which, incidentally, never came to the attention of the Foreign Office in London. But first a few words of background are in order.

In the previous March, and again in May, the Carrera brothers — Rafael and Laureano — had taken turns pillaging the prosperous San Jerónimo plantation of Marshall Bennett in Vera Paz, a property which formerly belonged to the Dominican Order. Though at first Chatfield hesitated to present these claims, undoubtedly because of Bennett and Meany's obstructionism in the past, the consul had a change of heart in late October.[85] He presented the claim with all the pertinent documents to Minister Alvarez on November 2.[86] Actual damages totaled 45,875 dollars, to which Chatfield added another 30,000 "to compensate for the delay of two years which it is calculated will occur before the estate is sufficiently recovered to resume its former activity and to be productive."[87] On November 13, in a letter to the "old rascal," Chatfield told him that if he ever hoped to collect on the claim of 75,875 dollars he would have to propose a "transaction" to the federal government. Here was the "deal" Chatfield had in mind:

> I would therefore suggest that you should give me a credit upon Mr. Charles Evans at Belize for 11,000 dollars, and authorize me to offer to advance 10,000 dollars in money to this Government on the condition that it will first deliver to me certificates for 85,000 dollars admissible as cash in the payment of duties at all custom houses of the Republick.

84. To Palmerston, No. 11, p. encl.s, February 13, 1839, F.O. 15/22.
85. To Carlos Meany, October 25, 1838, F.O. 252/6.
86. To Miguel Alvarez, November 2, 1838, F.O. 252/5.
87. To Marshall Bennett, pvt., November 13, 1838, F.O. 252/9.

The extra thousand dollars, he explained, would be used "for private distribution where it may seem useful." If Bennett disapproved, his chances of collecting the claim, once a change had occurred in the federal government, would be difficult at best.[88]

The consul further elaborated upon the loan proposal in a letter of the same date to Charles Evans in Belize.[89] In his opinion, the best time to offer the "bait of a present advance of money to the government" would be "when it has troops to maintain and not a hundred dollars in the Treasury." And for the scheme to work smoothly, Chatfield stressed, it was imperative that "I should have the money here because the power of telling the Government that they have only to send *across the street* for it will materially sharpen their inclination to listen to my proposals."[90] The utmost secrecy should be observed in this matter, Chatfield cautioned; not even Carlos Meany, Bennett's Spanish partner, should know of it at this time. Recognizing a good thing when he saw it, Mr. B. immediately replied in the affirmative; and Chatfield knew this, by December 20.[91]

What motivated the loan proposal and what did the consul hope to achieve with it? In the light of future events, several possibilities suggest themselves. First, let us exclude such motives as the protection of an Englishman's property and the desire to help the Republic. Chatfield dropped the claim too easily in the following year to justify the former; and, since he made the same offer to one of the states in 1839, we can rule out the latter. But there were other advantages that might result from the transaction: first and foremost, it could help to protect Belize from the competition of Santo Tomás. Bennett, who had earlier supported the renewal of the Eastern Company's grant, could now be counted upon, out of self interest, to support Chatfield's political design against the new port. It also should be noted that the consul wished to keep the project from Carlos Meany, a strong champion of the Eastern Company and the renewal of its contract on October 15, 1838. Certainly, the consul must have learned of Young Anderson's success by the time he outlined the loan proposal to Bennett. With 85,000 dollars in customs certificates, ranging from 100 to 500 dollars, Santo Tomás would have a difficult time getting started, to say the least. Underscoring the political motive was the fact that the certificates were valueless as cash, especially

---

88. *Ibid.*
89. To Charles Evans, November 13, 1838, F.O. 252/9.
90. My italics.
91. From Bennett, December 8, 1838, F.O. 252/6, received on December 20.

since customs revenues of the Republic had already been pledged two years in advance — and Chatfield knew this.[92]

Another political consideration of importance was the desire to commit General Morazán, and therefore his successors — either in the federal government or in the seceded states — to an obligation which would give the British consul a measure of control over them. This would be especially true if Chatfield could win the cooperation of the British navy. The loan transaction, therefore, revealed a slight shift in the consul's position, one that recognized the possibility of Morazán's defeat.

The change, however, was merely one of intent and did not involve any observable abandonment of the alliance with the federal government. In fact, the acceptance of the loan proposal by federal officials led Chatfield to adopt a strong pro-union course of action in early 1839. Certainly the Allied States had no reason to suspect that the consul favored them, as they grumbled at his insistence upon their proportional responsibility for the federal debt. The same was true for the soldiers of the invasionary force, poised near the Salvadorean border, who were irritated by the consul's reminders that they would be held responsible for any damages to Englishmen. A common rumor among them, in fact, was that General Morazán and company had sold out to England and Mr. Chatfield.[93]

As an ally of the British consul, Marshall Bennett also won protection for his share of the mining property of Guayavillas, near Tegucigalpa. In a blistering note of January 15, 1839, to the independent state of Honduras, Chatfield warned it would be held responsible for any abuses at Guayavillas. He would consider such action as "an insult to the dignity of Her Majesty the Queen of Great Britain and Ireland and an act of unprovoked hostility towards her said Majesty's Government in the person of one of Her Majesty's subjects for which full indemnification and reparation will be exacted."[94] To support his position, Chatfield again requested naval support from Admiral Ross of the Pacific Squadron on the 21st and justified this request in another letter of that date to Lord Palmerston.[95] It should be noted, moreover, that the brother of the Republic's vice president was Bennett's co-partner in the Guayavillas enterprise. And their Honduran challenger was Felipe Jáuregui, known to Chatfield as one of the prime movers in the secession of Hon-

92. To B. Wilson, December 20, 1838, F.O. 252/10.
93. From Richard MacNally, March 10, 1839, F.O. 252/6.
94. To Honduran Government, January 15, 1839, F.O. 252/14.
95. To Admiral Ross, January 21, 1839, F.O. 252/8; to Palmerston, No. 4, January 21, 1839, F.O. 15/22.

duras as well as a leading advocate of plans to invade the state of El Salvador.[96]

With the invasion of El Salvador a virtual certainty in early January, 1839, the opportune moment for the loan transaction was at hand. Someone — either Chatfield or Alvarez — crossed the street on the 5th of the month; the two men then discussed the San Jerónimo claim; Alvarez thought it should be scaled down; the consul had Bennett's authority to do this; and both agreed to write to General Morazán for his approval.[97] On the 17th, Morazán consented to the transaction.[98] Chatfield jubilantly announced the decision to Mr. Bennett: "This is a great step gained, and I shall immediately commence my conferences with the government for the arrangement of this business and I hope to hear from you and Mr. Evans that the necessary arrangements on your part are completed."[99] In short, the principals had agreed to proceed on the loan; all Chatfield needed now was the money "across the street."

Fighting for the survival of the Republic, her leaders could hardly refuse the British consul's offer. The Allied army was mobilizing near the Salvadorean border; rumors circulated that the states' righters and Carrera's agents were working closely together; and if the two bodies should ever unite in force, converging upon the federal capital, the Republic would fade into history. Yet heartening news reached San Salvador on December 30, 1838, producing salvoes of artillery and the joyous pealing of church bells. A week earlier, General Agustín Guzmán, commander of the federal forces in Los Altos, had agreed to a tentative truce with Rafael Carrera, in which the latter promised to turn over most of his arms (ca. one thousand). In late January, 1839, Morazán sanctioned the Carrera-Guzmán agreement. Shortly thereafter, Carrera turned over 320 muskets; and then, as part of the settlement, he was left in charge of the Mita district in Guatemala. For the time being, the treaty with Carrera nullified any potential alliance with the Allied States. That is why San Salvador celebrated wildly the news from Guatemala. But no one seriously thought that the man Carrera would keep his word for long. Certainly General Morazán had no illusions on this score.[100] He was merely buying time while he stopped the allied invasion of El Salvador.

---

96. To Marshall Bennett, January 20, 1839, F.O. 252/9.
97. From Alvarez, January 9, 1839, and to Morazán, pvt., January 9, 1839, F.O. 252/5; to Pedro N. Arriaga, May 24, 1839, F.O. 252/13.
98. From Morazán, pvt., January 17, 1839, F.O. 252/5.
99. To Bennett, January 23, 1839, F.O. 252/9.
100. Auguste Mahelin to Minister of Foreign Affairs, No. 10, December 31, 1838, A.A.E.P./CPAC, vol. 2; *idem* to *idem*, No. 11, February 3, 1839, A.A.E.P./CPAC, vol. 3; to Palmerston, No. 10, February 6, 1839, F.O. 15/22.

Even before receiving word of Chatfield's proposal, the lack of financial resources disposed Morazán to accept the Carrera-Guzmán truce.[101] The consul's offer, therefore, fitted perfectly into his plans and provided Morazán with the funds to carry out his strategy against the Allied States. By February 4, the general returned to the federal capital fully intending to proceed "to San Miguel, a town 40 leagues to the eastward of San Salvador, situated on the frontiers of Honduras and Nicaragua, to arrest by force the hostile movements in those states, and to check the disposition of Salvador to join them."[102]

At the last moment, however, the Morazán government decided upon one last attempt at compromise before resorting to civil war. Realizing his unpopularity and to counter the outcry that he wanted to perpetuate himself in power, Morazán formally resigned from the presidency of the Republic, even though constitutionally he had some three months to serve. On February 9, Vice President Vigil, pleading poor health, urged the states to organize a provisional government that would replace him as executive and serve until a convention were held to discuss reforms and to elect regular officials. In an accompanying document, dated the 11th, Minister Alvarez reviewed the federal government's efforts in behalf of reform and now requested the states to show their good faith by accepting the vice-president's peaceful offer. He warned, however, that they should not interpret the decree of the 9th as a sign of weakness; if they chose to reject the offer, insisting upon civil war, the federal authorities would meet force with force. Special envoys carried these documents to the governments of the Allied States.[103]

Opinions varied on the reasons for the compromise efforts of the federal government. Liberals like Pedro Molina of Guatemala hailed them as another indication of Morazán's patriotism, hoping to spare his country civil war.[104] Chatfield also attributed honorable motives to the move; and on February 15, apparently assuming that the states could not refuse such a peaceful offer, he wrote to Mr. Bennett that the loan would no longer be necessary.[105] Interestingly, in explaining Morazán's resignation and the subsequent compromise, Chatfield used the expression "on a review however of his resources."[106] In other words, Mora-

---

101. Broadside, Francisco Morazán, Guatemala City, January 12, 1839, F.O. 254/2.
102. To Palmerston, No. 12, February 15, 1839, F.O. 15/22.
103. See enclosures in No. 12; also in F.O. 254/2 and in No. 12, Mahelin to Molé, March 1, 1839, A.A.E.P./CPAC, vol. 3.
104. "Alocución dirigida al patriotismo," Pedro Molina, Guatemala City, March 1, 1839, F.O. 254/2.
105. To Bennett, February 15, 1839, F.O. 252/9.
106. To Palmerston, No. 12, February 15, 1839, F.O. 15/22.

zán could not proceed to San Miguel because he lacked the necessary financial support; and to be sure, Chatfield did not yet have in his possession the ten thousand dollars to loan the federal government. The Allied States, on the other hand, interpreted, or chose to interpret, Morazán's move as part of a conspiracy to disarm them. The true reason for rejecting the federal compromise, however, was their conviction that it indicated weakness on the part of the Morazán government; and they were determined to bring about the violent end of Francisco Morazán and his darling Republic.

The Allied reply to compromise was the invasion of El Salvador in the final days of February, 1839. On the 27th, news reached the federal capital that the invaders were in San Miguel.[107] Given the sudden turn of events, the loan proposal received new life. Chatfield urged Bennett to forward the money in all haste: "because if I am not to treat upon the basis of mutual accommodation, which can only be done by your sending the sum of money required, I must announce this alteration to the government to avoid compromising myself to do that which I afterwards find myself unequal to perform."[108] It is clear that the consul wanted to provide Morazán with the funds to stop the invasion of El Salvador. In the same dispatch, however, he wrote as follows: "The changes now occurring on the Government instead of delaying the settlement of this affair will perhaps accelerate it, for the want of money is so pressing that the newcomers will probably be glad to obtain funds at any price."[109]

This remark is conclusive proof that Chatfield had forwarded the loan proposal strictly for political reasons, as well as for the protection of his countrymen's interests. Though originally he intended the loan for the federal government, now he seemed disposed to offer it to the rebel forces when and if they successfully captured the federal capital.

With invasion a fact, General Morazán, as commander of the federal forces, mobilized and deployed his units swiftly to meet the enemy, an effort which required energy, patriotism, and money. Since Chatfield did not have the cash "across the street," the federal authorities called for a forced loan on March 4 and 5 and proceeded to make use of the tobacco revenues in the Salvadorean customhouses.[110] With these funds, as well as Morazán's superiority as a military strategist, the federal army routed the invaders in April, 1839. The Republic, it would seem, had been saved; but trouble did not stay away for long. The *serviles* of Guate-

---

107. Mahelin's No. 12 (see fn. 103)
108. To Bennett, February 28, 1839, F.O. 252/9.
109. *Ibid.*
110. To Palmerston, No. 14, March 6, 1839, F.O. 15/22; to Alvarez, March 22, and April 4, 1839, F.O. 252/5.

mala City gained the ear of Rafael Carrera and urged him to break his pact with General Morazán. On April 13, the chieftain again invaded Guatemala City; and Guatemala joined the ranks of the seceded states. The states' rights cause had thus won a new lease on life. But that is a story for the next chapter.

Chatfield's long alliance with the *Morazanistas* ended irrevocably on March 4, 1839, when the forced loan was levied in San Salvador. The break resulted from the consul's frustration and inability to supply the federal government with the money it needed to halt the invasion of the Allied States. He insisted angrily that no Englishman should contribute to the forced loan in question, a demand which the federal government respected and which thus further infuriated him. His frustration finally reached the point where he was prepared to insist that the federal government had no right whatsoever to levy forced loans, even upon its own citizens. But knowing that Palmerston would never support such a stand, he decided to apply his doctrine to all foreigners, not just Englishmen. In defense of the Spaniard Cosme Idígoras, Chatfield made the following threat on March 15 in a letter to Minister Alvarez: "should Mr. Idígoras be again molested in his peaceful commercial pursuits," the British consulate would "take such measures as will bring an early conviction to the mind of the Central American Government that the rights of foreigners in the country whether under the British or Spanish flag cannot be invaded with impunity."[111] To support his threat, Chatfield dispatched a hurried note to Colonel Macdonald in which he asked the superintendent to put on "a demonstration of force in our favour."[112]

———◆———

A new Frederick Chatfield was on the horizon, one reminiscent of the unknown consul at Warsaw who singlehandedly tried to bring down the Russian Bear. Five years of nurturing conscientiously an alliance with the *Morazanistas* had come to naught; and the Foreign Office had continually rebuffed him and had refused to accept the prolific series of doctrines and techniques by which he planned to advance British territorial designs and interests throughout Central America. All was not in vain, however; Lord Palmerston was now in a more receptive mood; and the experience and training had been invaluable. But in March, 1839, the future looked far from promising to the British consul.

---

111. To Alvarez, March 15, 1839, F.O. 252/5.
112. To Macdonald, No. 1, March 16, 1839, F.O. 252/15.

CHAPTER SEVEN

This Miserable Island

If Her Britannic Majesty had aspired to the possession of this miserable island, she would have displayed to this government the titles upon which she based her possessory right: she would not have invaded it outright as her Governor of Belize has done.[1]

— Miguel Alvarez, June 10, 1839

Mr. Morazán, and his friends, have always been averse to the meeting of a convention, from a suspicion that under a new order of things they will be unable to monopolise the power which they have so long exercised, without profit to the publick.[2]

— Chatfield, May 13, 1839

Upon learning of the Trujillo-Ruatán incident in the fall of 1838, Frederick Chatfield displayed statesmanlike qualities in contrast to the reaction of his superiors in London. Usually cautious and circumspect, Lord Glenelg of the Colonial Office bristled at the reports from Central America. As far as he was concerned, warning the Republic was not enough; British ships should be sent to protect Englishmen residing on Ruatán and to haul down any foreign flag on the island.[3] The Foreign Office was likewise irritated; and with Palmerston's recommendation, the Admiralty prepared for action.[4] Captain Thomas A. C. Symonds, in command of Her Majesty's sloop *Rover,* stationed in Jamaica, received orders on April 6, 1839, to pull down any "foreign flag which may be hoisted upon the island."[5] The die was cast. Great Britain had finally yielded to her aggressive agents in Central America.

One can well imagine the joy which overwhelmed Colonel Macdonald on April 16 when he learned of Symond's mission, especially since the superintendent was authorized to participate in it. A man of action, he would now back up his threats with deeds. On the 20th, the determined crew of the *Rover* arrived at Port Royal, Ruatán. To their annoyance, or perhaps satisfaction, they saw a "Montezumean flag" waving in the breeze. That flag had to come down immediately was the essence of the peremptory order from the *Rover.* Officials on the island

1. From Miguel Alvarez, June 10, 1839, F.O. 252/5; also enclosed in No. 21, to Palmerston, June 20, 1839, F.O. 15/22.
2. To Palmerston, No. 18, May 13, 1839, F.O. 15/22.
3. C.O. to F.O., p. encl.s, December 31, 1838, F.O. 15/21.
4. From Palmerston, No. 2, January 24, 1839, F.O. 15/22.
5. Peter John Douglas to Thomas A. C. Symonds, April 6, 1839, F.O. 15/22.

obeyed with amazing speed; then, in a spirit of defiance, they dramatically rehoisted Central America's colors. Blind with rage, Macdonald asked Symonds for a landing party and then led the assigned men ashore to remove the offending flag.[6] Overpowered by the invaders, twenty-odd subjects of Central America watched the scene helplessly: their flag came down and the union jack went up in its place. They were thoroughly humiliated.[7] To add insult to injury, Macdonald took five prisoners from among the island's officials and subsequently deposited them at Trujillo. Any attempt to rehoist Central America's colors at Ruatán, the Belizean superintendent threatened the commandant of the port, would most certainly incur the displeasure of the British government.

The bellicose Macdonald had spoken. But this time it was with the authority of his government — a most significant difference.[8] Hailing the returning heroes on April 27, the *Belize Advertiser* described the glorious events which had just taken place at Port Royal.[9] On the 30th, Macdonald notified Chatfield officially that Lord Palmerston had authorized the junket. For unknown reasons, except that there was some trouble with the mails, this dispatch did not reach San Salvador until May 23, 1839.[10]

Actually, the Ruatán events were known in El Salvador by May 15 and perhaps even a few days earlier. Chatfield admitted hearing of them early in May; and the French consul had exact details of Symond's mission on the 15th.[11] Ironically, Juan Galindo, who happened to be on the Atlantic coast when the incident occurred, was the one who spread the news of England's action in the most strident and nationalistic terms. This information appeared in a letter to the Guatemalan government, a copy of which was forwarded to Chatfield by George U. Skinner.[12] Certain undertones in the consul's correspondence of May 11 and 13, moreover, reflect an awareness of the events at Ruatán.[13] At any rate, we

---

6. Symonds to Douglas, May 27, 1839, F.O. 15/22.
7. Auguste Mahelin to Minister of Foreign Affairs (Molé), No. 15, May 15, 1839, A.A.E.P./CPAC, vol. 3.
8. Symonds to Douglas, May 27, 1839, F.O. 15/22.
9. From Alvarez, June 10, 1839, F.O. 252/5.
10. From Macdonald, April 30, 1839, F.O. 252/8; to Jefe de Chiquimula, May 20, 1839, F.O. 252/13.
11. To Palmerston, No. 21, June 20, 1839, F.O. 15/22; Mahelin's No. 15 (see fn. 7).
12. To Palmerston, No. 21.
13. To Palmerston, Nos. 18 (May 13) and 19 (June 21, 1839), F.O. 15/22.

can be fairly certain that he was aware of them by the 15th — a chronological point which has an important bearing upon political developments
in Central America.

Rather than accept the peaceful overtures of the federal government,
the expeditionary force of the Allied States — two thousand strong —
invaded El Salvador in February, 1839. During the following month,
there was little contact with the invader; and at one point, while General
Francisco Ferrera roamed near the Guatemalan border, he sent out
envoys to encourage Carrera's break with the provisional government of
Carlos Salazar in Guatemala City. Protesting his loyalty to the pact with
Morazán, the Indian *cacique* reported Ferrera's subversive mission. At
the same time, he asked for troops and money to defend Guatemala's
border. The Salazar government handled the request gingerly, suspecting
that it might lead to an act of treason. Rumors circulated, moreover, that
the *serviles* were conspiring with Carrera to join the cause of the states'
righters.

As it turned out, these rumors were accurate. On April 13, the
"Barbarian" and his followers again captured Guatemala City, this time
under the exclusive auspices of the old "Spanish Party." As a respectable
front, the *serviles* restored the moderate Mariano Rivera Paz to the governorship. On the 17th, Guatemala officially seceded from the union —
another partner in the states' rights column.[14] For all practical purposes
the Republic was dead by this time; it ceased to exist with Morazán's
resignation and the failure of the states, except for the federal district, to
hold national elections. The Republic thus had no body; it had only a
few caretaker officials in the executive branch.

The Guatemalan Revolution, however, came too late to be of any
help to the Allied army in El Salvador. On April 6, Ferrera led a surprise
attack upon Morazán's forces, encamped at Espírito Santo, near San
Vicente. Ignominiously deserted by his cavalry, the federal chief "by dint
of personal example and energy," Chatfield tells us, "got his men to stand
their ground for a time, and he succeeded in completely routing the dis-
orderly rabble opposed to him."[15] Despite the break with his erstwhile
ally, the consul's description of the victory at Espírito Santo evinces a
note of admiration for Morazán's military prowess. Indeed, the rout had

14. Guatemalan circular to governments of the Federation, March 22, 1839,
F.O. 254/2; Carlos Salazar to the people of the Republic, Quezaltenango,
May 19, 1839, A.G.N.G./LV; "Memoria," Mariano Rivera Paz, May 31,
1839, Guatemala City, B.N.G./HS, 1839.
15. To Palmerston, No. 16, April 20, 1839, F.O. 15/22.

been complete: three hundred invaders lost their lives, others were imprisoned, and most of them abandoned their arms, taking off to the four winds. According to the French consul, the Allied defeat had a sobering effect upon the governments of Honduras and Nicaragua; it brought to the fore men of peace in both states.[16]

The peace movement was also strong in Guatemala where the *serviles,* who had returned to full power in their state for the first time in ten years, were anxious to consolidate their political control. For this, peace was indispensable. In view of Morazán's recognized superiority in military matters, an aggressive policy would have been suicidal. Carrera undoubtedly was a brilliant *guerrillero,* but the military situation called for more than that. And no one, except perhaps Carrera himself, really felt that he had any chance whatsoever against Morazán in standard warfare. Yet, as Auguste Mahelin pointed out frequently in his astute evaluations of the political scene, men like Carrera and Ferrera with standing armies at their command posed a serious threat to the peaceful aspirations of the respective governments. From conceit or personal whim, these caudillos might easily commit their governments to a disastrous war with the ex-president.[17] Ironically, the Guatemalan peace advocates continually accused Morazán of having aggressive designs upon their state, when, as a matter of fact, their real source of anxiety was that Carrera might provoke Morazán into an invasion of Guatemalan territory. British sources, for example, in July and August, 1839, implied that Morazán had not committed any act of aggression; the caudillo Ferrera, on the other hand, had certainly done so, and it was not clear whether Carrera would join him.[18]

Victorious on the field of battle, the unionists could easily have dictated the terms of peace. Instead, they chose to offer their vanquished foes another compromise. On May 3, 1839, Vice-President Diego Vigil revived the federal decree of July 18, 1838, and urged the states to meet in convention for the reformation of the general government. Presumably, this would be followed by a national constituent assembly to be held in mid-July.[19] The states, however, demurred; they accepted the convention

16. Mahelin to Min. of Foreign Affairs, No. 14, May 1, 1839, A.A.E.P./CPAC, vol. 3.

17. See the following dispatches by Mahelin: Nos. 15 (May 15), 18 (August 1), and 19 (August 20, 1839).

18. From George U. Skinner, August 2, 1839, F.O. 252/18; also see, to Richard MacNally, July 1, 1839, F.O. 252/9.

19. Mem. on Central American Affairs, February 21, 1840, A.A.E.P./CPAC, vol. 3; *El Tiempo* (Guatemala), No. 12, June 21, 1839.

call but they were not disposed to follow this with a national assembly.[20]
When the Ruatán news broke, unionists were even willing to accept the
limited program of the states' rights type of convention. As a result, from
May to June, five of the Central American states had signed, or were
about to sign, treaties of peace and alliance in preparation for a convention at Santa Ana, El Salvador, on August 15 or shortly thereafter.[21]
Los Altos was the single exception; but even there, by mid-July, convention delegates had received instructions authorizing the negotiation of
treaties with the sister states.[22]

There were two different attitudes, or interpretations, concerning
these treaties of alliance; and the distinction was basic in the political
events which followed. Costa Rica, Nicaragua, Honduras, and Guatemala intentionally stressed the fact that ultimate and absolute sovereignty
lay with the state governments, as if to assure themselves that any future
general government, which might be agreed to at Santa Ana, would of
necessity be a loose confederation of sovereign states. At first, El Salvador appeared to favor this procedure and interpretation. Later, however,
with the Ruatán disclosures, it viewed the treaties as merely provisional
agreements which would become obsolete upon the establishment of a
more perfect union. Los Altos, also controlled by unionists, adopted the
same view.[23] Since the Republic no longer existed in fact, unionists
realistically accepted the treaty technique; and their state governments
took over certain functions which formerly were the responsibility of the
Republic. The important distinction, however, was that they regarded
this assumption of federal prerogatives as temporary.

Despite their different objectives, the prospects for a compromise
solution at the Santa Ana convention seemed promising, especially in
view of the British occupation of Ruatán Island. The Ruatán news
should have united the two factions against the common foe. But such
was not the case, providing a tragic commentary on the sentiment of
national consciousness in Central America. Not without some irony, the
unionists, who favored strong action in defense of the nation's territorial
integrity as well as the establishment of a national government which

20. "Dictamen," Guatemala, June 5, 1839, *El Tiempo* (Guatemala), No. 10,
June 12, 1839.

21. Practically all of the treaties negotiated during this period can be found in
the issues of *El Tiempo*. See, for example, the Treaty between Honduras
and Guatemala in the issue of June 21, 1839.

22. Decree No. 41, Quezaltenango, July 10, 1839, B.N.G./HS, 1839.

23. Article 21 of decree No. 42, Quezaltenango, July 10, 1839, B.N.G./HS,
1839, states that the treaties are valid only until "the new pact is sanctioned
and published." The states' rights point of view is presented in *El Tiempo*,
No. 24, August 16, 1839.

might command respect in the world, were depicted as unprincipled scoundrels and political opportunists by the states' righters. Undoubtedly this picture of the *Morazanistas* helped the defenders of the states to salve their consciences in not supporting the principles of the unionist program.[24] A basic political fact of this period, Ruatán signified to the champions of states' rights a potential loss of their newly won political power. It would have been difficult for them to argue at Santa Ana, or any other place, that what Central America needed most was a loose confederation of sovereign states — an untenable stand in view of the Ruatán news, and the states' righters were well aware of this. That is precisely why they extended themselves so desperately to paint the picture which they did of General Morazán and his partisans.

The unionists, on the other hand, favored an energetic policy toward Great Britain. At first, in the month of May, the less sanguine elements — the diplomats and the realists — dominated unionist policy. This group preferred to tone down the incident so as not to frighten the states' righters from canceling their plans to attend the Santa Ana convention. For this reason, as in the case of El Salvador, they were also disposed to accept the treaty device described above, confident that they could dominate, or sway, such a convention by an appeal to logic and to Central American nationalism. The presence of Guatemalan liberals, who were living in exile in Los Altos, assured the cooperation of the highland state in the convention. And to guarantee himself a voice at Santa Ana, General Morazán decided to run for the governorship of El Salvador in late May. He won the elections handily, and this news reached the other states by mid-June.[25] There is something to be said for the moderate approach of the unionists during the month of May, 1839, though its principal effect was to frighten the states' righters almost to death.

In the state of Los Altos, a more aggressive type of unionist policy soon prevailed and complemented Morazán's maneuvers in El Salvador. In response to a circular letter sent out to all the states on June 21 by Vice President Vigil, alerting them to the British danger and urging them to take the initiative in defense of the nation's honor, Los Altos modified her earlier instructions to convention delegates. On July 21, the legislature passed decree fifty-one insisting that priority at the convention should be given to measures strengthening the union and to the

---

24. Typical of the attack upon the *Morazanistas* was the apochryphal decree of Vice-President Diego Vigil, San Salvador, May 1, 1839, published in Comayagua, Honduras (B.N.G./HS, 1839). In it, Morazán is accused of selling Ruatán to the English.

25. Mahelin to Molé, No. 17, July 5, 1839, A.A.E.P./CPAC, vol. 3.

imposition of economic sanctions upon the foreign aggressor. Article two of the decree proposed the following action:

> First, that no import derived from the agricultural or manufacturing industry of any English possession be admitted, even though it may be brought here under the flag of any other nation; secondly, that no product coming from another nation, although it may be friendly, be admitted into our territory if it comes in an English ship; and thirdly, that these restrictions are to remain in effect during that time that England does not place Central America in possession of said Ruatán Island.[26]

On August 9, the Salvadorean constituent assembly voiced its approval of decree fifty-one as passed by the Los Altos government. In fact, at an even earlier date Governor Morazán had sent an envoy to Quezaltenango to negotiate a treaty embodying the above-mentioned decree. In view of Chatfield's political astuteness, there can be little doubt that he was aware of these actions, so inimical to his nation. On August 10, 1839, the two unionist-controlled states signed the so-called "Treaty of Quezaltenango." Los Altos ratified it two days later; and Morazán affixed his signature on September 12.

In many respects, this treaty was similar to those signed earlier in the year by other states. It recognized the absolute sovereignty of the signatory governments; it subscribed to the principles of non-intervention, non-aggression, arbitration, etc.; and it accepted the convention site of Santa Ana, as agreed to by the remaining states of the former Republic. Article eleven, however, insisted that the treaty would be obsolete upon the formation of a new union — a clause which was not characteristic of the other treaties.

Articles eight through ten, moreover, recommended — and this verb must be emphasized — a strong program of action against Great Britain. Article eight stipulated that priority at the Santa Ana convention should be given to strengthening the union and to the recovery of Ruatán. Article nine reproduced verbatim the above-mentioned Los Altos decree fifty-one. But article ten stated that the previous article would be inoperative, or non-binding upon the signatory states, "until it had been agreed to, and accepted by, the remaining states of the union." As we shall see, Frederick Chatfield stubbornly chose to ignore the condition in article ten. In ratifying the treaty, Morazán stated unequivocally that the proposed anti-British action depended upon its acceptance by the remaining

---

26. Decree No. 51, Quezaltenango, July 21, 1839, published in the *Gaceta del Gobierno de Los Altos* (Quezaltenango), September 11, 1839, B.N.G./V, leg. 836.

states.[27] From the Central American point of view, it is difficult to see any lack of principles in the unionist treaty of August 10; in fact, the tenth article reflects an unusual restraint — a concern for means — which can hardly be labelled unprincipled.

Honduras was the first to panic in the states' rights column. Precisely upon learning of Morazán's election to the governorship of El Salvador, she announced plans to ask her sister states that "as a measure of security, and as an act of justice and of good order," no ex-officers of the Republic should be permitted to have any say or any position in the Santa Ana convention.[28] Understanding the implications of Ruatán, Guatemala and other states'-rights governments seized upon the Honduran suggestion with alacrity.[29] A provision to that effect was included in Guatemala's treaty with Costa Rica, dated August 1. By then, Honduras and Nicaragua had likewise agreed to exclude *Morazanistas* from the convention.[30] In due time, terrified states' righters also found it expedient to change the location of the convention site from Santa Ana, El Salvador, to Los Llanos de Santa Rosa in Honduras. Then the convention was postponed — first to mid-October, later to December. Adding to the fears of the states' righters, Los Altos and El Salvador reiterated their desire to meet at the new location whenever the others wanted to assemble. For obvious reasons, however, they could not consent to the exclusion of unionist liberals from the meeting.[31] As a result, no convention was held.

Those in brief were the general lines of the celebrated convention issue during the year 1839. According to the propaganda of the states' righters and their abettors, *Morazanistas* were not in favor of holding the convention; all they wanted was to keep Central America in a state of turmoil in order to perpetuate themselves in power — ridiculous charges which revealed the sense of desperation among states' righters at the prospects of losing political power in their respective states. In July, and twice in August, Governor Rivera Paz of Guatemala wrote anxiously to

27. Treaty, Los Altos and El Salvador, Quezaltenango, August 10, 1839, B.N.G./HS, 1839, with notes on the ratification of the document by both states.
28. Coronado Chaves to Ministro General de Guatemala, Comayagua, June 13, 1839, *El Tiempo* (Guatemala), No. 15, July 10, 1839.
29. *El Tiempo* (Guatemala), Nos. 16 (July 13) and 17 (July 19, 1839). In No. 16, the editor refers to Francisco Morazán as *"el héroe malhadado."*
30. Treaty, Costa Rica and Guatemala, San José, August 1, 1839, *El Tiempo,* No. 33, September 21, 1839.
31. Mahelin to Molé, Nos. 18 (August 1) and 21 (September 28, 1839), A.A.E.P./CPAC, vol. 3; *El Tiempo,* Nos. 32 (September 8, 1839) and 65 (January 7, 1840).

the Salvadorean government, asking it to declare its intentions with regard to the convention and the maintenance of peace. Writing in early September, Morazán assured Guatemala that his state would honor the terms of its treaty of July 5, 1839, and asked the Guatemalan government to serve as mediator in Salvador's dispute with Honduras, whose forces had invaded El Salvador for the second time.[32]

Among the states' righters, there was also a belligerent faction led by the caudillos — Ferrera in Honduras, Carrera in Guatemala, and Braulio Carrillo in Costa Rica. The distance of Costa Rica from the center of events made it unlikely that Carillo would figure prominently in the disturbances, at least in Chatfield's opinion.[33] But Ferrera was another case altogether. Smarting from the defeat at Espírito Santo, Francisco Ferrera dreamed of revenge. He thus became the leader of the hostile states' rights group which aspired to key positions in any general government that might be established at a convention.[34] And Nicaraguan officials had agreed to support him on the forcible exclusion of *Morazanistas* from the convention.[35] In early August, moreover, Ferrera sent an agent to Carrera hoping "to seduce" him into joining the armed action against ex-president Morazán. Ferrera was the one who was "mad," George U. Skinner wrote to Chatfield on August 2. As for the possibility of Carrera joining Ferrera, Skinner's opinion was: "If we are not attacked he never will join any movement, but a march of Morazán's on Honduras would excite I much fear a serious matter to keep him quiet."[36]

Swollen with revenge, the headstrong Ferrera took the law into his own hands in July and for the second time during the year invaded El Salvador. In the circumstances, Governor Morazán had no alternative but to defend his state from the Honduran invaders. For more centralized control, and with the approval of Vice-President Vigil, the federal district was reincorporated; and San Salvador again became the capital of El Salvador. In August, as Ferrera's forces ranged throughout the state, Morazán declared a state of siege and deployed his forces.[37] Fearing that Carrera might join the invaders, he stationed a cordon of Salvadorean troops along the Guatemalan border — defense measures which any sensible military leader had to take in such an emergency. In Guatemala City, however, these measures were interpreted as part of Morazán's

32. Mahelin to Molé, No. 20, September 7, 1839, A.A.E.P./CPAC, vol. 3.
33. To Skinner, July 21, 1839, F.O. 252/18.
34. Mahelin to Molé, No. 18, August 1, 1839, A.A.E.P./CPAC, vol. 3.
35. Mahelin's No. 17, July 5, 1839.
36. From Skinner, August 2, 1839, F.O. 252/18.
37. To Palmerston, No. 26, October 8, 1839, F.O. 15/22.

plans to invade their state. The validity of this charge can be appreciated if we remember El Salvador's request for Guatemalan mediation. The real source of fear in Guatemala City was that Carrera might not be able to restrain himself, that he might accidentally commit the *serviles* to an armed conflict with Morazán. As a military strategist of no mean ability, Chatfield realized this danger and had no illusions with regard to Carerra's chances of success. No wonder the *serviles* sought peace, hoping that Great Britain would guarantee it.

Events in El Salvador reached their climax in September, 1839. On the 16th, an uprising of states' righters broke out in San Salvador with the rebels proclaiming their allegiance to the cause of the states. It was a short-lived revolution, however, for the city fell to Morazán's forces two days later. On September 25, the battle with Ferrera took place; and for the second time that year, he was defeated. Wounded and left for dead on the battlefield, the Honduran general effected a miraculous escape swearing to get revenge another day.[38] His head was indeed hard.

Ferrera's second defeat momentarily relieved the situation in Guatemala by discouraging Carrera's intervention. But *serviles* now feared that a victorious Morazán might be able to dominate the impending convention at Los Llanos de Santa Rosa in Honduras. The ex-president increased their anxiety by making a fresh appeal to settle the differences of the states at the convention so as to meet the real challenge to Central America — the British action at Ruatán. Clearly states' righters needed a pretext for not holding the convention, and a convenient one was at hand. They complained that Morazán's forces had entered Honduras and were in possession of a border section — a charge which was true, incidentally. With some justification, Morazán adamantly insisted that Honduras owed his state reparations for damages occurred in two successive invasions. Until Honduras agreed to a settlement, his forces would continue to occupy a section of that state. Thus, Morazán provided his enemies with an excellent excuse for postponing the convention until December. By then, as we shall see, other factors brought about a new delay.[39]

In the light of this brief political sketch of Central American history from April to September, 1839, Chatfield's actions can be placed in their proper context — a perspective which he denied his superiors in the For-

38. *Ibid.;* Mahelin's No. 22(?), October 26, 1839.
39. Mahelin's No. 21, September 28, 1839; *El Tiempo,* No. 51, November 23, 1839; from J. Guerrero, November 27, 1839, F.O. 252/16.

eign Office. The fulcrum of political action during that period was "this miserable island."

———◆◆———

After the break in Chatfield's alliance with the federal government in early March, he pursued an official policy of neutrality, at least for the first two months. By propagating the cynical picture of General Morazán and his followers, however, the consul was in fact committed psychologically against the movement to restore the Republic. In part, the metamorphosis in his thinking resulted from resentment over the failure of his loan proposal; but, more importantly, he was now deeply convinced that Morazán had outlived his usefulness in Central America. The state's righters would never permit him to restore the old Republic. For the ex-president to insist upon his dream of union in the circumstances was sheer folly. It could only lead to more chaos and anarchy, all of which would be to the detriment of British life and property.

From this it does not follow that he had any greater confidence in the rulers of the state governments. He correctly understood their contribution to, and responsibility for, the disorder in Central America; and he wasted no love for them. After all, they represented groups and interests which he had detested for a long time — the "coloured classes," the "romish" elements, and the people with "Spanish prejudices." They were the ones who sinned most in arousing anglophobia and in picturing all Englishmen as allies of the Devil. From Richard MacNally, a Jamaican who was held prisoner by the Allied army in the previous February, he learned of states' rights propaganda to the effect that Morazán had sold out to the heretical English and had sent a fortune to the Bank of England for a future day. And leading the Allied troops were such characters as Benito Méndez of Nicaragua and Francisco Ferrera of Honduras who had openly betrayed their aspirations to build up personal fortunes from the sale of Mosquitia's resources.[40] In short, Chatfield had little in common at this point with his future allies.

On the other hand, if the Foreign Office could be persuaded to back him up with naval support and if he could commit Lord Palmerston to a policy of direct intervention in the internal affairs of Central America, then perhaps he might be able to bring peace and order to the area. In effect, the consul envisioned a virtual protectorate of Central America with advantages to both peoples — British investors and entrepreneurs would thrive, and Central Americans would advance culturally by the exposure to enlightened English institutions. Similar aspirations had dic-

40. From Richard MacNally, March 10, 1839, F.O. 252/6.

tated the former alliance with liberal unionists; but those dreams of empire were smashed on the rocks of Central American politics, despite his conscientious efforts. He had no alternative now but to move toward a *modus vivendi* with the states' righters, while at the same time influencing a more forceful policy from London. This was a large order; but Mr. Chatfield was fully capable of thinking big and acting just as aggressively.

With regard to the states of Costa Rica, Nicaragua, and Honduras, the consul's goal was the acceptance of his doctrines on forced loans and the proportional responsibility of the states for the federal debt. He had remarkable success during the course of the year. In June, Costa Rica agreed to make an instalment on her share of the federal debt — somewhat scaled down because of her offer — by delivering a cargo of tobacco to Nicaragua, the logical market for the type of tobacco in question.[41] And in September, Nicaragua consented to permit John Foster, the English vice-consul, to dispose of the Costa Rican tobacco in that state, providing the government received a fraction of the sales. Part of Nicaragua's share, according to the agreement, would go toward her own administrative expenses and the rest, toward the liquidation of Nicaragua's indebtedness to British bondholders.[42] As for Honduras, Chatfield despaired of Ferrera's bellicose influence upon the government and contented himself with the state's acknowledgement of the debt obligation.[43] In short, those three states did not figure in the consul's calculations for a new political alliance; the British navy would suffice to keep them in line. Chatfield had not yet envisioned Costa Rica as a pivotal power point in his plans to control Central America. That would come many years later.

The logical power center for Chatfield to cultivate was Guatemala City, which for centuries had been the political and economic nerve center of Central America. And though the *serviles* were retrograde, they were at least white and with some semblance of civilization. If he could control them and educate them to the English way of life — if, in short, he could succeed where the liberals had failed — he might be able to prevent power from slipping into the hands of the non-whites. This dread had haunted Frederick Chatfield since his near brush with death at Zugapango, a few years earlier. Here again the British navy would be the weapon which would control the *serviles*.

41. To Palmerston, No. 11, February 13, 1839, F.O. 15/22; to Costa Rican Government, No. 3, June 15, 1839, and from Rafael Escalante, July 19, 1839, F.O. 252/14; from John Foster, July 20, 1839, F.O. 252/19.
42. From Foster, September 13, 1839, F.O. 252/19.
43. To Skinner, July 21, 1839, F.O. 252/18.

On May 13, 1839, for the first time, Frederick Chatfield prepared Lord Palmerston for his impending alliance with the decent people (*gente decente*) of Guatemala, apparently assuming, or gambling, that the master in the Foreign Office had not been paying very close attention to his former dispatches:

> I freely confess that I have no predilection for any party or persons in this country. I am not a partisan of expresident Morazán, or of his friends, the existing government, first because I perceive that Morazán has no administrative ability, and secondly, because I can feel no respect for Persons, who sacrifice the publick interests and resources to their own individual emolument. With regard to the servile party, although I may lean towards them as being persons of property and reputable conduct, nevertheless on publick grounds I cannot very cordially welcome the prospect of their return to power, from a suspicion that no permanent good will accrue from the govt of a Party embued with the old Spanish prejudices, and subject to the tyrannical influence of the Romish Priesthood; however, between the two evils of only the semblance of a govt without power or principle, as has long been submitted to here, and a substantial one based on obsolete principles, perhaps the latter is best, at any rate it may be the means of leading to the establishment of such outward forms of respectability and decency, as any future rulers will find difficult to dispense with.[44]

This important statement of political preference has to be put in its proper context — the impact of the Ruatán news in Central America and Chatfield's decision to seek an alliance with the *serviles*. Out of context, it can lead to erroneous interpretations of the consul's role in the political developments of the period.[45] On May 11, two days earlier, Chatfield reopened the correspondence on the Trujillo-Ruatán issue, announcing to Miguel Alvarez Palmerston's warning of a "collision" if Central America dared to hoist its flag on the island.[46] On the 13th, when he expressed a preference for the *serviles*, he raised for the first time a very shaky financial claim against the federal government with the objective, it would seem, of preventing it from raising money for any hostile venture against Great Britain. The William Barchard claim — that of a North American citizen, incidentally — reflected the consul's awareness of events at Ruatán. Ironically, the claim dated back to the years 1827–1828 when the *serviles* controlled the central government.[47]

---

44. To Palmerston, No. 18, May 13, 1839, F.O. 15/22.
45. See, for example, Karnes, *The Failure of Union,* p. 116 ff.
46. To Palmerston, No. 19, p. encl.s, June 1, 1839, F.O. 15/22.
47. To Miguel Alvarez, May 13, 1839, F.O. 252/5.

That Chatfield was applying economic pressure on the federal government for political purposes — to prevent a strong stand against Ruatán — was more clearly evident in an ultimatum of May 27 in which he insisted upon the payment of an instalment on the debt to British bondholders. In the government's reply, Miguel Alvarez acknowledged the Republic's responsibility to English creditors but pleaded the circumstances which had prevented the payment of an instalment, a point well understood by Chatfield. Nevertheless, the consul found the reply unacceptable; and on June 5, for the first time, he asked Lord Palmerston for British intervention in the affairs of Central America on the ground that the continuance of disorder was detrimental to, and at the expense of, English interests.[48] He conveniently kept from Palmerston the knowledge that a movement was afoot to resist Great Britain's actions at Ruatán and that he had already made overtures of alliance to the *serviles* of Guatemala City.

On July 5, Chatfield wrote his second request for direct intervention of Great Britain in the internal affairs of Central America, even though it contradicted Lord Castlereagh's circular of January 19, 1821. "It would be the height of presumption in me," he told Palmerston, "to aim at controverting those principles." Yet in typical style, he did presume to recommend a contrary policy; and to make it palatable, he suggested that England join France and the United States in such a program of intervention.[49] Actually, he preferred the unilateral intervention of Great Britain but he chose to conceal this from the Foreign Office at this time. Then, on August 20, a determined British agent made his third appeal for intervention.[50]

These various requests for direct interference in Central America's domestic affairs are meaningful in the framework of the consul's discussion with the federal government on Ruatán and his negotiations with the *serviles* of Guatemala City. First, let us consider the tempestuous correspondence with Miguel Alvarez. The Central American minister of foreign affairs did not reply officially to the May 11 dispatch on the Trujillo-Ruatán question until June 10, although he had discussed the matter privately with the consul. It would seem that Alvarez delayed his answer in the hope that states' righters might not panic and thus refuse to attend the convention. The more sanguine unionist faction, however, demanded action on the part of the federal government, forcing Alvarez's

---

48. To Palmerston, No. 20, p. encl.s, June 5, 1839, F.O. 15/22; from Miguel Alvarez, June 4, 1839, F.O. 252/5.
49. To Palmerston, No. 23, July 5, 1839, F.O. 15/22.
50. To Palmerston, No. 25, August 20, 1839, F.O. 15/22.

hand. Unquestionably Chatfield's ultimatum of May 27 also encouraged a stronger posture toward England. At any rate, the June 10 answer complained of the English action on "this miserable island" and presented the argument that the Bay Islands belonged to Central America by virtue of her "derivatory rights" from the King of Spain.[51] As formerly, Frederick Chatfield denied the validity of the Central American thesis, repeating his own interpretation that Central America was not a party to the negotiations between Spain and Great Britain in the eighteenth century and therefore had no legal say in the territorial question. Annoyed at the hint that the Republic would go over his head to the Foreign Office to seek satisfaction, he suggested that first the federal government should prepare a brief presenting its legitimate claims to Ruatán, excluding, of course, the nonsense about derivatory rights.

In describing the correspondence with Alvarez, Chatfield went out of his way to discredit the Central American interpretation, hoping that Palmerston would reject it in the event a delegation were sent to London. Instead, the consul urged a reconsideration of the various doctrines which had germinated in his mind over the years, all of which amounted to the old right of effective occupation. Since Spain had not held the area to the east of Lake Petén and Cahabón, he again recommended its occupation by the British.[52] All barrels were blazing away in Chatfield's desperate fight against the unionist challenger in Central America.

Considerable publicity attended the heated exchange of letters between Alvarez and Chatfield. Their correspondence was published and widely circulated throughout Central America. It inflamed the nationalistic spirit of unionists and pricked the guilty conscience of states' righters, who could not claim ignorance of the Englishman's territorial views.[53] On June 21, Vice-President Diego Vigil sent a circular message to the states in which he noted the federal government's impotency and urged the states to meet in convention to formulate a common stand against the British. The initiative, he insisted, was theirs. Only El Salvador and Los Altos heeded the call. And on June 25, there appeared in the federal capital an impassioned publication entitled "Roatán," in which the author pleaded for Central American unity and reviewed emotionally the fate of other disunited peoples throughout history. Rumor had it that Alvarez wrote the piece at the behest of General Morazán.[54] Be that

51. From Alvarez, June 10, 1839, F.O. 252/5.
52. To Palmerston, No. 21, June 20, 1839, F.O. 15/22.
53. *Gaceta* (San Salvador), No. 11, June 12, 1839, in No. 16, Mahelin to Molé, June 15, 1839, A.A.E.P./CPAC, vol. 3.
54. Enclosed in Mahelin's No. 19, August 20, 1839.

as it may, one can easily imagine the exacerbated state of the Central American mind during the months of June, July, and August, while Chatfield was recommending strenuously British intervention in the area. And during this period, states' righters were turning a frightened deaf ear to pleas for unity. They were concerned with other principles and they convinced themselves that *Morazanistas* were unscrupulous politicos out to perpetuate themselves in power.

So much for one phase of the proper context for Chatfield's statement of political preference. Let us now turn to the buildup of his alliance with the *serviles*. Technically, the initiative was taken by the Guatemalan government on April 26, when Governor Mariano Rivera Paz wrote to the consul requesting his mediation in the maintenance of peace in Central America. The governor feared that Morazán's victory at Espírito Santo might encourage the invasion of Guatemala. To erase any misgivings the consul might have, Rivera Paz assured him that Rafael Carrera sincerely desired peace for his country and was not the vicious sort of person some people had pictured him.[55] On the 28th, Guatemala sent a circular to all foreign agents proclaiming her respectability: all foreigners and their property would be safe within her borders.[56] And on May 13, a printed letter from Rivera Paz to the government of Nicaragua urged the latter to work for peace rather than listen to the disruptive advice of mischievous persons — an allusion, it would seem, to the alleged attempts of Morazán to invade Guatemala.[57] To Chatfield it was clear that the *serviles* of Guatemala City wanted two things: first, peace, and secondly, an ally. After the disclosure of the Ruatán events, the English consul likewise shared their aspirations. Though Guatemala had made the first move, the real impetus for the subsequent alliance came from the British consulate.

From May 9 to 24, Mr. Chatfield prepared the bases for such an alliance. In reply to the Guatemalan circular, he explicitly recognized the sovereignty of Guatemala in gracious terms which he had not used in his correspondence with other states.[58] On the 10th, he answered Rivera Paz's request for British mediation with these words:

> I am much gratified by the confidence which it implies towards me. I shall not mention having received from you an invitation to inter-

---

55. From Mariano Rivera Paz, April 26, 1839, F.O. 252/12.
56. Guatemalan circular, April 28, 1839, *Brief Statement ... Eastern Coast of Central America Commercial and Agricultural Company* (2nd ed., London, 1840), p. 143.
57. Broadside, Governor Rivera Paz to Nicaragua, May 13, 1839, F.O. 254/2.
58. To Pedro Arriaga, May 9, 1839, F.O. 252/13; *El Tiempo* (Guatemala), No. 8, May 24, 1839.

pose for the maintenance of peace in this Republick but I will . . . exert my good offices to deter this Government from the prosecution of a policy which promises destruction to the domestic and foreign interests of the country.[59]

It is conceivable that Chatfield may have known of Ruatán when he wrote those lines, but this cannot be definitely established. On the 13th, he stated his preference for the *serviles;* and on the 18th, he wrote to the Guatemalan government concerning the "malicious reports" of that "unnatural Englishman" Juan Galindo — very definitely a reference to Ruatán — and suggested that it disavow those reports, so dangerous to British life and property.[60]

By the 24th, in anticipation of a violent unionist reaction to Great Britain, Chatfield's political plans finally materialized. In a letter of that date to John Foster, he asked him to influence the Nicaraguan government in behalf of Guatemala's peace policy. If Nicaragua refused, Chatfield threatened to use economic pressure upon her since "Great Britain would not be pleased to see its resources squandered in an unjust war, for the gratification of Party Vengeance," resources which were pledged "to the satisfaction of the Foreign Debt."[61] In a letter to the Guatemalan government, dated the 24th, the consul presented the San Jerónimo claims of Marshall Bennett along with all pertinent documentation, including Morazán's acceptance of the "transaction." He offered the same terms to the state of Guatemala; if she did not accept, England would insist upon the prompt collection of the claim.[62] Whether she liked it or not, Guatemala *had* to join an alliance with Frederick Chatfield — the San Jerónimo proposal, interestingly, was the means, or weapon, which brought the two allies together. It was both a threat and an incentive for Guatemala desperately needed a loan of 10,000 dollars. Even before he learned Guatemala's answer, Frederick Chatfield had written his first request for intervention (June 5).

The intermediary in the subsequent negotiations between the consul and the *serviles* was George Ure Skinner, acting vice-consul at Guatemala City during the absence of William Hall. We cannot, however, account specifically for his whereabouts from May 7, when he acknowledged his temporary appointment, to July 5, when he wrote the first of a series of letters to Chatfield. But we do know that he personally relayed Galindo's letter on Ruatán to San Salvador and that he was absent from

59. To Rivera Paz, May 10, 1839, F.O. 252/13.
60. To Pedro N. Arriaga, May 18, 1839, F.O. 252/13.
61. To John Foster, pvt., May 24, 1839, F.O. 252/21.
62. To Arriaga, p. encl.s, May 24, 1839, F.O. 252/13; from Skinner, July 5, 1839, F.O. 252/18.

Guatemala City on June 17.[63] These fragments of information, certain inferences in the Skinner-Chatfield correspondence, and the complex nature of the alliance negotiations suggest the interpretation that Skinner spent most of his time in San Salvador discussing the prospective alliance with Chatfield.

In his talks with the consul, Skinner pointed out that the San Jerónimo proposal would cause the Guatemalan government no end of embarrassment, especially since Carrera and his brother — the guilty parties — were important props for the regime. Acknowledging the obvious, Chatfield insisted upon using the claim in order to maintain the upper hand over the Guatemalan government. On June 11, when Guatemalans answered that the pitiful condition of the state treasury prevented any payment of the San Jerónimo claims, Chatfield replied with a counteroffer. He would reduce the claim to the sum of 55,000 dollars which with a loan of 10,000 brought the total indebtedness to 65,000. A letter to Skinner, dated June 21 and probably written in the merchant's presence, contained the counteroffer.[64] With this document Skinner returned to Guatemala City.

The two Englishmen, moreover, had worked out an alternate plan, one which would go into effect providing the *serviles* met three conditions. First, Chatfield expected Guatemala to repudiate publicly article 43 in the decree of August 5, 1838, the one which had announced Guatemala's sovereignty over Belize. Secondly, Guatemala was also to apply formally for a British guarantee of the peace in Central America. And thirdly, she should become the champion of financial responsibility in Central America and should make arrangements for an instalment on her share of the federal debt. In return, Skinner had authorization to make the following promises: first, the consul would drop the embarrassing San Jerónimo claim; secondly, the Skinner-Klee house would organize a loan drive among Guatemalan merchants to satisfy the financial needs of the state; and finally, Chatfield would secure the cooperation of the Foreign Office and the Admiralty in guaranteeing the peace in Central America. By dropping the San Jerónimo proposal, moreover, it should be noted that it left Chatfield in possession of 10,000 dollars which could be used in behalf of the common cause.[64bis]

---

63. From Charles Klee, June 14, 1839, F.O. 252/6; to Palmerston, No. 21, June 20, 1839, F.O. 15/22.

64. To Skinner, June 21, 1839, F.O. 252/18.

64bis. From William Walsh and Thomas Phillips, executors of Marshall Bennett's estate, March 13, 1840, F.O. 252/14; to Charles Evans, August 21, 1839, F.O. 252/9.

The question arises: How did George Skinner fit into this plan? Why was he so interested in floating the loan among the city merchants and why did his house contribute handsomely to that loan? The answer is simple. Chatfield had promised to include in the federal debt of Central America the amounts of money, plus interest, owed to the Reid-Irving firm in London. On the ground of speculation, the Foreign Office refused to include the instalments which that house had paid on the original loan and the expenses of the Marcial Zebadúa mission to England. Since the Skinner-Klee house had obstructed Chatfield's mission in Central America, he likewise denied them recourse to the British consulate. But the situation now was different. In return for Chatfield's support, Skinner's London associates would put pressure on the Foreign Office to provide the consul with the naval support he needed.[65] And that is precisely what happened.[66]

With the consul's blessings, Mr. Skinner returned to Guatemala City. In the meantime, Guatemala had already given evidence of a willingness to listen attentively to her new master in San Salvador. She promised to take action against the rascal Galindo, if he dared show his face in the state.[67] On July 5, Skinner wrote his first letter: the counter-offer, according to the Guatemalans, was "most generous and equitable" but still embarrassing. Therefore, Skinner decided to shift to the alternate plan since Guatemala was prepared to meet Chatfield's terms.[68] On July 15, Skinner wrote again; and though the letter is not available, its contents can be inferred from Chatfield's reply of July 21. Guatemala wanted one further concession: the consul's support for her type of "convention," establishing a loose confederation of sovereign states, each with one delegate and headed by a supreme delegate. Whether or not the *serviles* asked for the exclusion of *Morazanistas* from the convention is not clear, though obviously Chatfield shared their apprehension on this score. What pleased the consul most was the willingness of the *serviles* to ask for British protection. Whenever they formally requested such a guarantee, he promised to accept it without reservations. Yet he noted: "It might give more force to the affair if invitations were sent to Honduras, Nicaragua, and Costa Rica to adopt a similar policy." If four states applied for British mediation, Chatfield added, it would strengthen his hand with the Foreign Office — a clear-cut admission of the relation-

65. From George U. Skinner, August 2, 1839, F.O. 252/18.
66. Sir Robert Campbell to Palmerston, p. encl., April 22, 1840, F.O. 15/24; from Reid-Irving Company, October 15, 1839, F.O. 252/6.
67. From Pedro N. Arriaga, June 21, 1839, F.O. 252/12.
68. From Skinner, July 5, 1839, F.O. 252/18.

ship between the Guatemalan negotiations and the three demands for intervention. And finally, he cautioned secrecy for the time being: "not that secrecy is requisite in publick affairs because the subject matter will not bear the light, but because inconvenience arises from discussions being permitted in publick without the full merits of the case being understood."[69] It should be noted that the British consul did not include in his project the states of El Salvador and Los Altos — the unionist strongholds.

To be sure, the state of Guatemala met the consul's terms, one by one, during the months of July and August, 1839. Editorial after editorial stressed the importance of financial responsibility — a principle to which the conservatives would give priority at the impending convention.[70] The "unprincipled" unionists, of course, favored no such priority. On July 13, El Tiempo prepared the ground for the repeal of article 43 of August 5, 1838, in a selection entitled "Cuestión Pendiente." By ridiculing the article in question, the writer implicitly recognized British sovereignty to Belize.[71] On July 27, the Constituent Assembly of Guatemala officially repealed the article.[72] An overjoyed British ally gloated: "I hope that the pretensions of Persons in Guatemala respecting Belize are now forever silenced."[73] Optimism was always one of Chatfield's qualities.

Considering the intensity of feeling over the Ruatán issue during the month of July, one can appreciate the desperation and anger felt by unionists upon learning of these Guatemalan acts. Atop his highland post in Quezaltenango, José Francisco Barrundia commented upon the repeal of article 43 in the pages of El Popular. The title of his selection, written on August 3, aptly revealed his sentiments: "Oh men born to be slaves."[74] The publication aroused the ire of both Skinner and Chatfield who demanded to know if the offending newspaper was an official organ and, if not, hinted strongly to the Los Altos government that it should be muzzled. Los Altos answered that it was not an official newspaper but that in any case freedom of the press would be observed within her boundaries.[75] The British Foreign Office never learned of this exchange

69. To Skinner, July 21, 1839, F.O. 252/18.
70. For example, see El Tiempo (Guatemala), Nos. 23 (August 11) and 31 (September 14, 1839).
71. El Tiempo, No. 16, July 13, 1839.
72. Decree, Guatemala City, July 27, 1839, B.N.G./HS, 1839; also enclosed in No. 24, to Palmerston, August 10, 1839, F.O. 15/22.
73. No. 24 (August 10).
74. El Popular (Quezaltenango), No. 8, August 3, 1839, B.N.G./V, leg. 836.
75. From William Hall, August 23, 1839, and to Hall, August 23, 1839, F.O. 252/18.

of notes, the beginning of Chatfield's campaign against the unionists in Los Altos.

Ferrera's second invasion of El Salvador tightened the bond between the English consul and his partners in Guatemala City. Led by the Skinner-Klee house, the city merchants pledged themselves to supply a substantial loan on condition that the government ask Great Britain to guarantee the peace in Central America, so indispensable for their economic activity. On August 1, until midnight, Skinner closeted himself with Mr. B. (Luis Batres), a leading conservative. "As far as we finished last night," he wrote to Chatfield, "it will be most satisfactory, and God grant that you my good Sir be the means of having the consolation that Your good offices bring about an end that must ensure the blessings of all in this state."[76] The allies were about ready to make their alliance official. In this key letter, George Skinner made the following observations which have served as part of the basis for the interpretation in this chapter:

> I have written strongly on this point to Mr. Irving and Sir J.n P. Reid (now Governor of the Bank of England this year) and probably you will receive a letter from one or other of those gentlemen. They [sic] I have urged to interest themselves at Headquarters that you be supported by the Government in any measures you may suggest as whatever they may be they are for the best purposes towards their and our interests. I send you on the part of the firm the claims made up to the 1st. January.[77]

The final consummation of the alliance took place in early August, 1839. On the 2nd, the Guatemalan government notified Chatfield of the repeal of article 43; on the 5th and 6th, in separate letters by Pedro Arriaga and Luis Batres, Guatemala requested Great Britain's guarantee of the peace.[78] In the meantime, Skinner had assured the consul that the merchants' loan was progressing satisfactorily.[79] All these letters of confirmation reached San Salvador by August 20, when Chatfield made his third request for British intervention in the affairs of Central America. In his letter to Palmerston, Chatfield asked for instructions on two points:

> 1. Whether I may guarantee for Her Majesty's Government, the performance of Treaties of Peace, concluded between States of Central America, which may solicit the British guarantee.

---

76. From Skinner, August 2, 1839, F.O. 252/18.
77. *Ibid.*
78. From Arriaga, August 2, 5, 1839; from Luis Batres, August 6, 1839, F.O. 252/12.
79. From Skinner, official and conf., August 5, 1839, F.O. 252/18. According to Mahelin, the loan totaled 50,000 pesos (No. 19, August 20, 1839).

2. Whether I may interpose my good offices to protect a state which solicits the mediation of Her Majesty's Government, against the hostility of another state, which does not solicit it.[80]

Lord Palmerston had come a long way in accepting the aggressive proposals of his underling in Central America, but the implication of Chatfield's second point was unacceptable to him. He assured the consul that Great Britain would always be honored to serve as mediator upon the request of *all* the states involved. But, in view of England's oft-stated policy of non-intervention, she could not interfere directly in the internal affairs of Central America, which is what Chatfield's second point implied.[81] Palmerston's first refusal was written on November 19, 1839; a second refusal came in February, 1840. In the next chapter, we shall point out the novel manner in which Chatfield utilized Palmerston's statements of non-intervention.

———

With battle lines drawn in mid-August, 1839, the British consul undertook a two-pronged offensive: one against the two unionist states in Central America and the other aimed at committing the Foreign Office to a policy of intervention. On the basis of the Ruatán mission, Chatfield surmised that perhaps the Foreign Office had also persuaded the Admiralty to send him the naval support he had asked for in January — a correct assumption, incidentally. The *Electra* under Captain Thomas Mainwaring appeared on the Nicaraguan coast in August. But before her appearance, Chatfield was merely guessing; and he had to be doubly sure that naval support would be forthcoming. Moreover, he hoped that eventually Great Britain would assign a permanent patrol to both coasts. To achieve these objectives, it was imperative to paint a cynical picture of the political struggles in Central America, and especially of General Morazán and his partisans as the enemies of the English nation. Rarely, if ever, did he use the term *liberales* in his correspondence with Lord Palmerston, thus avoiding the impression that there was any ideological basis for the instability of the area. And henceforth this became a standard feature of a technique by which the consul was able to influence policy decisions in London.

As far as the Foreign Office was concerned, Frederick Chatfield first learned of the Quezaltenango Treaty on August 29, when he received a copy of it in the mail. There can be little doubt, however, that he knew the nature of the impending treaty between Los Altos and El

---

80. To Palmerston, No. 25, August 20, 1839, F.O. 15/22.
81. From Palmerston, November 19, 1839, F.O. 15/22.

Salvador since early August and perhaps since late July. At any rate, on August 31, he wrote to Miguel Alvarez complaining of articles eight and nine and demanding to know whether the federal government existed or not.[82] In private conversations, Alvarez pointed out the conditional nature of the objectionable articles — an argument which fell on deaf ears. In fact, Chatfield deliberately refrained from mentioning article ten to Lord Palmerston, which made the previous two articles conditional. Thus, he distorted the treaty as well as the convention issue.[83] If the Foreign Office had taken the pains to read the enclosures, or translate those sections which Chatfield had failed to do, it would have recognized many of the distortions of fact. But it did not. The impression created in Palmerston's mind, therefore, was one of unscrupulous anglophobes and political opportunists struggling against the law-abiding, decent people of Guatemala.

In his correspondence with the Los Altos and Salvadorean governments, Chatfield seemed determined to commit them to a categorical recognition of the Republic's non-existence. He refused, moreover, to accept the condition in article ten of the treaty as a satisfactory explanation for the studied insults against England in articles eight and nine. By equating the August 10 treaty with others which had been signed in Central America, he concluded that both states had virtually admitted the non-existence of the Republic. They had taken over certain governmental functions such as the collection of the tariff which formerly were within the province of the federal government. Again, Chatfield conveniently ignored article eleven of the treaty, which stated that the treaty would become obsolete upon the formation of the new union. His objectives were obvious: to convince Palmerston that no republic existed and to impress him with the fact that the two states were acting irresponsibly in recommending a violent program against Great Britain.[84] It followed that the British navy should demand reparations as well as an apology.

In pursuing the tactic of the Republic's non-existence, Chatfield had local objectives as well. First, he intended it as a threat to the wayward states — by no means an idle threat, as we shall see in the next chapter. And secondly, it furthered the cause of his allies and the type of convention which they wanted. If no union existed, it would be difficult to perfect it. The issue at the convention, therefore, would be the establishment

---

82. To Alvarez, August 29, 1839, F.O. 252/5.

83. To Palmerston, No. 26, October 8, 1839, F.O. 15/22.

84. *Ibid.;* also see the printed correspondence, Chatfield and State of Los Altos, 1839–1840, T.P.C.G., especially doc. 1 (September 3) and 3 (November 28, 1839) by Chatfield.

of a new government, not a reformed one. Ironically, the British consul revealed these objectives in a very novel manner. Of all things, he put them in the mouth of ex-president Morazán who, in an interview on September 19, presumably told Chatfield:

> that the strongest weapon which he could give against himself in the present contest, which he frankly told me is not a war involving principles but simply a strife of persons, would be the formal disallowance of the federal government; as it would render the convocation of a provisional government unavoidable, composed of an individual from each of the six states of Central America, which would place him and his Party in a minority of votes. Moreover a provisional government would lead to a convention, which by the same calculation will be destructive to him.[85]

From August 20, when Chatfield made his third appeal for intervention, to October 8, he wrote only one dispatch to Lord Palmerston — and that one by instalments. It was the only document in English which presented the events of those crucial seven weeks to the Foreign Office. The quotation above is a good example of the picture sketched in dispatch twenty-six.

To show the tyranny of the ex-president, the Salvadorean coup of September 16 was depicted as a nobly inspired revolution by adherents of constitutional government. *Salvadoreños* had no free choice or any say in their government — a point emphasized in the propaganda of the *serviles,* incidentally. The revolutionaries, Chatfield explained wanted "to put an end to the present civil war, and its attendant troubles, by the deposition of the so-called federal government, and by the separation of Mr. Morazán from the command of the State, whose permanency therein is believed to be the chief impediment to the meeting of a National Convention, for the amendment of the federal constitution, and for the organization of the country."[86] In this quotation, we can see the states' rights bias and a distortion of the convention issue. It reflects, moreover, the secessionists' fear of the role which General Morazán might play at any convention of the states.

During the Salvadorean coup — if we are to accept the consul's account — the few remaining officials of the federal government acted ignominiously. Vice-President Vigil — a paralytic, by the way — had hidden himself like a coward while Minister Alvarez "mounted his horse and disappeared, leaving the town to its fate, without an effort to restore order, or to protect the inhabitants from outrage." Other accounts, and

---

85. To Palmerston, No. 26, October 8, 1839, F.O. 15/22.
86. *Ibid.*

especially the one by the French consul, give an entirely different picture. Vigil, Alvarez, along with Carlos Salazar, were immediately imprisoned and put aboard a ship as part of a plan to send them off into exile. But when Morazán learned of the uprising, he attacked the city and freed the federal captives on September 18.[87]

Did Frederick Chatfield have anything to do with the September coup, as charged by his liberal adversaries? He was certainly sympathetic to the rebel cause; but it is doubtful that a realist like the English consul would suppose that such a coup could succeed against the military might of General Morazán. From the propaganda point of view, however, the accusation was significant, especially since it was accompanied by a widely circulated rumor that the British agent had denied asylum to Mrs. Morazán and daughters.[88] Whether true or not, the rumor did not enhance Chatfield's name among the nationalistically inclined. Surprisingly, in view of his sensitiveness to charges of a personal nature, the consul never denied the rumor; in fact, he never mentioned it to Lord Palmerston.

On September 19, the day after his victorious entry into San Salvador, Governor Morazán called the British consul into his office. Was it because of the rumor concerning Mrs. Morazán? Chatfield did not say, though he admitted that Morazán had called him. What is surprising in his account of the interview is that nowhere does he mention what Morazán wanted. On the contrary, the impression is given that Chatfield presented the topics of conversation: the Los Altos Treaty, the existence or non-existence of the Republic, the justice of British claims to Ruatán, etc. In this context, Morazán presumably made the remarks quoted above about the lack of principles in the political struggles of Central America. Yet the "unprincipled" Morazán stubbornly refused to accept the justice of British claims to Ruatán and to retract his ratification of the Quezaltenango Treaty. This vindictive anglophobe, moreover, had ratified the treaty solely upon hearsay — a point stressed by Chatfield as if Morazán had not known the nature of the treaty before it was drawn up! And the description of the interview left no doubt as to the general's aggressive designs upon the peaceful denizens of Guatemala. Thoroughly frustrated by Morazán's lack of principles, Chatfield threatened that he had no alternative but to sever relations with Central America and leave San Salvador, if no retraction of the treaty was forthcoming. Morazán made no comment.

---

87. Mahelin to Molé, No. 21, September 28, 1839, A.A.E.P./CPAC, vol. 3.
88. Mahelin's No. 26, January 10, 1840.

After the interview, Chatfield reconsidered his threat of breaking relations, explaining to Palmerston: "I determined therefore to await the result of the action which in a few days would take place, and which if unfavourable to him might afford me a chance of obtaining satisfaction from his successor, while if he should be successful, it seemed to me that the motives for continuing the course against which I had remonstrated would be less urgent."[89] The final clause is ambiguous, unless he meant by it that there might be a delay in the calling of the convention, hardly a likely occurrence.

Be that as it may, General Ferrera fell before the superior forces of Morazán on September 25; and Chatfield prepared to leave San Salvador. But in the final days of September, he received encouraging news from Nicaragua; an official of that government complained to him that Captain Mainwaring of the *Electra* had humiliated them with his forceful tactics.[90] This could mean only one thing. Admiral Ross had heeded his call for naval support. Now he could command respect from these upstart Central Americans.

Emboldened by the news, Chatfield requested a second interview with General Morazán, and it was granted to him on October 3. Rather forcefully the consul demanded an immediate retraction of the Quezaltenango Treaty and handed the general a draft of a retraction which would be acceptable to the British consulate. If he refused, the *Electra* would demand reparations. The facts concerning the British ship do not appear in Chatfield's account. The impression is given, however, that Morazán seemed disposed to retract his ratification providing it had not already been published. How true this is, it is difficult to say. At any rate, by October 7, at a third interview, Morazán again changed his mind — indeed, a man lacking principle and honor! He "would give me no satisfaction," Chatfield lamented. "My office having been thus cut from under my feet without any fault of my own," he concluded, "I would take leave to request Your Lordship's permission to return home. I am quite disheartened at perceiving that I have no chance of acquiring notice for usefulness, whilst stationed in a country hardly removed from a state of barbarism."[91] With ten thousand dollars in his possession, Chatfield had been unable to budge the stubborn ex-president of the Republic.

As he finished the lengthy dispatch of October 8, the consul might well have complained that besides having his job cut out from under him

---

89. To Palmerston, No. 26 (October 8).
90. From C. Juares, August 25, 1839, F.O. 252/16, received on September 26.
91. To Palmerston, No. 26 (October 8).

the world was literally falling around his ears. A series of earthquakes, since the 1st, had leveled the former federal capital. "Not a house remains standing secure," he scribbled nervously from the corridor of the consulate, "ready to spring into the Court Yard on the slightest motion of the earth." Practically everyone had fled the city, while the rains poured down unmercifully upon their heads. During the day, Chatfield worked at a table in the corridor; and at night he slept out in the wet "under the cover of hides to avoid the accident which a fresh shock of violence might occasion." [92] Providence was not smiling upon the British consul, thoroughly dejected about the fruitless years he had spent in Central America. To add to his sense of failure, on October 12, General Morazán left the city without bidding him adieu, another example of the "barbarity of the country." [93]

—◆—

A born fighter, Frederick Chatfield did not stay down for long. Rather than return to Belize to await instructions from Lord Palmerston, as originally planned, the British consul decided to proceed to Nicaragua, ostensibly to arrange for an instalment on the foreign debt.[94] This decision provoked a host of rumors. Some said that the British agent, angered by the forced loans levied upon his countrymen as well as their imprisonment by the Nicaraguan government, was on his way to punish that state. Incidentally, these matters had preoccupied Chatfield and his vice consul John Foster for a greater part of the year. Others insisted that the consul was returning to Belize where he would head an expedition of two hundred men to occupy San Juan de Nicaragua on the Atlantic coast until Nicaragua promised to satisfy English grievances.[95] No one, it seems, seriously believed that Her Majesty's consul was leaving the area in defeat, as one might infer from his letters to the Foreign Office.

The fact was that the indefatigable enemy of the *Morazanistas* was mounting a new offensive. The purpose of his visit to Nicaragua was political in inspiration; he was trying to counter an action recently taken by General Morazán. After Ferrera's second defeat, the victorious general hoped to unite the seceded states behind the type of convention which he favored. He therefore had urged Nicaragua to take the initiative in approaching Honduras on this matter. On October 17, Nicaragua dutifully carried out Morazán's request; and on the last day of that month, Honduras sent a letter of inquiry concerning the terms for a possible

92. To Palmerston, No. 27, October 10, 1839, F.O. 15/22.
93. No. 30 (October 14).
94. No. 28 (October 10).
95. Mahelin to Molé, November 5, 1839, A.A.E.P./CPAC, vol. 3.

reconciliation with El Salvador.[96] A unionist convention appeared in the offing, and Chatfield knew only too well what this meant for his country, as well as for the *serviles* of Guatemala. But unionists' hopes were soon dashed, thanks in part to the irascible Ferrera who wanted revenge, not reconciliation. With the aid of the *Electra,* Chatfield likewise was determined to stop the *Morazanistas.* When he left San Salvador on October 18, he did not know that Captain Mainwaring had already returned to Chile.

It will be recalled that Chatfield's tone stiffened in late September when he learned of the *Electra's* presence. To justify the use of the warship, he thought that the time was ripe for a public statement by Central Americans requesting Great Britain to guarantee the peace in the area. Since there had been so much unfavorable publicity concerning the consul's relations with the *serviles,* he proposed an indirect approach. Guatemala should ask the Nicaraguan government to take the initiative in requesting the British guarantee, while Chatfield used the *Electra* to persuade, or bring about, Nicaragua's acquiescence. Luis Batres in Guatemala City did exactly as he was told. On October 14, he formally requested British intervention and enclosed a note which he had written to Jerónimo Carcache, dated October 1. In the enclosure, Batres urged his friend to persuade Pedro Solís or the governor of Nicaragua to initiate a circular letter to all the states, requesting the British guarantee.[97] As on a previous occasion, the intermediary was George U. Skinner who personally delivered the above-mentioned letters to Frederick Chatfield. On October 18, the two English companions left San Salvador for Nicaragua.

Little is known of Chatfield's whereabouts from October 18 to November 5, though much of the time was undoubtedly spent en route to León, Nicaragua. More than likely the two English agents proceeded to the Salvadorean town of San Miguel, where the indigo fairs were in progress, hoping to learn of the *Electra's* presence. Instead, they perhaps heard of Mainwaring's hasty departure from the Nicaraguan coast — distressing news to say the least. While at San Miguel, Chatfield perhaps also learned of the tobacco arrangement which Foster had concluded with the Nicaraguan government.

Despite this information, however, a determined British consul continued his journey to León. From November 6 to 9, he was remarkably successful in achieving his political objectives. Yet it is difficult to

---

96. Mahelin to Molé, No. 33, p. encl.s, March 24, 1840, A.A.E.P./CPAC, vol. 3; also enclosed in, from J. Guerrero, November 27, 1839, F.O. 252/16.

97. From Luis Batres, p. encl. (Batres to Carcache, October 1), October 14, 1839, F.O. 252/12.

account for his success. Apparently he managed to convince Nicaraguans that the British navy was at his beck and call. Or, it is conceivable that Chatfield may have accepted the military support of five hundred men which an ambitious caudillo offered him, believing that the Englishman had come to León "to enforce order at any price."[98] Whatever the means, there can be no doubt about the results. Nicaragua agreed to circulate a letter to all the states asking for the British guarantee of peace. In so doing, Nicaragua joined the alliance with Chatfield. To save face, however, the allies agreed that the consul should not be present when the circular letter was issued, that he should go back to San Miguel, and that they should continue their correspondence at a distance. Moreover, Chatfield agreed to write persuasive letters to Costa Rica and Honduras encouraging them to listen to any proposals which might be made by Nicaragua's authorities.

This is precisely what happened from November 15 to 23.[99] Later, Chatfield published and circulated widely his correspondence with the Nicaraguan government, as if to create the impression that majority opinion in Central America favored the following points: a British guarantee of the peace, the non-existence of the federal government, and the justice of England's claims to Ruatán Island.[100] It would seem that the consul had little respect for the sentiment of nationalism in Central America. Perhaps his dealings with the two allies convinced him that it was non-existent. On November 27, Nicaragua did as instructed; the circular in favor of a British guarantee of the peace went out to all the states.[101]

In the meantime, Frederick Chatfield was making some revealing statements in letters to Admiral Ross and to Lord Palmerston, which hinted at his political maneuvers in Central America. With regard to Mainwaring's indiscreet departure, he told the admiral:

> I think you will be able to estimate the political inconveniences that had arisen to our interests in this quarter through the omission to lend me the moral influence I should have derived from the presence of one of Her Majesty's ships on the coast at the present juncture, when I state that in August last I was engaged in a correspondence remonstrating against an act of the State of Salvador highly offensive to the British Crown and for which I had de-

---

98. To Palmerston, No. 31, November 19, 1839, F.O. 15/22.
99. To Minister of Honduras, p. encl. (Chatfield's letter of November 18, 1839, written from San Miguel), April 8, 1840, F.O. 252/14.
100. To Palmerston, No. 31 (November 19), enclosing the printed correspondence.
101. *El Tiempo* (Guatemala), No. 86, March 17, 1840, in No. 33, Mahelin to Molé, March 24, 1840, A.A.E.P./CPAC, vol. 3.

manded and obtained the promise of reparation — but which being subsequently denied to me, has compelled me to retire from the territory of the State. . . .

My course would have been firm and explicit could I have pointed to one of Her Majesty's ships to second me as I should have then declared that the application from Guatemala and the other States for the preservation of peace through the instrumentality of our Government was a sufficient ground for announcing to the Government of Salvador the necessity of suspending its hostilities against Guatemala until the pleasure of Her Majesty's Government can be taken respecting the guarantee solicited of them.[102]

From San Miguel, on November 19, Chatfield made his fourth request for British intervention in the internal affairs of Central America — ironically, on that date Lord Palmerston refused his first three requests. In previous dispatches, the consul admitted to Palmerston, "I hinted that I was indirectly moving the governments to apply for England to guarantee any political compacts which the states might conclude amongst themselves."[103]

And on the 22nd, Mr. Chatfield began to prepare his offensive against the unionist states of Los Altos and El Salvador. On that day, a party of grateful English merchants signed a letter commending Queen Victoria's representative for his unceasing efforts in their behalf. He enclosed this letter in his dispatch of November 23 which announced his future strategy in Central America:

Conceiving that Her Majesty's Government will insist upon the authorities of this State of Salvador making reparation for their behaviour towards Great Britain, I should wish to recommend that repayment of the forced loans which have at various periods been exacted from Her Majesty's Subjects in the State should be demanded with interest and expenses. Not having my Papers with me, I cannot furnish Your Lordship with the particulars of these cases now, but I will do so at the earliest opportunity, and I merely take leave to draw Your Lordship's notice to the matter in order that it may not be overlooked when the time comes for bringing the Government of Salvador to their senses.[104]

Thus, in late November, 1839, the political situation was essentially this: Chatfield's alliance now included the *serviles* of Guatemala and the conservatives of Nicaragua, who had circulated the request for

---

102. To Admiral Ross, November 9, 1839, F.O. 252/8; also see letter of November 18.
103. To Palmerston, No. 31 (November 19).
104. To Palmerston, No. 33 p. encl.s, November 23, 1839, F.O. 15/22.

a British guarantee to the other states. These allies stood for a convention of states' righters, hopeful of erecting a weak confederation under the superintendency of Great Britain and dedicated to the advancement of such principles and objectives as the establishment of public credit, honesty in government, the restoration of relations with the Papacy, etc. Since Costa Rica had refused to join the unionists of Los Altos against England, we may assume that she was in a similar mood, though not a member of the alliance.[105] On the opposing side were the unionist states which had to be brought "to their senses," Los Altos and El Salvador. Those two states would not waver from their commitments in the Quezaltenango Treaty. In fact, the Nicaraguan circular of November 27 merely intensified their determination to stand firmly against *"el ominoso Chatfield,"* one of the milder epithets of this troubled period.[106] And to the consul's chagrin, the Nicaraguan conservatives fell from power shortly after sending out the circular letter.[107]

---

105. From M. Guevara, No. 2, January 5, 1850, which encloses Costa Rica's answer to Los Altos, dated December 5, 1839, F.O. 252/14.
106. To Palmerston, No. 8, February 15, 1840, F.O. 15/23.
107. *El Atleta* (San Salvador), No. 3, December 25, 1839, B.N.G./V, leg. 836.

CHAPTER EIGHT

El Ominoso Chatfield

That Chatfield has mixed himself in our Revolution is a circumstance that needs no demonstration.[1]
Miscelánea, February 21, 1840

I will therefore merely assure Your Lordship, on my word, that I have never in any way mixed myself up with the factions of this country.[2]
—Chatfield, February 5, 1840

Upon sealing the dispatch which outlined his future strategy toward the unionist states, the English consul left the site of the indigo fairs in great haste. By nightfall of November 24, he had reached Umaña. And, at two o'clock on the following morning, a messenger aroused him from his sleep with stirring news of events that had just taken place in San Miguel. After scanning the various documents, Mr. Chatfield penned a strong letter of protest to Department Chief Gerardo Barrios in which he demanded the immediate release of William Kilgour, a British merchant from San Salvador; and with this peremptory letter in his possession, George U. Skinner rode back to San Miguel. Offering no explanation for his failure to return to the indigo center, the consul instead mounted his horse and traveled some twelve leagues in the direction of San Salvador. In a hut by the side of the road, he stopped to scribble a note to the state government explaining recent events and insisting upon the department chief's punishment for an offense against the British Queen in the form of one of her subjects. Though we have only the English version of the Kilgour episode, its significance is clear: Mr. Chatfield was initiating his campaign to bring El Salvador to its senses.[3]

During the indigo fairs, William Kilgour had voluntarily contributed eighty-five dollars to a state loan. In return, he received a certificate which, so he was told, might be used to pay duties at the fair. Upon presenting this i.o.u. to state officials for taxes which he owed on some bales of indigo, they refused to honor it. Kilgour complained vehemently, and the department chief was called in to settle the matter. Chief Barrios likewise rejected the i.o.u., and tempers flared. Expressing himself

---

1. *Miscelánea* (Cojutepeque), No. 7, February 21, 1840, in No. 12, to Palmerston, March 23, 1840, F.O. 15/23.
2. To Palmerston, No. 6, February 5, 1840, F.O. 15/23.
3. To Palmerston, No. 35, p. encl.s, December 20, 1839, F.O. 15/22.

"warmly" at the breach of faith, the English merchant tore the certificate into bits and threw it upon the table mumbling that the state's promises were worthless. For these "alleged disrespectful expressions," which Barrios considered an insult to the dignity and honor of his government, Mr. Kilgour was escorted "through the street like a felon to the common jail." On the 24th, while Chatfield was on the road, the aggrieved merchant received permission from none other than Chief Barrios to compile the pertinent documentation on the incident. A special messenger carried it to the itinerant British consul.

Upon perusing Mr. Chatfield's letter which prejudged the Kilgour case at a distance, Chief Barrios exploded with anger. Conveniently, Mr. Skinner was there to record the reaction with signed statements by witnesses. If the British consul had asked for a pardon, Barrios was heard to say, it would have been granted immediately. But Chatfield's imperious note was the last straw. The chief remarked with feeling:

> The time . . . has arrived when we must understand if we are a nation or not. If all my countrymen thought as I do, we should not have suffered what the National Government has put up with from his nation and it would be better that the English should come and hang us, or make us return to our colonial dependence, than that we should dishonour our dignity.[4]

Chatfield interpreted this statement as follows: "These people are absurd enough to fancy, that the uniform mildness and forbearance of Her Majesty's Government proceed from fear, or an inability to correct their misdoings — a notion so truly ridiculous, that the Persons who indulge it must be considered little superior in intelligence and civilisation to the Chiefs of an African tribe." Englishmen should be protected from the harassment of these people, the consul persisted: "I cannot cease to regret that none of Her Majesty's ships should be stationed upon the coast, or at least be ordered to visit it at stated periods."

The merits of the case notwithstanding, the fact remains that the evidence was one-sided and that the incident was prejudged. Frederick Chatfield placed himself above the judicial and police officials of El Salvador. Moreover, it should be noted that state authorities promised to investigate the episode. But Englishmen were impatient. Even the Foreign Office pronounced its verdict upon limited evidence. "The conduct of those authorities, upon that occasion," Lord Palmerston ruled, "appears to have been arbitrary, unjust, and oppressive; and Her Majesty's Government is entitled to insist upon satisfaction being made

---

4. *Ibid.*

to Mr. Kilgour."[5] Coming on the heels of the November 23 dispatch, Chatfield's actions on this matter appeared suspiciously deliberate.

———•◦•———

Since it raised the question of extraterritorial rights for Englishmen, the Kilgour incident understandably fired the nationalistic spirit of unionists throughout Central America. Other rumors further intensified the hostility toward Englishmen and foreigners in general — the report that Chatfield denied asylum to Mrs. Morazán, the tobacco transaction with Costa Rica and Nicaragua, and the gun-running activities of one Walter Bridge in Nicaragua. To the heated Central American mind a conspiracy was afoot to deliver the country over to the Court of Saint James. Because of this general feeling, Chatfield's life was in danger. There were Central American patriots who dreamed of ways to end the meddling consul's activities. In fact, it was claimed that the English agent had actually been stabbed by one of his enemies — a doubtful assertion since we can be sure that Chatfield would have exploited it in order to guarantee the support of the British navy.[6] And yet he recognized the danger and took precautions. Upon returning to San Salvador to pack up the consular archives in preparation for his trip to Guatemala City, the consul decided to take the circuitous water route from Acajutla to the port of Istapa, in Guatemala, rather than risk an ambush on the overland route.[7]

With bolstered morale, the *serviles* heralded the arrival of their British ally on December 18. Two days later, Chatfield met with Mariano Rivera Paz, now styled the President of Guatemala.[8] We perhaps shall never know exactly what was said at this meeting and who participated in it. But, in the light of subsequent events, there can be little doubt that the allies discussed their common enemy and the tactics which they would employ to thwart him.

By the 20th, the situation confronting the allies was as follows. The Nicaraguan government which sent out the circular of November 27 had already fallen from power, and its successor was pursuing a cautious policy. The real danger was that Nicaragua might join the *Morazanistas* at a convention controlled by unionists. Costa Rica, because of its offside position, would perhaps remain neutral. The British consul had no assurances as yet from the San José government that it had rejected

5. From Palmerston, No. 7, July 15, 1840, F.O. 15/23.
6. From Pedro Negrete, April 10, 1840, F.O. 252/14.
7. To Palmerston, No. 38, December 24, 1839, F.O. 15/22.
8. *El Tiempo* (Guatemala), No. 60, December 21, 1839, A.G.N.G.

unionist recommendations. With regard to Honduras, it seemed fairly certain that Ferrera's influence would work against any reconciliation with El Salvador, especially since Morazán was insisting upon reparations for the two invasions earlier in the year. To commit these three states to their cause, or at least assure themselves of their neutrality, the allies considered propaganda measures as well as the threat and use of the British navy.

With regard to the unionist states, the following strategy was out-lined. For his part, Chatfield promised to launch a claims campaign against El Salvador which inevitably would bring him naval support. He would implement, as it were, the strategy he had hinted at in the Novem-ber 23 dispatch. The Kilgour claim was a promising one, and there would be others. To frighten the Salvadorean government, he would also send copies of the dispatches, listing the claims, to at least three Pacific ports — Realejo, Acajutla, and La Unión — along with a letter to the commander of any British ship which might call there.[9] Unques-tionably Salvadorean officials would intercept one of these letters and thus learn that a naval force was on its way to protect British interests. This sobering fact presumably would make General Morazán think twice about attacking the *serviles* in Guatemala. The claims campaign, therefore, had a double-barreled purpose — first, it was to be used as psychological warfare against El Salvador; and, secondly, to commit the Foreign Office to forceful intervention in Central America. The *serviles,* on the other hand, would encourage subversive elements in the neighboring state to hamper any invasion plans which Morazán might entertain.[10]

More ambitious and daring, however, were the tactics outlined for the State of Los Altos. Here the allies were clearly prepared to risk war with the unionists. Certain developments help to explain the abandon-ment of the *serviles'* peace policy. To begin with, all members of the alliance desired the destruction of Los Altos. Chatfield, for his part, resented the Quezaltenango Treaty, and was determined to get a retrac-tion, regardless of the means he might have to use. In fact, this objective had become an obsession with him. Rafael Carrera also had his own personal reasons for wishing the downfall of Los Altos — the scene of the humiliating truce with General Guzmán, by which he was compelled to turn over three hundred and twenty muskets on January 23, 1839. Quezaltenango, moreover, was the haven of Guatemalan *liberales* who

9. To the Captain of Her Britannic Majesty's Ship at Realejo, La Unión, Aca-jutla, January 11, 1840, F.O. 252/8.
10. Auguste Mahelin to Minister of Foreign Affairs (Molé), January 10, 1840, A.A.E.P./CPAC, vol. 3.

continually insisted upon calling him an *"antropófago,"* which his more literate advisors told him meant "cannibal." This made him angry. The *serviles,* as their English ally, were especially sensitive to the barbed editorials in *El Popular,* which criticized their relations with the British consulate and which scored the bills passed by the Constituent Assembly of Guatemala as a return to the obscurantism of the colonial period.[11] In addition, they could never reconcile themselves to the highlands' secession, particularly because the establishment of an effective Central American republic was closely related to the survival of Los Altos.

Psychologically the allies were therefore ready to commit themselves to an aggressive stand. But more than this was needed. After all, there was still the factor of Morazán's invincibility in military affairs, which could not be shrugged off lightly. The allies' belligerent posture can be explained by the arrival of an arms shipment in Guatemala City sometime in late November, or early December.[12] Ironically, the thousand rifles in question belonged to the government of Los Altos, who had ordered them from Belize. But Guatemala intercepted the guns and refused to permit them to reach their destination. With these arms in their possession, it is to be noted that Guatemalans adopted a most aggressive tone toward the Quezaltenango government. On December 5, Carrera threatened to take action against the abusive articles in the highland press; at the same time he demanded the return of the rifles which he had given General Guzmán. And on the 18th — the day Chatfield arrived in Guatemala City — a Los Altos envoy was pressured into signing a treaty of friendship with Guatemala. Rather than a treaty, it might be more accurate to call it an ultimatum for it contained an article demanding the return of Carrera's guns. Furthermore, Los Altos was given thirty-five days in which to ratify the treaty, or until January 23, 1840.[13] As far as it is known, Frederick Chatfield had nothing to do with Carrera's threat or the treaty itself. Later, the ex-governor of Los Altos, Marcelo Molina, accused him of preventing the arms shipment from proceeding to the highlands.[14] Actually, as we have seen, the Guatemalan government was responsible for this; by his silence, however, the English consul sanctioned the act.

Precisely on the date of his interview with Rivera Paz, Chatfield

11. *El Popular* (Quezaltenango), No. 18, December 4, 1839, B.N.G./V, leg. 836.
12. *El Tiempo* (Guatemala), No. 52, November 27, 1839.
13. Treaty, Guatemala and Los Altos, Guatemala City, December 18, 1839, B.N.G./HS, 1839.
14. Marcelo Molina, *Esposición a la convención de los Estados Centro-Americanos protestando contra la Usurpación de los Altos* (Mexico, 1841), p. 14, T.P.C.G.

listed for Palmerston the first instalment of claims which eventually brought on the British blockades of the early 1840's.[15] Except for their use in psychological warfare — to frighten the enemy and bolster the courage of his allies — these claims were more important for their long-range effects. They established, as it were, a pattern for the future. It should be noted, moreover, that Chatfield strained hard to find legitimate claims against El Salvador and that, as a matter of fact, he had better claims against his own allies. For example, in January, 1840, he purposely refused to advance the San Jerónimo claims of Marshall Bennett, though he resurrected them at a later date when he began to have trouble with the Guatemalan government.[16] The pattern of pushing claims and then dropping them — a common occurrence in a later period — confirmed the fact that he was using the claim technique as a political weapon, pure and simple.

In describing the various claims presented in the two dispatches of December 20, 1839, we should keep in mind Lord Palmerston's observations about them for they help to demonstrate the effectiveness of Chatfield's technique.[17] As already noted, the Foreign Office had pronounced favorably upon the Kilgour claim. In addition, Mr. Chatfield advanced a series of claims involving the interests of a Canadian (Frederick Lesperance), a Jamaican (Richard MacNally), a North American (William Barchard), and Marshall Bennett.[18] Except for the "old rascal," these men had all assumed Central American citizenship in order to gain special favors from the government, a point which the consul minimized. In his opinion, no Englishman, or British subject, could ever give up his nationality — a basic assumption in his presentation of claims which raised still another nationalistic principle to frustrate his adversaries.

Mr. Lesperance had two claims against the Salvadorean government: one, a forced loan of fifty dollars; and second, a voluntary loan of one-thousand dollars. In the first case, Chatfield argued his version of forced loans, while Palmerston again rejected it and stated that under certain conditions forced loans were valid. In the second case, there appeared to be a misunderstanding concerning the liquidation of an i.o.u. The Canadian insisted that Morazán had promised to pay it *in toto* at the indigo fairs; whereas Salvadorean officials maintained that it could

---

15. To Palmerston, Nos. 34-35, December 20, 1839, F.O. 15/22.
16. To Domingo Knoth, January 6, 1840, F.O. 252/9.
17. From Palmerston, No. 7, July 15, 1840, F.O. 15/23.
18. To Palmerston, No. 34, December 20, 1839, F.O. 15/22.

be used in paying duties — the liquidation, in other words, would be gradual. As far as Chatfield was concerned, however, this was a clear case of "swindling." Nowhere does he indicate the Salvadorean view; and Palmerston correctly pointed out that the facts presented were insufficient to judge the matter.

The MacNally claim, which involved a forced loan levied on August 11, 1839, is a good example of one taken out of context and charged with such patriotic fervor that the Foreign Office had little alternative but to support it. It graphically demonstrates the consul's political orientation, as well as the dearth of claims available to him. In the enclosures, one can read the insulting remarks of Central Americans concerning England and her people which convinced Lord Palmerston that the MacNally case was truly "an act of extortion and oppression committed on a British subject." The Foreign Office would support this particular claim. As a matter of fact, Palmerston's verdict was fair and justified, regardless of how one interprets the documentation. But — and this is the tragic part of this case — the guilty parties who extorted money from MacNally and said such nasty things about England and Englishmen were the Honduran invaders under General Francisco Ferrera, not the Salvadorean government of General Morazán. If the Foreign Office had caught him in this distortion — and they could have done it if they had bothered to translate the enclosures — Chatfield undoubtedly would have argued that since it happened on Salvadorean soil the responsibility still rested with that state.

The claims of William Henry Barchard and Marshall Bennett likewise revealed political motivation. Ironically, both of them dated back to the late 1820's when the so-called "intrusive government" of President Arce and the Guatemalan *serviles* was in control. In either case, the documentation, as Lord Palmerston noted, was vague and inadequate.

To this initial series of claims which sparked the decision to assign British warships to Central American duty, the English consul added more legitimate claims that arose from the agitation and civil war during the early months of 1840. Of course, he did not reveal to the Foreign Office his personal contribution to the hostile climate of opinion which placed the lives of Englishmen in jeopardy. In reviewing these new claims, Lord Palmerston tried to be eminently fair, indicating the cases in which the evidence was insufficient. With consistency, Palmerston maintained that forced loans, providing they were general and not discriminatory, were an attribute of sovereignty; and Englishmen therefore had to contribute to them. In one case, involving a second claim for MacNally — an unsolicited one, as it turned out — "Old Pam" lost his temper. "You acted improperly," he said, "in taking up a case in which it appears that your assistance was neither requested nor desired."[19]

Still the fact remains that Frederick Chatfield succeeded in committing the Foreign Office to support his political designs even though London authorities believed that they were merely protecting British life and property. Without knowing it, in other words, England had been committed to her representative's imperialistic policy in Central America. And Lord Palmerston unwittingly made this possible by the leeway he gave his consul in the instructions of July 15, 1840. Frederick Chatfield was allowed to be both judge and jury in determining whether a forced loan was discriminatory or not. And it was the evidence which he compiled that served as the basis for action. It is significant, moreover, that Lord Palmerston had definitely placed the navy at the consul's disposal. The following instructions gave Chatfield the opportunity to wield a big stick in the internal affairs of Central America, attesting to the success of his program:

> I have accordingly to desire that you will examine carefully into the complaints made by British subjects, and that you will satisfy yourself of the justice of their claims. You will then prepare a written statement, setting forth the whole of the claims which you may consider yourself authorized, under these instructions, to lay before the Central American authorities.
>
> You will transmit that statement to the ruling authorities of Central America in an official note, explaining therein that you do so by order of your government whose duty it is to protect the persons and property of Her Majesty's Subjects, and who must see that justice be done to them. You will state that Her Majesty's Government has ordered the Commanders of Her Majesty's Naval Forces in the West Indies and in the Pacific to support the just claims of British subjects and you will accordingly put yourself into communication with those officers upon this subject.
>
> It is desirable also that you should communicate unreservedly with Her Majesty's Superintendent at Belize, who will be instructed to afford you every assistance in his power in bringing these matters to a satisfactory conclusion.[20]

◄━●━►

Of more importance, in the immediate scheme of affairs, was the action taken against Los Altos. Since mid-1839, the Quezaltenango government was a thorn in the allies' side, especially because of the comments of exiled Guatemalans in the highlands' press. José Francisco

---

19. From Palmerston, June 8, 1840, F.O. 15/23; to Palmerston, No. 37, December 23, 1839, F.O. 15/22.
20. From Palmerston, No. 7, July 15, 1840, F.O. 15/23.

Barrundia's remarks of August 3, on the repeal of the Belize clause, marked the beginning of a polemic between Chatfield and the Los Altos government. The consul complained, in a letter of September 3, 1839, of articles eight and nine in the treaty with El Salvador; and in subsequent letters, he raised all the same points which had come out in his various interviews with General Morazán. Los Altos, like the Salvadorean government, insisted steadfastly upon the conditional nature of the treaty, the existence of the federal government, and the temporary assumption of federal prerogatives. But Chatfield would not listen; and on November 28, he demanded the repeal of the offensive articles, expecting to receive such a retraction upon his return to Guatemala City. When he arrived in Guatemala, however, he found no envoy there from the highlands to bow humbly before him. On the contrary, Los Altos did not choose to answer Chatfield's ultimatum until January 3, 1840.[21]

The allies' decision to adopt violent measures against the highland state was also prompted by the criticism in the Quezaltenango press concerning Nicaragua's circular of November 27, 1839, and the steps taken subsequently by the Los Altos legislature. As might be expected, *El Popular* had some uncomplimentary things to say about the circular and its sponsors:

> The important island of Ruatán has been snatched away from us; practically all of the territory from Belize to the Petén has been usurped from us. A claim has been advanced to the entire country of the Mosquitos. The British consul Chatfield treats our National Government with contempt and even insolence, so unbearable to our patriotism; and this man is chosen to serve as the agent of our submission and as our solicitor in winning the concession of intervention by his cabinet! This agent, public enemy of America, advocate of the most anti-American and servile sentiments, special adversary of our nationality and of the republic of our country, and particularly and personally [the foe] of the Federal Executive, has broken relations without notice, has left the country; such is the nature of the man in charge of this wretched intrigue on the part of the savage faction in Guatemala, with which he is abundantly sympathetic in hating America's emancipation as well as all her institutions. A worthy and genuine instrument of our vandals, it is said that through his agency magnificent gifts have been given to the savage [Carrera], English armaments have been provided him, and foreign intervention has been agreed upon in order to support him against the party of *nacionalidad* and of the constitution. This public rumor is confirmed by the present appeal — a stupid and humiliating one — to this British consul by Nicaragua, request-

---

21. "Con la mira de que la cuestión....," 1840, T.P.C.G.; also enclosed in No. 5, to Palmerston, January 29, 1840, F.O. 15/23.

ing him to carry out the great diplomatic move and to place us in all respects under the yoke of his Government.[22]

The state government of Los Altos shared this opinion of the Nicaraguan circular, judging from the report of a special commission on the 21st of December.[23] Ten days later, the legislature passed two decrees which were signed into law on January 1, 1840, by Governor Molina. Except for one article, Chatfield failed to reproduce these decrees for the Foreign Office; and this omission was indeed significant for, in effect, it denied his superiors in London an insight into the ideological issues at stake. Article one of the first decree (number sixty) rejected the Nicaraguan proposal; and article two authorized the governor to propose a settlement of all differences between the states at the impending convention. By omitting this second clause, Chatfield continued his distortion of the convention issue. He did, however, reproduce the third article of the decree which urged the governor of Los Altos to encourage his counterparts in other states to enact a boycott against British goods until England returned the island of Ruatán. According to the terms of this article, the government would publish the answers received from the various states. Obviously the men who approved of this measure were anglophobes.

The second decree of January 1, 1840, which the British consul ignored — at least as far as its reproduction was concerned — evoked the "Western Hemisphere Idea." It read as follows:

> The Constituent Assembly of the State of Los Altos, sensitive to the outrages inflicted upon some American Republics and considering that without alliances, which are the only recourse of the weak against the strong, all American States are exposed to and can expect a similar fate, has decided it proper to decree and does decree:
>
> Article 1. The Executive will instruct the State's representatives to the National Convention to promote there without delay an initiative for a treaty with all the governments of the American Continent, in which it should be stipulated that when a foreign government hostilizes any of the new republics the rest of them should close their ports to it.
>
> Article 2. He shall also instruct them to initiate another agreement which should promote the reunion of the great American Diet which was installed in Panamá but which could not continue its sessions in Tacubaya.[24]

---

22. *El Popular* (Quezaltenango), No. 20, December 30, 1839, B.N.G./V, leg. 836.
23. Commission's Report to Asamblea Constituyente de Los Altos, Quezaltenango, December 21, 1839, B.N.G./HS, 1840.
24. Decrees, Quezaltenango, December 31, 1839, B.N.G./HS, 1840.

Copies of these two decrees reached Guatemala City by January 18 at the latest; considering their content, we can safely assume that they were received there by January 8. Dispatches usually took three to four days to travel that distance.

Annoyed by such decrees — and working from a position of strength — the allies in Guatemala City began to exert pressure upon the recalcitrant highlanders. The Indians of Los Altos, at the instigation of Guatemalan agents, were encouraged to bring their petitions to Guatemala City, as they had done for centuries. And Carrera was especially active in preparing them for rebellion against the Quezaltenango government.[25] On December 27, the "man" Carrera issued another proclamation which incited the Indians to rise against their oppressors — a move unquestionably sanctioned by the *serviles* to force Los Altos' commitment to the treaty of December 18.[26] On January 1, 1840, the day in which Governor Molina signed into law the two decrees mentioned above, he complained officially of Carrera's recent threat. Given these belligerent remarks, it would be folly for Los Altos to disarm herself by returning the three hundred and twenty rifles to General Carrera. In fact, Molina noted, under the terms of the Guzmán pact Carrera was still obligated to turn over an additional six hundred guns. To show his peaceful inclinations, however, the highlands' governor proposed that the matter of the guns be submitted to arbitration — a remarkable concession in the light of subsequent Guatemalan charges that Los Altos was planning aggression against them.

Singularly unimpressed with Molina's letter, Guatemala parried his complaint with the facetious remark that Carrera was speaking for himself and that this was the result of freedom of the press within her borders — an allusion to Los Altos' unwillingness to muzzle the Guatemalan exiles in the Quezaltenango press. Moreover, in a letter of January 8, there was the strong implication that if Los Altos did not ratify the treaty of friendship by the 23rd Guatemala would not be responsible for the consequences — a not too subtle threat that she would unleash the "Barbarian."[27] The implication was not wasted; Los Altos immediately alerted her ally in El Salvador.

---

25. Molina, *Esposición,* p. 17.

26. Rafael Carrera to the Inhabitants of the State, Guatemala, December 27, 1839, B.N.G./HS, 1839.

27. Auguste Mahelin to Minister of Foreign Affairs, No. 48, p. encl. (an anonymous tract published in Costa Rica, October 3, 1840), January 8, 1841, A.A.E.P./CPAC, vol. 3; also see Guatemala to Los Altos, January 8, 1840, in *El Tiempo,* No. 71, January 24, 1840, which in turn is enclosed in No. 3, to Palmerston, January 25, 1840, F.O. 15/23.

At the same time, the consul's correspondence with Los Altos deteriorated to the point of no return. On January 3, the highlanders replied firmly to Chatfield's strong November letter and repeated their stand on the various questions posed. Since he was only a consul, the government of Los Altos suggested that the matters in dispute were none of his business; therefore, it could no longer entertain further correspondence with him on those subjects. It is not difficult to imagine the explosion which rocked the British consulate in Guatemala City when those lines were read. On January 13, an irritated English agent cited the book and verse of international law which authorized consuls to serve as political functionaries. He was authorized therefore to conduct such a correspondence with the Los Altos government. Articles eight and nine of the Quezaltenango Treaty, he reminded the highlanders, were insults to Queen Victoria's government; he wanted them repealed immediately. For this purpose, he enclosed a draft of a retraction which would be acceptable to him.[28] In a second dispatch of the same date, which was not reproduced for the Foreign Office, Chatfield warned Los Altos that failure to sign the retraction would lead to punishment. He noted subtly that England "has many allies upon whose cooperation she can count in a matter of this kind."[29] Was Chatfield also threatening to unleash Carrera, just as the *serviles* had done five days earlier? Los Altos, at least, had little doubt that armed action was imminent, despite assurances from Guatemala City, as late as the 20th, that Carrera and company would not march up to the highlands.[30]

Events moved swiftly toward their climax in the second and third weeks of January. Los Altos' letter to General Morazán, which alerted El Salvador to the impending aggression of Guatemalans, was intercepted by Carrera's forces and served to raise the alarm that unionists were planning an invasion of Guatemala. From the 18th to the 22nd, both Chatfield and the *serviles* received negative answers to their respective ultimatums. And on the 20th, Carrera left Guatemala City. His forces invaded Los Altos on the 24th, ravaging the countryside and despoiling the capital city of Quezaltenango.[31] Within a week's time, the Los Altos government disappeared from the pages of history — the victim of an Englishman's rancor, a political faction's ambition to rule, and the revenge of an Indian caudillo.

Overjoyed at the results of their "machiavellian" policy — inciden-

28. "Con la mira . . ." (footnote 21).
29. To Secretario General de Los Altos, January 13, 1840, F.O. 252/13.
30. Mahelin's No. 48 (January 8, 1841).
31. Molina, *Esposición,* p. 17; "Informe," Mariano Rivera Paz, July 14, 1840, B.N.G./HS, 1840.

tally, an adjective used by the French consul — the *serviles* honored their Indian hero with the title of "Illustrious Protector of Los Altos."[32] No one seriously questioned who the aggressor had been in the highlands campaign; in fact, Governor Rivera Paz later admitted it even though he tried to justify it on the ground of self defense. Presumably his government had received definite information concerning unionist plans to invade Guatemala.[33]

Carrera's action in Los Altos meant that war with General Morazán was inevitable — a risk which the allies had accepted back in December, 1839. In the circumstances, more arms and ammunition were needed to defend Guatemala City. Significantly, on the 25th of January, while Carrera was marching through Los Altos, Frederick Chatfield sent an urgent letter to Colonel Macdonald. Aware of the fact that there were no longer any guns for sale in the British establishment, Chatfield asked the superintendent to send him from two to five hundred muskets from the militia stores.[34] This request for arms, coming when it did, implicated the English consul in the political developments outlined above.

Just as Rafael Carrera was completing his invasion of the highlands, Chatfield wrote his first report to Lord Palmerston on the lengthy correspondence with the State of Los Altos. He had published most of this correspondence in order to counteract a similar publication by the highland government.[35] As we have already noted, there were key omissions in the consul's version of the correspondence. In addition, he neglected to translate portions of the adversary's answers, thus further distorting the crucial Los Altos story. And, unfortunately, the Foreign Office was not interested in translating those sections of the correspondence.

In late March, 1840, the consul wrote up the final instalment on the events in Los Altos. It was simply a matter of Carrera's march up to the highlands; and after "faint resistance, he succeeded in putting down the opponents of this Government and in restoring to the Indian population their ancient customs and mode of government." The Indians were beside themselves with gratitude; Chatfield explained: "The refusal of the Indians to obey any government but this had produced the dissolution of the State of the Altos, and has caused its reincorporation with Guatemala." After all, there was no point in confusing the Foreign

---

32. Mahelin's No. 48 (January 8, 1841).

33. "Informe," Rivera Paz, July 14, 1840, B.N.G./HS, 1840.

34. To Macdonald, pvt. and conf., January 25, 1840, F.O. 252/15.

35. To Palmerston, No. 5, January 29, 1840; "Con la mira . . . ," footnote 21; Mahelin to Molé, No. 27, January 25, 1840, A.A.E.P./CPAC, vol. 3.

Office with facts; it was a tedious job to translate all those documents. And since the highland state no longer existed, Chatfield concluded sagely, it would no longer be necessary to have "any further correspondence with the Altos on the subject of the Treaty between Salvador and the Altos of August last."[36] That falls of its own weight, as the old Spanish saying goes.

Those were the highlights of Los Altos' demise, a little-known yet crucial episode in the chain of events which brought about the death of the unionist movement in 1840. And Frederick Chatfield, Her Majesty's consul in Central America, played an active part in the young state's disappearance.

———●◆●———

Small wonder that the British consul was a *persona non grata* among unionists in Central America, and especially in El Salvador, once the Los Altos news reached there. Everyone associated with him in the slightest way was watched carefully and his mail censored to prevent the forwarding of information to Guatemala City. Chatfield, in turn, protested against these anti-espionage measures and complained about the offensive remarks made in the Salvadorean press. That was more than freedom of the press, it was libel. And he felt that the government should punish the offenders. All this, he assured Lord Palmerston, stemmed from sheer vindictiveness on the part of the *Morazanistas* for he had never given them cause for such actions.[37]

Not only Englishmen but foreigners in general suffered from Chatfield's provocative statements and actions concerning El Salvador. Resentful of this, Auguste Mahelin instructed his vice-consul in San Salvador, Pablo Negrete, not to represent English subjects as he had been empowered to do by Chatfield before the latter's departure from the former capital of the Republic.[38] Furthermore, the French consul observed, the

---

36. To Palmerston, No. 13, March 24, 1840, F.O. 15/23.

37. See, for example, No. 6, to Palmerston, February 5, 1840, F.O. 15/23; also, from Marcos Idígoras, May 1, 1840, F.O. 252/24; to Palmerston, No. 17, p. encl.s, April 1, 1840, F.O. 15/23.

   On one occasion, John Lloyd Stephens, a famous American author and archaelogist who at the time was on a special mission for his government, was imposed upon while traveling in El Salvador to carry some letters to Chatfield. Later, he told his English colleague: "I was aware there you were no great favorite with the men of St. Salvador and thought that if some roving 'militares' should take the liberty of examining my trunks, letters from you would not be particularly useful to me." Then, jostling Chatfield, he added, "You must give up the Belize and that valuable island of Roatán and bring us all back into favor." (From Stephens, March 28, 1840, F.O. 252/24.)

38. Mahelin to Morazán, February 13, 1840, B.N.G./HS, 1840; Mahelin to Molé, No. 30, February 21, 1840, A.A.E.P./CPAC, vol. 3.

British agent seemed determined to provoke Salvadoreans to drastic action rather than to relieve the general hostility toward foreigners.[39] Thus English claims against the government proliferated during this period and especially in connection with William Kilgour and Richard MacNally, both of whom were suspected of spying for Chatfield — a correct suspicion, incidentally.[40]

And it was no coincidence that the abuses inflicted upon English subjects paralleled, and were in response to, the provocative actions of the British agent in Guatemala City. On January 24, 1840, for example, Chatfield and his allies published the recent correspondence with El Salvador on the freedom-of-the-press issue. The Salvadorean government, on the other hand, steadfastly maintained the cherished principle, while liberal writers — stimulated by Chatfield's complaints — advised him facetiously to seek redress for libel in the local courts.[41]

In preparation for the invasion of Guatemala — the inevitable consequence of Carrera's attack on Los Altos — General Morazán levied a forced loan of 30,000 dollars. The British consul immediately protested that Englishmen could not be compelled to contribute to such a loan. On January 28, therefore, the state legislature proposed a law, signed five days later by Governor Morazán, advising foreigners that if they failed to pay their share of the loan the government would be unable to protect them. They should therefore wind up their affairs and leave the state within eight days.[42] Chatfield objected, and was determined to make every English contribution a prospective claim against the state. In theory, Lord Palmerston again disagreed with him; but, in practice, since he allowed his underling to determine whether or not a forced loan was discriminatory, the consul had his way. The British navy was brought in to collect the claims that Chatfield raised as a result of the Salvadorean law of January 28-February 2, 1840.

Without question, Frederick Chatfield bore a considerable portion of the responsibility for the anti-foreigner movement in the first three months of 1840. He was by no means a disinterested party in the power struggle between *Morazanistas* and *serviles*. In fact, it might be argued that he was the recognized leader of the states' rights movement during this period, publishing all manner of correspondence to discredit El

---

39. *Ibid.*
40. From Richard MacNally, February 6, 1840, F.O. 252/24.
41. *El Tiempo* (Guatemala), No. 71, January 24, 1840, in No. 3, to Palmerston, January 25, 1840, F.O. 15/23.
42. Decree of El Salvador, Cojutepeque, January 28, 1840, signed by Francisco Morazán on February 2, 1840, *El Tiempo*, No. 77, February 16, 1840, B.N.G./V, leg. 837; to Palmerston, No. 8, February 15, 1840, F.O. 15/23.

Salvador and to win the support of the uncommitted states of Central America.[43] More important perhaps, these various publications demonstrated to the three states in question that Mr. Chatfield, and thus the British nation, was leading the challenge against Morazán. And the Carrera action in Los Altos was conclusive evidence that the consul and the *serviles* had decided to bring down Morazán by force, if need be.

Typical of the propaganda sent to the uncommitted states was an article of March 13, which Chatfield instructed John Foster to circulate in Nicaragua. It presented an idyllic picture of life in Guatemala, where the cause of the states prevailed in the hearts of all citizens. Carrera's influence was benevolent; the Indians loved him and they were well-disciplined; and the "Illustrious Protector of Los Altos" commanded the allegiance of an excellent officers' corps and could raise any number of troops when he so desired. All segments of society were well-treated and happy — proprietors, the clergy, foreigners; in short, all respectable people. As for the convention of the states, there had been delays; and it was doubtful that it would take place "while Morazán is around as a political figure." Where he might strike first, no one was sure; it might be Nicaragua, or Honduras, or even Guatemala. But if he tried it in Guatemala, he would have trouble.[44] This clever article exuded enthusiasm and strength in order to win over the states of Nicaragua and Honduras.

The unionist cause had its able propagandists as well. The talented pen of José Francisco Barrundia, who moved to San Salvador after the fall of Los Altos, appealed to the nationalism and common sense of Nicaraguans and Hondurans in such articles as *"Die Talum Advertite Cassus,"* or "God will not condone such a tragedy." Beware of the acts of "the stranger," and of European agents who are determined to frustrate the advance of liberalism and Americanism in the New World, obliging "us to solicit their protection and to reduce us once more to the degrading condition of colonists." He went on to explain:

> Without question we owe to them the present savage insurrection, the rupture of the National Unity, and the disunion of our best citizens. The work is near its conclusion, and whether it be in consequence of Mediators, or whether it be by exacting reparation for pretended insults of this or that state, or called in by the liberticide sellers of their country, who take refuge in Guatemala, it is prob-

---

43. Pedro Negrete to Chatfield, printed correspondence, San Salvador, February 1, 1840, B.N.G./HS, 1840; *El Tiempo,* No. 71, January 24, 1840, enclosed in No. 3 to Palmerston, January 25, 1840, F.O. 15/23.

44. "Noticia del Estado Político de Guatemala," March 13, 1840, F.O. 252/21.

able that very soon the daring footsteps of European Conquerors
will plant themselves again on our shores.[45]

In an effort to bring unity against the common enemy, El Salvador
wrote a letter to Nicaragua, intended also for the perusal of Honduras.
Fortunately, Chatfield rescued this document from oblivion and copied it
"to shew, that the attacks against Great Britain, and the bitterness mani-
fested towards me by the Salvadorean authorities, originated in feelings
of hatred and disappointment that I would not lend myself to the incon-
sistencies of a desperate and unprincipled faction."[46] For our purposes,
the most interesting sections of this letter, dated February 26, 1840, are
those which Chatfield chose not to translate for the Foreign Office, again
obscuring the ideological basis for the political struggles of Central
America.

In the translated portions of the letter, the Salvadorean minister
reviewed the military relations between his state and Nicaragua, commented upon Nicaragua's error in proposing a British guarantee of the
peace, and referred to the disgraceful and humiliating threats of the
English consul. Moreover, he warned the Supreme Director of Nicaragua that some day England would covet his state since it possessed the
logical route for the "Great Oceanic Canal." He should therefore ponder
these facts and recall "passed events." The translation ended at this
point. In the following section, the minister explained what he meant by
"passed events": how the *serviles,* in 1821, had favored annexation to
Mexico and the preservation of "hereditary distinctions," and how, in
1826, they had sided with President Arce in a civil war against the "independent party." "What would have become of the Republic then," he
asked, "if the three states of Nicaragua, Honduras, and Salvador had
not been allies?" Then he reminded the Nicaraguan government that
Guatemala had deprived Los Altos of her independence and sovereignty,
a matter which could not be overlooked by a defender of "the Sovereignty of the States." At this point, Chatfield renewed the translation: "It
is necessary that Honduras and Nicaragua disabuse themselves. Their
alliance with the actual Government of Guatemala is not a natural nor
a convenient one for them. The families who influence there tend either
to govern the republic for their own sake, or through the intermediary
of a powerful nation."

The second omission was even more significant, for it recognized
the importance of Los Altos in the reformation of the old republic:

45. "Die Talum Advertite Cassus," Cojutepeque, February 24, 1840, in No. 19,
to Palmerston, April 4, 1840, F.O. 15/23.
46. To Palmerston, No. 28, May 8, 1840, F.O. 15/23.

All states were in favor of the division of Guatemala and the establishment of Los Altos in order to minimize the excessive influence of the former. Can it be possible that now they approve of the forceful incorporation of the latter? Such an act gives one-half of the population and resources of all the Republic to Guatemala. What equilibrium or counterweight can there be found in the rest of the states if instead of uniting they weaken themselves by hostilizing each other.

And in the concluding section, part of which was translated, El Salvador offered to drop her claims against Honduras for the Ferrera invasions of the previous year — a significant concession which might have united the three states of Central America against the allies in Guatemala City.[47]

In a sense, the propaganda effort was superfluous. Nicaragua and Honduras waited cautiously for the results of the military campaign, ready to jump over to the winning side. They did just that when they learned of Morazán's defeat on March 19. With bravado, they committed themselves to the cause of the states and volunteered their arms to oust the hated enemy from Central America's soil. And, of course, they refused to believe the terrible things which had been said about England and her conscientious representative, Frederick Chatfield.[48] José Bustillos, the Honduran minister of war, excelled as a sycophant. Later, when the pesky liberals resurged to power in Honduras, Bustillos requested English citizenship. But, despite Chatfield's support, the Foreign Office rejected the petition on technical grounds — Bustillos could not assume English citizenship from that distance.[49]

Perhaps to salve his conscience, the British consul went out of his way to collect favorable expressions of opinion in order to prove that the good people of Honduras and Nicaragua had refused to believe the falsehoods about Great Britain:

To me personally this impartial testimony is of value, since it enables me to afford Your Lordship a sure proof, that the exceeding bitterness of the Salvador government against me, is unmerited, and that its calumnious language towards Great Britain has been used advisedly, to promote the lowest party purposes.[50]

---

47. El Salvador to Nicaragua, February 25, 1840, in No. 28 to Palmerston.
48. Ministerio de Relaciones (Nicaragua) to Ministro General del Gobierno (El Salvador), March 21, 1840, *El Tiempo* (Guatemala), No. 95, May 9, 1840, B.N.G./V, leg. 837; enclosures on Honduras are in No. 22, to Palmerston, April 7, 1840, F.O. 15/23.
49. To Palmerston, No. 40, p. encl.s, December 15, 1840, F.O. 15/23; from José Bustillos, March 21 and April 29, 1840, F.O. 252/14.
50. To Palmerston, No. 22, April 7, 1840, F.O. 15/23.

While it is true that the Foreign Office was committed to a program of naval support, we must remember that Chatfield had not received these assurances in the early part of 1840. A constant theme in all his dispatches, therefore, was the demand for naval support against those who flagrantly insulted Queen Victoria's government. In the meantime, he sent copies of the claims dispatches to three Pacific ports in hopes that Admiral Ross had acted upon his request for a warship. And, during the Los Altos' campaign, he asked Belize for arms — a request which Macdonald regretted he could not fulfill "without laying ourselves open to censure and animadversion from home."[51] Then, in February and March, Chatfield also sent several articles for publication to the *Belize Advertiser*. Employing the same arguments that the consul had used in previous dispatches to Lord Palmerston, the jingoistic selections called for British naval action and direct intervention in Central American affairs.[52] In short, every conceivable pressure group was encouraged to petition the Foreign Office to support the British consul with warships — Belize, Skinner-Klee and Reid-Irving interests, and the English Bondholders' Association. And Chatfield's campaign bore fruit.

On March 13, Salvadorean forces crossed the Guatemalan border. At the time, Chatfield was in Escuintla, some twenty leagues from Guatemala City. Although warned by friends that the *Morazanistas* would find some excuse to eliminate him if they found him in the capital, the consul hurried back to Guatemala City to inspire confidence among his allies and to protect his countrymen.[53] Upon his arrival, on the 16th, he wrote to Colonel Macdonald asking him to put on a "demonstration" on the Atlantic coast in order to show Morazán that England meant business.[54] Perhaps the letter's main objective was to stiffen the backbones of his allies, trembling at the thought of matching wits with the great Morazán. Be that as it may, the defense strategy of the *serviles* left nothing to be desired. If Carrera was responsible for it, then indeed he had native military ability; but the plans bear the marks of a professional. Could it be that Frederick Chatfield worked out the defense strategy? He was no slouch in military matters, it will be recalled. The documents, however, are silent on this point.

For some twenty-odd hours, starting on the 18th and ending on the 19th, Guatemala City experienced a genuine military engagement, not

51. From Macdonald, March 3, 1840, F.O. 252/8.
52. Auguste Mahelin to Molé, No. 35, p. encl.s (*Belize Advertiser*, No. 75, February 29, No. 77, March 7, Nos. 78-79, March 14, 21, 1940), April 18, 1840, A.A.E.P./CPAC, vol. 3.
53. To Palmerston, No. 12, March 23, 1840, F.O. 15/23.
54. To Macdonald, March 16, 1840, in *ibid*.

a skirmish as were most of the battles of that period. With fourteen hundred men, General Morazán marched toward the city and entered the main square without difficulty, almost as if it had been planned to allow him to do so. Then, from fortified positions around the square, the defenders caught the *Morazanistas* between two fires, while Rafael Carrera simultaneously attacked the reserve units in the rear and was soon free to reinforce the entrapment of Morazán's main body.[55]

No matter which account is consulted for the details of this famous battle, the fact emerges that General Morazán, hitherto invincible as a strategist, was out-maneuvered by the Guatemalan defenders — a terrible and final blow to his waning prestige in Central America. To be sure, he returned from exile two years later but only to meet a tragic death before a firing squad. The defeat of March 19, 1840, was a crucial turning point in the history of Central American unionism and in the career of its great leader.

According to the account of the *serviles,* Carrera's Indians, well-disciplined but poorly armed, fought valiantly during the entire engagement. On the other hand, the treacherous Morazán and some of his followers had managed to escape from the trap by a ruse, yelling "Long Live Carrera" and then sneaking away in the darkness. Providence had won the day for the forces of right; and *Te Deums* reverberated throughout the city and land of Guatemala. Such was the tableau sketched by the victors.[56]

The French consul's description of the battle seemed to be more exact and plausible. With emotion he recorded the bloody orgies and vindictive actions of the Indians during the fray, mitigated only occasionally by some conscientious priests. From Mahelin's account, we also learn that there was a bright moon on the night of Morazán's escape, hardly the best conditions for the alleged ruse mentioned above.[57] Strangely enough, the British consul — usually a prolific writer — had little to say about the famous battle. He merely forwarded the conservative version to London.

Perhaps we shall never know what Frederick Chatfield was doing during that key battle. But there were certain rumors about his actions which became legendary in Central America and elsewhere in the world. An English missionary, who for various reasons was not counted among the consul's friends, related this oft-told story in a book

---

55. Mahelin's No. 33, March 24, 1840.
56. To Palmerston, No. 18, p. encl. (Expedición de Morazán á la capital de Guatemala, Guatemala City, March 27, 1840), April 3, 1840, F.O. 15/23.
57. Mahelin's No. 33.

which he published. Some twelve to fifteen officers of the entrapped Salvadorean army, upon retreating from the enemy, had hidden themselves in the patio of the British consulate, near the plaza. When Carrera learned of their whereabouts — some say that Chatfield informed him — he ordered the consul to release them into his custody. Chatfield agreed to do so but only upon the condition that the prisoners be tried legally. Carrera said *sí*. But no sooner were the men taken into the street, they were shot down without any further ado.[58] A garbled version of this story, putting Chatfield in even a worse light, appeared in the *New York Herald* in 1845. While Carrera was liquidating the prisoners, the British consul was allegedly reading "his favorite Chapter of Ezekiel in a large Bible, a yard square which belonged to his mother's father, a preacher."[59]

◆◆◆

"Eternal glory to the invincible caudillo General Carrera," blared the victory edition of *El Tiempo*.[60] And after the battle, Carrera's forces joined with the states' righters of Nicaragua and Honduras to chase the remnants of the liberal army into exile. They succeeded by mid-April, 1840. Meanwhile, the victorious armies surrounded the Salvadorean capital and forced terms upon the new government which disavowed the actions of its predecessor and promised to exclude *Morazanistas* from public office. The mop-up campaign, followed anxiously by the British consul, was expeditiously carried out.[61]

Apparently upset by the traumatic experience of March 18-19, Frederick Chatfield sought to convince himself that his actions had not been morally wrong. He wrote these revealing lines to the Honduran government on April 18:

> The conduct of England from the earliest period of the Independence of South America of Spain has been uniformly regulated by a wish to assist the consolidation of her Power and her Commercial prosperity. It is altogether foreign to the aim of England to acquire possessions in America and to depress and weaken the New States: her true interests tend to the encouragement of their industry and to the organization on a permanent basis of their political institutions, and by an interchange of good offices to tighten the bonds of friendship which mutual interest has founded. England therefore does not as it is falsely pretended, seek to disorganize these Govts.

58. Frederick Crowe, *The Gospel in Central America* (London, 1850), p. 147.
59. *New York Herald* (New York), July 10, 1845, which contains a report from Guatemala City, dated May 15, 1845.
60. *El Tiempo* (Guatemala), No. 86, April 3, 1840, in Mahelin's No. 33.
61. Mahelin's No. 35, April 18, 1840, and No. 36, June 6, 1840; to Macdonald, May 15, 1840, F.O. 252/15.

by fomenting their intestine convulsions, but on the contrary she aims at convincing them that Peace and Tranquility are the essential foundations of National Prosperity.[62]

Chatfield seemed especially sensitive to the charge that he had connived to promote the movement for a British guarantee of the peace in Central America. To offset these rumors, he published a rebuttal in *El Tiempo* which, incidentally, he kept from the Foreign Office. The publication included his correspondence with some of the states proving that Great Britain did not favor intervention in the internal affairs of any country. The proof was indeed interesting. It consisted of an extract from Palmerston's letter of March 12, 1840 — the second refusal to accept the consul's recommendations on direct intervention. Out of context, the selection revealed an excellent statement of British nonintervention. And, of course, the English representative cleverly concealed the factors which prompted Lord Palmerston to restate Great Britain's policy — the consul's four requests for intervention in 1839.[63]

Though troubled by a guilty conscience, Chatfield could not admit to himself that he done anything wrong. In fact, the indomitable instincts of the fighter made him all the more determined to follow through on the course he had set. This was evident on April 14 when Lieutenant Robert Nichols arrived in Guatemala City, as the representative of Belizean magistrates, urging the government to respect British life and property. What annoyed the consul was the fact that the magistrates had addressed their letter to General Morazán on the assumption that he had been the victor in the recent battle. In no uncertain terms, he reprimanded them for their degrading message and their unwillingness to support him with a "demonstration," as requested on March 16.[64] Macdonald had urged forceful action, but the magistrates had outvoted him, favoring Nichol's diplomatic mission. As in the past, Chatfield's countrymen let him down again; and he was angry.

There was a brighter side to the Nichols mission, however. Macdonald's letters informed Chatfield of measures to establish a British protectorate of the Mosquito Shore. In February, 1840, the pliable Mosquito king — at Macdonald's suggestion — had appointed a special commission to govern his domains. As might be expected, the superintendent was the king's chief advisor, and other Belizean officials completed the roster of this select governing group. Incidentally, this step was taken without the authorization of the English government, another

---

62. To Honduran Government, April 8, 1840, F.O. 252/14.
63. *El Tiempo,* No. 108, June 28, 1840, A.G.N.G.
64. To Palmerston, No. 20, p. encl.s, April 6, 1840, F.O. 15/23.

fait accompli by an ambitious agent in the field. Chatfield was delighted. He later supported the project warmly in London.[65]

Thanks to the French consul, we are able to describe an interesting facet of Nichols' mission to Guatemala City. It seems that Chatfield tried to capitalize upon the lieutenant's presence by impressing the local citizenry with the fact that he had come there at his request. In other words, he could command military support whenever he wanted it. According to Mahelin, the British consul introduced Nichols to Rafael Carrera. When the discussion turned to the mop-up campaign in El Salvador, Chatfield presumably volunteered the services of four thousand Englishmen to complete the rout of Morazán and company. The "barbarian" then retorted angrily that his own forces were adequate and that he did not need the help of foreign soldiers and officers.[66] If the story is true, Frederick Chatfield had been humiliated in the presence of Guatemala's leaders. The "man," catapulted to prominence as an instrument of the *serviles,* was fast becoming an end in himself. More than ever Chatfield needed the support of the British navy to keep his allies in line.

There was another case of friction between Chatfield and Carrera in late May, when the caudillo returned from successful maneuvers in El Salvador, swollen with his own importance. According to the consul and the *serviles,* Auguste Mahelin had brought to Carrera's attention certain editorials in the *Belize Advertiser* which provoked a belligerent reaction in the Indian chieftain. Ironically, these were the jingoistic articles which were written to influence the Foreign Office toward a policy of direct intervention. But now these same editorials were contributing to rumors that British marines were going to land in Central America in August and that the *serviles* had actually invited them.[67] Perhaps these rumors account for Chatfield's publication of Palmerston's remarks on non-intervention — an attempt to placate Carrera and to protect his allies, the *serviles*. The appearance of the Eastern Company's colonists in the Gulf of Dulce area undoubtedly reinforced these invasion fears.[68] In addition, Governor Rivera Paz had given Lieutenant Nichols a letter for Colonel Macdonald, inviting him to visit Guatemala City — another

---

65. From Macdonald, March 3, 1840, F.O. 252/8; to Macdonald, March 26, 1840, F.O. 252/15.
66. Mahelin's No. 35, April 18.
67. To Palmerston, No. 28, May 8, 1840, F.O. 15/23; to Macdonald, May 9, 1840, F.O. 252/15; *El Tiempo,* No. 101, June 3, 1840; Mahelin to Molé, No. 36, p. encl.s (ext., *Belize Advertiser,* No. 86, May 9, 1840), June 6, 1840, A.A.E.P./CPAC, vol. 3.
68. Mahelin's No. 36; *El Tiempo* (Guatemala), No. 106, June 20, 1840.

item which was perhaps distorted in the public mind and added to the anxiety concerning an invasion.[69] At any rate, Carrera was in a violent mood.

To placate the caudillo, a few priests visited him and explained that the British consul had written those editorials prior to the attack upon Guatemala City in order to help him and the Guatemalan government against the common enemy. The explanation apparently pacified Carrera; and the danger completely passed when his religious advisors took him to a local studio where they were painting a huge life-size portrait of the "Illustrious Protector of Los Altos."[70] He liked it. This incident undoubtedly troubled the master of the British consulate. Had he won a battle and lost a war? He was convinced that only the British navy could keep the lid on this pot.

In late May, 1940, Frederick Chatfield received word that the Foreign Office had passed favorably upon his request for a leave of absence.[71] In hopes that he might be assigned elsewhere upon returning to duty, he felt it necessary to compile an impressive record of achievement for the six years he had spent in the New World. Concrete arrangements for the liquidation of the foreign debt would be helpful in this regard; and indeed his record here was outstanding. By the end of 1839, the states were committed to accept responsibility for their share of the total foreign debt, which also included the Reid-Irving obligation.[72] Costa Rica and Nicaragua had agreed to the "tobacco" transaction; and there was a strong likelihood that the new government of El Salvador might do likewise.

By the time of Chatfield's departure from Central America, moreover, he was completing arrangements with Honduras to liquidate her share of national indebtedness. These were interesting negotiations, especially since they were at the expense of General Morazán's property. Upon learning of the general's defeat, the Honduran government, in an attempt to please Chatfield, hinted that it was planning to rescind Morazán's wood grant of 1834 and suggested that perhaps the grant might be used to clear Honduras' indebtedness. With embarrassing speed, the British consul accepted the suggestion and forwarded a draft contract to the State of Honduras on May 14. According to this agreement, two-thirds of the proceeds would be applied to the debt and one-third to the state's

---

69. To Macdonald, April 9, 1840, F.O. 252/15; from Macdonald, April 20, 1840, F.O. 252/8.
70. Mahelin's No. 36, June 6.
71. To Palmerston, No. 30, May 30, 1840, F.O. 15/23.
72. To Costa Rica, November 7, 1839, F.O. 252/14; to Palmerston, No. 32, June 20, 1840, F.O. 15/23.

regular expenses.[73] By July 1, Honduras had partially accepted the contract though it still insisted upon certain modifications which held up the negotiations for several months. The important point, however, is that Chatfield could list these negotiations among his achievements.[74] And to be sure, the Bondholders' Association and the Reid-Irving house were deeply appreciative. They, in turn, helped him win over the Foreign Office to a policy of naval support in Central America.

The consul's allies in Guatemala City were likewise asked to give some evidence of fiscal responsibility. A series of anonymous editorials in *El Tiempo,* bearing the telltale syntax and hard-hitting style of an English author, prepared the reading public for impending negotiations on financial matters.[75] Guatemalan conservatives were "decent people," no doubt, but the consul felt that he had to guide them firmly down the path of fiscal soundness. The *serviles* agreed that priority would be given to a program of debt-liquidation and financial reform at the forthcoming convention of states. So as not to embarrass them, it was understood that this would be done after Chatfield's departure from Central America. He, in turn, promised to discuss the matter with the English creditors, hoping that they might be persuaded to offer a funding scheme along the lines suggested a few years earlier.[76] On paper, therefore, the consul's record of achievement on financial matters was a creditable one, to say the least.

Before leaving Central America in late June, 1840, the British consul also collected a series of tender testimonials concerning his great effort in behalf of British merchants throughout the area and at Belize. To these, he added the best wishes for a speedy return from his allies in Guatemala City.[77] After a stop at Belize where he discussed Macdonald's Mosquito commission and promised to forward it in London, Frederick Chatfield sailed back to England. As the coastline of Central America faded away in the distance, he perhaps wondered if he would ever return to the wars and problems of that troubled land. He hoped not.

—●●—

At five o'clock on Tuesday afternoon, November 3, 1840, Chatfield walked into Lord Palmerston's office, just as he had done eight years

73. To Honduran Secretary General, p. encl., May 14, 1840; from José Bustillos, March 21, 1840, and from Francisco Alvarado, March 21, 1840, F.O. 252/14.
74. To William Hall, July 20, 1840, F.O. 252/21; from Honduran Secretary, August 28, 1840, F.O. 252/14.
75. *El Tiempo,* No. 99, May 23, 1840, B.N.G./V, leg. 837; also No. 103, June 9, 1840.
76. To Palmerston, No. 32, p. encl., June 20, 1840, F.O. 15/23.
77. *El Tiempo,* No. 110, July 6, 1840; to Palmerston, No. 36, p. encl.s, July 18, 1840, F.O. 15/23.

earlier as the discredited consul from Warsaw. Again, no minutes remain of this particular meeting; but much of it can be inferred from subsequent and contemporary correspondence. Appreciative of the many policy suggestions made over the years, Lord Palmerston nevertheless reminded his consul that the political situation in England, being what it was, would not allow him to deviate drastically from traditional foreign policy, no matter what the justification might be. Chatfield agreed though he could not help thinking that Great Britain should never permit uncivilized peoples to assume that they could violate British life and property with impunity. Moreover, he explained, Central America was potentially one of the richest areas of the world with its untapped resources and raw materials, not to mention the important market which existed there for English goods. From John Baily, whom the federal government assigned to survey a possible oceanic route through Nicaragua, he learned that it was indeed a feasible project, not just a scheme for speculators.[78]

And, the consul warned, the United States had more than a passing interest in such a canal. One of its special agents, John L. Stephens, had seen Baily's survey documents and was excited by the possibilities of such a waterway.[79] If the United States government backed Stephens up in this matter — and Colonel Macdonald fully expected this to be the case — Great Britain had better prepare herself for this eventuality.[80] That is why he strongly recommended Colonel Macdonald's commission scheme, establishing, in effect, a British protectorate of the Mosquito Shore. And, by extending the domains of the Mosquito king to at least the port of San Juan de Nicaragua, if not farther to the south, the English could control the Atlantic terminus of any future canal through Nicaragua. The consul's reasoning impressed Lord Palmerston. The vision of empire was infectious.

About three weeks later, the Colonial Office forwarded to the Foreign Office the documentation on the Mosquito commission. For months, Lord John Russell had been studying Macdonald's action as well as its implications. Finally, he decided against it since it meant England's direct intervention in Mosquitia.[81] Nevertheless, he wanted to learn Palmerston's views on the matter. Influenced by the interview with Chatfield, "Old Pam" defended Macdonald's move. He foresaw the day when Great Britain and her subjects would control "the whole way along the coast from the Rio Hondo to the Boca del Toro; and it is not impossible

---

78. See correspondence from John Baily, 1837–1838, in F.O. 252/6.
79. John L. Stephens to John Forsyth, April 6, 1840, MDCIA, III, 158.
80. Alexander Macdonald to Lord John Russell, August 25, 1840, F.O. 15/24.
81. C.O. to F.O., November 27, 1840, F.O. 15/24.

that the Republic of New Granada may offer their English creditors land on the Isthmus of Panama in payment of the debt due by the Republic." In short, it was England's destiny to establish a protectorate of the Mosquito Shore:

> The object in view seems praiseworthy. . . . an endeavour to impart to a rude and barbarous Race of Men, some of the elements of social order, some rudiments of political organization and some instruction in the Truths of Religion. Such appears to have been the Intentions of the Governor of British Honduras in appointing the Commission, and of the Commissioners in their Proceedings; and although the technical forms of their minutes may be open to remark, and though the proceedings may leave many important matters as yet untouched, yet the Comissioners may allege in their defence that their object has been to lay a foundation for the Introduction of civilisation and Christianity among the Mosquito Nation.[82]

Over the years, Lord Palmerston was sold a bill of goods by Frederick Chatfield and his co-worker at Belize. "Honduras is ours by the best of all titles, that of the Sword," had been Palmerston's first step along the imperialistic path; then came his support of the Ruatán mission in April, 1839; and now, the protectorate of the Mosquito Shore. Clearly, the initiative in policy decisions had not always come from London.

---

82. F.O. to C.O., December 15, 1840, F.O. 15/24.

CHAPTER NINE

Quijano's Ransom

The Law of Nations is founded on the Law of Nature and would recognize such a temporary assumption of power, when justice, humanity and the absence of all immediate appeal to the proper tribunals, called aloud for its exercise.[1]

— Alexander Macdonald, October 7, 1841

Although I feel that my office in a country so radically disorganised as Central America, must in some measure be a thankless one, still I cannot but hope, that in the end it will be seen that my acts are ever guided by a desire conscientiously to perform the duties which belong to the station I have the honour to hold as a Servant of the Crown.[2]

— Chatfield, November 4, 1844

Late on the afternoon of August 12, 1841, the commandant of San Juan de Nicaragua strained his eyes to make out the colors of two ships which were entering the port. As they drew closer, he identified the union jack on the corvette, Her Majesty's Ship the *Tweed,* but was unable to determine the flag on the smaller vessel which he recognized as belonging to a resident of the northside. Could it be, he wondered, that Peter Shepherd's sloop was carrying the Mosquito flag and that England had decided to claim San Juan de Nicaragua for the Mosquito king? Troubled by these thoughts, Lieutenant Colonel Manuel Quijano hurriedly donned his dress uniform, bedecked with medals, and prepared to meet the newcomers. Boarding the customhouse launch, he sailed out toward the *Tweed,* anxious to learn the nature of her mission. As he approached the corvette, however, a disturbing scene took place. A group of distinguished-looking officials got into a launch, which had been lowered from the *Tweed,* and sailed away to the opposite shore, deliberately ignoring the brightly clad Quijano. Understandably, the commandant's feelings were hurt; he had little choice but to return to the commandancy on the southside. In the meantime, the north-bound launch discharged her passengers: King Robert Charles Frederick of the Mosquito Nation, Colonel Alexander Macdonald of Belize, their two secretaries — Thomas Haly and Patrick Walker, respectively — Commander H. D. C. Douglas of the *Tweed,* and Peter Shepherd, the Mosquito commandant for the

---

1. Alexander Macdonald to El Salvador, October 7, 1841, F.O. 15/25.
2. To Lord Aberdeen, No. 32, November 4, 1844, F.O. 15/37.

Middle District of Blewfields. The newcomers established their headquarters in Shepherd's home.[3]

Doubly anxious to know the intruders' mission, Colonel Quijano wasted no time in reaching Shepherd's door where he was greeted by Captain Douglas and Secretary Walker. When he asked to see Colonel Macdonald, however, they politely denied his request on the ground that the superintendent was not feeling well — a deliberate stall, Quijano surmised as he withdrew to his quarters. At seven-thirty that evening, he scribbled an official note welcoming the English visitors and at the same time urged them to account for their appearance at San Juan. In response to this greeting, Macdonald sent a committee of four (Douglas, Walker, Haly, and Shepherd) to explain their presence at the port. According to the commissioners' oral report, the superintendent had come to the Mosquito Shore to relay a message from his government to the King of the Mosquitos, as well as to ascertain the extent of the king's domains. These included, they maintained, San Juan de Nicaragua, Salt Creek (Matina), Boca del Toro, and the Great Corn Island, to which the states of Nicaragua, Costa Rica, and New Granada also had claims. Shaking with rage, Colonel Quijano rejected these assertions and railed against the bald attempt to attribute sovereignty to a horde of "uncivilised" savages — a mask for British economic and territorial ambitions in Central America. Threats poured forth from both sides of the table, and the English commissioners left in a huff.

At one o'clock on the following morning, the sleepless commandant wrote a second letter to Macdonald insisting upon a more suitable explanation for his presence at a Nicaraguan port. He warned that Central Americans, as well as New Granadians, would never accept the territorial pretensions announced by the committee on the previous evening; they knew their "sacred rights" and would defend then on the "field of honor" if need be.[4] Macdonald replied to this note a few hours later. The explanation was the same, but this time it was on paper. If Quijano had any further questions, he would gladly give him an interview at eleven o'clock that morning.[5] With documentary proof of Macdonald's objectives in coming to San Juan, Quijano categorically refused to see the superintendent. Instead, he alerted the port's garrison and the neighboring population for action against the invader. Anyone who aided or

---

3. William Hall to Aberdeen, October 16, 1841, F.O. 15/25; and Nicaraguan Secretary of State to Aberdeen, January 12, 1842, F.O. 15/29, contain the specific documents on the Quijano incident among the enclosures.

4. To Macdonald, August 13, 1841, F.O. 15/29.

5. Patrick Walker to Manuel Quijano, August 13, 1841, F.O. 15/25.

abetted the enemy would meet the fate of traitors to the State of Nicaragua, the commandant ordered.

When Macdonald learned of the preparedness program on the southside, as well as the threats Quijano had made, he sent out his commissioners for a second interview with the commandant. This time they warned Quijano that if he dared molest a single resident "within His Majesty's dominions, or in peaceful transit to them," he and his state would be held accountable. Moreover, they dropped the hint that in the near future a naval force would occupy the port in the king's name. Quijano's reply was equally violent; and to protect himself for the future, he wisely ordered a documentary account of this second interview.[6] On the northside, Colonel Macdonald was also preparing his legal case against the Nicaraguan adversary by receiving depositions from residents of San Juan who had been threatened by the commandant. All of them agreed, of course, that Quijano was an "infamous character." Any action taken against such a wretched fellow would be more than justified.[7]

The inevitable clash occurred on the morning of August 14, 1841 — an incident which reverberated in Central America for years. As a commotion developed outside of Shepherd's home, Macdonald strutted to the front door to find out who was causing it. To his surprise, he saw "a great many individuals armed with muskets, grouped together in various parts in the vicinity." And within fifty yards of where he stood, there was a line of men, many of whom were "busily engaged in manning a couple of small field pieces." Such audacity and affrontery, Macdonald reasoned, had to be met with firmness. He therefore ordered a contingent of marines to disembark from the *Tweed* and at the same time shouted at Quijano to disperse and withdraw his troops immediately. The commandant, described as "very much intoxicated with liquor," refused to obey; instead he waved his hands pugnaciously and screamed at the top of his voice that he "would fight to the death." And yet, when the *Tweed* party landed, Quijano capitulated without firing a shot. Was this due to cowardice or calculation? It is difficult to say; perhaps it was a little of both. At any rate, from the standpoint of later propaganda, it was a master stroke for it dramatized Macdonald's mistake in landing an English force at San Juan de Nicaragua.

Apparently, the superintendent realized immediately the implications of his action. Thinking ahead for a possible justification, he ordered

---

6. Quijano to Nicaragua, August 13, 1841, F.O. 15/29.
7. Peter Shepherd and United States citizens to Macdonald, August 14, 1841, F.O. 15/25.

Quijano to sign a document in which he promised not to molest British, American, and Mosquito subjects at San Juan. Since this would be tantamount to recognizing Mosquito sovereignty to the port, Nicaragua's representative refused to sign the paper — a refusal which infuriated Colonel Macdonald and caused him to lose his head. Compounding the initial error of landing British forces, the superintendent of Belize, in effect, kidnapped Nicaragua's commandant.

As a prisoner aboard the *Tweed,* Colonel Manuel Quijano was forced to accompany his English captors while they completed the southern tour of the alleged Mosquito dominions. Finally, they broke down his resistance; he meekly signed a declaration in which he confessed that the trouble at San Juan had all been the result of his "own imprudence." He also expressed gratitude for the "friendly treatment" he had received aboard the *Tweed.*[8] On the return voyage, he was allowed to disembark at Cape Gracias a Dios, along with King Frederick. Thus ended the celebrated "Quijano Affair" whose consequences would amount to a formidable ransom, both for Central America and England.

━◆◆━

The Macdonald expedition to San Juan and parts southward was a deliberate and an unauthorized move to claim disputed lands for the King of the Mosquitos.[9] In February, 1840, it will be recalled, the superintendent had set up an English commission to advise King Frederick — in effect, he established a protectorate of the Mosquito Shore. According to the terms of the arrangement, however, the British government had to sanction the commission before it could go into effect. Lord Palmerston, as we have seen, favored the idea of a protectorate; but Lord John Russell in the Colonial Office voted against it, precisely because it implied such an arrangement. In February, 1841, therefore, Lord John instructed his superintendent at Belize to disband the Mosquito commission.[10]

In the meantime, Colonel Macdonald acted upon the assumption that London would support him and thus involved himself in a heated correspondence with Costa Rica and New Granada on Mosquito matters. The upshot of this exchange was that Costa Rica decided to occupy Salt Creek and that the Bogotá government reasserted its rights to Boca del Toro and the Great Corn Island.[11] When Russell's negative reached

---

8. Quijano's declaration, August 22, 1841, F.O. 15/25.
9. Macdonald to C.O., July 12, 1841, F.O. 15/28.
10. Lord John Russell to Macdonald, February 8, 1841, F.O. 15/28.
11. M. Guevara to Palmerston, p. encl.s and subsequent correspondence, April 20, 1841, F.O. 15/25; George Upton to Palmerston, May 19, 1841, F.O. 15/26.

Belize, therefore, the superintendent found himself in an untenable and humiliating position. Nevertheless, he refused to humble himself before the Latin adversary; and like it or not, he was stubbornly determined to commit Great Britain to the idea of a protectorate. That was his primary objective in visiting Mosquitia.

The expedition left Belize on July 20, 1841, and soon appeared at Cape Gracias a Dios to take aboard the Mosquito king. Interestingly, even before the *Tweed* arrived in Blewfields, her mission was already known there.[12] From August 6 to 11, while in Blewfields, Macdonald and company secretly worked out the final details of the aggressive tour to the south. Apparently everyone was in the best of spirits. According to one English observer, the conspirators drank "lots of champagne" and toasted in succession "Queen Victoria, the King of the Moskito Nation her ancient Ally, the Queen and Family, the Duke of Wellington, and the Irish Nation, the Army, Navy, Captain Douglas, and the memory of Lord Nelson in Silence."[13]

Determined to set up a new English commission, one which could not be vetoed by the Colonial Office, Macdonald persuaded his alcoholic puppet to sign certain key documents during the stay at Blewfields. On August 9, King Frederick soberly proclaimed the establishment of a second advisory commission which contained the same personnel as the first but which was not conditional upon the approval of the British government.[14] Next, the king was imposed upon to change the line of succession to his throne from his eldest to his youngest son. And during Prince Clarence's minority, of course, the second commission would serve as regent—a very convenient change from the standpoint of Belize's control over Mosquito affairs. Finally, the king magnanimously freed the slaves at Blewfields. There was at least one Englishman who did not cheer this act, "the most nefarious I have ever met with." "The proprietors," he explained, "are to be paid for their slaves out of the revenue of St. Juan when given up by the Spaniards to the King of the Moskito Nation."[15] The minutes of a meeting held at Blewfields on the 10th likewise revealed the method of payment for slaves, all of which underscored the deliberate nature of the English expedition.[16] Two days later, the *Tweed* entered the port of San Juan de Nicaragua.

---

12. "Journal of a Voyage . . . to Blewfields," Mathew H. Willock to F.O., November 26, 1842, f. 201, F.O. 15/34.
13. *Ibid.*, f. 204.
14. Decree, King Robert Charles Frederick, August 9, 1841, enclosed in C.O. to F.O., December 24, 1841, F.O. 15/28.
15. "Journal," Mathew H. Willock, folios 204-205.
16. Minutes, Blewfields, August 10, 1841, F.O. 15/28.

Macdonald's visit to the ports south of San Juan merely confirmed what has already been said. The Costa Ricans and New Granadian governments, as might be expected, protested the Mosquito claims; and it should be noted that in the vicinity of Boca del Toro the superintendent left an impressive calling card — forty stands of arms among Indians who acknowledged allegiance to the Mosquito king.[17] After visiting the Great Corn Island, the *Tweed* sailed back to Cape Gracias a Dios, where King Frederick and the repentant Quijano disembarked. From there, the English party returned to its home base, arriving in Belize on the afternoon of September 4, 1841.

On that same afternoon, Colonel Macdonald began to justify his unauthorized tour to the south. He tried to explain his actions on humanitarian grounds — Quijano was a drunkard who had threatened the lives and property of respectable people at San Juan, as well as the assassin who had killed the beloved Juan Galindo in the recent civil war. Boca del Toro, moreover, was of strategic importance to Great Britain as a naval base, one which would give her control of the continent and prevent encroachments by the United States.[18] But these were arguments that the superintendent had used earlier without any effect. Lord Russell had to be approached in a different manner; perhaps it might be well, the superintendent reasoned, to borrow a page from Frederick Chatfield's book of procedures, so to speak. The claims which the British consul had raised against the unionists, prior to his departure from Central America, might again be used to serve a political goal — to establish a British protectorate of the Mosquito Shore.

For one reason or another — and especially the lack of detailed information on the claims — Colonel Macdonald and Vice Admiral Adam were not able to collect on them. In the meanwhile, all five states had been assigned a proportional share of those claims. Suspiciously, on September 4, 1841 — the day of his return to Belize — Macdonald's patience reached the breaking point. He demanded payment of the claims by December 1; conveniently, no copy of this ultimatum to the states of Central America reached the Colonial Office in London.[19] On the same day, however, Macdonald did write to Lord Russell recommending the "propriety of simultaneously taking possession of the Ports of Isaval,

17. Macdonald to Bustamente and Elkshilsend, August 19, 1841, F.O. 15/28; Manuel A. Bonilla to Aberdeen, September 13, 1841, F.O. 15/25.

18. Macdonald to Russell, September 8, 1841, F.O. 15/28.

19. Macdonald's circular to the States of Central America, September 4, 1841, A.A.E.P./CPAC, vol. 3, folio 176.

Trujillo, and Omoa," since it was obvious that Central Americans were stalling on the payment of the English claims.[20]

Interestingly, William Hall, the acting British consul in Guatemala City, noted the folly of using force on the claims issue just at a time when nationalistic spirit was at a fever pitch in Central America, thanks to the Quijano affair.[21] He did not realize, of course, that Macdonald's actions were deliberate; Central America's reaction to the Quijano incident would inevitably play right into the superintendent's hands. When the states refused to meet the December 1 deadline, Macdonald was able to interpret this refusal as the desire of Central Americans to welsh on their obligations to British creditors. It followed that a blockade was necessary to bring them to their senses.

Macdonald's strategem bore fruit in the two years following the Quijano kidnapping, despite reprimands from the home office and the initial reluctance of the British government to support a protectorate of the Mosquito Shore. Let us trace briefly the steps and circumstances which brought about this significant change in policy. To begin with, the British government disapproved of the "questionable proceeding" at San Juan de Nicaragua; it also rejected the second Mosquito commission.[22] And yet, just as in Chatfield's case earlier, Macdonald's superiors unwittingly provided him with enough leeway in his instructions so that he was able to accomplish his political objectives. Governor Charles Metcalfe of Jamaica, for example, had authorized him to settle both the Mosquito and claims issues, cautioning him, however, to do so in an impartial and amicable fashion. But whereas Metcalfe, seconded by the Colonial Office, had implicitly intended that the two issues be treated separately, the instructions were not specific on this point. This allowed Colonel Macdonald to mix them together, while conveniently ignoring the recommendation of impartiality. On November 9, 1841, he sent out a circular to the states in which he peremptorily insisted upon the settlement of the Mosquito question and the payment of claims.[23] When the Central American states categorically refused to deal with Quijano's kidnapper, they helped the superintendent achieve his political goals. By March, 1842, the British government was ready to follow Macdonald's lead; and on April 16, Admiral Adam issued his ultimatum. If the states did not

20. Macdonald to Russell, September 4, 1841, F.O. 15/28.

21. William Hall to Palmerston, No. 12, October 18, 1841, F.O. 15/25.

22. Charles Metcalfe to Macdonald, October 29, 1841, F.O. 15/28; F.O. to C.O., April 2, 1843, F.O. 15/36.

23. Macdonald to the Central American States, November 19, 1841, F.O. 15/32, folios 37-39; Macdonald to Metcalfe, December 1, 1831, F.O. 15/31.

pay their debts by June 1, the British navy would blockade the Atlantic ports of Central America.[24]

Macdonald's objective with regard to the Mosquito Shore had to wait a little longer. As Central Americans clamored for his recall and punishment, the superintendent of Belize stepped up his recommendations for violent measures against them, sketching in the process an unfavorable picture of the Latin adversary to further his cause.[25] Moreover, he added fuel to nationalist fires by flaunting English domination over the island of Ruatán, reopening an old wound. In August, 1842, he again urged the landing of "marines" at Omoa and Trujillo — a recommendation which the British government would not heed.[26] It did, however, listen to his suggestion that England revive the old practice of assigning a British resident to the Mosquito Shore, an institution which was used prior to the eighteenth-century treaties with Spain. And again, Central American demands concerning the Quijano affair, since they placed the British government on the defensive, abetted the acceptance of this old institution.[27] In late 1843, when news circulated that New Granada and the three unionist states of Nicaragua, Honduras, and El Salvador — signatories of the *Pacto de Chinandega* — had decided to occupy the Mosquito Shore effectively, Great Britain finally accepted the protectorate policy. Undoubtedly, Macdonald's presence in London was a deciding factor. Upon his recommendation, Patrick Walker, his former secretary at Belize, assumed the post of British resident on the Mosquito Shore in early 1844.[28]

━━◆◆◆━━

Central America's reaction to the Quijano affair very definitely contributed to the change in English policy toward Mosquitia. The news

---

24. See the following documents for the steps taken by Macdonald in setting up the first English blockade of 1842: Metcalfe to Lord Stanley, November 19, 1841, F.O. to C.O., January 15, 1842, and Macdonald to C.O., Decemmer 15, 1841, in F.O. 15/30; also see, Macdonald to C.O., December 21, 1841, *idem* to Metcalfe, December 1, 1841, Macdonald to C.O., February 2, 1842, Macdonald to Stanley, March 12, 1842, Metcalfe to Macdonald, March 31, 1842, blockade ultimatum in Adam to Macdonald, April 16, 1842 — all in F.O. 15/31.

25. Macdonald to Metcalfe, December 15, 1841, p. encl.s and subsequent letters, folios 19-40, F.O. 15/32.

26. Macdonald to Lord Elgin, August 4, 1842, and C.O. to F.O., October 15, 1842, in F.O. 15/34; also see C.O. to F.O., July 30, 1842, F.O. 15/32.

27. C.O. to F.O., p. encl.s and subsequent correspondence (folios 157-169), July 20, 1842, F.O. 15/32.

28. "Memorandum on the Musquito Shore," F.O., December 15, 1843; Macdonald to Aberdeen, December 20, 1843, in F.O. 15/36; and from Aberdeen, April 30, 1844, F.O. 15/37; also see, James S. Bell to Elgin, August 8, 1843, F.O. 15/36.

of Quijano's abduction spread like wild fire throughout the states; and a wave of anglophobia placed the lives and property of all Englishmen in jeopardy, especially in Nicaragua.[29] The León government immediately protested to the British Foreign Office and demanded reparations as well as Macdonald's punishment. Moreover, it urged the issuance of special instructions to all British subalterns so as to prevent such unauthorized acts in the future.[30] These demands, however justified, had the effect of putting the English government on the defensive, touching both its pride and pocketbook. A point of honor had been raised — a dangerous psychological corner from which there seemed to be only one avenue of escape for England, that is, to support her agents in the field. Chatfield was a master at working his country into these corners; it would seem that his colleague at Belize had also learned the lesson well.

Another important consequence of the Quijano affair was the momentary impetus it gave to the unionist movement in Central America. Though the states frequently had discussed the vaunted convention after Morazán's defeat, they apparently lacked any sustained desire to establish a confederation. Braulio Carillo of Costa Rica, for example, adamantly resisted the calling of a convention, fearful that it might upset his aspirations for a lifetime dictatorship.[31] Guatemala likewise opposed any general government which she could not control or which might interfere with the collection of tariff revenues. And both Honduras and Guatemala were victimizing their sister El Salvador, who had no port on the Atlantic, by collecting a twenty percent duty on goods destined to be sold on the Salvadorean market. Understandably, El Salvador favored a general government which could correct this abuse. And as for Nicaragua, she was still desirous of preempting the great canal project for herself. In view of these selfish state interests, therefore, it is not surprising that there were delays in holding the convention, that delegates held conflicting instructions, and that squabbling over the site of the meeting should take place.[32] Only an occasional voice, usually belonging to a former sup-

---

29. Broadside, Pablo Buitrago to Nicaraguans, León, August 27, 1841, F.O. 254/5; mem., by Frederick Chatfield, March 24, 1842, F.O. 15/29; to Aberdeen, No. 4, January 15, 1843, F.O. 15/35.

30. Nicaragua to Aberdeen, October 16, 1841, F.O. 15/25; *idem* to *idem,* January 12, 1842, and Guatemala to Aberdeen, January 12, 1842, F.O. 15/29.

31. From John Foster, April 29, 1841, F.O. 252/19.

32. "Situation of affairs in the different states," Captain J. C. Fitzgerald to Admiral Adam, May 18, 1842, F.O. 15/32; "Informe," Juan José Guzmán, San Vicente, September 17, 1842, F.O. 252/5; "Manifiesto," Chinandega, February 27, 1842, B.N.G./HS, 1842; "Manifiesto," Rafael Carrera, March 21, 1847, F.O. 15/45.

porter of Morazán, pleaded for union in order to command respect from foreign powers.[33]

This apathy toward union changed overnight with the news of Macdonald's action at San Juan de Nicaragua. The offended state, as might be expected, led the way. On August 30, 1841, Nicaragua sent out a circular to her sisters in which she related the facts of the Quijano affair and pleaded for common action against the unlimited ambitions of British agents in Central America. She refused to believe that Queen Victoria's government had authorized the abduction of her commandant from the port of San Juan. Upon receiving Nicaragua's note, the Central American states responded with uncharacteristic unity; they wrote to Colonel Macdonald, to William Hall in Guatemala City, and to the Foreign Office demanding an explanation for the outrage.[34] When Macdonald had the temerity to justify his action on humanitarian grounds, they fiercely rejected his explanation. "Who gave him the right to intervene in this matter," exclaimed Rafael Carrera on November 4, 1841. And voicing a common sentiment, he added:

> Could it be that because he took the island of Ruatán without anyone reclaiming it formally from him until now, or because in trespassing beyond the limits which were granted temporarily by the King of Spain to the establishment of Belize he has also taken over all the territory which exists from there to approximately the mouth of the Gulf [of Dulce], which was not demanded of him either, that he now considers himself the master of Central America?[35]

Carrera's manifesto illustrated the improved position of unionist liberals throughout Central America because of the Quijano affair. The states' righters had very little choice but to remain silent for the time being. Many of them now even came out in favor of union. When Nicaragua and El Salvador urged Guatemala to join the movement for reestablishing the central government, the "man" Carrera looked upon the suggestion with favor. On November 3, 1841, for example; a military junta made the following demands upon the Rivera Paz government; first that Guatemala join her sisters in forming a national power which could

---

33. "Protesta," Chinandega, June 30, 1841, and "Discurso," Patricio Rivas, León, February 26, 1841, in B.N.G./HS, 1841.

34. Nicaragua to Aberdeen, October 16, 1841, F.O. 15/25; Nicaragua and Guatemala to Aberdeen, January 12, 1842, F.O. 15/29; *Correo Semanario del Salvador* (San Salvador), No. 60, September 16, 1841, A.A.E.P./CPAC, vol. 3; "Documentos relativos a lo ocurrido en el puerto de San Juan," Nicaragua, B.N.G./HS, 1841.

35. Rafael Carrera to the States of Central America, November 4-12, 1841, printed, A.A.E.P./CPAC, vol. 3, folios 191-193.

protect the territorial integrity of Central America; second, that the government stop any further correspondence with Colonel Macdonald on the ground that it was degrading; third, that Guatemala insist upon a satisfactory explanation from William Hall for the Quijano action, suspending relations with his country if he refused to comply; and finally, that the government close all ports to the British until England promised to make amends for the insult to Central America's integrity.[36] It would seem that initially the *serviles* were willing to meet the junta's demands; but when Carrera realized that they did not seriously intend to implement them, he angrily dismissed the Rivera Paz government and replaced it with a sympathetic one. By January, 1842, Guatemala joined with Nicaragua in addressing the British Foreign Office; and there were rumors that she planned to send an envoy to the Court of St. James.[37]

At the same time, the states of Nicaragua, El Salvador, and Honduras sent representatives to the Nicaraguan city of Chinandega to discuss the possibilities of erecting a central government. The delegates' mood came out clearly in the "bases" for the future *Pacto de Chinandega*. According to the "bases," drawn up on April 11, 1842, the Supreme Delegate, or executive, was instructed to encourage the construction of the Nicaraguan canal, to work toward the calling of the "Great American Diet," and to protest the British occupation "of the Republic's territory and islands."[38] In short, Macdonald's action at San Juan brought into favor the old *Morazanista* platform. A copy of the "bases" reached Guatemala City by June, 1842. This chronological point should be kept in mind.

As in the Ruatán crisis three years earlier, however, the desire for political power subverted the new-born unionist movement. Nicaragua had sent a copy of the Quijano circular to Lima, Peru, where it was read carefully by General Francisco Morazán. Instead of embarking for Chile, as previously scheduled, Morazán decided to return to his native land. On February 15, 1842, he entered the Salvadorean port of La Unión and offered his services to the state authorities. He was willing, he told them, to take up arms against the British, once all diplomatic avenues had been exhausted in seeking redress for the Quijano incident.[39] Rather than accept his offer of assistance, the Salvadorean government — and the same was true later in the remaining states of Central America —

---

36. *Ibid.*
37. Guatemala to Aberdeen, January 12, 1842, F.O. 15/29; William Hall to Patrick Walker, December 8, 1841, F.O. 15/31.
38. "Pacto de Chinandega," April 11, 1842, in P. Caravajal to William Hall, May 31, 1842, F.O. 252/16.
39. William Hall to Aberdeen, p. encl., March 5, 1842, F.O. 15/29.

panicked with fear at the prospect that Francisco Morazán might now be able to restore his darling Republic. States' righters therefore took up arms against him and thus revived the civil war which had ended in 1840. The wild forays of General Francisco Malespín upon La Unión and Sonsonate, where followers of Morazán were gathering, announced graphically the change of heart that had taken place.[40]

Forced to leave El Salvador, Morazán's army worked its way into Costa Rica; and in April, Morazán overthrew Braulio Carillo and assumed the directorship of the new government. In the following months, rumors circulated that *Morazanistas* were planning an invasion of all the states. In Guatemala, the news of Morazán's return allowed the *serviles* to regain control over Rafael Carrera; they sent him westward in anticipation of a Mexican invasion of Soconusco. Rumor had it that *Morazanista* exiles in Mexico were planning a diversionary attack that would facilitate Morazán's invasion elsewhere in Central America.[41]

The resurgence of Central America unionism, therefore, was short-lived because of Morazán's reappearance on the political stage. On May 25, 1842, ironically, the ex-president's nemesis disembarked at Belize.[42] And though Frederick Chatfield had preferred an assignment elsewhere, particularly in Europe, he had little choice in the matter. Lord Aberdeen, now in charge of foreign affairs, felt that only Chatfield could rectify the deteriorating situation in Central America.[43] Thanks to George U. Skinner, the Bondholders' Association, and the Reid-Irving house, Mr. Chatfield now returned to the Central American wars with the augmented rank of "Consul-General."[44]

———◆◆◆———

With no illusions about the difficult task ahead of him, Chatfield realized that one of the first things he had to do was to reassert his authority over Central Americans and Englishmen alike. Colonel Macdonald in particular had to be put in his place and to a lesser extent Vice Admiral Charles Adam, both of whom had taken over many of the consul's functions during the past two years. These two officers,

40. Auguste Mahelin to Minister of Foreign Affairs, No. 71, March 10, 1842, A.A.E.P./CPAC, vol. 3.
41. "Informe," Juan José Guzmán, September 17, 1842, F.O. 252/5; Charles Adam to Admiralty, p. encl.s, June 1842, F.O. 15/32.
42. To Aberdeen, May 28, 1842, F.O. 15/29.
43. From F.O., February 28, 1842, F.O. 15/29; Hall to Palmerston, No. 12, October 18, 1841, and No. 13, to Aberdeen, December 8, 1841, F.O. 15/25; "Treatise . . . Guatemala," George U. Skinner, February, 1842, F.O. 15/30.
44. Robert Campbell to Aberdeen, March 23, 1842; F.O. to Campbell, March 31, 1842, F.O. 15/31; from F.O., No. 1, April 13, 1842, F.O. 15/29.

furthermore, had grown accustomed to regarding the acting consul in Guatemala City as their underling — a situation which Chatfield would no longer tolerate. Even before leaving England, he asked Lord Aberdeen certain questions which were clearly intended to restore his full authority. Should "British Civil and Naval officers," he inquired, correspond directly with Central American governments "independently of Her Majesty's agent in that country?" What compensation and explanation, if any, should be given to Nicaragua for the "violation" of her territory?[45] And in commenting upon Mosquito matters, he also implied a rebuke of Macdonald's aggressive tour to the south. It would be folly, he asserted, to claim ports to the south of San Juan de Nicaragua. England should restrict herself instead to the area from Cape Honduras to the north bank of the San Juan River since the latter point secured for Great Britain "that which is of chief importance to her in that quarter, vizt. the complete command of the intercourse with the Central American Province from which this river derives its name."[46] These remarks and questions revealed the consul-general's determination to strengthen his hand in Central America.

But Lord Aberdeen had a mind of his own, influenced by Macdonald's comments as well as the protests of Central American leaders. While, on the one hand, he instructed his agent to announce England's disapproval of the superintendent's action at San Juan; on the other, he wanted Nicaragua and Costa Rica to understand that Great Britain would not remain indifferent to any encroachment upon the territory of the Mosquito king. He argued, moreover, that since there was reason to believe that the territory where the incident had taken place did not belong to Nicaragua, there was thus "no grounds for compensation."[47] This position was hardly calculated to win friends for England among Nicaraguans. But the most annoying part of Aberdeen's instructions was the injunction that Chatfield assist other English officials in the collection of the claims, as if he were their subordinate.

During a brief stay in Belize, Chatfield discussed the impending blockade action with Colonel Macdonald and Vice Admiral Adam. In response to the April ultimatum, three states came to terms with the British: Costa Rica, Honduras, and Guatemala. With no port on the Atlantic, El Salvador felt free to stall in her answer to the British note and suggested instead that a tribunal be set up to study the justice of the claims — a preposterous suggestion from the English point of view.

---

45. Mem., to Aberdeen, March 24, 1842, F.O. 15/29.
46. Mem., to Aberdeen, April 12, 1842, F.O. 15/29.
47. From F.O., April 13, 1842, F.O. 15/29.

The consensus of opinion was that Admiral Richard Thomas, in charge of the Pacific squadron, should be asked to send ships to help Chatfield bring El Salvador into line during the annual fairs of October and November. And since Nicaragua defiantly refused to acquiesce, incensed at the use of Macdonald's name on the ultimatum note, it was decided to impose the blockade against her. If the other states reneged on their earlier promises — and Chatfield was to determine this — the blockade would be extended to them as well.[48]

The apparent harmony of the Belize meeting with fellow-English officers did not survive the consul's return to Guatemala City. On June 18, he urged Adam to instruct his officers to communicate directly with the British consulate through the port of Izabal. Since this letter passed through Belize, the superintendent had an opportunity to read it. He understood its implications only too well — Macdonald was not to be consulted on Central American affairs. With unusual politeness, the superintendent objected; but Chatfield stubbornly refused even to acknowledge receipt of his colleague's note, though he had read it.[49] On July 2, in another letter to Admiral Adam, Chatfield reminded him that according to Lord Palmerston's instructions of 1840 the navy was at the consul's disposal and not the other way around. These were the words he used: "With every desire then to attend to the suggestions and information which I may receive from you, or from Colonel Macdonald, for the benefit of the Queen's service, I decline, on public grounds, making myself liable to irregular instructions or subjecting the Trust I hold to an unasked intervention."[50] The admiral and the superintendent, as might be expected, did not take warmly to the consul's "unbefitting" conduct; and before long, both the Admiralty and the Colonial Office registered their complaints with the Foreign Office.[51] In no uncertain terms, Lord Aberdeen admonished his consul-general for an unwillingness to obey orders from London and for an uncooperative attitude toward other English officers.[52]

Undaunted by the stinging reprimand — only the first of many he

---

48. To Aberdeen, May 28, 1842, F.O. 15/29; Admiralty to F.O., p. encl.s, July 29, 1842, F.O. 15/32; *Centro-América y la Inglaterra,* by Unos Guatemaltecos, Guatemala City, 1843, B.N.G./F, 1843.
49. To Adam, June 18, 1842; from Macdonald and Houston, July 14, 1842, F.O. 15/34.
50. To Adam, July 2, 1842, F.O. 15/33.
51. From Adam, August 30, 1842, F.O. 15/33; Macdonald to Lord Stanley, August 23, 1842 (enclosed in C.O. to F.O., November 29, 1842), F.O. 15/34.
52. From Aberdeen, October 30, 1842, F.O. 15/29; from *idem,* No. 1, January 21, 1843, F.O. 15/35.

would receive from Lord Aberdeen in the next few years — the consul did not yield an inch to his superior. And the amazing thing is that he got away with it. He stubbornly denied Macdonald's charges that he was impeding "the course of Her Majesty's service"; and at the same time he accused the superintendent of unwarranted interference in Central American affairs. In crystal-clear terms, he assured Aberdeen that he would never be a party to lowering the prestige of the British consulate by making it subservient to the establishment at Belize. He found the attitude of "superiority," implicit in the letters of Adam and Macdonald, "quite inadmissible." Lord Palmerston's instructions had placed him in charge of the claims collection; and those were the instructions that he was going to follow.[53] There the matter rested, perhaps because the blockade ended in late 1842 or because the Foreign Office, though annoyed by his insolence, recognized Chatfield's ability. Nevertheless, the consul succeeded in reasserting his authority over British officials in the Central American area.

In short order, after his arrival in Guatemala City, Chatfield restored the old alliance with the *serviles*. The first indication of this was the support he gave to Guatemala's defense plans in Soconusco, urging his countrymen to pay their share of the forced loans levied for this purpose.[54] Later, he also accepted the private request of Juan José Aycinena, the Guatemalan secretary of state, to mediate the Soconusco matter.[55] Of more importance, however, were the plans which the allies evolved to check all challengers to their position in Central America. Little needs to be said about their desire to frustrate the *Morazanistas* and their goal of restoring the Republic. This was merely a revival of the past civil war. But the *Pacto de Chinandega*, signed by the delegations of three states on July 27, 1842, was another matter. It represented a more serious threat to Chatfield and his Guatemalan allies, precisely because it appealed to moderates and conservatives in Central America who felt that something had to be done to check English aggression. The British consulate, it will be recalled, had received a copy of the "bases" to the *pacto*, which embodied many planks of the *Morazanista* program in foreign affairs. Moreover, Honduras promptly ratified the pact in October, 1842; Nicaragua followed suit in January, 1843; El Salvador affixed its signature to the convention shortly thereafter; and all three states had agreed to ask Costa Rica and Guatemala to join the

---

53. To Aberdeen, No. 7, April 24, 1843, F.O. 15/35.
54. To Adam, June 18, 1842, F.O. 252/8; to British citizens, July 19, 1842, F.O. 252/12.
55. To Aberdeen, No. 6, p. encl., August 29, 1842, F.O. 15/29.

new confederation when political conditions permitted.[56] The Chinandega pact, therefore, was no paper threat; it was a reality which the allies had to face.

Primarily at Chatfield's instigation, the allies proposed a rival or substitute plan for union which, for purposes of clarity, we shall call the "Guatemalan Confederation." This third scheme of union — for it must be remembered that *Morazanistas* and *pacto* supporters were at odds with each other — had two major appeals. First, it was essentially a military alliance of anti-*Morazanistas* against Costa Rica, the state controlled by the ex-president. Secondly, its political program was of the type calculated to attract states' righters. Each state would have one delegate in the confederation, and the Supreme Delegate would be the executive of the state in which the diet were held. In short, the plan resembled the one championed by the *serviles* in 1839–1840.

Despite its attractive features, the "Guatemalan Confederation" was intended to place power in the hands of Guatemala City and the British consulate. How could this be so since on paper it seemed such an equitable instrument? The answer is to be found in a promise which Chatfield had made his allies. He would recognize the independence of Guatemala; and as an independent nation, she would then be eligible to negotiate a trade treaty with Great Britain. The benefits and provisions of such a treaty could then be extended to any other state who sent a delegate to Guatemala City. It followed therefore that Guatemala, having an English treaty, would always be the site of the prospective confederation. This clever scheme, in other words, satisfied the *serviles'* ambition to control the general government while at the same time allowing Chatfield to thwart any action against English territorial aspirations. The consul-general first announced the "Guatemalan Confederation" to Lord Aberdeen on August 30, though he had conceived of it shortly after his return to Guatemala City.[57]

Capitalizing upon the fear of General Morazán in the *pacto* states, Chatfield wasted no time in advancing the "Guatemalan Confederation" among them. While the British blockade was in progress, he informed Nicaraguan officials that Guatemala had consented to guarantee Nicaragua's share of the claims. If they accepted this proposal "in writing," he would then recommend lifting the blockade. When the Nicaraguan gov-

---

56. Francisco Castellón to Aberdeen, p. encl. (Pacto de Chinandega, July 27, 1842), Paris, F.O. 15/39; "Informe," Mariano Rivera Paz, Guatemala, November 4, 1842, B.N.G./HS, 1842.

57. To Aberdeen, No. 7, August 30, 1842, F.O. 15/29; No. 36 (November 18, 1844), F.O. 15/37, which refers to a note by Chatfield, dated July 4, 1842, in which he discussed Guatemala's desire to become an independent country.

ernment gave its approval, the British naval force evacuated San Juan de Nicaragua. In one fell swoop, Frederick Chatfield enhanced his prestige throughout Central America by showing that he could call off the English navy; he also made Nicaragua beholden to the State of Guatemala. The next step politically was an obvious one.[58]

A similar tactic with regard to El Salvador, however, met with no success. Yet it is significant that in championing the "Guatemalan Confederation" the British consul was definitely willing to recognize the absolute sovereignty of the states in contrast to a policy which he subsequently developed.[59] As a sovereign state, El Salvador could accept Guatemala's offer to serve as guarantor for her share of the claims; and she could also send a delegate to Guatemala City, thus benefiting from the impending treaty with Great Britain. But the Salvadorean government resisted the tempting offer and instead proposed to allow Mr. Chatfield to take over "one of the maritime custom houses" — an attractive concession if his sole concern had been the claims. Since his objective was political, however, he refused to accept the Salvadorean offer "partly because I consider such a mode of payment, in the actual stage of this negotiation, inadmissible, and partly, because I wish Salvador to feel, that in declining to accept a proposal dictated for its own convenience and relief, I resent the offensive course which it has so long pursued towards us."[60] Just what the proposal was Chatfield never said; fortunately, a Salvadorean document revealed it. Guatemala not only offered to serve as guarantor for the claims but also agreed to drop the tariff on goods going into the sister state from twenty to nine percent — a substantial concession, it must be admitted.[61] The Salvadorean refusal, of course, displeased the British consul-general. When he learned that Her Majesty's ship the *Champion* was awaiting him on the Pacific coast, Chatfield left Guatemala City on September 29, 1842, determined to bring the recalcitrant state into line.

No sooner had their English ally left the capital than the *serviles* formally announced their confederation scheme. On October 9, 1842, commissioners representing four states agreed to a nine-article *pacto de unión*. The consul-general's close friend Manuel Francisco Pavón signed for Guatemala; Pedro N. Arriaga, for Honduras; and Joaquín Durán, for Nicaragua and El Salvador — all three gentlemen were Guatemalan offi-

58. To Aberdeen, No. 7, August 30, 1842, F.O. 15/29; to John Foster, No. 7, August 19, 1842, F.O. 252/21; from Simón Orosco (Nicaragua), September 12, 1842, F.O. 252/16.
59. From El Salvador, July 27, 1842, and to *idem,* August 5, 1842, F.O. 252/20.
60. To Aberdeen, No. 8, September 1, 1842, F.O. 15/29.
61. "Informe," Juan José Guzmán, September 17, 1842, F.O. 252/5.

cials. A supporting declaration on the 19th underscored the military alliance against Costa Rica. With a British ship at his command, moreover, Mr. Chatfield's assistance was indispensable; it could help implement the *serviles'* dream of a confederation dominated by them.[62]

—•••—

The British action on the Pacific coast from October to December, 1842, was only partially successful. In cooperation with Admiral Richard Thomas, Chatfield was able to force settlements on the outstanding claims. The English worked expeditiously and without any regard to the suggestions and sensibilities of the governments concerned. This, of course, deepened the rancor toward all things British throughout Central America and helps to explain the unmitigated failure of the consul-general's political program.[63]

Another contributing factor to the failure of the "Guatemalan Confederation" was the elimination of the *Morazanista* threat to the *pacto* states. When news reached them that on September 15 General Francisco Morazán had lost his life before a Costa Rican firing squad, there was less reason, or incentive, to join the Guatemalan movement. For awhile, in October and November, the threat persisted in the form of a few ships commanded by the Frenchman Isidore Saget, a supporter of Morazán who was beseiging Puntarenas in Costa Rica. Fearing that Saget might attack them, Nicaragua and El Salvador appealed to Admiral Thomas for naval support. Though he refused to provide assistance, the issue by then was academic. Saget's blockade of Puntarenas was actually broken by the appearance of the *Champion*. Chatfield had sent her to Costa Rica; but it is not certain that he did so intentionally to defeat Saget's maneuvers. Be that as it may, the *Morazanista* threat no longer existed. On her return trip, the *Champion* brought a representative of the new Costa Rican government to negotiate with Chatfield in Nicaragua.[64]

Complications in the consul-general's negotiations with Nicaragua further weakened the prospects of achieving the political objective. Relations had begun amicably enough on October 20; but by the end of the month a rift was beginning to develop ostensibly because of Aberdeen's

---

62. Pacto de Unión, Guatemala, October 7, 1842, B.N.G./HS, 1842; *Gaceta Oficial* (Guatemala), No. 70, October 28, 1842.

63. To Aberdeen, No. 18, December 24, 1842, F.O. 15/29; Richard Thomas to Admiralty, p. encl.s and subsequent correspondence, November 3, 1842, F.O. 15/36.

64. To Aberdeen, No. 18, p. encl.s, December 24, 1842, F.O. 15/29; from Simón Orozco, October 18, 1843, F.O. 252/16; Richard Thomas to José Astiguieta, November 6, 1842, and Thomas to Admiralty, November 29, 1842, F.O. 15/36.

position on the Quijano affair. Perhaps even this obstacle might have been surmounted if the *Morazanista* threat had prevailed. To complicate matters, however, another incident, which was similar to the Quijano affair, took place in late September and early October as the British blockade was lifted. Before leaving the port of San Juan, the commander of the *Charybdis* threatened José de la Tijera, Nicaragua's commandant, and forced him to sign a document to the effect that San Juan de Nicaragua belonged to the Mosquito king. By coincidence — an unfortunate one, it would seem — the officer's name was James Macdonald, the nephew of Quijano's abductor. Upon learning of the episode, the Nicaraguan government formally protested to Chatfield. The latter argued that Tijera was exaggerating the incident. When Nicaragua persisted in presenting documentary evidence, Mr. Chatfield lost his temper. On November 2, he threatened as follows:

> It becomes my duty now to assure the Supreme Government of Nicaragua, that the whole of this correspondence shall immediately be laid before Her Majesty's Government; and if it should be found on investigation that Mr. Tijera has willfully traduced the honour of the Queen's Service, the Supreme Government of Nicaragua must be prepared to expect, that Her Majesty's Government will require and exact ample reparations for the offense.[65]

All chances for a peaceful settlement were now out of the question. Chatfield assured himself that coercive action was again necessary. Since Nicaragua refused to listen to reason on the Quijano matter, he urged Lord Aberdeen to consider the forceful occupation of San Juan's north bank for the Mosquito king. And, at the same time, he announced to the Nicaraguan government that Mosquitia's boundaries extended from Cape Gracias a Dios to the north bank of the San Juan River.[66] To guarantee himself the support of the home office, Chatfield again resorted to the old technique of raising claims against the recalcitrant government. At first, he presented the cases of Jonas Wilson Glenton and Thomas Manning, both of whom had won favorable decisions in the state's courts. The outstanding issue therefore was the method and time of payment. On his own, the English consul-general decided that Nicaragua was stalling. He therefore demanded immediate payment to his two countrymen and instructed them to abandon any further litigation in the

---

65. To Aberdeen, No. 14, p. encl.s (To Orosco, November 2, 1842), November 17, 1842, F.O. 15/29.

66. *Ibid.;* to Aberdeen, No. 15, p. encl.s, November 21, 1842, F.O. 15/29; Pablo Buitrago to James Buchanan, November 12, 1847, MDCIA, III, 255.

courts.[67] On November 8, he brought forth a third claim involving damages to the property of Walter Bridge, which had resulted from the anti-English feeling in the state after the Quijano incident.[68] On the 9th, he issued an ultimatum to the State of Nicaragua; it had to agree to settle all these claims within fifteen days. When state officials refused to meet these terms, Chatfield wrote to Lord Aberdeen, on the 30th, recommending a second blockade of San Juan de Nicaragua.[69] In March, 1844, Great Britain heeded his request. As in the blockade two years earlier, the motive of the British agent was political.

From Nicaragua, Chatfield proceeded to El Salvador where he joined Admiral Thomas in forcing that state to pay claims. In early December, he returned to Guatemala City, thoroughly frustrated at having failed to advance the "Guatemalan Confederation." Always the optimist, he made one more attempt to salvage the situation by encouraging his allies to take the initiative on the liquidation of the Bondholders' and Reid-Irving debts. In January, 1843, the *serviles* dutifully sent out a circular requesting the states to send delegates to Guatemala City in order to settle the financial question with Chatfield. The states demurred; they wanted no part of the "Guatemalan Confederation."[70]

With Chatfield's departure from the Pacific coast of Central America, the Nicaraguan and Salvadorean press unleashed a volley of articles which teemed with hatred for all Englishmen, who were variously described as pirates, buccaneers, and "abominable monsters." Threats of reprisals and warnings by Admiral Thomas and Frederick Chatfield did not deter the anglophobes, many of whom were ex-*Morazanistas* who were allowed to come back into the states.[71] Macdonald and Chatfield were their principal targets. Unionist writers attacked the superintendent of Belize for his treatment of Quijano; pleaded for effective union against the *serviles* of Guatemala, who had treacherously sold out to the British consulate; and urged the calling of the "Great American Diet" to prevent the abuse of Old World nations in the Western Hemisphere. *El Granadino* in Nicaragua and *El Amigo del Pueblo* in San Salvador were especially active in spreading this unionist and anti-British propaganda. With anger and vehemence Chatfield accused the Salvadorean government of

---

67. To Aberdeen, No. 16, p. encl.s, November 30, 1842, F.O. 15/29; from Orozco, November 9, 16, F.O. 252/16.

68. To Aberdeen, No. 4, p. encl.s, January 15, 1843, F.O. 15/35.

69. To Aberdeen, No. 16, November 30, 1842, F.O. 15/29.

70. To the Salvadorean Government, No. 19, December 7, 1843, F.O. 252/20.

71. Admiral Thomas to the Nicaraguan Government, December 22, 1842, F.O. 15/36; to Secretary of Nicaragua, January 7, 1843, F.O. 252/16.

"connivance" in these publications and threatened to hold it responsible for the licentiousness of its press.[72]

By raising the freedom-of-the-press issue, the consul-general unwittingly aided the unionist cause and further damaged his popularity in Central America. Salvadoreans charged that the English representative believed in the cherished principle only for his countrymen while he hypocritically denied it to the citizens of the New World. And to a large extent their accusation was true. Chatfield maintained firmly that the principle had no application in areas where the governments controlled the press. These remarks, in turn, were published at Salvadorean expense and circulated widely with impressive results.[73] Even in Guatemala City, a newspaper called *El Tambor* (The Drum) managed to publish a few issues in which it scored British aggression in Central America and pleaded for unity against the "enemy." Furious at learning of "this disgraceful print," right in his own backyard, Chatfield demanded its immediate suspension. Otherwise, he threatened, "I shall have no alternative but to withdraw my presence from this territory." Embarrassed *serviles* assured him that it would never happen again.[74] As Aberdeen learned of these squabbles between his agent and Central American governments, he refused to support the consul-general's position and cautioned him to use more diplomatic language in his correspondence with sovereign states.[75] No wonder Chatfield was angry and frustrated in late 1843.

————

The prospects of concerted action against British interests in Central America increased daily as the unionist movement gained momentum. On April 10, 1843, El Salvador pleaded with her sister states for harmony and unity. By that time, three states had ratified the *Pacto de Chinandega;* and Guatemala and Costa Rica had formally been asked to join them.[76] Frederick Chatfield had no alternative; the time to act had come.

Since there was more than sufficient evidence to justify the resumption of the Nicaraguan blockade, the British consul-general trained his

---

72. To Aberdeen, No. 9, p. encl.s (to Salvador, May 26, 1843, and *Amigo del Pueblo,* San Salvador, No. 4), May 27, 1843, F.O. 15/35.
73. *Correo Semanario del Salvador* (San Salvador), No. 104, June 2, 1843, in No. 11, to Aberdeen, June 10, 1843, F.O. 15/35; to the Salvadorean Government, No. 13, June 10, 1843, F.O. 252/20.
74. To Aberdeen, No. 19, p. encl.s, July 24, 1843, F.O. 15/35.
75. From Aberdeen, No. 8, October 1843, F.O. 15/35.
76. To Aberdeen, No. 9, p. encl.s, May 27, 1843, F.O. 15/35; "Memoria . . . Costa Rica," José María Castro, San José, June 2, 1843, B.N.G./F, 1843.

guns primarily on the states of El Salvador and Honduras. With regard to the former, he utilized a technique whose assumptions were diametrically opposed to the position he had established in advancing the "Guatemalan Confederation." Though he first described the new policy in 1845, its initial application was during the period under discussion. Commenting upon the anti-foreigner legislation of the various Central American states, Chatfield announced:

> I never intend allowing the Constitution of 1824 to expire, until all the states have assembled and formally agreed to annul it. It is our only sheet anchor against the capricious attacks of the State governments, who would otherwise be hourly devising laws to render the sojourn of foreigners in this country unbearable.[77]

Whereas in furthering the "Guatemalan Confederation," he had agreed to recognize the absolute sovereignty and independence of certain states, he now maintained that they had no such attributes and would not acquire them until they met to abrogate the former constitution — a virtual impossibility, and he knew it. On the surface, this "sheet anchor" policy appeared to be unionist in sympathy; but the irony of it was that the consul-general used it consistently as an anti-union device, against the very states who wanted to restore the old republic and who favored a strong policy against Great Britain. It would seem that Mr. Chatfield had special policies — oftentimes contradictory ones — to meet all occasions.

El Salvador was the first to feel the weight of the sheet anchor in a case which involved the English merchant Thomas Manning. Back in December, 1842, Manning had imported a consignment of goods from Nicaragua into El Salvador. When Salvadorean officials demanded payment of a twenty percent ad valorem tariff, Mr. Manning resisted on the ground that he had paid such a duty in Nicaragua when the goods first landed there. Another twenty percent duty clearly would have been abusive; and yet El Salvador, as a sovereign nation, had a right to collect duties upon goods which were to be sold within her boundaries. Both sides, it would seem, had valid points. However that may have been, when Chatfield assumed this case, he became the judge and the jury. Justice was with Mr. Manning and no one else. The Salvadorean government then countered with a decree which stated that merchants refusing to pay the tariff would not be allowed to trade in the state. Whereupon Chatfield replied pontifically: "I now disallow the right of the Government of Salvador to regulate anything affecting the Foreign Trade of this

---

77. To John Foster, March 12, 1845, F.O. 252/21.

country, or to rescind or to change the laws constitutionally established upon this head, by the Legislature of the Nation."[78]

Incidentally, this new hassle with El Salvador raged concurrently with the freedom-of-the-press dispute; and in both cases, the correspondence was published by the state government to the detriment of Chatfield's popularity. In the meantime, the consul-general insisted upon naval action against El Salvador, hoping that British ships would arrive in October or November during the annual indigo fairs. The presence of those vessels, he assured Lord Aberdeen, would have a "beneficial effect," discouraging the anglophobes "who are jealous of Guatemala" and her "British connexion."[79] Since eventually warships helped to collect the "sheet anchor" claims, we have here another illustration of Chatfield's success in committing his government to a divide-and-conquer policy in Central America.

The situation in Honduras was somewhat more complex since it was tied up with Guatemalan developments. In this case the consul-general's weapon was the Marshall Bennett claim to the Guayavillas mining property, discussed in Chapter Six. After Mr. Bennett's death in October, 1839, the Guayavillas case made its way through the courts of Honduras; and they passed favorably in behalf of Felipe Jáuregui's interests. The evidence seems to indicate that Jáuregui, as vice-president of the state, used his political office to influence these decisions. At any rate, no doubt existed in Chatfield's mind about this. Again as judge and jury, he decided that the Honduran courts were in error. The claim therefore had to be paid immediately to Bennett's heirs.[80] Honduras, of course, protested that Englishmen had to abide by the decisions of her courts; but Chatfield was unimpressed. He again asked Lord Aberdeen for naval support: "Unless I am authorized to follow it up as proposed by making the local government accountable for the irregularities of its tribunals, I candidly avow a belief, that ere long no Englishman's property will be safe from invasion in Central America."[81]

The key to the consul's strategy in Honduras was to be found in the tightening bond between him and the *serviles,* who had been asked recently to bring their government into the *Pacto de Chinandega.* In a pamphlet which appeared in Guatemala City on June 22, 1843, Guatemalan writers openly supported British action in Central America and attacked the irresponsibility of the *pacto* states. Unionists, of course,

---

78. To Aberdeen, No. 12, p. encl.s, June 12, 1843, F.O. 15/35.
79. No. 13 (June 15).
80. No. 17, p. encl.s, July 15.
81. No. 22 (September 16).

promptly denounced these writers for their lack of *nacionalidad* and their defense of the meddling British consul.[82] On July 5, moreover, the Guatemalan government formally rejected the Chinandega pact.[83] Though sensitive to the "malicious charges" in the unionist press concerning their motives in refusing to join the new pact, the *serviles* persevered in aligning themselves with Chatfield.[84] He, in turn, promised them a trade treaty; and the state legislature went on record favoring these negotiations. Writing on November 13, Father Juan José Aycinena told the British consul-general that he hoped other Central American states would welcome the opportunity to benefit from this economic contact with Great Britain.[85] Obviously, the allies had not abandoned their confederation scheme.

By applying pressure — the Guayavillas claim — upon Honduras, Chatfield was attacking the weakest link in the *Pacto de Chinandega*. He wanted to dissociate President Francisco Ferrera from any aggressive action which the signatory states might decide to take against Guatemala and her pro-English government. The strategy worked perfectly. Both Ferrera and Jáuregui wrote to Father Aycinena asking him to stop Chatfield on the Guayavillas business; it was creating a situation, they said, which might topple their government and throw political power into the hands of the *Morazanistas*. With assurances that Honduras would listen to reason, the British agent suspiciously dropped the Guayavillas claim. And Honduras was informed, in early November, that she might share in the impending treaty between Guatemala and Great Britain. She accepted.[86]

Determined to advance the "Guatemalan Confederation" at all costs, Chatfield issued a circular to the states on December 7, 1843, in which he reminded them of their debt to British creditors. To his "infinite surprise and disappointment," the states had not heeded Guatemala's call earlier in the year — a negligence which he now termed "reprehensible." "The time does not seem far distant," he added, "when the British government for the protection of the Publick whose interests are confided to its care, will probably have to enforce a compliance with the

82. *Centro América y la Inglaterra,* by "Unos Guatemaltecos," June 22, 1843, B.N.G./F, 1843; *El Amigo del Pueblo* (San Salvador), No. 12, July 20, 1843, B.N.G./V, leg. 837.
83. "Orden de la Asamblea Constituyente del Estado de Guatemala," July 5, 1843, B.N.G./HS, 1843; also in M.A.E.B./CPSG.
84. *Gaceta Oficial* (Guatemala), No. 114, August 4, 1843, B.N.G./V, leg. 837.
85. From Juan José Aycinena, November 13, 1843, F.O. 252/12.
86. Felipe Jáuregui to Aycinena, September 9, and Francisco Ferrera to Aycinena, September 11, 1843, F.O. 252/24; from Aycinena, November 16, 1843, F.O. 252/12.

Bondholders' claims."[87] It behooved the states, therefore, to send envoys at once to arrange a settlement with him in Guatemala City.

Since the Chinandega states had recently decided to hold a meeting in the Salvadorean town of San Vicente, scheduled for late January, 1844, the consul's debt circular had definite political undertones. For example, he told them in that message: "The altered circumstances of the country since the events of September 1842 render it essential that the several states should by a formal instrument discharge each other from all liability for more than their relative proportion of the Foreign Debt." To satisfy this requirement, amounting to a denial of any right to form a central government in the future, Chatfield appended a "draft of a release." If the states refused to sign the release, he added, "the obligations of the late federation towards the bondholders bound each State for the whole amount of the Debt."[88] In other words, if the Chinandega states had signed such a release, they could not have legally formed the Confederation of Central America which resulted from their 1844 meeting. Presumably the December circular was also intended to stop Costa Rica, who had paid most of her obligations, from joining the new general government. These political objectives were implicit in the analysis of the Belgian consul, who incidentally was on friendly terms with Frederick Chatfield.[89]

The allies' victory in bringing Ferrera within Guatemala's orbit spurred unionists to adopt military plans against them. On August 16, 1843, El Salvador and Nicaragua signed a pact in which they committed each other to the forceful overthrow of Ferrera in Honduras, replacing him with the unionist General Cabañas, and to an attack upon Guatemala City.[90] Assigned to lead the invasionary forces were General Francisco Malespín for El Salvador and Manuel Quijano, now sporting the rank of general, for Nicaragua. In a moment of exhilaration, the ex-commandant of San Juan de Nicaragua publicly challenged Frederick Chatfield to a duel. The consul-general noted disparagingly that the challenge was made in San Salvador, at a safe distance of two hundred miles.[91]

Without a doubt the situation was critical, especially since Costa Rica had partially committed herself to the *Pacto de Chinandega* in late

---

87. To Salvadorean Government, No. 19, December 7, 1843, F.O. 252/20.
88. *Ibid.*
89. Martial Cloquet to Minister of Foreign Affairs (Compte Goblet d'Alviella), No. 38, December 21, 1843, M.A.E.B./CST.
90. *Ibid.*, p. encl.s.
91. To Aberdeen, No. 3, p. encl.s, January 9, 1844, F.O. 15/37.

December.[92] Moreover, for several months Nicaraguan unionists had been considering the possibility of sending their foreign minister Francisco Castellón on a special mission abroad to expose Chatfield's political maneuvers in Central America and to gain support — moral and financial — for the new confederation government.[93] From the consul's point of view, he had to prevent Castellón's departure from Central America, to discourage the formation of an anti-British confederation government, and to block the military invasion if possible. Fortunately, his good friend Manuel Francisco Pavón, who worked in conjunction with Bishop Jorge Viteri in San Salvador, successfully thwarted the invasion of Guatemala by feeding Malespín's suspicions that *Morazanistas* were merely using him and would eventually sacrifice him. As far as it is known, Chatfield had no direct influence upon the changing scene in El Salvador, though obviously he welcomed the results.[94]

In the meantime, the consul was counting heavily upon naval support on the Pacific coast, hoping that it would arrive by October at the latest. To expedite matters, he sent written instructions to various ports on the Pacific, in which he suggested what actions naval captains should take after their arrival.[95] British ships, however, failed to appear as expected, thus weakening Chatfield's pressure upon the unionist states. Later he vented his anger and disappointment in a blistering message to Admiral Thomas. The latter immediately relayed the insolent letter to the Admiralty, but the Foreign Office took no corrective action. Perhaps it shared the consul-general's opinion that the Pacific squadron was derelict in carrying out instructions from London.[96] At any rate, there can be no question about Chatfield's disappointment at not receiving naval aid.

Offsetting the annoyance with Admiral Thomas was the welcome news he received in mid-November from Lord Aberdeen and the admiral in charge of the Atlantic squadron. In a dispatch dated August 26, 1843, Aberdeen agreed to support his agent's request for a second blockade of San Juan de Nicaragua. Following through on this decision, Admiral

92. "Reformas al pacto de Chinandega propuestas por la Asamblea Constituyente de Costarrica a los Gobiernos Confederados," San José, December 6, 1843, in *Eco* (León), No. 15, December 21, 1843.
93. From John Foster, November 6, 1843, F.O. 252/19; also see the documentation on the Castellón mission to Europe in F.O. 15/39.
94. From Manuel Francisco Pavón, January 6, 1844, F.O. 252/20; to Aberdeen, No. 6, January 28, 1844, F.O. 15/37; Martial Cloquet to Min. of Foreign Affairs, No. 38, December 21, 1843, M.A.E.B./CST.
95. To British Naval Officer at Realejo, August 3, 1843, F.O. 252/8.
96. Richard Thomas to Admiralty, p. encl.s, November 18, 1844, F.O. 15/41, including Chatfield's letter of July 27, 1844, to Thomas.

Adam asked the British consul for information on the Glenton, Manning, and Bridge cases.[97] Assured of naval support, the consul-general's tone in the correspondence with unionist states stiffened noticeably. In fact, he issued an ultimatum which required Nicaragua to settle the above-mentioned claims by February 16, 1844. Completely ignoring Nicaraguan protests, Chatfield referred the claims to Admiral Adam on December 30, just as he had threatened.[98]

The fruitless correspondence with Nicaragua continued for a few months longer. But Chatfield's mind was made up, especially since his informants in Nicaragua had told him that the Ramón Solórzano-Francisco Castellón government was having its share of internal problems. Apparently he wanted to force the government's downfall with the threat of a second blockade.[99] Furthermore, Minister Castellón had refused to accept and to sign the release document on the foreign debt, suspecting its political implications. He promised nevertheless to bring up the debt question at the impending meeting of the *pacto* states at San Vicente.[100] Annoyed at the Nicaraguan's clever maneuver, Chatfield was all the more determined to settle the matter by force. Besides, he wrote to Aberdeen, Castellón was a two-faced scoundrel who had written to the states alleging that "I arrogate the right to dispose of cases pending in its law courts, and insinuating that my demand is a mere cloak to hide some more important end."[101] Compulsion was the only answer, he told Admiral Adam; and it pleased him to know that the British government was recognizing this truth.[102]

Desperately hoping to prevent the threatened blockade of San Juan, Nicaragua beseeched the *serviles* of Guatemala to intercede in her behalf. On his part, Father Aycinena tried to convince his English colleague that a display of force at this juncture might have harmful political and economic consequences. But the Englishman would not listen.[103] In fact, he even refused a last-minute proposal, made on March 8, 1844, by

---

97. From Aberdeen, Nos. 5-6, August 26, 1843, F.O. 15/35; Aberdeen to Admiralty, August 26, 1843, especially folios 221-223, F.O. 15/36; from Adam, October 20, 1843, in No. 2, to Aberdeen, January 3, 1844, F.O. 15/37.
98. Enclosed in No. 2, to Aberdeen, January 3.
99. From J. W. Glenton, pvt., December 22, 1843, F.O. 252/30; from Foster, January 5, 1844, F.O. 252/19.
100. To Aberdeen, No. 9, p. encl.s, February 5, 1844, F.O. 15/37; *Eco* (León), No. 17, January 18, 1844.
101. To Aberdeen, No. 7, February 1, 1844, F.O. 15/37.
102. To Adam, December 30, 1843, in No. 2, to Aberdeen, January 3, 1844, F.O. 15/37.
103. Enclosures in No. 11, to Aberdeen, February 21, 1844, F.O. 15/37.

which Nicaragua offered to pay the claims under protest, using the revenues of San Juan de Nicaragua.[104]

The second blockade of Nicaragua commenced on March 30 and ended on July 28, 1844. At first the naval pressure had little or no effect. But on July 5, when the *Daphne* reached the Pacific port of Realejo, the end was in sight. Nicaragua was brought to her knees.[105] To the victors went the spoils. Glenton and Manning gained control of the Nicaraguan tobacco monopoly for a period of two years; and Bridge received credits on future import duties.[106] Satisfied with these impressive results, Her Majesty's consul-general felt that he had buttressed his oft-stated argument that with the navy at his command he could protect British life and property in the "rude and uncivilised" states of Central America.

Quijano's ransom was indeed costly for Central America, thanks to the maneuvers of aggressive British agents like Alexander Macdonald and Frederick Chatfield. In pursuit of political objectives, they encouraged two blockades and committed their country to a protectorate of the Mosquito Coast. In effect, they influenced, or brought about, a divide-and-conquer policy in Central America. Ironically, England was unaware of the manner in which she was being used by her representatives in the field.

Just as Father Aycinena had predicted, the forceful British action on the coasts of Nicaragua opened up pandora's box in Central America. Two chaotic years of little benefit to anyone ensued; and every state, bar none, passed anti-foreigner legislation as ex-*Morazanistas* strengthened their political position. Even Chatfield's allies had to desert the ship. Ferrera's state reopened the thorny Ruatán issue; and the *serviles* lost their preeminence in Guatemala City. The fact is that the British consul-general was alone during those years and wielded no political power to speak of. To protect his countrymen from abuse, he resorted to the above-mentioned "sheet anchor" policy, applying it not only to economic matters but also in the diplomatic sphere. For example, he argued that Honduras had no legal right, as an isolated state of the former republic, to approach Great Britain on the Ruatán issue. On occasions, British ships were called in to support his doctrines; but, in any case, no permanent stability resulted from the consul's efforts. In fact the peremptory

---

104. Decree, León, March 8, 1844, in Adam to Admiralty, August 14, 1844, F.O. 15/38.
105. Richard Thomas to Admiralty, p. encl.s, October 23, 1844, F.O. 15/41.
106. "Memorandum on Blockade," July 6, 1844; Adam to Admiralty, October 2, 1844, F.O. 15/38.

and disrespectful tone of his correspondence with the various states merely intensified the hatred for all foreigners.[107]

Although initially the union movement gained from the English blockade of 1844, it soon shattered upon the rocks of Central American politics. As scheduled, the *pacto* states met at San Vicente and on March 29, 1844, created the Confederation of Central America.[108] Leading an ephemeral existence, the new general government had a short life; it lost whatever authority it had by August, 1844, though it lingered on officially for another year. Since Mr. Chatfield's alliance with Guatemala and Honduras dissolved itself, the British agent had little to do with the demise of Central America's second government. Rather, its failure resulted from two factors which had plagued the area for decades: first, the ideological struggle between unionists and states' righters; and, secondly, the baneful effect of *personalismo* — the irresponsible and opportunistic rivalry of such caudillos as Malespín in El Salvador, Ferrera in Honduras, and Carrera in Guatemala. There is little point, therefore, in recording the shifting sands of Central American politics during those chaotic years, except to note the general trends mentioned above.

Francisco Castellón's mission to Europe — in the wake of the second blockade — likewise ended in failure. On the Continent, the Nicaraguan envoy labored diligently to win recognition for the Confederation of Central America, especially in France. In addition, he hoped that France would agree to finance the construction of the Nicaraguan canal. His achievements, however, were limited and disappointing, perhaps because Great Britain stood against him.[109]

In London, Lord Aberdeen granted him several interviews in which they thrashed out the points of contention. But when placed on the defensive, the British foreign secretary ended up by defending the actions of his aggressive agent in Central America. As far as he was concerned, Chatfield was faithfully carrying out instructions from the Foreign Office and had not acted upon his own initiative. He would therefore not recall him. With regard to the issue of recognition, Lord Aberdeen maintained — an argument suggested to him by his consul-general — that England could not accept the new general government since it did not represent all five states of Central America. And, as for the Nicaraguan suggestion to arbitrate the claims which provoked the recent blockade, he would

107. Raymond Baradère to Min. of Foreign Affairs, No. 7, December 19, 1844, A.A.E.P./CPAC, vol. 4; to Aberdeen, No. 2, January 6, 1845, F.O. 15/40.

108. *Eco* (León), No. 21, April 22, 1844.

109. Castellón to Aberdeen, August 28, September 15, 25, October 17, November 4, 14, 23, and December 4, 1844, F.O. 15/39.

not hear of it. Since Nicaragua had indemnified the three Englishmen in question, he argued speciously that she had virtually admitted the validity of those claims. There was thus nothing to arbitrate.[110] To be sure, Castellón's mission accomplished little in London, but its very failure contributed to a healthy revival of the union movement in 1846. Henceforth no one seriously doubted that the British government was solidly behind Chatfield's activities in Central America. This knowledge underscored the urgency of union and the need for a counterpoise to Great Britain. Perhaps, many reasoned, the United States might be willing to serve in that capacity.

The disclosures of the Castellón mission, moreover, alerted the Foreign Office to Chatfield's involvement in the internal affairs of Central America. It exposed, so to speak, many of his techniques of operation, especially the slanting of reports by the deliberate omission of materials. And Lord Aberdeen was miffed, to say the least. He questioned the validity of the consul's "sheet anchor" policy, though he had in effect accepted it when he refused to recognize the Confederation of Central America.[111] And he strongly reprimanded Chatfield for failing to send the Foreign Office a copy of the *Pacto de Chinandega,* thus denying his superiors pertinent information concerning the unionist movement. This carelessness had to stop, Lord Aberdeen scolded: "I trust I may not again have to make any remarks upon this subject."[112]

Despite the reprimands, however, the Foreign Office never seriously considered recalling Chatfield even though it was clear that he would not mend his ways. In 1845, when the Guatemalan secretary of state, José Antonio Azmitia, again demanded the consul's recall, Lord Aberdeen refused to acquiesce.[113] The fact that Guatemala was the state recommending Chatfield's dismissal illustrated graphically the political effects of his insistence upon a second blockade. Hampered by Aberdeen at every turn and discouraged by his continual nagging, Chatfield despaired and grew weary.

His spirits revived and his outlook changed, however, when he learned the good news that in mid-1846 Lord Palmerston had again taken over the portfolio of foreign affairs. Another period of aggressive British policy in Central America was in the offing. "Old Pam" understood him and appreciated his talents.

---

110. Aberdeen to Castellón, November 26, 1844, F.O. 15/39.
111. From Aberdeen, Nos. 6-8, October 1, 1845, F.O. 15/40.
112. From Aberdeen, Nos. 4-6, November 15-16, 1844, F.O. 15/37.
113. From Aberdeen, No. 6, October 1, 1845, F.O. 15/40.

CHAPTER TEN

Old Predilections

I should have expected that [Felipe] Molina, by his connection with Wallerstein, and long residence out of C. A., would have acquired better ideas, and not have acted in the sense of the perverse and mischievous liberales of this country; but it seems old predilections are not to be overcome.[1] — Chatfield, August 3, 1846

The Treaties which Your Lordship has instructed me to conclude with Guatemala and Costa Rica will do a good deal towards preventing these states from forming themselves again into a single state.[2] — Chatfield, January 12, 1849

As "Doyen" of the corps, the British consul-general was chosen to represent his colleagues at an important interview with General Carrera, scheduled for May 23, 1846.[3] He was somewhat apprehensive about the way the "man" might receive him, especially considering the strained relations with the Guatemalan government in the previous two years. In the best circumstances, moreover, it was difficult to predict how the young Indian chieftain, now in his early thirties and very much impressed with his own importance, would react on any given occasion. Scarcely a year earlier, Carrera had vowed to kill the English agent for having denied Guatemala's nationality in a series of claims which were accompanied by the ever-present threat of naval force.[4] Matters worsened when Lord Aberdeen refused to grant the Guatemalan request for the consul's recall.[5] Yet despite the potential danger to himself, the situation in early 1846 called for action; Chatfield had to take his chances.

The purpose of the interview, as it turned out, was to raise doubts in Carrera's mind concerning two of his cabinet members: General Jerónimo Pais, minister of finance and war, and José Antonio Azmitia, minister of foreign affairs. Some political observers, including members of the consular corps, had the impression that Pais, former commandant of Izabal and a close friend of Carrera, was promoted to the cabinet post

---

1. To John Foster, August 3, 1846, F.O. 252/21.
2. To Palmerston, No. 6, January 12, 1849, F.O. 15/57.
3. To Palmerston, No. 21, July 1, 1846, F.O. 15/42.
4. Raymond Baradère to Min. of Foreign Affairs, August 28, 1845, A.A.E.P./ CPAC, vol. 5; to William Hall, pvt., October 20, 1845, F.O. 252/18; to Aberdeen, No. 41, December 10, 1845, F.O. 15/40.
5. From Lord Aberdeen, No. 6, October 1, 1845, F.O. 15/40.

in order to assure the loyalty of the military forces. Azmitia, on the other hand, who was known for his liberal predilections, had been chosen to moderate Pais's actions and to divert the government's unpopularity from Carrera to himself. But this ingenuous political maneuver had misfired, according to Chatfield, producing a contrary result. By supporting Pais's aggressive stand against foreigners, Azmitia was deliberately working to discredit Carrera and to bring about the downfall of the government.[6] At least, this is what Chatfield thought.

Though Azmitia's presence at the interview was an inhibiting factor, the English speaker presented his arguments effectively, and was pleasantly surprised at Carrera's attentiveness. It was of the utmost importance, he lectured his listener, for Guatemala to remain on friendly terms with other foreign powers, thus encouraging the inflow of foreign capital and immigrants whose "know-how" was so essential to the development of the state. Yet Minister Pais had, in fact, jeopardized relations with European nations by his arbitrary acts toward their consuls, rescinding, for example, their old privilege of importation without the payment of duties. Furthermore, he had raised the duties on foreign goods entering Guatemala; and he had officially circulated broadsides which discredited European consuls and incited the public's wrath against them. Actions of this nature could only lead to reprisals from the aggrieved countries. France, for example, had already decided to use force if the harassment of her nationals continued.[7] In addition, the commandant of Izabal (Marcelino Marchamé) — perhaps under orders from Pais, Chatfield hinted — had written to Colonel John Fancourt at Belize in terms which were calculated to revive the thorny territorial issue with Great Britain. Such provocative moves were certainly not intended to serve Guatemala's best interests; in fact, the underlying objective, Chatfield insinuated, was the downfall of the regime's leader. This last point registered visibly upon Carrera's face. Could it be that his erstwhile comrade in arms had political ambitions?

After taking leave of the Indian chieftain, Chatfield stepped into the adjoining room to pay his respects to General Pais, who undoubtedly must have heard the entire conversation — accusations and all. A *persona non grata* among Europeans living in Guatemala, General Pais was pictured by them in the most derogatory colors as a drunkard, an atheist, and a man lacking *savoir vivre*. The Belgian consul recalled how Pais

6. To Palmerston, No. 21, July 1, 1846, F.O. 15/42; Martial Cloquet to Min. of Foreign Affairs (Deschamps), No. 206, February 15, 1846, M.A.E.B./ CPC, vol. 2 (1841–1850).

7. To Palmerston No. 21 (July 1); and Cloquet's No. 206 (February 15).

had boorishly received the French consul while serving as commandant of Izabal. Later, when Raymond Baradère failed to invite him to a dinner honoring Carrera, the vindictive Pais swore that he would have revenge. Presumably, this slight had triggered the offensive against the consular corps and especially against French citizens.[8] The following description of Chatfield's brief conversation with General Pais is self-evident:

> He spoke of Europe, and especially of England, as north and south Americans sometimes will speak, tauntingly; that worn out Europe and its decrepit institutions were fast giving way to the superior vigour and intelligence of this precious hemisphere; perfectly careless of the fact, that if the constant infusion of European blood into America were stopped for a few years, the European race would in all probability wear out, since it is seen, that Europeans degenerate on this continent, as well as plants and animals transferred hither.[9]

The interview with Rafael Carrera produced the desired effect, especially when followed up by a confidential letter from the British consulate.[10] In early July, 1846, Pais lost his cabinet post.[11] And by the end of the year, Azmitia's influence over Carrera was waning. Guatemalan liberals, who thanks to the second British blockade had increased their political power, were now on the decline. Frederick Chatfield had once again entered the political arena.

———◆———

The prospects of a successful union movement — one that might secure the support of the United States of America — had prompted the consul's decision to move his residence from Antigua back to Guatemala City. Earlier, this was unnecessary, for any political observer could see that while the battle of the caudillos raged in Central America there was little likelihood of a unionist victory.[12] But the *Morazanistas,* nonetheless, had made substantial gains as a result of Castellón's failure in Europe. A constant barrage of rumors announced the impending occupation of San Juan de Nicaragua, now called San Juan del Norte — all of

8. Cloquet's No. 206.
9. To Palmerston, No. 21 (July 1).
10. To Rafael Carrera, conf., June 8, 1846, F.O. 252/13; also enclosed in No. 21 (July 1).
11. To Aberdeen, No. 24, July 11, 1846, F.O. 15/42; to John Foster, July 8, 1846, F.O. 252/21.
12. To Foster, March 12, 1845, F.O. 252/21; Cloquet to A. Deschamps, No. 210, March 15, 1846, M.A.E.B./CPC, vol. 2, containing an excellent analysis of caudillos as deterrents to union.

which underscored the need for united action. And, significantly, in the various treaties signed in 1845 — Nicaragua and El Salvador (May 6), Honduras and Guatemala (July 19), and Honduras and El Salvador (November 27) — the states repeated their desire to reconstitute the general government of Central America in order to regularize their relations with other foreign nations and to counter effectively the territorial aggression of British subjects.[13] To achieve these ends, they agreed to meet in January, 1846, at Sonsonate, in El Salvador. After some delays, the delegates opened their sessions in June.

Typical of the revived enthusiasm for union, a publication appeared in San Salvador on November 15, 1845, which happened to represent the official views of the state. Under the lengthy title "A writing which demonstrates and urges the only measure which it is convenient to take in order to establish easily a national government which will give being to Central America," the article reviewed the weaknesses of the 1824 Constitution and the various attempts to reform it. The author argued convincingly that the 1835 reforms, though they were not ratified by the requisite two-thirds vote in all of the five states, had nonetheless represented the wishes of the majority in Central America. He therefore urged a reconsideration of those reforms along with two modifications: first, that a majority vote in each state would suffice for ratification; and secondly, that Central Americans should abandon the system of delegates-at-large, insisting that all politicians of the new government be required to live at least two years in their districts. The writer of the *Escrito* also repeated the view that the time had come for a genuine imitation of the United States Constitution. In the addenda and accompanying chart, he demonstrated that the new government would not cost more than 104,000 pesos annually — a nominal figure compared to the expenses of war and the anarchy of the past. Interestingly, in view of Chatfield's subsequent actions, the author of the article suggested that the tobacco revenue would more than meet the cost of the proposed general government.[14] It should be noted, moreover, that the *Escrito* received wide circulation. In fact, it even encouraged an anonymous states' righter in Guatemala City to publish a rebuttal in the local gazette.[15]

The unionist movement was particularly strong in Guatemala where

---

13. Cloquet to Deschamps, No. 207, February 20, 1846, M.A.E.B./CPC, vol. 2.
14. "Escrito . . . ," by "Un hijo del Salvador y ciudadano de Centro-América," San Salvador, November 10, 1845, in M.A.E.B./CPC, vol. 2, and in B.L./ CAP, vol. 8, which is more complete since it includes a final resumé and chart.
15. "Contestación al communicado sobre nacionalidad inserto en la Gaceta Official de Guatemala Núm. 21," February 5, 1846, B.L./CAP, vol. 2.

José Antonio Azmitia and Mariano Padilla persuaded General Carrera to lead the cause of reform, just as the liberals had done prior to Chatfield's return to Central America in the summer of 1842. Dr. Padilla, moreover, was sent on a special mission to encourage the participation of El Salvador, Nicaragua, and Honduras in the Sonsonate meeting. On January 12, 1846, the Guatemalan envoy delivered an impassioned plea to the Salvadorean government in which he urged common action against the usurpers of Central American territory: Great Britain, Mexico, and New Granada. Salvadorean officials replied enthusiastically and promised to appoint a special agent to accompany Padilla on his tour of the states.[16]

Considering the unionists' penchant for the "Western Hemisphere Idea," it is not difficult to understand why the British consul-general decided that he could no longer remain aloof from politics. In the opening quotation of this chapter, Mr. Chatfield was referring to Felipe Molina's nationalistic outburst in a Costa Rican paper concerning the exchange of correspondence between the commandant of Izabal and superintendent Fancourt of Belize. Molina, it would seem, shared the "old predilections" of the *Morazanistas* on territorial questions.[17] Irony would have it, however, that Molina eventually became one of Chatfield's agents in Central America.

At Sonsonate the obstacles to union again proved insurmountable. Unionist liberals led the deliberations but they were unable to convince their states' rights colleagues, who only reluctantly had come to the reunion because of the overwhelming sentiment for union in their states. At the meeting, however, they raised objections which led eventually to inaction — the fate of the unionist movement in the crucial 1840's.

Conflicting and limited instructions, coupled with the non arrival of some delegates, also frustrated the Sonsonate meeting. Yet the delegations managed to agree to hold another reunion in the following year at Nacaome, in Honduras. They hoped that by then all five states would authorize their representatives to consent to the calling of a national constituent assembly which would draw up a new federal pact.[18] It should be noted that the secrecy which surrounded the discussions of the impending meeting at Nacaome visibly disturbed the master of the British consulate.[19]

---

16. Cloquet's No. 210, p. encl.s.
17. To Foster, August 3, 1846, F.O. 252/21.
18. Sebastián Salinas to the Legislature (Nicaragua), in No. 23, to Palmerston, March 19, 1849, F.O. 15/57.
19. To Palmerston, No. 29, September 4, 1846, F.O. 15/42.

But again his apprehension was unfounded; only three states sent delegations to the Honduran site in June, 1847. On October 7, they signed the *Pacto de Nacaome* which, when ratified, would have set up a provisional government empowered to represent the states until the calling of a national constituent assembly. Interestingly, from informants in Nicaragua and Honduras Chatfield learned that those two governments did not intend to ratify the pact; they had merely sent delegates there to assuage the public mind.[20] In short, they were insincere; only the state of El Salvador labored in good faith. Guatemala and Cost Rica, safely under the control of Mr. Chatfield by then, refused categorically to send representatives to Nacaome. That the three states of the "center" eventually ratified the pact in early 1848 was due more to developments concerning Mosquitia than to any sincere desire for union.

<hr>

If unionist liberals found it difficult to overcome their "old predilections," the same was true of the *serviles* and their English leader. The pattern of 1842–1843 repeated itself as they resurrected the "Guatemalan Confederation" to distract the unionist movement. Interestingly, after the second British blockade and with the *serviles'* loss of political power, Mr. Chatfield had abandoned the confederation tactic.[21] And with the *liberales* controlling Carrera's ear, his opinion of Guatemala and her leaders changed abruptly. Guatemala was not one iota better than her sister states; and following his "sheet anchor" policy, he denied her a right of nationality.[22] An alteration in the political climate, in other words, caused a shift in the consul-general's views concerning the Guatemalan government, formerly his ally.

But all this changed with the resurgence of unionism in late 1845. Upon his return to Guatemala City, Chatfield again promoted the political fortunes of his erstwhile allies, "Chico" Pavón and Luis Batres in particular. By attacking Pais and Azmitia in the interview with Carrera, the consul-general in effect was aiding their cause. In an important dispatch to Lord Aberdeen, dated April 25, 1846, we have the first evidence of the restored alliance between Chatfield and the *serviles*.[23] He discussed in this letter the prospects of the Sonsonate meeting, which he described as far from promising. The *Morazanistas,* he noted, were strongly en-

20. From Thomas Manning, October 11, 1847, F.O. 252/33; to Manning, July 3, 1847, F.O. 252/36; from Juan Lindo, October 25, 1847, F.O. 252/14.
21. From Manuel Francisco Pavón, October 26, 1844, F.O. 252/12; to Pavón, No. 23, November 18, 1844, F.O. 252/13.
22. To Foster, March 12, 1845, F.O. 252/21.
23. To Aberdeen, No. 15, April 25, 1846, F.O. 15/42.

trenched in El Salvador; and the Honduran President Juan Lindo was fearful that the *coquimbos,* a derogatory term for the unionist liberals, might capture control of the meeting. Describing the unionists' plan as impracticable, Chatfield then told Aberdeen that Central Americans would do well to consider the enclosed report written by "two of the most intelligent and enlightened men in the country" — Manuel Francisco Pavón and Luis Batres. In their opinion, the formation of a national government would be a futile gesture. They recommended instead a "Council of Union" consisting of one delegate per state and under the jurisdiction of Guatemala's president.[24] When these two learned gentlemen were appointed to represent their state at Sonsonate, Guatemala was well on her way to deserting the cause of union. By then liberals and conservatives were engaged in a fierce competition for control of the "man" Carrera.[25]

The dispatch of April 25, 1846, also marked the first indication of a real concern for the possibility that the United States might encourage the unionist movement in Central America — a fear which thoroughly obsessed Frederick Chatfield from this time forward. Although indirectly expressed, the allusion was nonetheless there. In reference to the remarks made by General Mariano Paredes on December 15, 1845, by which that Mexican officer had declared himself in favor of a monarchical form of government, Chatfield noted that Guatemalan conservatives were favorably impressed. He too felt that monarchical institutions should be supported in the New World as opposed to the anarchy of "republicanism."

The context for this allusion is what is important. From a Nicaraguan informant, Chatfield learned that Prince Louis Napoleon of France was considering a plan to establish a monarchy in Central America, and perhaps eventually in Mexico, as a counterpoise to the advance of North Americans into that area — a harbinger of the Maximillian Empire a decade and a half later. Knowing that Prince Napoleon had escaped from jail and was in London, Chatfield, in the above-mentioned dispatch, may have been encouraging his government to condone the imperial project.[26] At any rate, the objective of the Napoleonic scheme is what interested him: to thwart the advance of the United States into Middle America. In later dispatches, Chatfield minced no words on this matter. "Brother Jonathan" might easily prove to be the difference between success and failure for the unionist movement; and the liberals' type of union would

---

24. *Ibid.,* enclosure dated March 23, 1846.
25. Cloquet's No. 206.
26. From John Foster, February 25, 1846, F.O. 252/21; to Aberdeen, No. 29, September 4, 1846, F.O. 15/42.

be disastrous for Great Britain. When José Antonio Azmitia learned of the conservatives' interest in monarchy, it should be noted, he formed an "American party" in Guatemala, dedicated to the spread of republicanism in the New World.[27]

Though the British agent pretended that the Sonsonate meeting had little chance of success, for he was sure that his allies would obstruct it with a confederation scheme, he nonetheless had some doubts. To guarantee the failure of the meeting, he wrote two selections against the unionist movement, which he sent to his friend and correspondent in San Salvador, Marcos Idígoras. They were published in *El Salvador Rejenerado,* one under Idígoras' name and the other anonymously — a remarkable illustration of Chatfield's meddling in the internal politics of Central America. Incidentally, he reprimanded Idígoras for signing the first article.[28] Everybody, of course, knew who the real author was.

As a brutal realist in politics, the English consul-general deliberately appealed to the selfish interests and aspirations of factions in the various states of Central America. The major point in his overall strategy was to control the peripheral states of Costa Rica and Guatemala. As for the "center" states, his principal goal was to attract them to one of the outlying states, especially Guatemala. The means were varied. He might appeal to them along ideological lines, as conservatives or states' righters, who might also be liberal. In these cases, he exploited sectional rivalries on occasion. His objective was simply to divide-and-conquer so that factions hostile to Great Britain would not flourish. At the time in question, Chatfield hoped to bring Honduras into the Guatemalan camp by appealing to the Juan Lindo-Francisco Ferrera faction of states' righters with a conservative bent. And, in Nicaragua, he favored the León party of José Guerrero as opposed to their liberal rival from Granada. Whenever convenient, he likewise encouraged Nicaraguan conservatives — Padre Solís, Jerónimo Carcache, etc.— the group which had sought British protection in the civil war of 1839. In other words, expediency and local circumstances governed his relations with the "center." He despaired, however, of the "troublesome" State of El Salvador, by far the most consistently unionist of the five states. Here the use of claims, collected by the British navy, was the most effective instrument of control.

The rapprochement with Costa Rica definitely began in early 1846, when Chatfield learned that the San José government was anxiously

---

27. To Palmerston, No. 1, political, October 12, 1846, F.O. 15/42.

28. To Marcos Idígoras, June 19, July 10, 17, 1846, conf., F.O. 252/29; from Idígoras, July 10, 1846, F.O. 252/33.

seeking British protection.[29] Alarmed at New Granada's offensive with regard to the Mosquito Shore — a subject which will be treated in more detail subsequently — Costa Rica wanted British support for her claims to the area south of the San Juan River. Moreover, realizing that the outlet to the Atlantic from San José to Moíns (Matina, or Salt Creek) was inadequate, she was hopeful that Chatfield would assist her in establishing a new route via the Serapiquí River to its junction with the San Juan, leaving only some thirty miles from that point to the ocean. For this purpose, Costa Rica needed an assurance from Nicaragua which would guarantee the free navigation of the San Juan River; and she was willing to pay her neighbor a sizable amount for this concession in the form of tobacco.[30]

The Costa Rican proposal contained some very real advantages for the British consulate. To begin with, Nicaragua would thus have revenue to make a substantial payment on the English debt; this was no mean consideration since the creditors in Great Britain by this time were justifiably impatient. But to Chatfield the political advantages were far more attractive. By encouraging the Costa Rican-Nicaraguan tobacco arrangement, he could gain the gratitude of the southernmost state, thus preparing it to join the "Guatemalan Confederation." Furthermore, it is interesting to note that in advancing the project the British agent asked for the Nicaraguan tobacco monopoly (*estanco*) for the period 1847–1848, that is, after the expiration of the Glenton-Manning contract which had resulted from the second British blockade. At the same time, he was pressuring El Salvador for a similar arrangement.[31]

Control of the tobacco revenues was important to him not only to assure the liquidation of the British debt but also as an anti-unionist measure — to deprive any general government which might be established in Central America from its principal source of revenue, as suggested in the *Escrito* mentioned above. Though the *estanco* proposals failed to materialize, for many reasons which do not concern us here, the fact remains that a working alliance with the Costa Rican government resulted from the overture. This was especially obvious from October, 1847, forward.[32]

After the Sonsonate meeting, the British consul-general redoubled

---

29. From Edward Wallerstein, January 20, February 5, 20, 1846, F.O. 252/33; also see, from Ignacio B. Calvo, October 1, 1845, F.O. 252/14; and, to Foster, February 5, 1846, F.O. 252/21.
30. To Aberdeen, No. 15 (April 25).
31. To Principal Secretary of Nicaraguan Government, conf., August 3, 1846, F.O. 252/16; to Foster, August 3, 1846, F.O. 252/21.
32. From José M. Castro, October 20, 1847, F.O. 252/14.

his efforts to advance the "Guatemalan Confederation" before "Brother Jonathan" appeared on the scene to nullify his long Central American career. From English and North American newspapers, which he received regularly, he watched the Oregon crisis develop and subside. Then came the war with Mexico, convincing him that in due time the Yankee juggernaut would overpower Central America. On September 4, 1846, in letters to both John Foster and Thomas Manning, he recommended that they persuade the Nicaraguan government to send an envoy to Guatemala City so as to benefit from a treaty which would be negotiated shortly between Guatemala and Great Britain — an important phase of the "Guatemalan Confederation" plan, it will be recalled. Moreover, he wanted Nicaragua to urge her sister states to do likewise, thus forming a "bold front" against both Mexico and the United States.[33]

On the same day, Chatfield wrote to Lord Aberdeen requesting permission to negotiate the Guatemalan treaty in accordance with his instructions of 1834. Whereas earlier under liberal control Guatemala had been unfavorably described, now the British agent observed that the calibre of her leaders and the nature of her economic resources fully warranted the negotiation of a separate trade pact with her. To make the move more palatable, Chatfield shrewdly contrived another technique which he pursued vigorously henceforth. He announced to Aberdeen that the Hanse Towns of Germany were likewise disposed to negotiate such a treaty with Guatemala.[34] In short, Mr. Chatfield was using his influence in the consular corps to encourage the negotiation of treaties with Guatemala, thus forever disassociating that state from her sisters. He was driving another nail into the unionist casket.

For a brief period, in October, 1846, Azmitia with his "American Party" nearly frustrated Chatfield's strategy. Somehow or other Azmitia managed to persuade Carrera to send a special mission to the United States. According to the plan, this Guatemalan envoy would try either to negotiate an alliance with the United States or request the establishment of an American protectorate over his state. In return, the United States would guarantee the reincorporation of Chiapas and Soconusco, territory which Guatemala had lost to Mexico. But Azmitia's influence over Carrera did not last long. By the end of the month, the "English Party" was in control of the situation.[35]

---

33. To Foster, September 4, 1846, F.O. 252/21; to Manning, September 4, 1846, F.O. 252/29; from Manning, October 15, 1846, F.O. 252/33.
34. To Aberdeen, No. 29, September 4, 1846, F.O. 15/42.
35. To Palmerston, Nos. 1-2, political, October 12, 22, 1846, F.O. 15/42,

Following their ally's lead, the tractable government of Guatemala announced its intention, on January 26, 1847, to proclaim its independence, thus breaking the bond with its Central American neighbors.[36] In effect, by this declaration Guatemala accepted the implications of Frederick Chatfield's "sheet-anchor" thesis; her former declarations of independence and absolute sovereignty had been so much paper. Although Central Americans had consistently denied the validity of Chatfield's position — for that matter so had Lord Palmerston — Guatemala now accepted it.[37] It might be argued — that is, providing we accept Chatfield's premise — that Her Britannic Majesty's consul-general to Central America had single-handedly created the Guatemalan Republic. Later, he was also responsible for the birth of the Costa Rican Republic.

In explaining why he condoned Guatemala's action, as well as the negotiations of a trade treaty with her, Chatfield said the following to Palmerston:

> In considering this question, it will also be proper to take into view the political condition of Mexico at this juncture, and the probable consequences of the aggression of the United States to the interests and stability of the adjacent republics; and looking at the actual course of events in Mexico, where no elements seem to exist for the restoration of a government entitled to respect, and capable of successfully arresting the dissolution of the Country by foreign conquest, involving the temporary separation, if not the ultimate loss, of the Californias and the northern provinces, it becomes proper to consider in what manner the State next in succession for attack should secure itself from subjugation, or at least how it may best delay that event; also in what way European governments might contribute to thwart the superior domination which in a few years, the United States will probably claim the right of exercising upon this part of the Continent.[38]

The rest was just a question of time. To the sound of rhetoric, Guatemala once again declared her independence and sovereignty on March 21, 1847 — this time with Chatfield's consent. In a thirteen-page *"Manifiesto,"* the illiterate Carrera explained in grandiloquent terms why Guatemala had decided to abandon the union with her sister states.

---

36. From José Mariano Rodríguez, January 26, 1847, F.O. 252/12; to *idem,* January 27, 1847, F.O. 252/13.

37. From Palmerston, No. 4, February 22, 1847, F.O. 15/44, which provides a clear expression of Palmerston's attitude toward the "sheet anchor," or the non-recognition of a state's nationality.

38. To Palmerston, No. 3, January 28, 1847, F.O. 15/45.

Costa Rica, he prophesied uncannily, would soon join her in this move.[39] And, of course, neither Guatemala nor Costa Rica bothered to send delegates to the Nacaome meeting which convened on June 16, 1847.

Instead, Guatemalans busied themselves negotiating a treaty with the British consul-general. They worked, it would seem, from an advantageous bargaining position. To avoid the troublesome Belize question, the negotiators adopted the wording "Territories, Dominions, or Settlements of Her Britannic Majesty" rather than "Territories, Dominions and places in the possession or occupation of Her Britannic Majesty."[40] Later, when Guatemala insisted upon the insertion of a clause that the treaty need not affect any arrangement which she might desire to make in the future on the subject of boundaries, Chatfield hurriedly concurred; so did the Foreign Office.[41] Moreover, the British negotiator consented to an article which favored Guatemalan shipping for a period of twelve years, rather than the six years stipulated in his 1834 instructions. Though this was later cut down to seven years by the Foreign Office, it nevertheless demonstrated Chatfield's eagerness to negotiate the treaty: an important step in his plan to establish a "Guatemalan Confederation."[42]

By mid-1847, the English agent also sent out feelers to the various states concerning their accession to the Guatemalan treaty. He wrote a personal note to Juan Lindo of Honduras to this effect; and through his agents in Nicaragua, he approached Director José Guerrero discouraging his state's participation in the Nacaome meeting and urging him instead to join the Guatemalan system.[43] Chatfield's greatest success, however, occurred in Costa Rica. In February, 1848, a Costa Rican envoy signed an "act of accession" to the Guatemalan treaty, which the San José authorities ratified in September.[44] But Lord Palmerston, apparently unmindful of Chatfield's political objectives, discouraged the act of accession and instructed his agent to negotiate a separate treaty with Costa Rica.[45] In November, 1849, Chatfield negotiated such a treaty, so

---

39. To Palmerston, No. 12, p. encl.s, March 22, 1847, F.O. 15/45; also can be found in F.O. 252/12.
40. To Palmerston, No. 24, p. encl., June 28, 1847, F.O. 15/46.
41. To Palmerston, No. 34, July 10, 1847, F.O. 15/46; from José Mariano Rodríguez, conf., June 10, 1847, and July 8, 1847, F.O. 252/12.
42. From Palmerston, No. 23, October 30, 1848, F.O. 15/50.
43. To Juan Lindo, conf., July 17, and October 2, 1847, F.O. 252/14; from Foster, August 28, 1847, F.O. 252/21; to Manning, July 3, 1847, F.O. 252/36.
44. To Palmerston, No. 18, p. encl.s, February 24, 1848, F.O. 15/51.
45. From Palmerston, No. 23, October 30, 1848, F.O. 15/50.

that by then the indefatigable British agent was unquestionably in control of the two peripheral states of Central America.

—◆•◆—

To ward off the challenge of the United States in as many ways as possible, Mr. Chatfield outlined a fantastic imperialistic project which was only partially supported by the British government. We have already mentioned his suggestion with regard to Costa Rica's outlet to the sea. In that same dispatch of April 25, 1846, he not only urged Lord Aberdeen to support Costa Rica against New Granada but also extolled the value of Boca del Toro as one of the best harbors on the Atlantic coast of Middle America. He then suggested the implementation of the program which he had recommended in November, 1842 — the occupation of San Juan del Norte by the Mosquitos. As for the Pacific coast of Central America, he urged the periodic visits of British ships to Puntarenas to safeguard the burgeoning economy of Costa Rica, so closely linked to English markets and interests. He also noted the valuable ports of Realejo (Nicaragua) and La Unión (El Salvador) in the Gulf of Fonseca, as if to suggest the importance of controlling those points.[46] Although addressed to Lord Aberdeen, this key dispatch was read by Lord Palmerston, who returned to the Foreign Office in June, 1846. Did it reinfect him with the vision of empire he had had in 1840? It would seem so.

Certainly the British consul-general had no room to complain about the cooperation of the Foreign Office under Lord Palmerston's leadership. When he asked Admiral Seymour for naval support on the Pacific coast, Lord Palmerston seconded the request.[47] And when relations with Honduras took a turn for the worse, the Foreign Office again sanctioned the consul-general's appeal for naval assistance on the Atlantic coast. In short, he was promised the use of naval units on both coasts of Central America.

The squabble with the Honduran government had another significant consequence. It raised the basic question of sovereignty to the Mosquito Shore and whether or not Englishmen should be allowed to cut wood on the right (east) bank of the River Aguam, off Cape Honduras. The Hondurans complained to the superintendent of Belize that the British had no such right. Chatfield, on the other hand, countered this complaint with his "sheet-anchor" thesis — since Honduras had no

---

46. To Aberdeen, No. 15, April 25, 1846, F.O. 15/42.
47. To Aberdeen, No. 24, July 17, 1846, F.O. 15/42, with Lord Palmerston's note, dated September 15, 1846.

nationality, she could not engage in such a discussion with English authorities.[48] In the correspondence dealing with this matter, moreover, Chatfield expressed his opinion as to what the extreme limits of the Mosquito Shore should be — from Cape Honduras to San Juan del Norte. And these remarks reached Lord Palmerston before June 30, 1847.[49] This is an important chronological point since it will permit us to assess Chatfield's influence on Palmerston's decision to announce the territorial limits of Mosquitia.

On January 29, 1847, just at the time that he was encouraging Guatemalan independence and the negotiation of the trade treaty, the British agent presented a detailed plan whose avowed objective was the control of the Pacific coast of Central America "in anticipation of the Americans." As in the previous April, he pointed out to Lord Palmerston that the ports of Realejo and La Unión, both in the Gulf of Fonseca, were the most valuable ones between Peru and California. The former was the logical terminus of any interoceanic passageway through Nicaragua and the latter had the best harbor for any extended traffic with the Californias. It was to England's best interests, he argued, to dominate both ports. The island of Cardón, outside of Realejo, might serve in this capacity, as would the islands in the Bay of Conchagua with regard to the Salvadorean port. If Palmerston were to approve of this suggestion, he should then urge the Admiralty to conduct a secret reconnaissance mission in the Gulf of Fonseca. In the meantime, Chatfield promised to aid the cause along by continuing a program which he had begun in the latter part of 1846, namely, to get Englishmen to purchase property behind La Unión, extending from the port to the town of San Miguel. He had already encouraged a gentleman from Belize, who owned property in that vicinity, to establish a clear title to it; and he was also urging a London mining company to purchase "a powerful mineral district lying between San Miguel and the harbour of Conchagua [La Unión], being persuaded in my own mind that territorial possessions in that direction will offer immense advantages in a few years to Great Britain as well as to her subjects." He hinted, moreover, that he might be able to use the British debt and claims effectively against the Central American states in order to bring about the sale of the best control points.[50]

Although that was the substance of Chatfield's grand project, which three years later produced a crisis in Anglo-American relations, there

---

48. To Aberdeen, No. 22, July 6, 1846, F.O. 15/42.
49. From Palmerston, No. 13, June 8, 1847, F.O. 15/44, acknowledging receipt of Chatfield's No. 11 (March 13, 1847), F.O. 15/45.
50. To Palmerston, No. 4, January 29, 1847, F.O. 15/45.

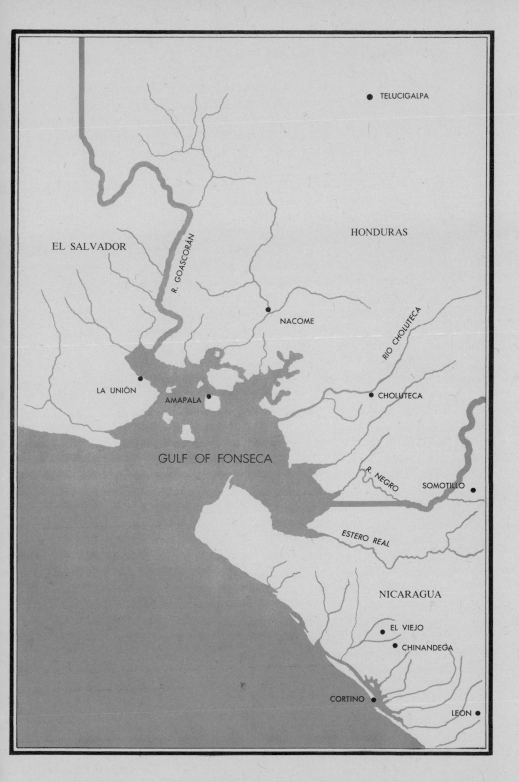

Gulf of Fonseca Region

was a noteworthy distortion of fact in his prospectus. To begin with, there was no "gentleman from Belize" involved in his scheme; the gentleman was a Guatemalan — none other than Manuel Francisco Pavón who owned the property of Encuentros near San Miguel.[51] And Chatfield was trying to persuade the English mining company to purchase Pavón's land, as well as other property in that vicinity. With or without the approval of the Foreign Office, moreover, the fact remains that the English consul-general devoted the next four years to gaining possession of the land behind the port of La Unión: and he applied all manner of pressure upon the government of El Salvador to this end.[52] His efforts, however, were not successful for various reasons. First, suspecting that a political objective was involved in advancing Pavón's title, the Salvadorean government opposed it.[53] Secondly, English mining interests, primarily interested in profits, did not consider it a good investment. And, finally, many propertyholders in the area deliberately held up their prices, knowing how desperately Mr. Chatfield wanted their lands.[54]

In contrast to previous projects of an imperialistic nature, the Foreign Office was not disinterested in this latest scheme. On April 15, 1847, Lord Palmerston relayed the proposal to the Admiralty for its consideration — an indication of some interest in the plan, to say the least.[55] The Admiralty, moreover, sent Captain Thomas Henderson, aboard the *Sampson,* to reconnoiter the Gulf of Fonseca. The secret survey was conducted in early December, 1847. Captain Henderson revealed his findings to Frederick Chatfield in a confidential letter of December 17. The island of Cardón, he said, was not suitable for controlling Realejo; instead he recommended the occupation of positions on shore which could be held by strong and commanding batteries. As for La Unión, there was no question about it; the best island was Tigre. Perhaps, he added, Great Britain might also want to occupy the nearby islands of Sacate Grande and Miaguera.[56]

---

51. From Manuel Francisco Pavón, December 15, 1846, F.O. 252/33.
52. To Coode Brown and Kingdon, pvt., December 19, 1849, F.O. 252/29; to the Salvadorean Government, No. 4, January 15, 1847, and others in this same volume, F.O. 252/20; from John Baily, January 14, 1848, F.O. 252/33.
53. From José Altiguieta, March 8, 1847, F.O. 252/33.
54. To Marcos Idígoras, June 27, 1848, F.O. 252/36. Most of the correspondence on the mining story can be found in F.O. 252/33. For a good review, see, to Henry Patteson, August 7, 1847, F.O. 252/36, as well as the dispatch to Idígoras cited above.
55. F.O. to Admiralty, April 15, 1847, F.O. 15/49; also see Palmerston's note on Chatfield's No. 4 (January 29, 1847).
56. From Thomas Henderson, conf., December 17, 1847, in No. 62, to Palmerston, December 20, 1847, F.O. 15/47.

It goes without saying that Captain Henderson's letter brought joy and elation to the British consulate in Guatemala City. To Chatfield it could mean only one thing: "Old Pam" favored his grand project, just as any good Englishman would have done in view of the impending challenge from the United States. He told Palmerston that the three islands mentioned by Captain Henderson were of little or no value to the states of El Salvador and Honduras, their proprietors. Besides, they could not hold them "for a moment after the Americans had found a pretext for taking them." Then he remarked:

> To prepare the way to an arrangement with the governments of Salvador and Honduras, both of whom I understand, claim these islands, I will cautiously ascertain how they consider their respective rights to stand, so as to profit, if necessary by their disagreement, by playing off the claim of one against that of the other, for a cession by either Party, irregardless, will be valid.

In addition, he would press the two states for an early payment of the British claims — 72,000 pounds sterling for El Salvador and 80,000 for Honduras. Then he made the interesting observation that the claims "could be compounded to the satisfaction of the claimants, for less than half their amount," revealing the "water" in the claims. Implicit in the statement, moreover, was the offer that the state willing to cede the islands to Great Britain could reduce its indebtedness by half. And, to avoid arousing the suspicions of the two states, "the Islands might be applied for as a Coal Depot; or as a place where coal may exist (though being volcanic that is not likely) or they might be purchased in connexion with the projected English mining establishments on the mainland in their rear." These, however, were points for Lord Palmerston to decide. Chatfield concluded humbly: "Although I may not live to see the effect of our presence on the Coast, as herein contemplated, I feel convinced that a British station in Conchagua will ensure the internal peace of Central America, and give us a permanent and powerful influence in the country."[57]

Apparently Lord Palmerston did not lose interest in the project. Upon reading the dispatch quoted above, he called for a good map of Central America; and without making any observations, he ordered copies sent to the Admiralty on April 3, 1848.[58] We can only conclude therefore that he favored the scheme at this time; certainly he was not against it. That later he changed his mind is another matter and due to other circumstances. In the present context, however, his approval

---

57. No. 62 (December 20).
58. Palmerston's notes on No. 62.

throws a new and more meaningful light upon his Mosquito policy in 1847.

━●◆●━

It should be recalled that Lord Palmerston had not only provided Chatfield with naval support but had also read the latter's dispatches in which the agent suggested what the southern and northern limits of Mosquitia should be. On June 30, 1847, the Foreign Office officially announced that the boundaries of the Mosquitio Nation extended from Cape Honduras to San Juan del Norte.[59] What had prompted Lord Palmerston to make the announcement at this particular time?

In view of the foregoing discussion, the best explanation is that he was convinced that the United States was, or would soon be, a real threat to British interests in Central America. In short, Mr. Chatfield was not the only one concerned with the so-called "bogey" of American intervention.[60] On January 20, 1847, when he first contemplated the move, Palmerston hinted that the decision resulted from a discussion with the New Granadian ambassador Tomás Cipriano de Mosquera, who had proposed a settlement of the Mosquito's southern boundary at San Juan del Norte. Presumably, in such an agreement, England would have had to recognize New Granada's rights to the area to the south. Palmerston therefore asked Chatfield for his opinion on what the Mosquito limits should be. And although the underling's reply did not reach London by June 30, Palmerston had in fact — before then — received Chatfield's opinion in other dispatches.[61]

Palmerston's reference to New Granada likewise implied an awareness of a possible challenge by the United States. On December 12, 1846, the American agent in Bogotá, Benjamin Bidlack, negotiated a treaty with New Granada by which the United States guaranteed the neutrality of the Isthmus, as well as New Granada's sovereignty to that territory, in return for an American right-of-way across the Isthmus of Panama. As Professor Joseph B. Lockey has pointed out, this was clearly an anti-British move on the part of the New Granadian govern-

---

59. From Palmerston, No. 14, June 30, 1847, F.O. 15/44, a copy of which was also sent to the British Agent in Bogotá, New Granada.

60. Richard Van Alstyne, "The Central American Policy of Lord Palmerston, 1846–1848," *Hispanic American Historical Review*, Vol. XVI (August, 1936), p. 347, argues that Lord Palmerston was not affected "by the same bogey, certainly not to the same degree, and there is no proof other than that of coincidence in time that he acted in Mosquito to anticipate the United States."

61. From Palmerston, No. 2, January 20, 1847, F.O. 15/44; also see footnote 49 in this chapter.

ment.[62] Apparently, Mosquera had tried to pressure Lord Palmerston into a settlement of the Mosquito line; and when this failed, the New Granadian government turned to the United States for support. In any case, the "bogey" of American intervention was gaining reality; it perhaps also explains why Lord Palmerston had countenanced the project in the Gulf of Fonseca.

In Chatfield's official reply on the Mosquito limits, he again demonstrated remarkable research ability, as he thoroughly demolished New Granada's claim to the right bank of the San Juan River.[63] That claim, he insisted, rested upon flimsy evidence, a military order of 1803 which was never implemented. Other documentation led to the same conclusion: Great Britain should not dignify the claim by entering into an agreement with New Granada. Besides, New Granada's real motive in advancing her claim was merely to frustrate any interoceanic passageway which might compete with the Chagres-Panama crossing. "Moreover," he concluded, "looking at the probable destinies of these Countries, considerable advantages might accrue to England in after times, by receiving for settlement with Central America or Costarica (the only proper parties) the rights of Mosquito beyond St. John's River."[64] In making these suggestions, the British agent undoubtedly was guided by a desire to advance Costa Rica's interests. He had, for example, applied considerable pressure upon Nicaragua to free the navigation of the San Juan River.[65]

Upon receiving Palmerston's official pronouncement on Mosquito limits, the consul-general relayed it to the states of Nicaragua and Honduras. On his own initiative, however, he added one qualification — he inserted the clause "without prejudice to the right of the Mosquito King to any territory south of the River San Juan."[66] In his explanation to Palmerston, Chatfield admitted that this was done deliberately to frustrate the aspirations of the New Granadians, who in the past year had been playing both ends against the middle.[67] New Granada had no friend in Frederick Chatfield.

---

62. See MTUSA, V, 115-160 for text of treaty; also, Joseph B. Lockey, "A Neglected Aspect of Isthmian Diplomacy," *American Historical Review,* Vol. XLI (January, 1936), 295-305.
63. To Palmerston, No. 16, April 15, 1847, F.O. 15/45.
64. *Ibid.*
65. To Palmerston, No. 14 (March 29).
66. Circular to Honduras and Nicaragua, September 10, 1847, in No. 44, to Palmerston, September 11, 1847, F.O. 15/47.
67. *Ibid.;* also see No. 33 (July 17, 1847), F.O. 15/46, and No. 46 (September 29, 1847), F.O. 15/47.

As might be expected, Palmerston's decision on Mosquito limits complicated matters for Chatfield in Central America. The reaction in the "center" states was particularly violent, undoubtedly encouraging them to draw up the *Pacto de Nacaome* which was signed on October 7, 1847. But no general government was set up at this time for the reasons discussed earlier in this chapter. In addition, since August, 1847, it was rumored that the Mosquitos planned to occupy San Juan del Norte in the near future — a common rumor for years, however. Then, on September 1, Patrick Walker, the British resident in Mosquitia, let it be known to the Nicaraguan authorities at San Juan that before long their government would receive important information on Mosquito limits. In other words, before September 10, when Chatfield wrote officially on the subject, Nicaraguans were already in an ugly mood.[68]

The situation worsened in the remaining months of the year, especially when Central Americans learned that a British ship had visited the announced termini of the Mosquito Shore. On October 25, 1847, the *Alarm,* commanded by Captain Granville G. Loch, took George Hodgson, one of the Mosquito king's old advisors, to San Juan del Norte. In the conversation with the commandant at the port and in subsequent letters to the Nicaraguan government, the fact emerged that Mosquito forces would occupy San Juan del Norte on January 1, 1848.[69] In December, 1847, moreover, the same Captain Granville carried a similar message to the authorities at Trujillo, Honduras.[70] In short, Lord Palmerston had announced the Mosquito limits; and the British navy, presumably with the support of the Foreign Office, had set and announced the deadline for occupying those limits effectively.

Understandably, Nicaragua tried every conceivable measure to prevent the takeover of San Juan on January 1, 1848. Her agent in Europe, José de Marcoleta, received instructions to gain the support of France, Holland, and Belgium in dissuading Palmerston from occupying the port.[71] The appeal also went out to the United States. In a letter to Secretary of State James Buchanan, Pablo Buitrago wrote: "the object of Great Britain in taking possession of this key of the continent is not to protect the trifling tribe of Mosquitos, but to establish her dominion at the northern extremity of the line, affording the greatest facility for a canal connecting the two oceans, her mercantile preponderance in the American Continent, and her direct relations with Asia the East Indies,

---

68. No. 44 (September 11, 1847), F.O. 15/47.
69. "Memoria," Pablo Buitrago, León, December 25, 1847, B.L./CAP, vol. 3.
70. To Palmerston, No. 6, January 22, 1848, F.O. 15/51.
71. "Memoria," Buitrago, p. 21.

and other important parts of the earth."[72] This letter, written by Nicaragua's foreign minister, marked a revival of the United States' interest in Central American affairs.

In similar fashion, Nicaragua appealed to her sister states for assistance, both moral and physical. Costa Rica turned a deaf ear; and Guatemala demurred, or at least this was so in late October, 1847.[73] The "center," on the other hand, was more cooperative. After Captain Loch's appearance at both Trujillo and San Juan, Honduras sought common action with her neighbor; and El Salvador scored the "immense wickedness" of subaltern English agents in numerous publications. The remarks in the Salvadorean press especially annoyed the master of the British consulate in Guatemala City, who was determined to check the "fiery" tendencies of the Salvadoreans "by a severe demonstration."[74]

And finally, the Nicaraguan government sent a mission to the Mosquito coast with the object of acquiring a signed deposition from Princess Agnes Ana Federico, the eldest sister of the Mosquito king, in which she stated her disapproval of San Juan's impending occupation. In fact, Princess Agnes went beyond that; she even recognized Nicaragua's sovereignty to the area in which she lived. This in turn served as the pretext for declaring it a department of Nicaragua on November 4, 1847.[75] Chatfield was furious when he learned of this move. Apparently the English alone could enjoy the luxury of the Mosquito farce.[76]

In mid-October, 1847, both Nicaragua and Honduras replied to Chatfield's message on the Mosquito limits. Politely, yet in a determined tone, they presented their claims to the Mosquito Shore. It had belonged to Spain for centuries, they argued; and when Spanish rule ended, they had inherited their former king's right of sovereignty to the area. Even Great Britain in the blockades of 1842 and 1844 had in fact acknowledged Nicaragua's sovereignty to San Juan del Norte — indeed, this was a point which the English conveniently overlooked. But arguments of "derivative" rights had never been acceptable to Chatfield before; he was in no mood to countenance them now. He hoped that the states would comprehend these "truths," once and for all.[77]

---

72. Pablo Buitrago to James Buchanan, November 12, 1847, MDCIA, III, 257.
73. José Mariano Rodríguez to Nicaraguan Government, October 27, 1847, in No. 50, to Palmerston, November 4, 1847, F.O. 15/47.
74. To Palmerston, Nos. 47 (October 16) and 51 (November 8, 1847), p. encl.s, F.O. 15/47.
75. "Memoria," Buitrago, p. 23.
76. To Palmerston, No. 27, March 4, 1848, F.O. 15/51.
77. To Palmerston, No. 52, p. encl.s, November 16, 1847, F.O. 15/47.

In fact, the British consul-general had reason to believe that Nicaragua was by no means as united as her reply to him would seem to indicate. On October 26, 1847, Thomas Manning wrote as follows: "The Chief Authority requests me to say that the question of the Mosquito affair, treaty of Commerce and that of the Debt would all be arranged, but *their* drift, and it is now a *very general one amongst all classes* is to call upon Her B. Majesty for Protection." "Protection they seem determined to have," Manning repeated in his letter, and "these are the sentiments of Carcache, Padre Solis, the government and in fact everyone."[78] John Foster's information buttressed the same contention. It was only because of such nationalistic leaders as Pablo Buitrago and Sebastián Salinas, and the fact that there was a strong faction of Granadians in the state legislature, that the León government presented such a bold front on the Mosquito question. The conservatives were not anxious to fight at all, Foster pointed out. There was another group, moreover, led by the liberal Francisco Castellón, who felt that it would be futile to resist the British by force. It preferred instead to negotiate the matter with Chatfield in Guatemala City or with Palmerston in London. Castellón, it seems, was willing to sign a treaty with the British recognizing San Juan del Norte as English, but he adamantly refused to consider the recognition of the Mosquito Indians.[79] That was the essence of Castellón's position which the León government adopted. After deciding to seek Guatemalan mediation, Nicaragua appointed envoys to discuss a settlement with the British consul-general in Guatemala City.[80]

Encouraged by Manning and Foster's reports, Chatfield wasted no time in exploiting the possibility of establishing a protectorate over Nicaragua. He approached Palmerston indirectly by asking him if the Mosquito Nation had any claim to the south bank of the San Juan River; then he proceeded to argue that both in the colonial and independence periods there had been a fortification on the south bank of the river's mouth.[81] Clearly, Chatfield wanted England to yield on this point as a concession to the Nicaraguans; and Lord Palmerston had no trouble in reading between the lines. He replied that Nicaragua had no

---

78. From Manning, October 26, 1847, F.O. 252/33. It is not clear who underlined the words in this dispatch. Extracts of this key letter are included in No. 53 to Palmerston, November 16, 1847, F.O. 15/47, though they are not attributed to Thomas Manning.

79. To Palmerston, No. 53 (November 16, 1847), contains extracts from John Foster's letters.

80. "Memoria," Buitrago, pp. 21-22; from Sebastián Salinas, November 13, 1847, in No. 55, to Palmerston, December 3, 1847, F.O. 15/47.

81. To Palmerston, No. 53.

bona fide claim to the south bank; in fact, she had no right to come down any lower than the Serapiquí River — an observation which revealed how closely Palmerston was following his agent's advice with regard to Costa Rica. He agreed, however, that Nicaragua should have free access to the sea; and he authorized both Chatfield and Patrick Walker, the British resident at Mosquitia, to transmit to him any proposition which Nicaragua, or any other state, might wish to make concerning "an alliance or closer connection with Great Britain."[82] Palmerston's fever for empire was rising.

The negotiations in Guatemala City failed dismally because Chatfield refused to consider the "derivative" thesis.[83] Significantly, the *serviles* found themselves embarrassed by the territorial question of Mosquitia; and when a Cuban article attacking British policy in Central America managed to appear in a Guatemalan paper, Chatfield forced the government to knuckle under to him immediately — a humiliating episode which aided the revival of liberal influence in Guatemala.[84] In the attempts at mediation, the Guatemalan government hoped to win a four-months' suspension of the Mosquito occupation of San Juan. The assumption, ironically, was that Chatfield was responsible for the English decision to occupy San Juan; but he quickly reminded the Guatemalan foreign minister that the order "did not proceed from me."[85] So there the negotiations ended; as a result, the conservatives' political power began to ebb. This was well illustrated by the ad interim appointment of José Antonio Azmitia to the position of minister of foreign affairs in mid-December, 1847.[86]

As the occupation deadline approached, all Central America, with the exception of Costa Rica, was afire with indignation. The Salvadorean press was particularly incensed. One writer remarked that the occupation of San Juan del Norte would inevitably focus world attention upon Central America. And when that occurred, the "American Continent" would rise up against Europe to prevent her from putting "a foot on any

---

82. Palmerston's note on No. 53, dated February 6, 1848; from Palmerston, No. 6, February 29, 1848, F.O. 15/50, in which the expression "closer alliance" was scratched over and replaced by "closer cooperation."

83. To Palmerston, No. 55 (December 3, 1847), F.O. 15/47.

84. No. 57, p. encl.s, December 10, 1847.

85. No. 59, p. encl.s, December 13, 1847.

86. No. 63, p. encl.s, December 24, 1847.

part of the World of Columbus."[87] Brother Jonathan most certainly would heed that call.

◆◆

Anglo-Mosquito forces occupied San Juan del Norte on January 1, 1848. Within hours, Patrick Walker announced a tariff schedule for all goods passing through the port, now renamed Greytown. Under Colonel Antonio Salas, Nicaraguans rallied and regained control of the port by January 10; they took as prisoners the Mosquito governor, George Hodgson, and the captain of the port, S. W. Little.[88] Then came the British counterattack. With the help of two warships and a force numbering from two hundred and fifty to three hundred men, the Mosquitos and their English allies retook the port two weeks later.[89] Under the command of Captain Granville Loch, the expedition proceeded up the San Juan River to its junction with the Serapiquí, where the Nicaraguans had established a defense point. After a brief battle, on February 8, in which the Nicaraguans suffered most of the casualties, Captain Loch advanced his forces to San Carlos at the entrance of Lake Nicaragua. From the fort at that location, he wrote to the Nicaraguan government demanding the recognition of Greytown's occupation by Mosquito forces. On March 4, Francisco Castellón and two other Nicaraguan commissioners arrived at San Carlos. Realizing the futility of opposing the British by force, they signed a truce on March 7, 1848, by which their state recognized the "undisputed occupation of the mouth of the San Juan," pending negotiations between Great Britain and Nicaragua.[90] Might had again made right. Alexander Macdonald had been vindicated.

More important for our story was the world's reaction to the events described above. In the United States, the advocates of "Manifest Destiny" demanded a strong stand against Great Britain for this flagrant violation of the Monroe Doctrine. And, as we shall see in the next chapter, an important and articulate segment of British society likewise opposed Palmerston's aggressive diplomacy in Middle America. The immediate effect, as far as Nicaragua was concerned, was to make that state an armed camp physically and psychologically. The nationalists rallied behind the leadership of Pablo Buitrago. Communications via the San Juan were prohibited; and all Englishmen became targets for heated

---

87. No. 58, p. encl., December 11, 1847.
88. MTUSA, V, 705; to Palmerston, No. 9, February 12, 1848, F.O. 15/51.
89. *El Noticioso* (León), No. 11, February 6, 1848, in No. 24, to Palmerston, March 4, 1848, F.O. 15/51; MTUSA, V, 706.
90. To Palmerston, Nos. 33, p. encl.s, March 17, and 36, p. encl.s, March 30, 1848, F.O. 15/51.

Nicaraguan minds. Thomas Manning, for example, had to leave the state in a hurry; and the Mosquito prisoners were rigidly questioned. Hodgson, it seems, told his captors everything they wanted to hear and thus jeopardized the lives of other Englishmen in Nicaragua. Unionism, moreover, gained in the bargain. Whereas earlier José Guerrero and Juan Lindo had sent their envoys to Nacaome with no intention of ratifying the *pacto,* they now became vociferous exponents of union.[91] By February, 1848, the "center" had ratified the *Pacto de Nacaome,* and the way was clear to establish a general government for Central America.[92] Among the important objectives of the new government would be to establish a republic, to seek the aid of a powerful nation against England, and to encourage "the reunion of the great American Diet."[93] Manning and Foster simply could not understand how they had misjudged the thinking of Nicaraguans.

Interestingly, French agents capitalized upon prevailing anglophobia by offering the protection of their country, especially in Chatfield's strongholds of Costa Rica and Guatemala. They failed in Costa Rica, where it should be recalled that on February 24, 1848, in the heat of the San Juan crisis, Costa Rica had agreed to the "Act of Accession" to the Guatemalan treaty.[94] Urging the Foreign Office to accept Costa Rica's "Act," Chatfield argued that it would check "offers of protection" from other powers and prevent "the interference of the French and North Americans in this country."[95] In Guatemala, where Azmitia and the liberals had worked their way back into the government, the French challenge was almost successful. With the support of highland Indians, the liberals threatened Carrera's life if he did not give up the government on February 4, 1848. If he resigned peacefully, however, a French ship would take him away from Central America. Presumably the new government would seek the protection of France. But Carrera's friends, the "clergy, Notables, Merchants, and principal Strangers," rallied to his support and won over to their cause leading military figures. They thus prevented Carrera's resignation. The British consul-general wrote jubilantly that after the victory the Indian leader "selected Ministers from those who are disposed to serve him and who believe

91. To Palmerston, Nos. 7, February 7; 23, March 4; and 25-27, March 4, 1848, p. encl.s in all of them, F.O. 15/51.
92. To Palmerston, Nos. 11, February 15; and 27, March 4, 1848, p. encl.s in both, F.O. 15/51.
93. "Dictamen sobre el pacto de erección de un gobierno provisorio," Comayagua, 1848, B.L./CAP, vol. 1.
94. To Palmerston, Nos. 3, January 14; 18, February 24; and 19, February 25, 1848, p. encl.s in the first two dispatches, F.O. 15/51.
95. No. 18 (February 24).

Carrera is the best guarantee for peace and well being of the Republic."[96]

Faced with the resurgence of liberalism in Guatemala, the *serviles* again turned to England for a guarantee of their state's independence. They were even disposed to place their country under British protection "to the same extent as Mosquito has done." Aware that Palmerston had rejected a similar proposal years earlier, Chatfield maintained that conditions were now changed: "One reason for listening to this proposal may be found in the conterminous situation of Belize and Mosquito to Guatemala and another, in the expediency of securing an early hold in the Bay of Conchagua, within the States of Salvador and Honduras."[97] Palmerston appeared interested in the proposal, but he preferred to wait for a "formal communication." "Perhaps it may not be made," he added.[98] Although a British protectorate of Guatemala never materialized, the mere proposal illustrated graphically the political upheaval which attended the occupation of San Juan del Norte.

And as the unionist and liberal position improved in Central America, so did the likelihood of North American intervention. Even before the display of force at Greytown, a report reached Chatfield that an American expedition of five hundred men had landed at Tehuantepec, in Mexico, presumably to survey the area for a potential transit route.[99] Moreover, he learned that the American consul in Granada, Francis J. Clark, had visited Costa Rica in search of information and documentation for a prospective canal route through Nicaragua.[100]

Acting upon these reports of American activity, Chatfield proposed to Palmerston on December 18, 1847, the appointment of regular vice-consuls throughout Central America in order to consolidate British influence in the various states. Considering "Old Pam's" penchant for economy in government, the fact that he accepted the recommendation confirms the interpretation that he too was concerned about the North American challenge.[101]

After the occupation of San Juan, the *Pacto de Nacaome* states declared themselves in favor of seeking the help of a powerful nation. El Salvador, and the newspapers of that state, especially taunted Chatfield with the prospect of American intervention in Central America.

---

96. Nos. 4 (January 17), 5 (January 22), and 8 (February 8, 1848), F.O. 15/51.
97. No. 4 (January 17).
98. *Ibid.*, folio 38 which contains Palmerston's note of April 22, 1848.
99. To Palmerston, No. 38, August 14, 1847, F.O. 15/47. He received this news from an informant in Los Altos, writing in late July.
100. To Palmerston, No. 41, p. encl.s, August 21, 1847, F.O. 15/47.
101. To Palmerston, cons. No. 14, December 18, 1847, plus Palmerston's note of March 5, 1848, F.O. 15/48.

Parades were permitted in San Salvador during which the crowds invoked "the aid of the United States," Chatfield told Palmerston. Clippings from the New York *Herald* and the New York *Advertiser,* dramatizing the need for an interoceanic canal and boasting that before long New York would overtake London as the commercial mart of the world, did not lessen Chatfield's anxiety. El Salvador, moreover, had sent Ignacio Gómez on a mission to Washington in order to spread the alarm of England's encroachments in Central America.[102]

Obsessed with the prospects of "Brother Jonathan's" intervention, it is not surprising that Great Britain's consul-general repeatedly urged the Foreign Office to adopt strong defensive measures. In dispatches dated March 7 and 28, 1848, he recommended the purchase of the three islands in the Gulf of Fonseca, as well as the fort of San Carlos at the head of the San Juan River. In addition, he urged the use of the British navy to force Nicaragua and Honduras into a settlement of their inland boundaries with Mosquitia. By using force and by getting the British government to assume a considerable portion of the Central American debt, Mr. Chatfield could thus preserve Great Britain's hegemony in Central America.[103]

At this point, Lord Palmerston drew the line, apparently because of the English reaction to his Mosquito policy. "I'm afraid," he told Chatfield, "that Parliament will not accept this arrangement."[104] He therefore refused to sanction his agent's suggestions.[105] Interestingly, in the dispatch containing the refusal, Palmerston enclosed a copy of the papers presented to the House of Commons on Mosquito affairs.[106]

It does not follow, however, that Lord Palmerston had abandoned his concern for the possibility of an American intrusion in that part of the world. On the contrary, he wrote confidentially to Chatfield on November 1, 1848, that the United States, at the instigation of the New Granadian ambassador, had decided to send Elijah Hise as a special envoy to further union in Central America, so as to resist British activity in Mosquitia. If that were truly the case, Chatfield was authorized to defeat the policy of the United States "as far as its object is hostile to the interests of Great Britain."[107] The crisis was mounting; and the battle lines were forming. "Brother Jonathan" was on the horizon.

---

102. To Palmerston, Nos. 5 (January 22, 1848); 12 (February 15); 14 (February 17), and 15 (February 19, 1848), p. encl.s for first two, F.O. 15/51.
103. Nos. 29 (March 7) and 35 (March 28, 1848), F.O. 97/88, which are missing from the F.O. 15/51 files.
104. This remark, made on May 29, 1848, appears on folio 234, F.O. 15/51.
105. From Palmerston, No. 15, June 17, 1848, F.O. 15/50.
106. *Ibid.*
107. From Palmerston, No. 24, conf., November 1, 1848, F.O. 15/50.

CHAPTER ELEVEN

Brother Jonathan and the Tiger

It will I think be necessary to take a high hand with the North Americans, if we are to hold our ground in Central America.[1]

— Chatfield, November 2, 1849

Indeed the whole history of British relations and diplomacy here has been characterized by an effrontery and unscrupulousness almost incredible and absolutely unprecedented.[2]

— Ephraim George Squier, December 13, 1849

The French Revolution of 1848 spurred on the resurgence of liberalism and unionism in Central America, further complicating matters for Mr. Chatfield. Determined to promote her own selfish interest and even hopeful of a protectorate, Costa Rica alone remained firm in her allegiance to the British.[3] As in Guatemala's case, she too accepted the "sheet anchor" on August 3, 1848, when she expressed the desire to become a separate republic; and barely a week later, she ratified the "Act of Accession," which her envoy had signed in the previous February.[4] Since Palmerston decided in favor of a separate treaty, however, the British consul-general had to commence negotiations with Costa Rica by mail, expecting to settle the matter in the fall of 1849 when he planned to visit the peripheral state.[5]

The liberals' challenge in Guatemala seriously disrupted the alliance between the *serviles* and the British consulate. Though the February coup aborted, the insurgents from the highlands and the liberal leaders who were inflamed by the French example in Europe regrouped their forces and successfully toppled the Carrera regime in August, 1848. It is interesting to note — a fact which the British agent never mentioned in his dispatches — that the sixth state of Los Altos drew life again, and

---

1. To Palmerston, No. 102, November 2, 1849, F.O. 15/60.
2. Ephraim George Squier to John M. Clayton, December 13, 1849, MDCIA, III, 457.
3. William D. Christie to Palmerston, Nos. 13-14, October 14, 19, 1848, F.O. 97/88.
4. To Palmerston, Nos. 98-99, October 14, 1848, and 101, November 1, 1848, F.O. 15/53.
5. To Thomas Manning, January 19, and July 27, 1849; to John Foster, February 24, 1849, F.O. 252/43.

was immediately recognized by El Salvador and Nicaragua.[6] In fact, the Salvadorean director Doroteo Vasconcelos had played an important role in the various liberal victories of that period, even in Guatemala. Indeed, the future looked bright for the reestablishment of the old republic.[7] To Chatfield's discomfort, the highland insurgents cited his name in a publication which listed the grievances that had prompted the revolution. As usual, however, liberal rule in Guatemala did not last long because of partisanship among the liberals and dissension among the highland leaders. A hostile British agent did not help matters. By the spring of 1849, it was already evident that Rafael Carrera would soon return to power.[8] The storm had been weathered, but not without some apprehensive moments for "Don Federico."

The "center" states — with the surprising exception of Nicaragua — continued their spirited resistance to English influence and aspirations in Central America. Yet Nicaragua, who had suffered most from Anglo-Mosquito aggression, weakened the unionist effort at a time when its chances for success looked promising, especially while liberals controlled the government of Guatemala. In July, 1848, Chatfield learned that the Nicaraguan leader José Guerrero was in favor of establishing a separate republic and of adjusting his state's differences with Great Britain.[9] Except for earlier attempts to wean Nicaragua from the unionist movement, there is no evidence to indicate that English agents were responsible for this change of heart. Palmerston's willingness to negotiate with a Nicaraguan envoy undoubtedly played into the hands of Francisco Castellón, who previously had favored an amicable settlement with the British. Significantly, Castellón was chosen to represent his state in London for that purpose as well as to attract British capitalists into financing the canal project.[10] Thus, in pursuit of her own selfish interests, Nicaragua abandoned the *Pacto de Nacaome,* at least for awhile. In the spring of 1849, however, when the news reached León that Lord Palmerston had rejected Castellón's territorial views, disillusioned Nicaraguans returned

6. "Manifiesto . . . Estado de Los Altos," Manuel J. Fuentes, Quezaltenango, October 10, 1848, B.L./CAP, vol. 5. For an account of this August Revolution, see, to Foster, August 4, 1848, F.O. 252/21; to Palmerston, Nos. 58 (June 23) and 80 (August 18, 1848), F.O. 15/52.

7. Decree, Guatemala, No. 2, August 18, 1848, F.O. 254/3.

8. To Palmerston, Nos. 87 (September 9), 88 (September 16) and 101 (December 15, 1848), F.O. 15/53; to the Guatemalan Government, September 7, 1848, F.O. 252/13.

9. From John Foster, June 26, 1848, F.O. 252/21; to Palmerston, No. 94, September 30, 1848, F.O. 15/53.

10. To Palmerston, No. 89, September 16, 1848, F.O. 15/53; on the Castellón mission, see letters from John Foster, who accompanied Castellón, December 31, 1848, to June 16, 1849, F.O. 252/43.

to the unionist fold with a vengeance.[11] By then, Guatemala was again safely in the states' rights column.

On the other hand, the two states who owned the coveted islands in the Gulf of Fonseca never once wavered in their opposition to the English adversary. Both Honduras and El Salvador had officially disapproved of the March 13, 1848, Nicaraguan truce with Captain Loch; and their newspapers kept Chatfield in a continual rage. He reacted in typical fashion by raising new claims against them, some of doubtful validity which even the Foreign Office refused to support. And, of course, he expected the navy to collect these claims for him.[12] In the meantime, he had not lost sight of the fact that Tigre Island belonged to Honduras and the smaller islands to El Salvador.

When Chatfield learned of Palmerston's unwillingness to sanction the aggressive proposals of March, 1848, concerning the purchase of the three islands and the forceful settlement of the Mosquito limits, he understandably expressed disappointment even though he could appreciate the political context for the refusal. The rejection, however, left the British vulnerable to the North American peril, he pointed out to the Foreign Office. This fact was driven home graphically in early November, 1848, when Chatfield received word from one of his informants that the Salvadorean government had granted important concessions to an American steamship line. The Americans planned to begin operations there by January 1, 1849, in connection with their runs from Panama to San Francisco. This was a tangible threat to British interests, Chatfield argued; he therefore asked Palmerston to reconsider the proposal of occupying the key islands in the Gulf of Fonseca. To make the project attractive, he proposed that the islands might be taken over as *security for* the claims owed to British creditors.[13] Chatfield made this "lien" suggestion on November 24, 1848. In customary fashion, he began its implementation even before Palmerston could pass judgment upon it.

From November 30 to December 27, English ships blockaded El Salvador while the indigo fairs were in progress and succeeded in bringing Doroteo Vasconcelos to his knees. Unable to withstand the complaints of merchants at San Miguel, Vasconcelos had no choice but to acknowledge the list of claims presented by the British consul-general.

11. To Palmerston, Nos. 23, 25, March 19, 1849, F.O. 15/57; Thomas Manning to Palmerston, p. encl.s, March 4, 1849, F.O. 15/61.
12. To Palmerston, Nos. 63 (July 10), 71-72 (July 31), and 77 (August 2, 1848), F.O. 15/52; to Palmerston, No. 81, September 1, 1848, F.O. 15/53; from Palmerston, No. 2, January 31, 1849, F.O. 15/56, in which he refuses to support the Samuel Gibbeson claim.
13. To Palmerston, No. 108, p. encl.s, November 24, 1848, F.O. 15/53.

These included some which the Foreign Office had officially rejected. In what seemed to be a noble gesture, Chatfield did not insist on the immediate payment of all claims. Instead, he suggested an instalment plan whereby El Salvador would pay fifteen thousand pesos a year. Actually, there was little nobility in this proposal since it turned out that the British agent did not want a total liquidation of the debt. A complete payment would have interfered with the "lien" technique which he had recommended to Lord Palmerston. The longer El Salvador postponed the payment of her debts, the longer he would be able to claim a so-called "proprietary" right to islands which he felt might fall into North American hands. On January 5, 1849, he admitted this strategy to both Palmerston and Admiral Phipps Hornby of the Pacific squadron.[14] It followed, of course, that Honduras would also have to come under the new plan. On January 26, 1849, he wrote to the Honduran government outlining the instalment scheme and threatening that if it did not approve he would assume a lien on Tigre Island.[15]

Sensitive to opposition in the House of Commons over the Greytown episode, Lord Palmerston had no alternative but to reject Chatfield's new approach. In a letter of May 1, 1849, he told his agent: "Parliament would be very little disposed to take upon the Public the settlement of those claims in exchange for the Islands in question, the occupation of which might be looked upon as productive of doubtful advantage but certain expense."[16] This key letter reached Guatemala City by mid-July, a chronological point of no small importance. Though Palmerston had asked his underling to keep a close watch over American agents in Central America, he was not willing to sanction procedures which would inevitably embroil relations with the United States.

In late November, 1848, Elijah Hise arrived in Guatemala City carrying instructions to negotiate treaties with Guatemala and El Salvador and to further Central American union — a standard objective of American policy which was never implemented previously to any great extent.[17] Given his suspicious nature, the British consul-general needed no encouragement from London in placing a continuous surveillance on the American chargé d'affaires. Hise's every action and statement were

---

14. To Palmerston, Nos. 4 (January 5) and 8 (January 16, 1849), F.O. 15/57.
15. To Palmerston, No. 14, p. encl., February 24, 1849, F.O. 15/57. In the meantime, Chatfield continued to persuade English interests to buy property in the area of La Unión — in other words, he had not given up his imperialistic project. See, to Carlos Meany, March 9, 1849, and, from Young Anderson, pvt., February 15, 1849, F.O. 252/46.
16. From Palmerston, No. 7, May 1, 1849, F.O. 15/56.
17. James Buchanan to Elijah Hise, June 3, 1848, MDCIA, III, 30-35.

immediately known to Chatfield. In fact, one of Chatfield's conservative friends played chess with Hise regularly! Contrary to the erroneous picture often painted of Mr. Hise — undoubtedly inspired by his later actions in the United States — Chatfield described him as a harmless "lame-duck" appointee of the retiring Polk administration who was sent there merely to negotiate treaties; and the Englishman was correct in his analysis, incidentally. As for the treaty objective, the British agent was more than glad to assist his American colleague; in fact, Hise's unauthorized general treaties with Honduras and Nicaragua carried the blessings of the British consulate.[18] The reason was obvious if we recall Chatfield's goal of dissociating the states from the union. To an informant in Nicaragua, he confided that the impending treaty between Guatemala and the United States would put an end to unionist agitation in Central America.[19] In short, American recognition of Guatemalan independence, added to that of Belgium, France, the Hanse Cities, and Great Britain, suited the British consul's anti-union policy to the letter.[20] The same was true of Hise's treaties with other states of Central America.

Although Salvadoreans received Mr. Hise like a conquering hero, they refused to consider a separate treaty with his country. Instead they preferred a general treaty between the United States and all five Central American states which they had instructed Ignacio Gómez to negotiate in Washington.[21] Nevertheless, in the reception honoring Hise, the Salvadorean government warmly praised "Americanism" and the "Monroe Doctrine."[22] And reports received in Guatemala City — perhaps calculated to annoy Mr. Chatfield more than anything else, for it must be remembered that a British blockade was in progress during Hise's visit — described projects by which El Salvador planned to annex herself to the United States over a twenty-year period. Unionists, moreover, did not conceal their eagerness to grant further concessions to American steamship interests — an objective in which Elijah Hise showed more than a passing interest. These reports brought uneasiness to the British consulate.[23]

In the negotiations of general treaties with Nicaragua and Honduras,

---

18. To Palmerston, No. 107, November 24, 1848, F.O. 15/53; to *idem,* Nos. 6 (January 12) and 13 (February 24, 1849), F.O. 15/57.
19. To Thomas Manning, January 26, 1849, F.O. 252/43.
20. To Palmerston, No. 21, March 5, 1849, F.O. 15/57; to *idem,* Nos. 40 (May 14) and 45 (June 1, 1849), F.O. 15/58; to Manning, May 5, 1849, F.O. 252/43.
21. To Palmerston, No. 20, March 3, 1849, F.O. 15/57.
22. To Palmerston, No. 115, December 15, 1848, F.O. 15/53.
23. To Palmerston, Nos. 20 (March 3) and 12 (February 1, 1849), F.O. 15/57; to *idem,* No. 114, December 15, 1848, F.O. 15/53.

the Nicaraguan emissary was eager to establish a stronger bond with the United States. By May, 1849, it should be recalled, Nicaragua had rejoined the unionist movement of the "center," especially upon learning of Castellón's failure to convince Lord Palmerston. That is why Buenaventura Selva was sent to meet Hise in Guatemala City. After his arrival, Selva contacted the Honduran agent and proposed that they should approach Hise on the establishment of an American protectorate of their two states. But the Honduran representative, Pedro N. Arriaga, who subsequently became the foreign minister of the conservative government in Guatemala, betrayed this information to Chatfield. In a note to Selva, strongly influenced by the British agent, Arriaga rejected the proposal. As a result, Hise was only allowed to negotiate general treaties — an outcome which pleased the English political boss in Guatemala City.[24]

It turned out, however, that Mr. Selva had the last laugh. Managing to escape curious eyes in Guatemala City, he negotiated a secret treaty with Hise on June 21, 1849. If it had been ratified, the so-called Hise-Selva Convention would have placed Nicaragua under the protection of the United States and would have given either the American government, or a company endorsed by it, exclusive control over any canal constructed in Nicaragua. What is often forgotten in discussions of this celebrated agreement is that it was the product of Nicaragua's frustration and not the result of Hise's scheming.[25] Nicaragua — and unionists in general — desperately wanted an effective counterpoise to Mr. Chatfield and the nation he represented. The Hise-Selva Convention, moreover, stimulated Anglo-American negotiations which led to the Clayton-Bulwer Treaty of 1850.

Suspecting that perhaps Selva might have successfully concluded an arrangement with the American chargé d'affaires, Chatfield assigned his personal secretary Charles Booth to return to the United States with Hise. On July 2, the American agent and his English companion left Guatemala City; before reaching Izabal, Booth learned the contents of the secret treaty and immediately relayed the information to Guatemala City. By July 11, Chatfield knew the terms of the secret convention.[26] Of interest also was a letter which Mr. Booth wrote from New York on September 4, 1849:

> I observe here that the Yankees have their eyes fully set on *Tigre*.
> Your move regarding it does not seem to be known as yet; and

24. To Palmerston, Nos. 41 (May 15), 42 (May 17), 44 (May 22), and 45 (June 1, 1849), F.O. 15/58.
25. To Palmerston, No. 57, July 11, 1849, F.O. 15/59.
26. *Ibid.;* to Palmerston, No. 65, July 27, 1849, F.O. 15/59.

when it is, I doubt not but a great outcry will be raised. I hope the Government at home will take some decided step at once. It is a great pity your first suggestion was not acceded to.[27]

In other words, before Booth's departure from Guatemala City, Chatfield had decided upon the occupation of Tigre Island in keeping with the "lien" approach. And this is all the more remarkable when we consider that by July 27, 1849, he had already received Palmerston's letter of May 1, refusing to condone the "lien" strategy. Moreover, on July 27, Chatfield again insisted strenuously upon the occupation of the Tigre.[28] All of which, in addition to other factors which we shall discuss shortly, indicate conclusively that the dramatic occupation of Tigre Island on October 16, 1849, had been deliberately planned for some time — a fact which might have led to war with the United States if it had been widely known.

* * *

Although Hise and the secret treaty gave substance to the North American challenge in Central America, this was merely the beginning. On June 22, 1849, even before Hise's departure from Guatemala City, his replacement landed at Greytown, an appointee of the new Whig administratioin of General Zachary Taylor. A believer in the "Evident Destiny" of the United States, Ephraim George Squier was to become the greatest personal threat to Chatfield's position in Central America.

At the official reception for him in León, Nicaragua, Squier sounded the clarion to action. Like Don Quixote rushing toward the windmills, the champion of "Americanism" and the Monroe Doctrine thrilled his Central American audience with this thrust:

A cardinal principle in this policy is a total exclusion of foreign influence, from the domestic and international affairs of the American Republics. And while we would cultivate friendly intercourse, and promote trade and commerce with all the world, and invite to our shores and to the enjoyment of our institutions the people of all nations, we should proclaim in language firm and distinct, that the American continent belongs to Americans, and is sacred to Republican Freedom.[29]

Squier spoke too of the glorious interoceanic canal, soon to be con-

---

27. From Charles Booth, September 4, 1849, F.O. 252/46.
28. To Palmerston, Nos. 67-68, July 27, 1849, F.O. 15/59.
29. *Correo del Istmo* (León), No. 6, July 16, 1849, in No. 64, to Palmerston, F.O. 15/59; *Daily National Intelligencer* (Washington), October 12, 1849. For the use of the term "Evident Destiny," see, George L. Wyke to Clarendon, No. 25, July 28, 1853, F.O. 15/79.

structed; and he reminded Nicaraguans that President Taylor would not allow territorial aggression to go unchallenged in Central America. With Hise's secret treaty, and now the remarks of his successor, small wonder that on July 27 Frederick Chatfield was ready to take the "Tiger," with or without Palmerston's blessing.

Furthermore, subsequent activities of North Americans confirmed every suspicion that the British agent had ever harbored about "Brother Jonathan." The electrifying news of gold discoveries, followed by a veritable invasion of North Americans on their way to the promised land of California, made Squier's remarks and actions all the more meaningful and terrifying to Mr. Chatfield. On March 16, 1849, David Brown, who represented the New York and New Orleans Steam Navigation Company, had negotiated a contract with Nicaragua, in which the company promised to use whatever influence it might have to gain the United States' cooperation against the Anglo-Mosquito occupation of Greytown. Moreover, the contract called for the establishment of four customhouses along the proposed transit route from the Atlantic to the Pacific oceans, one of which was to be located at Greytown.[30] Chatfield instantly challenged the Brown contract on the ground that the port belonged to Mosquitia and that Nicaragua's customs duties were already pledged to the liquidation of British claims.[31]

Due to this opposition as well as other factors, the Brown contract never materialized. Later, however, Squier encouraged the Nicaraguan government to make similar concessions to other Americans; and on August 27, 1849, a contract to build a canal across Nicaragua was awarded to the Atlantic Pacific Ship Canal Company, a New York firm whose main directors were Joseph L. White, Cornelius Vanderbilt, and Nathaniel Wolfe.[32]

In the meantime, Squier had begun negotiations with Nicaragua for a general treaty, following the lines of the 1826 convention between the United States and the Central American Republic. Signed on September 3, 1849, it included article thirty-five, which recognized the exclusive rights given to the Vanderbilt company. On September 28, 1849, Squier also negotiated a general treaty with Honduras which contained a special protocol whereby that state temporarily (for a maximum period of eighteen months) ceded Tigre Island to the United States of America — an

---

30. To Palmerston, No. 87, p. encl., September 15, 1849, F.O. 15/59; to *idem,* No. 49, p. encl., June 8, 1849, F.O. 15/58.

31. To Palmerston, No. 38, May 5, 1849, F.O. 15/57; and Nos. 47 (June 2) and 51 (June 20, 1849), F.O. 15/58.

32. William Oscar Scroggs, *Filibusters and Financiers: The Story of William Walker and his Associates* (New York, 1916), p. 79.

act confirmed by the Honduran decrees of October 9 and 13.[33] The news of Squier's treaties reached Frederick Chatfield on October 15, 1849; the English occupied the Tigre on the 16th.[34]

Presumably, or at least that was the belief of many contemporaries, Squier's actions brought about Chatfield's unauthorized seizure of the Tigre; actually, as we have shown, the move had been planned for some time. Moreover, it should be noted that a report of the impending occupation of the island had leaked out prematurely; Squier, for example, knew about it as early as September 12, 1849, when he wrote the following to the American secretary of state:

> I am not authorized to give the name of my informant, in respect to the matter of Tigre, — but he is in the Secrets of the English, and has the proofs of their designs in his hands. I heard myself, accidentally, the adjurations of the British Vice-Consul here, that he would exercise the utmost caution, not to excite the suspicion of any one, but especially of this Legation [American]. I shall arrange things if possible so that I *can* interfere if necessary, but shall act only *when* necessary. I know this step may seem somewhat extraordinary; but the Gulf of Fonseca *must* be *free* or the Canal will be worthless, for it will inevitably terminate there, unless there is some insuperable natural obstacle not now present.[35]

The wording of the Honduras Treaty (September 28), along with the protocol, also reveals the fact that the concession was made to Squier in the hopes that it would deter Chatfield from occupying the Tigre. On October 9, 1849, moreover, the French consul in Guatemala City likewise announced the impending occupation of the island — conceivably, he may have been Squier's original source of information.[36]

Emboldened by Squier's aggressive leadership, the states of the "center" defied the English opponent with impunity, eliminating the niceties of speech which formerly characterized their correspondence

---

33. MTUSA, V, 724-725; *Gaceta del Salvador* (San Salvador), No. 50, February 15, 1850, B.L./CAMN, vol. 5; from Thomas Manning, p. encl.s, August 16, 23, and October 4, 1849, F.O. 252/43; to Palmerston, No. 86, September 7, 1849, F.O. 15/59; to *idem*, Nos. 99 (October 26), 103 (November 5, 1849), p. encl.s in both, F.O. 15/60, and No. 13, January 25, 1850, F.O. 15/64; MDCIA, III, 393-401.

34. From Thomas Manning, October 9, 13, 1849, F.O. 252/43, received by Chatfield on October 15.

35. Squier to Clayton, pvt., September 12, 1849, Mary W. Williams, "Letters of E. George Squier to John M. Clayton, 1849–1850," *Hispanic American Historical Review*, Vol. 1 (1918), p. 428; also see *idem* to *idem*, December 13, 1849, MDCIA, III, 452-463.

36. Fourcade to Min. of Foreign Affairs, No. 3, October 9, 1849, A.A.E.P./CPAC, vol. 9.

with him.[37] The press, as might be expected, kept up a constant barrage of anti-English propaganda and pro-American utterances; at every turn, Central American newspapers liberally quoted Squier's remarks and described enthusiastically his efforts and measures to defend Central America from Old World powers.[38]

Squier's challenge, however, awakened the fighting instincts of his English rival. It will be recalled how Chatfield had immediately questioned the Brown contract; incidentally, he gained Palmerston's unqualified support on this matter.[39] Then, to explain the British position on Mosquito matters, he published a lengthy letter which was sent to the State of Nicaragua on September 5, 1849. Again it should be noted that Palmerston fully sanctioned the expenditure of public revenue in the publication of two hundred copies of that letter.[40] In the meantime, the British agent continued to add new claims to El Salvador's list, especially a sizable one of twenty-three thousand pesos.[41] He seemed determined, in other words, to raise the debts high enough so that the "lien" technique would not misfire.

More particularly, Chatfield's relations with Honduras exposed the political objective which he had in mind. When he wrote to Honduras on January 26, 1849, suggesting a possible lien on the Tigre, he received no immediate answer — a fact which annoyed him during the month of March.[42] It was from anger, incidentally, that the Honduran government demurred. Hoping perhaps that the consul-general might listen to reason, however, it answered Chatfield in April that it was prepared to arbitrate or discuss the claims with him.[43] The Englishman found this reply unacceptable. The claims could not be discussed with Honduran commissioners; they could only be paid. Then, as in El Salvador's case, he tacked on an additional claim involving Marshall Bennett and Felipe Jáuregui, a prominent Honduran official.[44]

---

37. To Palmerston, Nos. 66 (July 27), 74-76 (August 20), and 84 (September 6, 1849), p. encl.s, F.O. 15/59.
38. *La Unión* (San Salvador), No. 4, August 1, 1849, B.L./CAMN, vol. 5, is typical of this literature.
39. See footnote 31; also, from Palmerston, Nos. 11 (June 28) and 13 (June 30, 1849), F.O. 15/56.
40. To Palmerston, No. 84, p. encl., September 6, 1849, F.O. 15/59; also in F.O. 252/45; from Palmerston, No. 28, December 12, 1849, F.O. 15/56.
41. To Palmerston, No. 90, p. encl., September 24, 1849, F.O. 15/59.
42. To Palmerston, No. 29, April 2, 1849, F.O. 15/57; to Marcos Idígoras, March 23, 1849, F.O. 252/46.
43. To Palmerston, Nos. 103 (November 5) and 105 (November 6, 1849), p. encl.s, F.O. 15/60.
44. To Palmerston, No. 37, p. encl., May 3, 1847, F.O. 15/58.

The resurrection of the Guayavillas claim, as well as its subsequent disposal, was perhaps the most flagrant example of using financial obligations for achieving political objectives. The tactic of raising and dropping claims, as he had previously done with this particular one, was well known to Central Americans; even Squier and his French colleague Fourcade noted the practice.[45] Apparently, the Foreign Office was the only uninformed source, though it is doubtful that Palmerston was that naive. Yet the important thing is that Lord Palmerston assured his agent of naval support for October, 1849, on both coasts of Central America. With this knowledge, Chatfield wrote to Honduras on September 20, announcing the impending use of coercion on both the Atlantic and Pacific shores of the state.[46]

Not an idle threat indeed, British ships completed their assignments as scheduled. On October 4, 1849, Captain Matthew S. Nolloth in command of the *Plumper* appeared before the port of Trujillo and demanded the immediate payment of 111,061 pesos and 5 reales — the total amount of claims listed for Honduras. If no payment followed, he threatened to raze the city. Of course, the Nicaraguan commandant had no such sum at his disposal, so Nolloth sent a landing party ashore to take the fortress. According to the Honduran account of the incident, English marines poured through the streets destroying property and manhandling many of the port's residents. Finally, the English withdrew but not before receiving 1,200 pesos, the sum offered by the Hondurans to spare the city. It would seem that the spirit of the buccaneers had not died. This was precisely the interpretation given to the *Plumper* action in the Central American press.[47] At a later date, even Chatfield admitted that Nolloth's tactics had been in poor taste.[48]

Leaving Guatemala City on the first of October, accompanied by his good friend "Chico" Pavón — now his personal secretary — Chatfield and party weathered the drenching rain to the coast. Because of the heavy surf at Istapa, they were unable to board the *Gorgon,* commanded by Captain James Paynter, until the 9th. Two days later, the *Gorgon*

---

45. Squier to Clayton, November 2, 8, 1849, MDCIA, III, 427-434, 441; Fourcade to Min. of Foreign Affairs, No. 6, November 12, 1849, A.A.E.P./ CPAC, vol. 9.

46. To Palmerston, No. 106, p. encl., November 6, 1849, F.O. 15/60; also see, to the Honduran Government, September 20, 1849, F.O. 252/45.

47. *Gaceta del Salvador* (San Salvador), No. 40, December 7, 1849, B.L./ CAMN, vol. 5, which contains the Honduran version and documentation of the incident. For the English account, see the documentation in F.O. 15/62 sent to the F.O. by the Admiralty (September 6 to October 13, 1849); also, from Palmerston, No. 29, December 12, 1849, F.O. 15/56.

48. To Palmerston, No. 118, December 18, 1850, F.O. 15/66.

arrived off La Unión; and on the 12th, the British consul-general — also bearing the added title of chargé d'affaires to Guatemala since the ratification of the English treaty with that state — issued an ultimatum to El Salvador on the claims. On the 15th, Chatfield received Manning's reports concerning Squier's treaties with the two states of Honduras and Nicaragua.

At 1:45 p.m., on October 16, 1849, five launches were lowered from the *Gorgon,* and sailed toward the port of Amapala on the Tigre. Eighty well-armed men, accompanied by three officers and Frederick Chatfield, disembarked at the port and within minutes had pulled down the Honduran flag, replacing it with the English colors. To the chorus of "Long live Queen Victoria," British marines fired three rifle volleys and twenty-one cannon shots. Great Britain had acquired a "Tiger." At three o'clock that afternoon, the conquerors reboarded the *Gorgon,* satisfied that the island was now safely theirs.[49] It is noteworthy that Chatfield does not mention his own participation in the action; nor does he refer to the presence of Manuel Francisco Pavón on the tour — the man recognized as the leader of Guatemala's *serviles* and called by his enemies the "Pseudo Central American." Only indirectly was Pavón's participation alluded to in the Admiralty's documentation on the Tigre incident.[50]

On October 20, Chatfield appointed Carlos Dárdano Gota as British superintendent of the Tigre, assigning a police force to assist him. Before leaving for Costa Rica on November 14, Captain Paynter also stationed a platoon of English marines on the island, under Lieutenant Charles H. Young, to prevent an invasion by the Honduran army.[51] Against specific orders from the Foreign Office, therefore, Frederick Chatfield had again taken the law into his own hands — another in a long list of accomplished facts. This particular one had been over three years in the making.

—◦•◦—

Understandably, Central America's reaction to Tigre's occupation was violent, as it was in the United States where the New York *Herald*

---

49. *Gaceta del Salvador* (San Salvador), No. 40, December 7, 1849, B.L./ CAMN, vol. 5, which includes the letter of Vicente Lechuga to Trinidad Muñoz, Amapala, October 16, 1849. Chatfield's version can be found in No. 95, to Palmerston, p. encl.s, October 17, 1849, F.O. 15/60.

50. The Admiralty's correspondence and documentation on the Tigre incident can be found in F.O. 15/68, including Captain Paynter's reports of November 18, 27, and December 11, 1849; *El Progreso* (San Salvador), No. 5, May 9, 1850, B.L./CAMN, vol. 2.

51. To Palmerston, Nos. 97 (October 20) and 111 (November 14, 1849), p. encl.s in both, F.O. 15/60; also see Chatfield's correspondence with Dárdano in F.O. 252/44.

trumpeted the misdeeds of "Mr. Chucklehead Chatfield."[52] Its immediate impact was to encourage "Americanism" and unionism in the states of the "center." The offended state of Honduras wasted no time in dispatching circulars to her sisters detailing the events at Trujillo and the Tigre — episodes which involved "a national question," as a prominent Honduran general put it. Looking forward to the help of the United States, Hondurans exclaimed: "Long live republican governments! Long live the enlightened descendants of the immortal Washington!"[53] Also, as threatened on October 12 when she learned of the *Plumper*'s actions, Honduras declared an embargo against British trade on both coasts.[54]

Decrees and publications from Nicaragua breathed the same fire. Pablo Buitrago proclaimed the "Declaration of Managua," which proscribed monarchical institutions from the New World as well as European intervention in the internal affairs of America.[55] On October 19, Buitrago sent out a circular to the states in which he repeated Squier's statement "The American Continent belongs to Americans, and is sacred to Republican Freedom."[56] Five days later, he published a lengthy exposition of Nicaragua's rights to Mosquitia. Great Britain should get out of Greytown, Buitrago concluded; and while in retreat she might also consider a withdrawal from Belize and Ruatán.[57] No time for timidity, the lion's tail had to be pulled in style. Significantly, the demand for a complete British withdrawal from Central America was the major theme of the newspaper *Integridad de Centro-América,* born in Granada on December 11, 1849.[58] Squier's star was most definitely in the ascendant.

To justify the forceful occupation of the island, Chatfield argued that Honduras' acknowledgment of his January 26 letter had in fact established England's "proprietary right" to the Tigre. Conveniently he overlooked the fact that Palmerston had vetoed the "lien" technique. Moreover, the embattled Englishman maintained that Honduras had no national attributes and therefore could not alienate her territory to a third party, namely, the United States.[59]

---

52. As quoted in the *Times* (London), February 2, 1850.
53. *Gaceta del Salvador* (San Salvador), No. 40.
54. To Palmerston, Nos. 106 (November 6) and 108 (November 8, 1849), p. encl.s in both, F.O. 15/60.
55. In No. 100, (October 29, 1849).
56. *Correo del Istmo* (León), No. 15, December 1, 1849, B.L./CAMN, vol. 5.
57. In No. 124, to Palmerston, December 24, 1849, F.O. 15/60.
58. Prospectus, *Integridad de Centro América* (Granada), November 30, 1849; issue No. 1, December 11, 1849, B.L./CAMN, vol. 5.
59. To Palmerston, Nos. 95 (October 17) and 98 (October 25, 1849), F.O. 15/60; to Honduran Government, November 2, 1849, F.O. 252/45. Chatfield tried to convey the notion that Honduras had resorted to the temporary cession of the Tigre in order to cheat British creditors (see, No. 120, to Palmerston, December 15, 1849, F.O. 15/60).

These arguments failed to convince anyone, least of all Mr. Squier who in terms which might have done justice to his English colleague told him that they had no basis in international law. The "lien" tactic and the "sheet anchor" were so much tommyrot — that was the essence of Squier's reply.[60] When Chatfield persisted, Squier repeated the American position.[61] Annoyed at his rival's remarks, the British agent declared a blockade of El Salvador on October 26, insisted upon payment of the debts, and prohibited the alienation of Salvadorean islands in the vicinity of Tigre Island. On November 5, moreover, he sent an imperious circular to the unionist states instructing them to send envoys to Guatemala City by March, 1850, in order to effect a settlement of the claims issue.[62] Mr. Chatfield was swinging wildly.

Except for his ideological strength — no mean consideration, to be sure — Squier lacked the physical force to oppose the British agent. Yet he worked effectively with what he had — an idea. Largely because of Squier's efforts, ably assisted by Chatfield's counteractions and remarks, the three center states signed a *pacto* on November 8, 1849, in which they agreed to establish a general government for Central America, dedicated to the defense of her territorial integrity.[63] This pact, incidentally, gave birth to the *Representación Nacional* in January, 1851.[64] What Chatfield had dreaded most had come to pass. He refused, of course, to admit that his own conduct had in any way contributed to this result.

To subvert the unionist pact of the 8th, the English agent agreed to a compromise with the Salvadorean government, which was sorely pressed by merchants who were suffering from the blockade. Commissioners Miguel Montoya and Juan Antonio Alvarado boarded the *Gorgon* on the 12th; and after being wined and feted at Captain Paynter's expense — a suggestion made by "Chico" Pavón and seconded by his English colleague — the Salvadorean representatives approved of two conventions. In the first of these, El Salvador consented to the instalment plan and agreed to make the first payment on the claims by January 1,

---

60. From Squier, October 23, 1849, F.O. 252/46.

61. From Squier, November 2, 1849, F.O. 252/46.

62. To Salvadorean Government, No. 18, October 26, 1849, F.O. 252/45; to Squier, October 27, 1849, F.O. 252/46; to Palmerston, Nos. 107 (November 7) and 112 (November 14, 1849), F.O. 15/60.

63. The twenty-two articles of this pact, signed in León on November 8, 1849, were printed in *El Correo del Istmo* (León), No. 16, December 16, 1849, B.L./CAMN, vol. 5.

64. "Consideraciones sobre la posibilidad de establecer un Gov.no jeneral en Centro-América," Tegucigalpa, September 13, 1852, B.L./CAP, vol. 2.

1850; she also stipulated that the islands near the Tigre could not be alienated to anyone but citizens of the state. A second convention called for the official recognition of Marco Idígoras, an Andalousian by birth, as the legitimate representative of the British government at San Salvador. These two agreements represented a compromise — the clause on the islands was a case in point; also the fact that Chatfield knew that the blockade would be ineffective if the Salvadoreans refused to honor their promise on the first of the year. Chatfield's reasons for accepting these arrangements are implicit in this statement to Admiral Phipps Hornby: "My opinion is that this little convention with Salvador will defeat Mr. Squier's plan for uniting the three states of Nicaragua, Honduras, and Salvador into a single state, or Federal Republic, against British interests and influence." [65] Interestingly, without waiting for the state's ratification of the two agreements, Chatfield lifted the blockade on November 12.

In addition to the anti-union motive, another important reason for the compromise was the distressing news of troubles in Costa Rica. On August 16, 1849, and again on October 1 and 20, Squier had written to the Costa Rican government about reports that it was seeking a British protectorate in violation of the Monroe Doctrine. Although Costa Rica refused to give Squier a satisfactory answer — she argued that it was none of his business — she anxiously sought Chatfield's aid against the "American party" which had developed since Squier's appearance in Central America. [66] It was precisely to thwart a rumored liberal uprising in Costa Rica that Chatfield came to terms with the Salvadorean government. On November 14, after stationing the platoon of English marines at Amapala, the *Gorgon* left for Costa Rica; she arrived at Puntarenas two days later. By that time, a revolution had broken out in San José, forcing the resignation of President José María Castro. This turn of events represented a defeat for General Juan José Flores, renowned adventurer, former president and dictator of Ecuador, contractor of the tobacco revenues with Nicaragua, and the leader of the "English Party" in Costa Rica. [67]

Unionist forces throughout Central America hailed the news of a

---

65. To Hornby, November 12, 1849, in No. 112, to Palmerston, November 14, 1849, F.O. 15/60; Hornby to John Parker, p. encl.s, December 18, 1849, F.O. 15/68.

66. *El Costaricense* (San José), No. 50, November 10, 1849, in No. 4, to Palmerston, January 7, 1850, F.O. 15/64; from Thomas Manning, p. encl.s, October 13, 1849, F.O. 252/43; to Palmerston, No. 102, p. encl.s, November 2, 1849, F.O. 15/60; Squier to Clayton, December 27, 1849, MDCIA, III, 468-477.

67. Colonel R. Wright Warren to Palmerston, p. encl., January 12, 1850, F.O. 97/88.

liberal victory in Costa Rica. And hoping that now the wayward southern sister would return to the flock, the Honduran Felipe Jáuregui was sent to San José to encourage her to join the *pacto* of November 8, 1849.[68] Happily for the British cause, however, the conservatives soon recaptured control of the government — a development undoubtedly influenced by the *Gorgon's* presence at Puntarenas. The new government under President Juan Rafael Mora greeted Frederick Chatfield with open arms on November 23, when he entered San José; and on the 27th, Costa Rica signed the long-awaited English treaty.[69] Mr. Chatfield now became the chargé d'affaires to two-fifths of Central America.[70]

With the renewal of the Anglo-Costa Rican alliance, rumors flourished that Nicaragua was planning to revolutionize the border district of Guanacaste at Squier's suggestion. To thwart the projected invasion, Chatfield made it clear to both the Nicaraguan government and to Squier that England would stand against such an invasion. The recent treaty, though it had not yet been ratified, would justify the English position, Chatfield argued. His instructions indicated that ratificatioin would soon follow. As far as he was concerned, therefore, the treaty went into effect on November 27.[71] Despite his questionable legal pronouncements, Chatfield's expeditious actions since leaving Tigre Island — it must be admitted — had saved Costa Rica for the English side.

He was also able to undermine the Jáuregui mission to San José. The envoy of the *pacto* states was Marshall Bennett's adversary in the Guayavillas mining case, a claim which had been added recently to Honduras' list. After some brief conversations with Felipe Jáuregui, the English *caudillo* made him a firm proposition: he would drop the Guayavillas claim if Jáuregui and General Santos Guardiola would join the English side — an excellent illustration of the use of claims for political purposes. And the unscrupulous Jáuregui agreed. By the terms of the convention signed on December 29, 1849, Jáuregui promised that Honduras would declare her independence and then negotiate a trade treaty with England just as Guatemala and Costa Rica had done. Furthermore, and this perhaps was one of Chatfield's demands in return for dropping the Guayavillas claim, Mr. Jáuregui promised to work in behalf of a permanent transfer of Tigre Island to Great Britain.

Thus, a mission which was sent to further unionism in Costa Rica

68. Squier to Clayton, December 13, 1849, MDCIA, III, 462; to Palmerston, Nos. 121 and 123, December 15, 1849, F.O. 15/60.
69. To Palmerston, No. 113, November 24, 1849, F.O. 15/60.
70. Nos. 114 (November 28) and 115 (December 3, 1849).
71. No. 116, p. encl., December 15, 1849.

had ended by serving the opposite cause. Without any pretense or disguise, Chatfield admitted his anti-union objective explicitly in a dispatch to the Foreign Office. And since Palmerston sanctioned the Jáuregui convention, except for the provision on the permanent transfer of the Tigre, we must conclude that he shared his agent's objectives.[72] It should be noted, moreover, that from the time Chatfield had received Palmerston's letter on Hise, he no longer bothered to conceal his political machinations from the Foreign Office.

Palmerston's support of Chatfield's actions was likewise evident in the negotiations with Washington. When the Tigre news reached the United States in December 1849, it nearly wrecked the discussions which preceded the Clayton-Bulwer Treaty. Given the uproar in the American press against Chatfield and his nation, John M. Clayton demanded the evacuation of Tigre Island and a disavowal of the act. Why Secretary of State Clayton neglected to mention the premeditated nature of the Tigre's occupation, since Squier had definitely written to him on this, is a mysterious point which remains to be answered. Palmerston complied insofar as the evacuation of the island was concerned; yet he qualified it by the face-saving statement that if Admiral Hornby of the Pacific Squadron decided otherwise, after surveying the situation personally, the Foreign Office would support him. Despite Palmerston's disapproval of the specific method of coercion which was used by the British consul-general, he nevertheless stubbornly maintained England's right to collect claims due to her citizens. Interestingly, Palmerston did not reveal the fact that Chatfield had disobeyed explicit orders from the Foreign Office not to apply the lien technique.

Washington found Palmerston's qualified apology unsatisfactory; and on March 19, 1850, President Taylor took a strong anti-British stand in his annual message to Congress. He also submitted to the Senate such papers as the Hise-Selva Convention and the Squier Treaty of September 3, 1849 — documents which were previously withheld in order to facilitate a peaceful settlement with Great Britain.[73] That Sir Henry L. Bulwer and John M. Clayton were able to negotiate their famous treaty subsequently, in view of the conditions described above, was really a tribute to their diplomatic ability.

And Palmerston defended Chatfield in yet other ways. He sanctioned the various acts and expenditures incurred since the occupation

---

72. No. 126, p. encl., December 31, 1849; to Palmerston, No. 6, January 12, 1850, F.O. 15/64.

73. See MTUSA, V, 737-742, 755-764, also, from Palmerston, No. 1, January 17, 1850, F.O. 15/63.

of the Tigre. He approved of the Jáuregui convention though he rejected the plan to acquire Tigre Island permanently — a concession, it would seem, to English opposition more than anything else.[74] Furthermore, Palmerston's correspondence with the American minister Abbott Lawrence on Mosquitia and on the occupation of the Tigre indicates that he had only begrudgingly accepted a conciliatory policy toward Central American affairs. Frederick Chatfield, at least, gratefully acknowledged the implied support in the Lawrence-Palmerston correspondence.[75]

＊＊＊

Despite the successes of his English adversary, Mr. Squier was by no means asleep, especially on the ideological front. "Americanism" and unionism grew apace, as liberal newspapers constantly preached the gospels of territorial integrity and *nacionalidad*. El Salvador, moreover, instantly rejected the November 12, 1849, agreement on claims which her commissioners had signed; Honduras expatriated "the traitor" Felipe Jáuregui for selling himself to the British; and when it was learned that on November 19, 1849, Costa Rica had ratified a canal contract with an English company (via the Serapiquí and San Juan rivers), both Squier and the Nicaraguan government registered protests.[76] In short, the English victories were more apparent than real; Squier had not conceded defeat. And the British rival found it all most irritating: "I really wish some check could be put on the advances and misrepresentations of Mr. Squier."[77]

But brute force and political maneuvers were not the only weapons in Chatfield's arsenal. Beginning with mid-December, 1849 — at least this was when he first admitted it to Palmerston — he entered the ideological arena with a clever propaganda campaign of his own. To bring about a more correct view of the English position, he published all types of documentation — for example, the Lawrence-Palmerston correspond-

---

74. Palmerston's note of March 5, 1850 to Chatfield's dispatch No. 6, January 12, 1850, F.O. 15/64; also see, mem., F.O. to Admiralty, June 13, 1850, F.O. 15/68.

75. To Palmerston, Nos. 3 (January 7) and 46 (June 29, 1850), F.O. 15/64; from Palmerston, Nos. 25 (November 16) and 28 (December 13, 1849), F.O. 15/56; from Edward Wallerstein, November 16, 1849, F.O. 252/54, informing Chatfield that the London *Times* was against him and Palmerston.

76. *Gaceta del salvador* (San Salvador), No. 63, May 12, 1850; *Correo del Istmo* (León), No. 18, January 16, 1850, plus *Alcance* to No. 18 (January 26, 1850); *Integridad* (Granada), Nos. 1-2, December 13-18, 1850 — all in B.L./CAMN, vol. 5; "Contestación," Guatemala, November 5 to 21, 1849, T.P.C.G.; from Thomas Manning, December 20, 1849, F.O. 252/54; to Palmerston, No. 10, p. encl.s, January 23, 1850, F.O. 15/64.

77. To Palmerston, No. 8, January 14, 1850, F.O. 15/64.

ence on Mosquitia as well as "Documents" exchanged "between some states of Central America and England."[78]

The English champion of Central American conservatism, assisted handsomely by his colleague Pavón, launched a double-barreled attack upon "The Western Hemisphere Idea" and *nacionalidad* in a series of broadsides and pamphlets entitled *Cuestión del Día,* propaganda that was also published in the faithful Costa Rican press. In number one, the anonymous author discussed "The Nationality of Central America and the Exclusive American system, Uninfluenced by European Monarchical Governments," contending that Central Americans could not isolate themselves from the markets and advanced civilization of the Old World without backsliding.[79] The third number continued the attack on the "American System" and the "Monroe Doctrine," as well as the imitation of all things American. In number two, the writer spoke against *"integridad nacional,"* an allusion to the newspaper *Integridad* which had frequent articles on *nacionalidad* and which stridently demanded a British retreat from Central America. In this same number, he attacked Squier as a "loco-foco" in American politics, a party composed of "socialists, communists, and disorganizers" bent upon extending their selfish objectives throughout the Americas. And judging from President Taylor's remarks on December 4, 1849, the author insinuated that Squier was pursuing an unauthorized course in Central America.[80]

The deliberate smear of Mr. Squier, and Americans in general, was fully developed in the third "Issue of the Day," also written in Costa Rica. The writer insisted that the United States was a poor example for Central America; that the American government was weak as evidenced by recent events foreboding civil war; and that even President Taylor had admitted as much in his December 4 message to Congress. To be sure, the Northern Republic had prospered in the past; but this was due to European influences and capital. One more point which all Central Americans should ponder was the dislike of their northern brethren for mixed races. What kind of an "American System" could be built upon this basis, he asked. It might be well for Central Americans to remember what Europe had done for them and how Great Britain, for example, had

---

78. To Palmerston, Nos. 119 (December 13) and 122 (December 20, 1849), p. encl.s, F.O. 15/60; to *idem,* No. 3, January 7, 1850, F.O. 15/64.

79. *Cuestión del Día,* San José, January 28, 1850, in No. 14, to Palmerston, January 29, 1850, F.O. 15/64; and also published with editorial comments in *Gaceta del Gobierno de Costa Rica* (San José), No. 62, February 2, 1850.

80. *Cuestión del Día,* San José, February 9, 1850, in No. 16 (February 12, 1850); and in the *Gaceta,* No. 64, February 16, 1850.

helped them in their emancipation from Spanish rule. Many sensible people in Costa Rica and Guatemala had already seen the light; the center states should not wait. Lord Palmerston, it should be noted, sanctioned the publication of these tracts.[81]

Through official channels as well, Chatfield carried on a relentless attack upon Squier, picturing him as a demagogue and the rascal who had enticed Honduras into giving up the Tigre — a vicious act of "collusion to defraud a creditor." Palmerston in London as well as Henry Lytle Bulwer and John F. Crampton in Washington received this stereotype of the American chargé and relayed it to the State Department.[82] And E. George Squier was recalled in mid-1850, not so much because of his rival's campaign — though the latter like to believe so — but rather because the Whig administration of Zachary Taylor and Millard Fillmore had decided to settle matters peacefully with Great Britain. Squier was thus sacrificed; and when he returned to the United States, he indicated his displeasure at this example of truckling to the British.[83] But when the State Department expected a reciprocal concession — Chatfield's recall — Lord Palmerston demurred on the ground that, as Professor Van Alstyne has put it, "Chatfield was an efficient servant in defending the private rights of British subjects in Central America."[84] That could cover a multitude of sins. To the last days of his tenure in the Foreign Office, Lord Palmerston stubbornly resisted the frequent demands for Chatfield's dismissal.

Before Squier's departure from Central America, the American agent and his allies had genuinely troubled the British chargé, provoking him to new counterprojects which we shall discuss subsequently. Jáuregui's betrayal came in for some acid comments from the unionist press, especially in view of the manner in which the British evacuated Tigre Island. When Admiral Hornby received news of the *Gorgon's* unauthorized participation in the Tigre incident, he immediately reprimanded Captain Paynter and ordered him back to evacuate the island. All this

81. *Cuestión del Día,* San José, March 2, 1850, in No. 22 (March 2, 1850); and in the *Gaceta,* No. 67, March 9, 1850; from Palmerston, No. 29, June 26, 1850, F.O. 15/63.

82. To Palmerston, Nos. 4 (January 7) and 13 (January 25, 1850), F.O. 15/64; to Bulwer, January 3, 5, 23, F.O. 252/52.

83. From Crampton, conf., November 29, 1849, F.O. 252/52; to Palmerston, No. 107, p. encl., November 28, 1850, F.O. 15/66; Squier to Clayton, pvt./conf., September 2, 1850, Mary Williams, *op. cit.,* pp. 432-434, in which Squier attributed his dismissal to Daniel Webster's hostility to everything which Clayton had done, as well as to Bulwer's duplicity.

84. Richard W. Van Alstyne, "British Diplomacy and the Clayton-Bulwer Treaty, 1850–1860," *Journal of Modern History,* Vol. XI (June, 1939), p. 165.

was done without consulting Chatfield. On December 26, 1849, Paynter carried out his orders; and on the following day, the naval officer wrote an indiscreet letter to the former superintendent of the Tigre commenting upon the consul-general's "bad role" in the entire affair. Lord Palmerston reacted angrily to Paynter's remarks; but when he sought satisfaction from the Admiralty, a spokesman noted that in the past Chatfield had not been very discreet in his comments about naval officers — a very accurate observation, it must be admitted.[85] To the unionist papers of Central America the evacuation of Tigre Island could mean only one thing: the British government had repudiated its agent's actions. They therefore clamored for his recall.[86]

Admiral Hornby's order to evacuate the Tigre proved embarrassing to Mr. Chatfield, especially since it was implemented three days before the signing of the Jáuregui convention. If Hornby had contacted him first, Chatfield scolded, the situation might have been salvaged for then he could have argued that the evacuation of Tigre Island and the Jáuregui agreement had been part of the same arrangement. Thus the English could have haved face.[87] Chatfield was not alone in disapproving of the manner in which Hornby had handled the matter. John Foster commented acidly that the admiral had little appreciation or knowledge of Spanish character — the *Plumper* of the Atlantic squadron had been more realistic.[88] Ground had been lost as a result; and precisely because of this, the British consul-general undertook the ideological campaign described above. He was particularly annoyed by the remarks and insinuations in *El Correo del Istmo* of January 16, 1850. Although he composed a rebuttal proving that the British navy had not revoked his actions at all, at the last minute Chatfield decided against its publication.[89]

To ascertain conditions in Central America for himself, Admiral Phipps Hornby arrived at Puntarenas on March 10, 1850. From there he wrote to Chatfield explaining that he was on his way to the Gulf of Fon-

85. To Palmerston, No. 7, January 14, 1850, F.O. 15/64; Francis Baring to Palmerston, June 21, 1850, F.O. 15/68.

86. To Palmerston, No. 15, p. encl.s, February 5, 1850, F.O. 15/64.

87. To Phipps Hornby, January 14, 1850, in No. 7, to Palmerston, January 14, 1850, F.O. 15/64.

88. From John Foster, January 1, 12, 1850, F.O. 252/50; from Thomas Manning, January 12, 1850, and from Young Anderson, February 17, 1850, F.O. 252/54.

89. *Correo del Istmo* (León), No. 18, January 16, 1850, B.L./CAMN, vol. 5. Interestingly, Chatfield's reply appears after this issue with a scribbled note stating that it would be best not to publish it. It would seem, therefore, that some of the newspaper materials at the Bancroft Library may have come from Chatfield's personal archives. This particular document, for example, is not in F.O. 252.

seca; if he wanted a ride in that direction, he had only to say. Although originally the consul-general's plans were to return to his home base in March via the Pacific, he now decided against it in order to carry out another important scheme, which will be described in the next section. Besides, since the annual fairs were over, a new blockade would have been useless. On the other hand, the presence of the Pacific squadron's leader might have a salutary effect by correcting the impression created by the evacuation mistake. In any case, the admiral should carry out Chatfield's suggestions.[90]

And this is precisely what happened during the months of March and April, while Hornby was in Central American waters. The admiral wrote to Honduras urging her to ratify the Jáuregui convention; he reprimanded El Salvador for reneging on her agreement to pay the British claims and to respect Marcos Idígoras as the English representative; and he expressed his displeasure with the hostile remarks in the newspapers of the center states. Provoked by the tireless Squier, who reportedly raised the American flag on Tigre Island when the Admiral appeared in the Gulf of Fonseca, the governments of the "center" defied the leader of the Pacific squadron. According to the rank-conscious Chatfield, who was having a running fight with the rival states for calling him "consul" rather than "chargé d'affaires," the Salvadorean government had deliberately insulted the admiral by calling him "Mr. Hornby." In short, Admiral Hornby received no royal welcome in Central America; and before his return to Chile, he made it clear to all concerned that the British navy would be back in October to collect debts and to teach them manners.[91]

Hornby's presence in Central America, as well as his communications with the governments of the "center," further enhanced Squier's stature among unionists. With greater intensity and fervor, the press scored *los malditos ingleses* (those wretched Englishmen) and their piratical ways. On May 9, 1850, *El Progreso* of San Salvador, edited by José Francisco Barrundia, wounded Chatfield to the quick with these remarks, which the Englishman translated as follows:

> The ravages of the small pox, the cholera — Civil War — bloody revolutions — tyranny — barbarism — a Malespín — and a Carrillo — all these pass away. Carrera also will pass away. But there is an evil, horrible and interminable, there is a living curse which cor-

---

90. To Palmerston, No. 37, p. encl.s, April 10, 1850, F.O. 15/64.
91. To Palmerston, Nos. 48 (July 1) and 52 (July 31, 1850), p. encl.s, F.O. 15/64; Z. M. Rojas to Phipps Hornby, March 28, 1850, MDCIA, III, 518.

rodes the vitals of Central America — and this is Chatfield, the eternal Agent of England.[92]

In the light of Squier's effective challenge and the territorial pronouncements of the unionist center, England's "eternal Agent" decided to return to Guatemala City via the Atlantic rather than the Pacific route. The purpose of what might be called his "grand tour" was to consolidate Great Britain's hold on Greytown, Mosquitia, Belize, and the Bay Islands. And he succeeded remarkably well, while at the same time establishing precedents for the future.

After their departure from San José on March 12, Chatfield and company proceeded to Greytown, which was on the verge of anarchy when they arrived there a week later. Rebellious North Americans and Nicaraguans had no respect for the King of the Mosquitos, his people, or the acting British Resident James Green, who was the recognized leader of the port. Rumor had it, moreover, that on March 26 a packet-boat would arrive at Greytown bringing word of the United States' decision to force the Anglo-Mosquito evacuation of the controversial port. Tension mounted; an explosion was imminent; it came on the eve of the 26th.

Some twenty-five Nicaraguan sailors, hailing from Granada, had just come into town; and after some drinks, a few of them began to strum their guitars, as sailors will. Another recent arrival was Raimundo Selva, a Nicaraguan gentleman on his way to the United States. Since he was passing through Greytown, a friend of his had instructed him to collect some debts owed by Louis Beschor, a German resident at the port. According to the Nicaraguan version, Beschor denied these obligations, and was instantly supported by the British consul-general. All of this happened on the morning of the 25th. That afternoon Selva harangued his celebrating countrymen from Granada; and before long they attacked the director of customs at Greytown. The local police then fired into the crowd and restored order; and at Chatfield's insistence, the boatmen were tied up and Mr. Selva was put in jail. At six o'clock on the following morning, according to the English version, the sailors received two dozen lashes apiece, and Selva was forced to witness the whippings. To impress Nicaraguans with respect for authority, Frederick Chatfield demanded further "exemplary punishment" — the distinguished Mr. Selva was also subjected to the lash.

92. As translated by Chatfield in No. 43, to Palmerston, June 25, 1850, F.O. 15/64; *El Progreso* (San Salvador), No. 5, May 9, 1850, B.L./CAMN, vol. 5.

Nicaraguans claimed that on the night of Selva's encarceration Chatfield had visited him, and after pulling a cigar from the prisoner's mouth, had then cuffed him with his sword. This account of the Selva incident appeared first in the Nicaraguan press and was republished by *El Progreso* on May 9, along with the Chatfield-is-a-curse quotation cited above.[93] Whatever the correct facts of the case may have been, the consul-general's popularity — if one can properly call it that — reached bottom in the center states. The Selva incident, moreover, heightened Squier's influence in Central America and also contributed to the angry defiance of Admiral Hornby. Furthermore, *El Progreso*'s account of the episode so enraged Mr. Chatfield that it led him to conceive further plans and projects against unionism in Central America.

Anticipating the Central American reaction to the Selva incident, the British agent devoted the following week to the consolidation of English control at the strategic port. And the Foreign Office sanctioned most of the recommendations and measures taken. To begin with, Chatfield maintained that Greytown needed an efficient police force; and later, in Jamaica, he appointed and paid former members of the West Indian Regiment to serve in this capacity. Secondly, to prevent an uprising or a Nicaraguan attack upon the port, he recommended to naval authorities, and to the Foreign Office, that a British warship be kept on permanent duty at Greytown. Thirdly, to pay for the added expenses of government, he suggested and drew up a customs and tariff schedule which went into effect on April 1, 1850. The contract for collecting these duties was farmed out to Louis Beschor, whom Chatfield had befriended in the Selva case, and to Phillip Auguste Barruel, a French merchant. Fourthly, he urged James Green, at the earliest opportunity, to establish an effective municipal government at Greytown. And finally, he made minor recommendations concerning mahogany licenses and other matters which might improve the port's revenues. His genuine concern for strengthening the British position in Mosquitia was clearly evident in his recommendation that the King of the Mosquito's yearning for a "white woman" be satisfied. Palmerston would not hear of this last suggestion; the decision, in his opinion, should be left solely to the damsel in question, a Miss Bell. Yet the mere fact that a confirmed white supremacist like Frederick Chatfield could make such a suggestion was indeed significant.[94]

---

93. To Palmerston, No. 29, April 8, 1850, F.O. 15/64; *Correo del Istmo* (León), No. 28, April 18, 1850, and *El Progreso* (San Salvador), Nos. 4-5, May 2-9, 1850, in B.L./CAMN, vols. 5 and 2 respectively.

94. To Palmerston, Nos. 26-35, March 21 to April 8, 1850, p. encl.s, F.O. 15/64; Customs Regulations, Greytown, March, 1850, F.O. 252/52; for Palmerston's approval of these various acts, see F.O. 15/63.

While in Greytown, the British consul-general learned from his Costa Rican ally that Felipe Jáuregui was unable to win his government's approval for the December 29 treaty. In conjunction with General Santos Guardiola, Jáuregui had then led a revolution against President Juan Lindo; and when it failed, he fled to Nicaragua where he was detained upon Lindo's request. In a letter to Hornby, Chatfield urged the admiral to remonstrate with the Honduran government and to support the Jáuregui-Guardiola faction if it were at all feasible.[95] The Jáuregui debacle, of course, worried President Mora of Costa Rica; and from a distance, his English ally tried to bolster his confidence. According to Chatfield, Mora had written to him recently asking for a concrete alliance, if not a protectorate, with Great Britain.[96]

From the Mosquito port, the British party took a circuitous route to Belize which included stops at Cartagena in New Granada, Jamaica, and Cuba. On the way, Chatfield had an opportunity to converse with some notable personages — the famous Mexican general Antonio López de Santa Ana who was suffering one of his periodic exiles, Governor Charles Edward Grey of Jamaica, Commodore Thomas Bennett of the British Navy, and the Captain General of Cuba — and he sounded them out on various issues. In Jamaica especially he won full support from Bennett and Grey for the measures he had taken to consolidate Great Britain's position on the Atlantic coast.[97]

Because of unionist demands with regard to Belize and the Bay Islands, Chatfield again recommended the establishment of royal colonies at those locations. During the month of May, 1850, he personally helped to circulate a petition among the residents of Belize which requested colonial status. Citing the danger of North American adventurers at Ruatán in the Bay Islands, he made a similar recommendation for residents of those islands.[98] And London acted upon these recommendations; the Bay Islands became a royal colony by the Queen's warrant of March 20, 1852.[99] Belize, however had to wait another decade because of complications in England's relations with the United States. It is interesting to note, nevertheless, that Lord Palmerston urged the Colonial Office

---

95. From Juan R. Mora, March 16, 1850, F.O. 252/53; to Palmerston, No. 37, p. encl., April 10, 1850, F.O. 15/64; to *idem,* No. 119, p. encl., December 20, 1850, F.O. 15/66.
96. To Juan R. Mora, March 20, 23, 1850, F.O. 252/53; to Palmerston, No. 27, April 6, 1850, F.O. 15/64.
97. To Palmerston, No. 36, April 10, 1850, and No. 1, sep., April 30, 1850, F.O. 15/64.
98. To Palmerston, Nos. 39 (May 20) and 49 (July 26, 1850), p. encl.s, F.O. 15/64.
99. C.O. to F.O., p. encl.s, September 24, 1850, F.O. 15/68; MTUSA, V, 786.

to set up definite markers on the western and southern boundaries of the establishment according to the principle of effective occupation.[100]

During his stay at Belize, Chatfield received the issue of *El Progreso* which referred to him as a curse and reproduced the Nicaraguan version of the Selva incident.[101] Angered at the uncomplimentary description of himself, he composed another broadside attack against the unionists; and assisted by his secretary Pavón, he actually published the selection and signed it: *Los Conservadores*. In no uncertain terms, "The Conservatives" attacked the "Red Republicans," and their demogogic leaders: Doroteo Vasconcelos, the Salvadorean chief; and José Francisco Barrundia, the Guatemalan exile who edited *El Progreso*.[102] The publication, moreover, served to remind unionists that Chatfield was back from his tour and ready to begin the next phase of the battle.

To his dismay, the British chargé also learned the distressing news that during his absence the Guatemalan government had issued a decree (January 16, 1850) which proclaimed Santo Tomás the official port of entry on the Atlantic in place of Izabal. As the French consul correctly noted, this could never have happened if Chatfield had been there. His policy had always been to keep Guatemala subservient to Belize and to prevent the Belgian Colonization Company, which had received its contract in 1842, from making Santo Tomás a rival to Belize.[103] To ascertain the situation at Santo Tomás, Chatfield *et al.* passed by that port on their way back to Guatemala City. It was just as unsanitary as ever, the English chargé wrote to Palmerston; and what was worse, the port settlers were living immorally. Why even boys seven and eight years of age could be found drunk in the streets or smoking cigars. In short, Mr. C. had decided that the January decree had to go. On July 26, while back in Guatemala City, he predicted that the law would not be implemented.[104] And to be sure, on September 6, 1850, the Guatemalan ally complied by rescinding the Santo Tomás decree. The Belgian Colonization Company had no friend in Mr. Chatfield, that is certain.[105]

From Zacapa, near the Honduran and Salvadorean borders, the British chargé launched another offensive against the unionist liberals,

---

100. To Palmerston, No. 85, October 9, 1850, with Palmerston's note of January 19, 1851, F.O. 15/65; C.O. to F.O., p. encl.s, September 24, 1850, F.O. 15/68; P. Wodehouse to Sir C. S. Grey, December 5, 1851, F.O. 252/73.
101. To Palmerston, No. 43, p. encl., June 5, 1850, F.O. 15/64.
102. To Palmerston, Nos. 40 (May 23), p. encl.s, and 43 (June 5).
103. Fourcade to Min. of Foreign Affairs, January 22, 1850, A.A.E.P./CCG, vol. 4.
104. To Palmerston, No. 50, July 26, 1850, F.O. 15/64.
105. To Palmerston, Nos. 74 (September 14) and 84 (October 8, 1850), F.O. 15/65.

while awaiting an escort to Guatemala City. Knowing that Squier was about to return to the United States, he wrote to various governmental officials, as well as private parties, demanding the suppression of anti-English propaganda in the newspapers of the center states. Sprinkled in these letters were veiled threats that the navy would be back in October, 1850. His anti-union tactics were especially evident in letters sent to the directors Juan Lindo of Honduras and Norberto Ramírez of Nicaragua.[106]

But the states of the "center" were not in a listening mood. On the contrary, Nicaragua complained that the tariff schedule at Greytown was a violation of the Loch-Castellón truce of March, 1848. To aggravate matters, some private interests in Granada had attacked and destroyed Beschor's boats in retaliation for the levying of duties at Greytown. Though the Nicaraguan government maintained that local courts would take up the matter, Chatfield insisted upon reparations for Beschor's losses; and Lord Palmerston concurred by authorizing the British navy to collect for the damages suffered by the German tax collector of Greytown.[107] On September 10, 1850, furthermore, Captain Robert Smart of the *Indefatigable* arrived at Greytown for permanent duty and forthwith announced to the Nicaraguan government that he would protect the King of the Mosquitos from rebellion at Greytown or any attack upon his dominions.[108] In an angry mood already, Nicaraguans understandably rejected the overtures from the British agent in Guatemala.

Relations with Honduras were no better. Chatfield insisted upon protecting Felipe Jáuregui and even encouraged his candidacy for the directorship in the coming elections. But when Juan Lindo was reelected handily, English tactics had to change. Chatfield tried to disengage Lindo from the unionist movement by promising to support him as dictator of Honduras. He also tried to bribe the government, in a manner of speaking, by promising to turn over the license money for wood cut by a Mr. James Walsh on the left bank of the Roman River. This was providing, of course, that Honduras yielded on the Mosquito question.[109] All his

---

106. To Palmerston, Nos. 58 (August 20) and 60 (August 21, 1850), p. encl.s in both, F.O. 15/65; to Juan Lindo, October 1, 11, 1850, and to Norberto Ramírez, September 9, 1850, F.O. 252/53.

107. To Palmerston, No. 67, p. encl.s, September 3, 1850, F.O. 15/65; from Sebastián Salinas, September 23, 1850, in No. 94, to Palmerston, October 14, 1850, F.O. 15/66; from Louis Beschor, July 3, 1850, F.O. 252/54; to Palmerston, No. 112, p. encl.s, December 6, 1850, F.O. 15/66.

108. To Palmerston, Nos. 98 (October 24) and 100 (November 5, 1850), p. encl.s in both, F.O. 15/66.

109. To Palmerston, No. 68, September 5, 1850, F.O. 15/65, and No. 93, October 14, 1850, F.O. 15/66; to Lindo, October 1, 11, 1850, F.O. 252/53.

efforts were in vain, however. Honduras wanted no part of the English-man's schemes.

As for the recalcitrant state of El Salvador, there was only one conceivable approach in Chatfield's opinion — a naked display of force. He therefore peremptorily demanded the suppression of libelous remarks in the Salvadorean press; to which Director Vasconcelos replied that free-dom of the press would be observed in his state.[110] Certain that English ships would arrive in October Mr. Chatfield issued his ultimatum in late August, 1850. He demanded that El Salvador satisfy him on these three points: first, she had to implement the arrangement signed on November 12, 1849, aboard the *Gorgon;* secondly, she had to recognize Idígoras' diplomatic immunity as the English representative; and thirdly, he insisted on an unequivocal apology for the scurrilous remarks in the Salvadorean press.[111] The brilliant pen of José Francisco Barrundia answered the ultimatum: the demands were ridiculous and absurd. War had been declared. In the Salvadorean answer, the term "consul" was used no less than forty-five times. Chatfield had counted them.[112]

All attempts to bring about a compromise, especially those of the French consul, ended in failure. His English colleague would simply not listen; all he wanted was to humble the Salvadoreans once and for all. With the arrival of the *Champion* in early October, a state of war existed in Central America: on the one side, the Anglo-Guatemalan forces; on the other, the unionists of the "center," in particular the governments of El Salvador and Honduras.[113]

Even with the arrival of a second ship, the *Gorgon,* the British blockade of El Salvador proved to be ineffective. The reason for this was that merchandise destined for the San Miguel fair was allowed to land on Tigre Island and then was transhipped to the nearby Honduran coast, proceeding overland from there to El Salvador. To stop this, on December 12, 1850, Chatfield assumed full responsibility for extending the blockade to Honduras. He urged the navy to enforce the blockade until March, 1851, when the trading season ended.[114]

These measures were all futile and only encouraged Salvadoreans and Hondurans to arm an offensive against Guatemala. Their expedi-

110. To Palmerston, No. 53, p. encl.s, August 1, 1850, F.O. 15/65.
111. No. 61, p. encl.s, August 21, 1850.
112. No. 66, p. encl.s, September 2, 1850.
113. To Palmerston, Nos. 96 (October 23) and 101 (November 5, 1850), F.O. 15/66.
114. To Palmerston, Nos. 102 (November 5), 103 (November 6), 110 (December 2), and 118 (December 18, 1850), p. encl.s in all, F.O. 15/66.

tionary force, however, met defeat on November 16, 1850.[115] Then they began to mount an even larger force to invade Guatemala in the opening months of 1851, representing the *pacto* states of the "center." By January 9, 1851, a new general government of Central America (*Representación Nacional*) came into existence; and the prospects of success in the impending action against Guatemala looked bright, especially considering the ineffectiveness of the British blockade.

Accordingly, Frederick Chatfield again reached the conclusion that he had to commit the Foreign Office to drastic measures. Though Squier was no longer present, that agent had planted mischievous seeds which had to be rooted out at once. Thus, on December 5, 1850, in letters to the governments of Nicaragua and Honduras, the British agent pontifically set down the inland boundaries of those states with Mosquitia, knowing full well that they would be rejected.[116] He admitted as much on the 26th: his purpose in setting those limits — he told the Foreign Office — had been to commit Palmerston to a forceful policy in Central America. In this letter, the belligerent underling also outlined for his superior a grandiose plan for the deployment of British ships, some on permanent and others on temporary assignments on both Central American coasts. Only in this way, he argued, could England suppress the "loud boasting of the Americans." Realizing that the implementation of Chatfield's project would mean war with the United States, Palmerston chose not to be committed.[117] Besides, it would have violated the Clayton-Bulwer Treaty, signed on April 19, 1850.

◆◆◆

Despite the rantings of anglophobes in the United States, the Taylor administration had opted for a conciliatory policy with Great Britain on Central American matters. As indicated previously, these negotiations had met with a severe set back when the Tigre news was received in Washington; the same was true when Palmerston only partially disavowed the act. President Taylor's address of March 19, 1850, reflected the strain. Yet Sir Henry L. Bulwer met the situation with consummate skill. By pointing out to his American colleagues that no canal company would be able to carry out its enterprise without British capital, he convinced them that it would be wise to sign a canal convention without dealing with the territorial questions. The assumption, of course, was that the two states

115. No. 109, p. encl.s, December 2, 1850.
116. No. 114, p. encl.s, December 13, 1850.
117. No. 120 (December 26, 1850), which contains a note by Palmerston.

would be able to iron out the territorial differences under more peaceful conditions.[118]

The Clayton-Bulwer Treaty was a compromise, pure and simple. And what is often forgotten by American critics of the pact is that Great Britain, at the height of its power in Central America, had chosen to begin a retreat from its former policy. In this respect, the Treaty represented a significant victory for the United States, a second-rate nation sorely divided by sectional conflict at that time. The following selection from the powerful London *Times* helps to explain graphically why the British chose to abandon Palmerstonian diplomacy in Central America:

> The most specious, but, in our opinion, the most fallacious assertion which is advanced in favour of Lord PALMERSTON'S policy in the administration of our foreign affairs, is that he has a paramount claim to be considered as an English Minister, and that whatever causes of complaint he may have given to the rest of the world, he has represented with unrivalled spirit and success the interests and the opinions of this country. Those who can trace in Lord PALMERSTON'S career the faithful reflection and the stubborn principles of England's policy must entertain very strange notions of the nature of those principles, and of the objects an English Minister is especially bound to pursue. They are led, in fact, by a vulgar fallacy to suppose that what is detested and dreaded abroad ought by so much the more to be cherished and defended at home; and their estimate of Lord PALMERSTON's merits is inordinately great only because it is calculated by the injuries he has done to others, not by the services he has rendered to ourselves. But we utterly contest the assumption that the principles and interests of Great Britain are so diametrically opposed to the principles and interests of the rest of the civilized world that it is only when we are at variance with all mankind that we can be said to be at the height of our glory. That sort of power which inspires dread and hatred might, indeed, be coveted by States relying chiefly on despotic authority or military force; but the fundamental conditions of the just influence of England are a steadfast adherence to the great principles of international law, and to that frank, temperate, and upright conduct which is the best ornament of true greatness. In proportion as we have forsaken that accustomed mode of directing the foreign transactions of England, her name has lost the weight it once possessed, the attachment it once inspired; and the same want of public consideration has not been unfelt on the

118. MTUSA, V, 671-801, is an excellent documentary source as well as commentary on the Clayton-Bulwer Treaty. For the most recent and authoritative review, see Van Alstyne, "British Diplomacy . . . ," pp. 149-183. Though dated, also see Mary W. Williams, *Anglo-American Isthmian Diplomacy, 1815–1915* (Washington and London, 1916), pp. 67-109.

private relations of British subjects, whose position abroad is now rendered unsafe and unpleasant by the spirit of altercation which is unhappily supposed to accompany their residence.[119]

Those were the momentous issues being debated in the famous "Don Pacifico" case of early 1850, which brought about a vote of censure against Lord Palmerston in the House of Commons. In June, however, this decision was reversed by a vote of confidence — 310 to 264— much of which was due undoubtedly to the negotiation of the Clayton-Bulwer Treaty.[120]

As far as the positive aspects of the treaty were concerned, there was no cause for controversy. Both powers agreed to protect the canal company which had recently obtained a contract from the Nicaraguan government — that is, the Vanderbilt company. If it failed to implement the contract or to give evidence of a faithful execution of its terms within a year's time, then the United States and Great Britain would support any other company willing to undertake a similar project through Nicaragua, Panama, or Tehuantepec. They stipulated, however, that there would have to be free ports at the termini of the interoceanic route.

On the negative side, the two countries gave up all pretensions to exclusive control over the waterway. It was to be a common enterprise, which other nations of the world might join by acceding to the convention. In addition, the signatory powers promised not to fortify, colonize or settle in Central America; nor interfere with the canal project by virtue of any connection which either might have with political entities in that area. The Mosquito Nation was included. This was the essence of Article One, which led to troubled relations between the United States and Great Britain during the decade of the fifties.

As usual, Mr. Chatfield could be counted upon to provide his own interpretation of the Treaty, a copy of which reached him in May, 1850. To counteract the Central American unionists interpretation — that Great Britain had thereby renounced her rights to Mosquitia, the Bay Islands and Belize — he interpreted the treaty for the center states while he was in Zacapa. "It seems to me," he told Palmerston, "that the advantages are chiefly on our side— and that North America has secured no greater benefit, than that of exercising a voice, to a certain extent, in Nicaragua." It most certainly precluded an American monopoly of the canal zone, he added; and it left the Mosquito question untouched "except that North America, on behalf of its protegé — Nicaragua — admits the existence

---

119. *Times* (London), June 22, 1850.
120. *Times* (London), June 29, 1850; also see Philip Guedalla, *The Palmerston Papers: Gladstone and Palmerston, 1851–1865* (London, 1928), p. 35.

of a Mosquito Shore, and that the shore is as distinct a state or country in regards to Nicaragua, as Costa Rica or any part of Central America."[121] To this astute analysis of the treaty, he added in a message to a Nicaraguan correspondent that the treaty had actually made the Monroe Doctrine obsolete, since the United States had recognized the existence of Mosquitia — a conclusion also shared by a recent scholar.[122]

Though Palmerston agreed with Chatfield's interpretation, he did not feel that his agent should discuss it with the Central American states. "Such a discussion," he said, "can only have the effect of raising unnecessary jealousies in regard to a Treaty which was intended to have the effect of extinguishing jealousies."[123] And in supporting the various measures which the consul-general had adopted during the "grand tour," especially since they were sanctioned after the Clayton-Bulwer arrangement had been signed, Lord Palmerston clearly demonstrated that he had no intentions of abandoning the British protectorate of Mosquitia. The only concession which Palmerston had made was to rescind Chatfield's tariff schedule, declaring Greytown a free port, effective January 1, 1851.[124] With regard to the American demand for Chatfield's recall, however, he refused to comply.[125] For obvious reasons, on the other hand, he could not accept the aggressive proposals which Chatfield made to him on December 26, 1850. That would have meant risking war with the United States and exposing the Foreign Office to even greater criticism and opposition to his type of diplomacy.

---

121. To Palmerston, No. 58, August 20, 1850, F.O. 15/65.
122. To Jorge Viteri, August 3, 1850, F.O. 252/53; Van Alstyne, "British Diplomacy," p. 182.
123. From Palmerston, No. 42, November 9, 1850, F.O. 15/63.
124. From Palmerston, Nos. 45 (November 15) and 46 (December 7, 1850), F.O. 15/63.
125. From Edward Wallerstein, December 16, 1850, and June 16, July 16, 1851, F.O. 252/60; Van Alstyne, "British Diplomacy," p. 165.

CHAPTER TWELVE

Prometheus and Hamlet

I cannot nor will not recognize any authority here and I will not pay unless I am made by force.[1]
—Cornelius Vanderbilt, November 21, 1851

But if you escape squabbles in Central America it is by special inter-position *and* mercy *of* Providence *and by no order of ours or Mr. Chatfield.*[2]
—Sir Francis Baring, December 21, 1851

With Greytown opened up as a free port on January 1, 1851, Mosquito officials found themselves financially pressed. It was difficult for them to maintain the requisite police force without the revenues from the tariff schedule which Chatfield had enacted. Noisy and adventuresome Americans, California-bound, defied Mosquitia's officialdom brazenly and incited restless Nicaraguans to recapture the port for their state. To meet this challenge, British Resident James Green decided to establish a municipal government at Greytown — another one of Chatfield's recommendations. On May 1, 1851, the town fathers voted through a list of nominal harbor dues; and with this income, plus an occasional subsidy from the Foreign Office, Greytown authorities were able to offer some protection to their denizens.[3]

Posing the greatest threat to Mosquito rule at the port was the Atlantic and Pacific Ship Canal Company, favored by the Clayton-Bulwer Treaty. Thanks to Sir Henry L. Bulwer and Lord Palmerston, Cornelius Vanderbilt and Joseph L. White were well received by London bankers during their visit in August, 1850; and the Foreign Office assured them that Greytown officials would not interfere with their project. Buoyed up by the prospects of English financial support, the company hastened to commence operations. In April, 1851, it received permission from the Nicaraguan government to alter its contract. While the company proceeded with its surveys for the canal, it could also form an "Accessory

---

1. As quoted in James Green to Lord Palmerston, No. 1, p. encl.s, January 6, 1852, F.O. 53/29.

2. Sir Francis Baring to Lord John Russell, December 21, 1851, R.P. 30/22/ box 9, in reference to the *Prometheus* affair of November 21, 1851.

3. "Laws and Regulations of the Port of Greytown," in Green's No. 1; Green to Earl Granville, March 6, 1852, F.O. 53/29; Palmerston to Green, sep./sec., November 29, 1851, F.O. 53/26; draft, Palmerston to Abbott Lawrence, December 30, 1851, F.O. 5/538.

Transit Company," inaugurating passenger service across the Central American Isthmus. Steamships would bring passengers from New York to Greytown; smaller steamers and land conveyances would cover the interoceanic area; and another large steamship would ply the Pacific route to San Francisco. On July 1, 1851, the steamship *Prometheus* brought the first passengers from New York.[4] And just a few weeks before the opening of the transit service, Greytown authorities allowed the company to establish a "temporary depot," on the south side of the harbor, at Punta Arenas, for the storage of coal and the assembling of "iron steamers."

With Vanderbilt's arrival on the *Prometheus,* however, relations deteriorated. The company began to construct permanent buildings on the south side, and its officials insisted that the land in question belonged to Costa Rica. Furthermore, on several occasions the captain of the *Prometheus* had refused to pay the harbor dues levied by the municipality of Greytown.[5]

For the fifth time, on the morning of November 21, Mr. Robert Coates boarded the *Prometheus* to demand the payment of 123 pesos for harbor dues. In the process, he handed Captain Churchill a copy of the "Laws and Regulations of the Port," which the latter promptly turned over to the owner of the ship, Mr. Cornelius Vanderbilt. The "Commodore" greeted the port collector's document with the saucy retort that opens this chapter. "I am sorry it is your determination not to pay," Mr. Coates answered, "as you will throw us on the disagreeable alternative of compelling you." Mr. Vanderbilt could not care less; the Mosquito port collector disembarked in a huff.

Ashore, Mr. Coates obtained a legal attachment for debt and then returned to the *Prometheus* to serve it upon Captain Churchill. "Blood will be drawn," the old captained threatened, if the Mosquito government should persist. Undeterred, Coates ordered a constable to serve the papers on him. The attempt to do so brought fire from Mr. Vanderbilt, who snatched the document and shouted wildly "Let them seize the vessel if they can." Still determined to prevent the departure of the *Prometheus* for New York, the port collector ordered all fires put out; and when the crew disobeyed, he instructed his small police force to seize Captain

---

4. *Ibid.,* to Palmerston, No 76, p. encl., July 21, 1851, F.O. 15/71, and No. 134, October 30, 1851, F.O. 15/72; Joseph L. White to Palmerston, conf., November 12, 1851, F.O. 5/537; Van Alstyne, "British Diplomacy," pp. 165-166.

5. White to Palmerston, November 12, 1851, *loc. cit.;* P. J. Martin to James Green, June 11, 1851, and H. G. Foote to Martin, June 12, 1851, in Green's No. 1, *loc. cit.*

Churchill. By this time, Vanderbilt was beside himself with rage as he boomed threats that if Coates did not get off the vessel instantly he would "get under way" and leave him "on some Desert Island." "This," Coates later wrote, "I dared him to attempt." The deciding factor, as it turned out, was the actions of the crew and some five hundred passengers who were anxious to return home. Surrounding the Mosquito agents, they literally pushed them off the ship.[6]

Although the incident had its amusing moments, it also had significant implications. Vanderbilt argued that the collection of duties by the Mosquitos was in direct violation of the Clayton-Bulwer Treaty which had called for free ports at the termini of the transit route, not to mention Palmerston's assurance to the canal company that Greytown officials would not interfere with the canal company. On the other hand, the British resident — with some justification — had grounds to fear the precedent that was being established. When Coates returned to shore, therefore, Green wrote to the commander of the British brig-of-war *Express* and asked him to support the demands upon the *Prometheus.* Acting under vague orders, Captain William F. Fead maneuvered the *Express* into position to stop the *Prometheus,* which had pulled up her anchor and was drifting away from port. To the surprise of everyone, he opened fire on her.[7]

Regardless of the account referred to, it is a fact that a British war vessel fired at an American ship in order to collect duties owed to the King of the Mosquitos. Widely publicized in the United States and in Great Britain, Captain Churchill's account noted that the *Express* "fired a round shot over the forecastle, not clearing the wheel house over ten feet — in a few moments another shot was fired, which passed over the stern so near that the force of the ball was distinctly felt by several passengers." And when he asked Captain Fead for an explanation, the officer replied that "it was to protect the authorities of Greytown in their demands, and if we did not immediately anchor he would fire a bomb-shell into us, and ordered his guns loaded with grape and canister shot." The display of force had its effect. The *Prometheus* returned to port; her captain paid the duties under protest; and then she proceeded full steam to the United States bearing her explosive tale. On December 2, 1851, New York newspapers blared the story to their readers.[8]

---

6. Robert Coates' account in Green's No. 1.
7. Admiralty to F.O., p. encl.s, January 9, 1852, FO. 53/30.
8. Henry Churchill to Editors of the New York *Express,* San Juan, November 21, 1851, in Abbott Lawrence to Lord Palmerston, December 19, 1851, F.O. 5/538; William F. Fead to Foxhall A. Parker, January 3, 1852, in Green's No. 1, *loc. cit.*

Convinced that they had been justified in their actions, British and Mosquito agents at Greytown took steps to consolidate their position. On November 22, the day after the incident, the town council passed new regulations concerning port procedures and the navigation of the San Juan River; these innovations clearly discriminated against the Vanderbilt interests at Punta Arenas. On December 6, the company's representative was told that the south side would have to be evacuated by January 1, 1852. And to undermine whatever accusations might be made by Vanderbilt *et al* in the United States, an American group which was hostile to the "Commodore" signed a petition praising the orderly government at Greytown. On the 8th, the town council again insisted upon the payment of harbor duties by another American ship, the *Daniel Webster*. On that occasion, the acting chairman of the town council was none other than Captain Fead of the *Express*.[9]

<hr>

The *Prometheus* news shocked the reading public in the United States, especially in New York and Washington, where editors and politicians demanded an immediate apology from England for grossly insulting the American flag and for violating the Clayton-Bulwer Treaty. Nationalistic sentiment was at a fever pitch; even moderates had taken offense at Captain Fead's peremptory actions. Fearful of an imminent break in relations between the United States and Great Britain, the stock market and financial houses mirrored the violent American reaction.[10] As might be expected, the canal company led the clamor for revenge. With Vanderbilt vouching for Captain Churchill's account of the incident, the board of directors issued a strong resolution on December 1, 1851, in which it urged the State Department to protect their interests at Greytown by sending a naval force there.

The Millard Fillmore administration responded immediately. Secretary of State Daniel Webster wrote instructions to Abbott Lawrence in London; and to deliver these, the steamship *Atlantic* delayed her departure from New York until the 6th. She arrived in England on the 18th;[11] and on the following day, the United States minister demanded

<hr>

9. John F. Crampton to Palmerston, Nos. 79-80, p. encl.s, December 20, 29, 1851, F.O. 5/531.

10. *Morning Chronicle* (London), December 19, 1851; *New York Herald*, December 6, 1851; Robert Bunch to Palmerston, No. 43, p. encl.s, New York, December 2, 1851, F.O. 5/533, was the first to send news of the *Prometheus* incident to London via the *Africa*, which reached England on December 15.

11. J. F. Crampton to Palmerston, No. 64, p. encl.s, December 7, 1851, F.O. 5/531; *Morning Chronicle* (London), December 18, 1851.

an unequivocal explanation and apology for the "outrage" committed upon the *Prometheus*. If the *Express* had acted upon orders from the Foreign Office, Lawrence noted, President Fillmore would consider the act a violation of the 1850 treaty "by which Great Britain has stipulated not to make use of any protection which she may afford Nicaragua, the Mosquito Coast, or any part of Central America, for the purpose of assuming or exercising dominion over the same."[12] Lawrence had cited a key section from the controversial first article of the treaty.

The Whig administration correctly gauged the mood of the American public. Dominated by the opposition Democrats, Congress requested all pertinent information on the *Prometheus* affair; Senator Lewis Cass, for example, sponsored a resolution to this effect on December 12. A few days later, President Fillmore explained what actions the executive had taken on the matter. He particularly highlighted the instructions which were sent to Commodore Foxhall A. Parker on the 15th by the Secretary of the Navy, orders to the commander of the West Indian Squadron which left no doubt as to the policy of the United States government:

> Whatever may have been the merits of the question between the Captain of the Prometheus and the authorities of Nicaragua, the United States acknowledges no rights to the government, or a vessel, of Great Britain to exercise any police or supervision over American merchant vessels in Nicaragua or elsewhere, out of British dominions.[13]

A dangerous situation was at hand, if we recall the actions taken by Anglo-Mosquito officials in the weeks after the *Prometheus* affair. In fact, the prospects of an armed collision haunted negotiations between the United States and Great Britain for the next few months. Tension heightened at Greytown with the arrival of the *Saranac* on January 1, 1852, followed shortly thereafter by the *Albany*. As instructed, Commodore Parker wrote to the Greytown council and to Captain Fead stating unequivocally that the United States would not tolerate British intervention in the collection of duties. This did not mean, he observed, that he would sanction the non-payment of duties to Nicaraguan authorities — a fine point, for it should be noted that Parker referred to Greytown officials as Nicaraguans, whereas Captain Fead recognized Mosquitia's sovereign rights to Greytown. This crucial difference implied rival inter-

---

12. Abbott Lawrence to Palmerston, December 19, 1851, F.O. 5/538; also in MDCIA, VII, 444-445.

13. Crampton to Palmerston, No. 77, p. encl.s, December 19, 1851, F.O. 5/531; *Times* (London), December 27, 1851.

pretations of the Clayton-Bulwer Treaty and added to the explosiveness of the moment.[14]

Fortunately, the "judicious conduct" of the English Vice Admiral George F. Seymour averted the expected clash between the two naval forces. In reply to Captain Fead's report on the *Prometheus,* Seymour had reprimanded him in no uncertain terms and had cautioned him not to use the *Express* for any further collection of harbor duties. Since Fead received these notes from his superior before Commodore Parker stated the American position, his hands were therefore tied. By that time, moreover, the British chargé in Washington, John F. Crampton, had also instructed Green not to implement the recent legislation against the canal company.[15]

The situation at Greytown remained critical, however. The mere presence of American ships — with some of their officers boasting more than was necessary — might easily encourage dissident Nicaraguans to attempt a political coup. In this event, Captain Fead would have been fully justified in resisting such an uprising according to his instructions for this would not have been just a case of collecting duties. Moreover, the American faction at Greytown, which was hostile to the Vanderbilt company, might also be the source of trouble between rival naval units. But here again Admiral Seymour displayed the imagination and foresight of a statesman. During the month of January, he dispatched at least three additional ships to Greytown in support of the *Express,* outnumbering the American vessels by two to one, a power move that deterred any potential rebels and leashed the tongues of American naval officers for the time being. More importantly, the admiral had assigned Captain Robert Spencer Robinson of H.M.S. *Arrogant* to explain the *Prometheus* affair to Commodore Parker. The burden of his message was that Captain Fead's actions had been unauthorized. Parker accepted this explanation and thus relieved the tension at the port. Rumors then circulated that in the near future the *Saranac* would proceed southward to Chagres on the Isthmus. Although Robinson had instructions to withdraw the *Express,* at the last moment he decided against it, perhaps because a point of honor was at stake.[16]

On January 20, 1852, Captain Robinson wrote a dispatch to his

14. Enclosures in Green's No. 1, *loc. cit.*
15. John F. Crampton to Green, December 24, 1851, in No. 80, Crampton to Palmerston, *loc. cit.;* George F. Seymour to W. F. Fead, December 18, 1851, in Admiralty to F.O., January 9, 1852, F.O. 53/30; Crampton to Palmerston, No. 1, p. encl.s, January 4, 1852, F.O. 5/544; Earl Granville to Crampton, No. 16, January 23, 1852, F.O. 5/542.
16. George F. Seymour to Admiralty, p. encl.s, January 26, 1852, F.O. 53/30.

superiors in which he stressed the urgency of a provisional arrangement with the United States in order to keep the peace at Greytown. One of the most striking things about Greytown, he told Admiral Seymour, was its American nature. It was American in population, in institutions, in the type of houses and food imports, and in its commercial enterprises. And these Americans were certainly a squabbling lot. The anti-Vanderbilt faction made no secret of its plans to attack the company's holdings at Punta Arenas on the south side. If this were to happen, Robinson predicted that there would be reprisals when the company's ships returned to Greytown. Such "recourse to violence on the part of the citizens of Greytown," he reasoned astutely, "would bring about a collision between the ships of war of the United States, and our own, which might be present." This was a disturbing prospect. The captain concluded with these words, almost prophetic in the light of subsequent developments:

> The onus of this protectorate of American property and American interests will fall more and more heavily upon us year after year. We really have no interest whatever in the matter except that of keeping ourselves clear of other people's quarrels: The fight, if fight there is to be, will be between rival and petty interests of American citizens. We ought not to risk the good understanding now existing between the two countries, for a cause that is not our own.[17]

The Foreign Office took Robinson's advice seriously. On March 1, 1852, another naval officer confirmed the captain's analysis: American factions were jockeying for power in Greytown politics.[18]

The *Prometheus* news reached London on December 15 and received only scant attention in the London press, dwarfed as it was by another story which held greater interest for the English reader — the revival of the debate on Palmerstonian diplomacy. After Louis Napoleon's coup of December 2, 1851, Lord Palmerston had indiscreetly expressed his approval of the French revolution; and in so doing, had violated Lord John Russell's policy of neutrality. Both the London *Times* and the *Morning Chronicle* instantly seized upon this incident to revive the discussion which was silenced in mid-1850. Presenting the anti-Palmerston position effectively, the *Morning Chronicle* made the following statement on the 16th:

17. Robert Spencer Robinson to Seymour, January 20, 1852, F.O. 53/30.
18. Arthur A. Cochrane to Peter McTeehal, March 1, 1852, F.O. 53/30.

The real question for the country to decide is, whether Lord Palmerston has shown himself fit to direct the policy of Great Britain in a European crisis of no ordinary magnitude; and the true answer to this question is, that he has alienated nearly every foreign Power, whilst his advocacy of Liberalism is proved by the event to be either a miserable failure or a worse than miserable sham.[19]

Despite a lively defense of Lord Palmerston by both liberal and conservative newspapers — for different reasons, of course — Lord Russell decided that he could no longer support him; and for violations of prudence and decorum," he chose to dismiss his foreign secretary. Palmerston's absence from the special cabinet meeting on the 22nd marked the end of his long tenure in the Foreign Office, one of the most controversial in British diplomatic history.[20] The official explanation — and the Russell papers confirm it — signaled out the "French Question;" but it was more than that, if we consider the implications of the *Prometheus* incident. Since other partisans of Lord Palmerston also resigned from the cabinet in succeeding weeks, the press hostile to Russell attributed his acts to cheap political expediency. With tongue-in-cheek, the *Morning Chronicle* quipped: "It is not an unusual thing for a sinking vessel to heave its lumber overboard; and, no doubt, of such a Cabinet, each member parted with is one reproach less to the Government, and one clear gain to the country."[21]

Lord Russell's critics were not being very fair in their accusations. To be sure, the embattled Russell ministry had a political objective in mind; but this should not obscure the fact that the basic reason for the shakeup was Palmerston's brand of diplomacy. Since the spring of 1848, for example, Lord Grey of the Colonial office had strongly opposed Palmerston's Mosquito policy which involved England in the protection of a "mock king."[22] For that matter, as we have seen in earlier chapters, Lord Russell had also opposed the establishment of the protectorate. But out of loyalty, or what have you, he had defended his foreign secretary in the great debate of 1850. Then came the Clayton-Bulwer Treaty which helped to rectify matters somewhat. But now, in addition to the embarrassment of "Old Pam's" remarks on Louis Napoleon, there was

---

19. *Morning Chronicle* (London), December 16, 1851.
20. Russell to Palmerston, December 24, 1851, R.P. 30/22/box 9. The newspapers cited are in the Colindale Newspaper Collection of the British Museum in London.
21. *Morning Chronicle* (London), February 2, 1852.
22. Grey to Russell, March 6, 1848, R.P. 30/22/box 7; also reproduced in Richard W. Van Alstyne, "The Central American Policy of Lord Palmerston, 1846–1848," *Hispanic American Historical Review*, Vol. XVI (August, 1936), pp. 357-358.

the gloomy prospect of trouble with the United States undermining one of the diplomatic trophies of the Russell ministry.

Although English newspapers preferred to emphasize European events, it does not follow that Lord Russell did not see the broader picture. In the second quotation which introduces this chapter, Sir Francis Baring, Lord of the Admiralty, was discussing the *Prometheus* case in his letter to Russell of December 21, 1851, the day before the special cabinet meeting took place. And the fact that Sir Francis mentioned Chatfield's name in connection with an incident in which that agent was only tangentially involved merely underscored the real issue — Palmerstonian diplomacy, of which Mr. Chatfield was a leading exponent. Moreover, the sense of urgency which permeated the correspondence on the *Prometheus* affair, as well as the significant change which resulted in Great Britain's Central American policy, reveals Russell's awareness of the incident's significance in the larger scheme of things.

Ironically, Lord Palmerston drafted the official reply to Abbott Lawrence on December 22, 1851, the day of the cabinet meeting. He explained to the United States minister that Captain Fead had not acted under orders from the Foreign Office and that England did not intend to sanction proceedings which were "at variance with" the Clayton-Bulwer Treaty. He also regretted the affront to the American flag. But his entire apology was couched in a tentative framework, that is, pending the receipt of information from the Admiralty. This explanation, after some inconsequential changes by Earl Granville who succeeded Palmerston in the Foreign Office, was presented to Lawrence at an interview on December 30.[23]

The matter did not rest there, however, since the American minister refused to consider the note as "an unreserved disavowal of this act." Although surprised and ruffled by the rejection, Granville promised to write again upon receiving a report from the Admiralty.[24] It should be noted, moreover, that Lord Russell was not indifferent to these negotiations. On January 1, 1852, he told Granville: "The Prometheus you will settle here." As for the more basic issues — the settlement of the Greytown and Mosquito problems — he preferred to send Sir Henry Bulwer back to Washington because of his popularity with the Americans.[25]

On January 10, after receiving Seymour's dispatches from the West

---

23. Draft, Palmerston, December 22, 1851, F.O. 5/541; draft, Palmerston, December 30, 1851, and Granville to Abbott Lawrence, December 30, 1851, F.O. 5/538.
24. Lawrence to Granville, and Granville to Lawrence, January 2, 1852, F.O. 5/555.
25. Russell to Granville, January 1, 1852, R.P. 30/22/box 10.

Indies, Earl Granville wrote an unqualified apology which was acceptable to Minister Lawrence.[26] And thus the *Prometheus* incident came to an end; its expeditious and relatively quiet settlement undoubtedly accounts for its cursory treatment in studies of Anglo-American diplomacy.

The aftermath of this minor incident, however, is what makes it worthy of our attention. Since it marked the beginning of the end for Palmerstonian diplomacy in Central America, one of the first casualties, understandably, would be Frederick Chatfield. And so he was. On January 8, 1852, Granville decided to recall Palmerston's efficient servant. The rank of chargé d'affaires was abolished; and his replacement, Captain Charles Lennox Wyke, carried with him to Central America the title of consul-general.[27] Despite Lord Russell's earlier preference, Sir Henry L. Bulwer was also relieved of his American assignment. In this case, however, the reasons for the recall were different. The recall was due more perhaps to John F. Crampton's harmonious relationship with Daniel Webster and to the fact that Bulwer's presence in Washington, since he had been a principal in the 1850 negotiations, might prove to be an obstacle to the settlement of the Greytown problem. Moreover, it would seem that Queen Victoria had a voice in the decision.[28]

The Russell ministry, significantly, went out of its way to convince the public as well as Parliament, which opened its sessions on February 3, that Great Britain was returning to her traditional form of diplomacy. In connection with an incident which involved an attack upon a British subject and for which the Foreign Office expected an apology, Earl Granville replied to an interrogator as follows:

> When I say that one nation should behave towards another as it would wish that nation to behave towards itself, without making any concession where honour or good faith is at stake, I mean to assert that, when a nation is clearly in the wrong, it ought not to be too proud to say so; and I may be permitted to make that declaration in consequence of the position in which I, as the Foreign Minister of this country have been recently placed. I have not been enunciating now principles which we do not apply in our own case. Of one thing I am justly proud, that I have made an apology in the name of Her Majesty's Government in a case which I thought it to be justly due. An unfortunate circumstance recently took place, in which, by the neglect of his instructions, a naval officer and civil servant of the State committed an act of insult and aggression towards the United

---

26. Granville to Lawrence, January 10, and Lawrence to Granville, January 13, 1852, F.O. 5/555.
27. From Granville, cons. Nos. 1-2, January 15, 1852, and F.O. mem. (folios 177-178), F.O. 15/77.
28. Granville to Crampton, Nos. 12-13, January 23, 1852, F.O. 5/542.

States. My noble predecessor in office began a friendly communication on the subject with the Minister of the United States now residing in England; but, on the very day after I had entered on the duties of my office, I was able to disavow that act of violence which had occurred, and to express our regret that such an act had been committed. I am not ashamed to say that I should have pursued the same course if a weak State had complained instead of a powerful one; for it was the only course that was consistent with the just pride and dignity of this nation.[29]

Although the London *Times* hailed Granville's remarks as a turning point in British diplomacy, the Russell ministry failed to placate the opposition.[30] The *Morning Chronicle,* for example resented the manner in which Granville had made his statement in Parliament, as if it had been done intentionally to blacken Palmerston's name for political purposes alone.[31] Liberals and conservatives, who defended "Old Pam," felt likewise. As might be expected, Palmerston himself disliked the entire proceedings. It is not surprising therefore that Russell's ministry fell on February 20, 1852, after a defeat on a minor issue — the militia bill; and that Palmerston had been instrumental in bringing about the downfall of his former colleague.[32] The Earl of Malmesbury took over the duties of foreign secretary in the caretaker ministry which followed. From the standpoint of diplomacy, however, this did not represent an interruption in Granville's new policy toward the United States and Central America.

In close cooperation with Sir Henry L. Bulwer, Earl Granville worked out the details of Great Britain's policy toward Mosquitia, later embodied in the Webster-Crampton Agreement of April 30, 1852. Although England desired to settle the matter peacefully, and was willing to accept alternate solutions which reflected a desire to withdraw from Central America, a basic requirement was that the solution had to satisfy her point of honor, or *pundonor* as the Spaniards call it. Indeed, this is crucial to the understanding of the British position vis-a-vis Central America in the troublesome decade of the fifties. Earl Granville expressed it well when he said that Great Britain "cannot act with regard to the Mosquito Question in any manner derogatory to its character, or in abandonment of the principles which it has hitherto maintained."[33] And one of those principles was the "protection" of the Mosquitos.

---

29. As quoted in the *Times* (London), February 13, 1852.
30. *Times* (London), February 14, 1852.
31. *Morning Chronicle* (London), February 13, 1852.
32. *Times* (London), February 21, 1852.
33. Granville to Crampton, No. 14, January 23, 1852, F.O. 5/542.

Explaining Article One of the Clayton-Bulwer treaty, Sir Henry Bulwer remarked:

> It does not preclude Great Britain from protecting the Mosquitos but simply restricts the British government within certain limits as to the sort of protection to be afforded; nor does it by any means follow that if one state lends its forces to another in order to procure due respect being paid to the laws of that other, its ally, it exercises, in so doing any act of self-sovereignty.[34]

Any convention arrived at with the United States, therefore, had to satisfy these two basic points, which were not mutually exclusive. By accepting "the protection" of the Mosquitos, the United States would also satisfy the British *pundonor* and thus make it possible for England to retreat gracefully from Central America. Granville concurred with Bulwer; and instructions to this effect were forwarded to John F. Crampton in Washington.[35]

The immediate task, however, was to get "Grey Town out of its present embarrassing position," Bulwer advised. To achieve this objective, he therefore recommended a provisional agreement which would permit a joint Anglo-American commission to supervise Greytown until a permanent solution were reached.[36] After reading Captain Robinson's evaluation of the Greytown scene, the suggestion made sense to Granville. He modified it, however, to the extent that Crampton should propose to Webster the joint recognition of Greytown's *de facto* government, which would also be supported by both American and English naval units.[37] This is precisely what happened. Webster instructed Parker to back the scheme on March 13, 1852; and Malmesbury wrote a similar dispatch to Seymour on April 6.[38] Thus, the two powers managed to neutralize the explosive situation at Greytown while they worked out the the details of a permanent solution.

——◆◆——

Although the Webster-Crampton negotiations represented the first genuine attempt to solve the Greytown problem, there were important antecedents which should be considered briefly. It might be argued, in fact, that the idea of a graceful retreat from Mosquitia in general and

---

34. Bulwer to Granville, February 16, 1852, F.O. 5/544.
35. Granville to Crampton, No. 24, February 20, 1852, F.O. 5/542.
36. Bulwer's February 16 letter.
37. Granville to Crampton, No. 25, February 20, 1852, F.O. 5/542.
38. Crampton to Granville, No. 31, p. encl., March 14, 1852, F.O. 5/544; Malmesbury to Crampton, No. 31, p. encl., April 6, 1852, F.O. 5/542.

Greytown in particular emerged soon after the occupation of San Juan del Norte on January 1, 1848. The London *Times,* for example, represented this current of English thinking as did Lord Grey in the Colonial Office. Lord Grey, it will be recalled, did not approve of the initial occupation of Greytown and of the increased expenditures which it involved. Yet his country had already taken the step; and she could not abandon the venture hastily without serious damage to her reputation. Therefore, on March 6, 1848, he proposed this face-saving formula: Nicaragua should recognize Mosquitia; and the King of the Mosquitos would then sell Greytown back to Nicaragua.[39] However ridiculous the proposal might seem to the non-English reader, it demonstrated graphically the basic British position in subsequent negotiations. Also, it was the first mention of an indemnity as a potential means for the English retreat.

The next person to suggest a graceful withdrawal was Secretary of State John M. Clayton in the fall and winter of 1849. He first brought it up in a conversation with John F. Crampton. In return for an indemnity to the King of the Mosquitos, he also proposed that Nicaragua should receive Greytown. But in addition, he recommended that the Nicaraguan government should agree to the relocation of the Mosquito Indians on a special reservation where they would be placed under the guarantee and protection of the British government. In this way, Nicaragua "might in perfect accordance with Her claim under the Spanish title, which the United States holds to be valid, proceed, as the United States have often done in similar cases, to extinguish the Indian title by granting an annuity to the Indians."[40] Clayton repeated this proposal in his instructions to Abbott Lawrence; and on December 26, 1849, he added that the United States would have "no objection to the confirmation of the [land] titles of all the British settlers in Nicaragua" — another key ingredient of the subsequent Webster-Crampton Agreement.[41]

The English, however, were in no mood to countenance Clayton's proposals at that time. Instead, and strongly influenced by Chatfield's propaganda, Lord Palmerston advocated the sale of Greytown to Costa Rica and pointed out that if Nicaragua were agreeable, she might receive favorable consideration on the Guanacaste dispute with her neighbor.[42]

---

39. Grey to Russell, March 6, 1848, R.P. 30/22/box 7.
40. Crampton to Palmerston, No. 85, October 1, 1849, F.O. 5/501; also in MTUSA, V, 717-719.
41. Clayton to Lawrence, October 20 and December 26, 1849, *ibid,* pp. 730, 739.
42. Van Alstyne, "British Diplomacy," pp. 163-164; from Palmerston, No. 46, December 7, 1850, F.O. 15/63; Granville to Crampton, No. 14, January 23, 1852, F.O. 5/542.

Despite the Foreign Office's preference for this solution in the months following the ratification of the Clayton-Bulwer Treaty, Daniel Webster and the Nicaraguan agent in Washington refused to take it seriously; so it was abandoned.[43] Then, in mid-1851, British and American negotiators returned to a plan reminiscent of the one Clayton had proposed earlier; but the Nicaraguan representative, claiming that he had no authorization from his government, discouraged this new attempt to implement those clauses in the Clayton-Bulwer Treaty which envisioned the settlement of territorial disputes.[44] With the impact of the *Prometheus* incident, however, it was imperative to resume these negotiations: to end once and for all the pesky Mosquito and Greytown problems.

Upon Bulwer's recommendation, Earl Granville accepted the Nicaraguan solution which Clayton had proposed and which negotiators had discussed in June, 1851; and he instructed Crampton accordingly.[45] At the same time, however, Granville suggested two alternate solutions which were to be presented to Webster only in the event the American secretary wavered on the preferred program. The willingness even to consider these alternate programs, also suggested by Sir Henry, reveals the anxiety of the Foreign Office to achieve a reasonable settlement with the United States. More importantly perhaps, it reflects Great Britain's determination to abandon Palmerstonian diplomacy in Central America.

The first alternate proposal, from the standpoint of Granville's preference, called for a free port at Greytown under Anglo-American protection or under a mutual guarantee of its neutrality — a solution which Palmerston had never favored. By the terms of the second alternate plan, the five Central American states were to have joint jurisdiction over Greytown; moreover, they would be required to establish a Court of Arbitration to settle all territorial disputes and to keep the peace in Central America — a harbinger of the United States' experiment in the twentieth century. Interestingly, this particular proposal envisioned the eventual liquidation of British protection over Mosquitia by making provision for the Mosquitos to annex themselves to a nearby state.[46] On June 18, 1852, Granville's successor also looked forward to the end of

---

43. *Ibid.*

44. MTUSA, V, 780-781; Edward Everett to John Bozman Kerr, January 5, 1853, MDCIA, IV, 31-37. For an excellent account of these negotiotions, see Mary W. Williams, *Anglo-American Diplomacy*, pp. 110-119.

45. Bulwer to Granville, January 19, 1852, F.O. 5/544.

46. Granville to Crampton, No. 14, January 23, 1852, and No. 15, same date, conf., F.O. 5/542.

Great Britain's protectorate of Mosquitia.[47] In short, the *Prometheus* had led to a significant change in England's Central American policy.

With one eye on the explosive Greytown situation, and following Granville's instructions to the letter, Crampton worked harmoniously with his American colleague, who was likewise determined to reach an equitable solution of differences and who was conscious of the basic English requirements. As instructed, Crampton astutely gave Webster the impression that the latter was directing the negotiations.[48] Consequently, the American secretary allowed his English friend to draw up the prospectus of the agreement which bears their name.[49] They signed the "Bases," another term used for the Webster-Crampton Agreement, on April 30, 1852. Since the Costa Rican representative in Washington had objections to some of the clauses, Webster appointed Robert M. Walsh, as special envoy, with orders to explain to the Costa Rican government the United States' determination to see the Agreement implemented with or without its consent.[50] Accompanying Walsh was Chatfield's successor, Charles Lennox Wyke, who was routed through Washington for this purpose. John Bozman Kerr, the American chargé in Nicaragua, was also instructed to assist them on their mission of persuasion. If and when the two Central American states agreed on the "Bases," they would forthwith send minister plenipotentiaries to Washington to sign a quadropartite treaty with the United States and Great Britain, these two serving as guarantors for the convention.[51]

As Crampton put it, there were two "branches" to the Webster-Crampton Agreement — one dealing with the Greytown, or Mosquito, problem, and the other, the boundary dispute between Costa Rica and Nicaragua. According to the first one, Nicaragua would receive Greytown and an adjacent territory extending to just below Blewfields in exchange for an indemnity — a certain percentage of the port dues annually. If, however, Nicaragua preferred to pay a set sum all at once, this might also be arranged. But, Crampton emphasized, a "fair indemnity from Nicaragua to the Mosquitos," was a "sine qua non." Nicaragua, moreover, had to honor land titles in the area according to the principle

47. Malmesbury to James Green, No. 4, conf., June 18, 1852, F.O. 53/29.
48. Crampton to Granville, pvt., February 10, 1852, F.O. 5/544.
49. Crampton to Granville, Nos. 30 (March 8) and 31 (March 14, 1852), p. encl.s in both; also see enclosure in Bulwer's letter of January 19, 1852, all in F.O. 5/544.
50. Webster to Walsh, April 29, 1852, MDCIA, IV, 14-17.
51. Webster-Crampton Agreement, April 30, 1850, MTUSA, V, 782-785; also in Crampton to Wyke, May 7, 1852, F.O. 252/73. Later amendments to the "bases" are included in *idem* to *idem*, May 13, 1852, F.O. 252/73.

of actual possession; and she was to respect the Indians in the land reserved for them under the "Bases."[52]

As for the second "branch," the problem was to reach a settlement of differences between three parties: the Atlantic Pacific Ship Canal Company, Costa Rica, and Nicaragua. The "Bases" honored the company's contract, recognizing its exclusive rights to the steam navigation of the San Juan River and to certain specified sections along the banks of that river. Costa Rica was called upon to abandon her claim to the south shore of Greytown in return for an outlet at the more southerly Colorado River. From the junction of the Colorado with the San Juan and from there to the Serapiquí River, the south bank would belong to Costa Rica. In addition, Costa Ricans were to receive a favorable decision in the territorial dispute with Nicaragua over Guanacaste; and they would also have free navigation of the San Juan, except for steamers during the life of the company's contract. Those were the principal terms of the Webster-Crampton Agreement, embodying ideas which had originated with John M. Clayton and had been elaborated upon by Lord Palmerston and Sir Henry Bulwer — a remarkable attempt to settle territorial differences and to implement the Clayton-Bulwer Treaty.

From the time of their arrival in Greytown, the Anglo-American commissioners met with one obstacle after another. To begin with, the anti-Vanderbilt faction of Americans, who had won the recent elections, was in complete control of the council and threatened revolution if their right of self-government were jeopardized by turning the port over to the Nicaraguan government.[53] The English supporters of the Mosquito king likewise opposed the commission. James Green, for example, had explained the "Bases" to the King of the Mosquitos, who reportedly flew into a blind rage. This was the British resident's way of saying that his countrymen at Greytown were also against the Webster-Crampton Agreement. He did not fool the Earl of Malmesbury who wrote him a blistering reprimand for obstructing the commissioners' efforts.[54]

In Central America proper, Wyke and Walsh met with further resistance. Costa Rica accepted the "Bases" though she felt that she was called upon to make more sacrifices than were necessary. She feared, moreover, that Nicaragua would not honor the pact in question.[55] At

---

52. Crampton to Wyke, May 7, 1852, *loc. cit.*
53. Walsh to Webster, May 28, 1852, MDCIA, IV, 279; Wyke to Malmesbury, No. 2, p. encl.s, May 23, 1852, F.O. 15/76.
54. Malmesbury to Green, No. 6, October 27, 1852, F.O. 53/29.
55. Wyke to Malmesbury, No. 3, June 25, 1852, F.O. 15/76; Joaquín Bernardo Calvo to Wyke and Walsh, June 16, 1852, MDCIA, IV, 284-286.

first the Nicaraguan government rejected the plan outright, while at the same time offering to submit its claims to arbitration.[56] Subsequently, however, Nicaragua agreed to accept the "Bases" providing certain alterations were made, most important of which were the incorporation of the Mosquito reservation as a department of the state and a different arrangement on the boundary line with Costa Rica.[57] To complicate matters further, the unionist liberals elsewhere in Central America came out openly against Anglo-American intervention on the "Mosquito Question."[58]

The Wyke-Walsh mission, in other words, failed to solve the troublesome Greytown problem. Yet the two nations had learned an important lesson: in any future agreement, additional concessions would have to be made to both Nicaragua and to the citizens of Greytown. In the meantime, however, the potential for mischief was ever present at the controversial port. A case in point was the celebrated bombardment of Greytown in 1854 by American naval forces.

Except for the "grand tour" of 1850, Frederick Chatfield had had little to do with the incident which brought about his recall and, as it turned out, the end of his diplomatic career. The *Prometheus* episode, however, was not the sole reason for his recall; his forceful diplomatic maneuvers in 1851 contributed to that end because they antagonized powerful English economic interests in Central America.

The British blockade of the Salvadorean and Honduran coasts during the winter of 1850–1851, it will be recalled, had no success whatsoever.[59] Nor had Chatfield convinced Palmerston of the need for an expanded naval program in Central America, which might have led to war with the United States. On top of that, unionism had taken giant strides forward. The *Representación Nacional* was born on January 9, 1851, at Chinadega, Nicaragua, later moving its capital to León. On the 20th, the R. N. raised the Central American flag on Tigre Island; and it demanded an explanation from Chatfield for the blockade of the Pacific ports.[60] In the meantime, both Nicaragua and Honduras had angrily

---

56. John Bozman Kerr to Francisco Castellón, June 23, 1852, and Castellón to Kerr, p. encl., July 20, 1852, MDCIA, IV, 286-288, 293-295.

57. Castellón to Kerr, p. encl., July 29, 1852, *ibid,* pp. 301-303; Wyke to Malmesbury, No. 4, p. encl., July 23, 1852, F.O. 15/76.

58. Wyke to Malmesbury, No. 12, November 29, 1852, F.O. 15/76.

59. To Palmerston, Nos. 14 (February 6) and 25 (March 1, 1851), p. encl.s in both, F.O. 15/70.

60. Nos. 18, p. encl.s, February 24; 23 (February 25), and 35 (March 10, 1851), F.O. 15/70.

rejected the tentative boundaries for Mosquitia, which the British chargé had delimited on December 5, 1850.[61]

The unionist challenge reached its peak during the month of January, 1851, despite Anglo-Guatemalan efforts to thwart it. In a manifesto of the 10th, Doroteo Vasconcelos appealed to his citizens and to those of other states for a united front against the enemy, who was threatening the security of El Salvador. The Honduran government heeded his call to arms, even though Chatfield had tried to disengage it from the impending invasion of Guatemala.[62] Nicaragua alone, of the center states, demurred; in so doing, she weakened and divided the leadership of the unionist movement.[63] On February 2, 1851, consequently, the unionist invaders again suffered a disastrous defeat at Arada, in the Guatemalan department of Chiquimula. The bells pealed in Guatemala City. Providence had again pulled Chatfield's chestnuts out of the fire. He was indeed grateful.[64]

Following through on the victory, General Carrera moved into El Salvador and brought about the downfall of the Vasconcelos government, which had antagonized Chatfield for years. With the concurrence of the British chargé, it was decided to withdraw Carrera from El Salvador before he overextended himself. While Carrera's forces were marching through El Salvador at will, however, Captain Paynter of the *Gorgon* moved to the Guatemalan coast and volunteered a platoon of marines to guard the British legation in Guatemala City. Though Chatfield graciously refused this offer, he nevertheless invited Paynter to visit the capital. From late February to March 6, Captain Paynter enjoyed the company of his countryman in Guatemala City. On the eve of his departure, Carrera returned from the battlefield.[65] In other words, there was some substance to the unionist charge of collusion between the *serviles* and the British. It was no abstraction at all.

Fearful of a unionist rally, which this time might appeal effectively to Nicaragua and Costa Rica, Chatfield revived an old project which dated back to 1839 when similar conditions existed. On February 5, 1851, he proposed that Central America be "partially mediatized" and

61. Nos. 11, p. encl.s, February 5, and 13, p. encl.s, February 3(?), 1851, F.O. 15/70.

62. "Manifiesto," Doroteo Vasconcelos, January 10, 1852, in No. 8, to Palmerston, January 27, 1851, F.O. 15/70; from Honduran Government, January 21, 1851, F.O. 252/60.

63. From John Foster, January 21, February 11, 1851, F.O. 252/58.

64. To Palmerston, Nos. 15 (February 10), 17, p. encl., February 24, and 18 (February 24, 1851), F.O. 15/70.

65. James Paynter to Phipps Hornby, March 21, 1851, F.O. 15/74.

that the United States and Great Britain serve as guarantors of the peace.[66] He personally vouched for the cooperation of both Guatemala and Costa Rica while the United States, if Webster agreed, should try to influence Nicaragua's acceptance of what amounted to a protectorate, or superintendency, of Central America. The remaining two states — the unionist strongholds, we might add — did not count; they would have to fall into line whether they liked it or not. Guatemala, as might be expected, promptly championed the plan and suggested the addition of Spain as a third guarantor of the peace.[67] Costa Rica, though somewhat more hesitant, likewise acceded, providing that some other state took the initiative in the matter.[68] The peripheral states were dancing to their fiddler's tune.

Chatfield's old friend Felipe Molina, formerly a liberal, took charge of the Washington front. Not by coincidence, Guatemala appointed her native son, who was Costa Rica's agent in the United States, to represent her there as well. And in July, 1851, Molina proposed the protectorate idea to Daniel Webster.[69] Meanwhile, Chatfield continued to encourage Bulwer and Palmerston to further the project. Sir Henry Bulwer agreed that the idea had merit, but he cautioned Chatfield to be sure that all five Central American states favored a superintendency.[70] Apparently Sir Henry Bulwer did not realize the political motives which had given rise to the suggestion. Lord Palmerston, on the other hand, correctly understood the political implications; and though he offered to support the project, he reminded Chatfield that Guatemala should not rely exclusively upon other foreign powers for her defense.[71] The superintendency proposal never materialized though it may have conceivably influenced, or buttressed, the partnership approach implicit in the Webster-Crampton Agreement. In a letter to Sir Henry, Chatfield had emphasized the point that the idea of a superintendency was consistent with the Clayton-Bulwer Treaty.[72]

As in 1839, the proposal for a superintendency reflected the British chargé's apprehension that unionists might achieve the goal of establishing a strong republic which could embarrass Great Britain. In early July,

66. To Palmerston, No. 10, February 5, 1851, F.O. 15/70.
67. From Pedro N. Arriaga, February 24, 1851, F.O. 252/60.
68. To Joaquín B. Calvo and to Juan R. Mora, June 20, 1851; from Calvo (July 22) and Mora (August 12, 1851), F.O. 252/60.
69. To Palmerston, No. 54, May 15, 1851, F.O. 15/71; Felipe Molina to Daniel Webster, July 17, 1851, in No. 121, to Palmerston, October 20, 1851, F.O. 15/72.
70. From Bulwer, March 24, 1851, F.O. 252/58.
71. From Palmerston, No. 16, May 16, 1851, F.O. 15/69.
72. To Bulwer, No. 2, February 24, 1851, F.O. 252/59.

1851, the *Representación Nacional,* which Chatfield had refused to recognize, issued a decree calling for a national constitutional convention, thus putting the issue of unionism squarely before the states. On the 24th, moreover, it also withdrew Chatfield's exequatur because of his refusal to recognize the general government.[73]

To stem the unionist upsurge, the British agent consolidated his hold over the peripheral states and tried to disengage as many states of the "center" as he could. He was remarkably successful. Guatemala, of course, posed no problem whatsoever. In fact, by the end of 1851 the *serviles* had finally managed to enact a constitution of their liking, one which was virtually monarchical in form and which called for the dictatorship of Rafael Carrera.[74] The Costa Rican scene, however, constituted a greater problem especially in the early months of 1851. During the previous blockade, Chatfield had requested arms from his old friend General Juan José Flores, the leader of the "English Party" in Costa Rica. For one reason or another, Flores was unable to send him the weapons he needed — a fact which annoyed his English colleague no end. Then, the report circulated that Flores was leaving for Ecuador, or Peru, and that the Mora government had insisted upon his departure, which seemed to indicate that Costa Rica might be tempted to join the center states.[75] Fortunately for Chatfield's cause, this never materialized, perhaps because of the presence of British ships in Central American waters during the month of May, 1851. Thereafter Costa Rica was willing to accept the superintendency plan — an indication that it was again safely in the states' rights column.

Fortuitous circumstances, along with some direct intervention of British agents, neutralized Nicaragua's participation in the unionist movement. The main cause for the civil war that raged in Nicaragua during 1851 was the perennial rivalry between Granada and León. Strongly influenced by John Foster, General Trinidad Muñoz of León came out against unionism; the evidence also suggests that Chatfield may have dissuaded Pablo Buitrago, also from León, from continuing to participate

73. Decree, Representación Nacional, July 24, 1851, in No. 94, to Palmerston, August 21, 1851; also see, to Palmerston, No. 78, July 25, 1851, F.O. 15/71.

74. The political regime is explained and justified to Palmerston in dispatches 128 (October 27), 131 (October 28), 135-136 (November 5) and 140 (November 8, 1851), F.O. 15/72.

75. To Palmerston, Nos. 38 (March 25) and 42 (April 16, 1851), F.O. 15/70; to Juan José Flores, February 13, 1851, F.O. 252/62; to Juan R. Mora, March 25, 1851, and from Mora, May 21, 1851, F.O. 252/60.

in the *Representación Nacional.*[76] In the meantime, the British chargé had also written to Fruto Chamorro, a conservative minister in the government of Laureano Pineda which had won the spring elections. The letter clearly discouraged him from having anything to do with unionism.[77] At this point the situation became confused. First, the Pineda government refused to accept the R. N.'s decree calling for a constitutional convention, which in turn provoked a revolution by the Leonese in August, 1851. The rebel government came out in favor of the R. N.[78] Then the Pineda government, which finally settled in Granada, accepted the help of unionist forces from Honduras on the condition that it would support the R. N. By this time, and because of unsettled conditions in Nicaragua, the R. N. had moved its capital to Tegucigalpa, Honduras.[79] In short, because of sectional rivalry and civil war, Nicaragua was of no value to the unionist movement; in fact, she weakened it.

As for the two unionist states of the "center" — El Salvador and Honduras — Chatfield's only solution was the use of force. He would bring in the navy again in the fall of 1851. No sooner had the previous blockade been lifted, the British chargé wrote to both Admiral Hornby and Lord Palmerston asking for naval support later in the year.[80] The response was immediate and gratifying. Though soon to be replaced by Rear Admiral Fairfax Moresby, Hornby promised to win the support of his successor; and Lord Palmerston also sanctioned the deployment of British ships on the coasts of Central America.[81]

As it turned out, Admiral Moresby proved to be more than eager to assist the British chargé in Guatemala. In fact, with a squadron of five ships, he personally visited the Gulf of Fonseca in May, 1851, to apprize himself of conditions in Central America. Of course, Chatfield exploited the opportunity to the utmost by publicizing Moresby's presence.[82] Undoubtedly, as suggested above, this is what brought Costa Rica back into line. It should be noted, moreover, that Chatfield's political objective was explicit in his correspondence with the admiral.

---

76. From John Foster, June 24, 1851, F.O. 252/58; to Bulwer, July 11, 1851, F.O. 252/59; to Buitrago, conf., June 13, 1851, F.O. 252/60.
77. To Fruto Chamorro, July 11, 1851, F.O. 252/60.
78. To Palmerston, No. 130, p. encl., October 27, 1851, F.O. 15/72.
79. To Palmerston, Nos. 145 (November 20) and 151 (December 8, 1851), p. encl.s for both, F.O. 15/72.
80. To Fairfax Moresby, March 3, in No. 33, to Palmerston, March 10, 1851; also see No. 41, April 7, 1851, F.O. 15/70.
81. To Palmerston, No. 25, p. encl.s, March 1, 1851, F.O. 15/70; also see, in same volume, Palmerston's note of July 25, 1851, to Chatfield's No. 41 (April 7, 1851).
82. To Moresby, May 20, 1851, in No. 56, to Palmerston, May 26, 1851, F.O. 15/71.

With the defeat of the Vasconcelos government after the battle of Arada, the successor governments of El Salvador anxiously sought an agreement with the British legation.[83] Moresby's presence in the Gulf of Fonseca removed all doubt in Salvadoreans' minds; it was now merely a question of attenuating Chatfield's three demands upon the state. They were especially worried about the humiliating apology concerning the press and the recognition of Marcos Idígoras as the British vice-consul. Despite the fact that many of the claims were not justified, the Salvadorean government was willing to pay them. Finally, on August 20, 1851, a settlement was reached because Chatfield permitted a slight modification in the wording of the apology to him.[84] Thus, the recalcitrant state of El Salvador, just as in 1840, had been brought to her knees. The tide had definitely turned. Rumors circulated that by 1853 El Salvador would declare herself a separate republic.[85] And, to be sure, this did come to pass.[86]

That left only Honduras supporting the *Representación Nacional*. Director Juan Lindo, though his record had been spotty in the past, welcomed the establishment of the R. N.'s capital at Tegucigalpa, an event which took place in November 1851. His government, moreover, supported the decrees calling for a national constituent assembly and the withdrawal of Chatfield's exequatur.[87] Of course, these various acts did not endear Lindo to the master of the British legation in Guatemala City, who was determined to use naval force on the Atlantic and Pacific coasts to quash unionism once and for all.[88]

In view of the foregoing, it would appear that Frederick Chatfield, after years of effort, was on the threshold of success — only Honduras stood in his way. Irony would have it, however, that his own countrymen again deprived him of his trophy.

The unsuccessful blockade of 1850–1851 had been the subject of vigorous discussions in both the United States Congress and in the English Parliament. Sir Francis Baring had questioned Lord Palmerston

---

83. From Marcos Idígoras, March 1, 1851, F.O. 252/58.

84. To Palmerston, No. 97, p. encl.s, August 27, 1851, F.O. 15/71.

85. From Idígoras, May 22, June 10, 13, July 10, August 22, 1851, F.O. 252/58.

86. Marcos Idígoras to British Secretary of State, No. 1, p. encl., March 30, 1853, F.O. 15/80.

87. To Palmerston, No. 116, p. encl., September 26, 1851, F.O. 15/72.

88. To Palmerston, No. 106, p. encl., September 1, 1851, F.O. 15/72; to Carlos Meany, conf., September 26, 1851, F.O. 252/62.

about it in the House of Commons.[89] And it was the powerful Chalmers-Guthrie Company which had been primarily responsible for the questioning that embarrassed the Russell ministry in England.

During the course of 1851, company officials had conducted an acid correspondence with the Foreign Office concerning Mr. Chatfield. And despite the company's convincing documentation, Lord Palmerston had not only condoned the use of naval force again in Central America but also had refused unequivocally to recall his aggressive agent.[90]

The argument began in January 1851, when it was learned that the company's ship *Texian* had incurred losses stemming from the blockade and Chatfield had done nothing to help her. Palmerston replied that he was sorry but that El Salvador, not Great Britain, had been responsible for those losses.[91] On April 9, 1851, after the blockade issue had been discussed in the House of Commons, company officials wrote a lengthy letter to the Foreign Office containing valuable information on the political situation in Central America. Since Palmerston had parried questions in Parliament with the retort that he had no further information, the company — with tongue-in-cheek, no doubt — volunteered to fill the void. The lengthy enclosures, written by two Spanish merchants in Guatemala City who were associated with the company, exposed Chatfield's political maneuvers, especially the use of claims for political purposes, and concluded that he actually did more harm than good for British interests. Since it would be folly to occupy Central America militarily — the United States would not permit it — it behooved England to change her policy in Central America and to remove her representative, so closely identified with the *serviles* of Guatemala. Palmerston replied angrily that it was none of the company's business; he alone was running the Foreign Office; and he considered the company shortsighted for accepting the testimony of non-Englishmen and for going against Great Britain's policy.[92]

On May 15, the Chalmers-Guthrie Company answered Palmerston's "undignified" letter and reminded him that it was one of the largest shippers to Central America. They were not shortsighted; they merely

---

89. To Palmerston, No. 39, p. encl.s, April 1, 1851, F.O. 15/70, alluding to Senator Shield's motion in the Senate on January 22, 1851; Chalmers-Guthrie Company to Palmerston, May 15, 1851, F.O. 15/74; from Edward Wallerstein, February 15, 1851, and to Wallerstein, April 17, 18, 1851, F.O. 252/60.

90. From Edward Wallerstein, February 15 and July 16, 1851, F.O. 252/60.

91. Chalmers-Guthrie Company to Palmerston, p. encl.s, January 19, 23, 1851, and Palmerston's note, January 25, 1851, F.O. 15/74.

92. Chalmers-Guthrie Company to Palmerston, p. encl.s by Juan and Manuel Ortiz, April 9, 1851; Palmerston to *idem,* April 19, 1851, F.O. 15/74.

wanted peaceful conditions for their trade in that part of the world. Moreover, they did not expect to be insulted by their foreign minister. The implication was obvious: Palmerston might face problems in England if he persisted in condoning Chatfield's actions in Central America. Although reiterating that he was sorry for the inconvenience the company had suffered from the previous blockade, "Old Pam" stubbornly maintained that the company had received "misinformation" about Central American affairs. In the reply, the company insisted that it was the Foreign Office that was misinformed. Since the blockade had been lifted, company officials wanted to know if they might be allowed to trade with Central America or would there be another "shooting season in August," they asked facetiously. Annoyed, the master of the Foreign Office haughtily referred them to the Salvadorean government for the answer to their question.[93] Shortly after the conclusion of this correspondence, Palmerston again sanctioned a new blockade for El Salvador. He was overjoyed, of course, to learn that the Salvadoreans had accepted Chatfield's terms on August 20, 1851, thus relieving the pressure from his opponents in London.[94]

But the Foreign Office had not heard the last word from Chalmers-Guthrie and Company. On December 29, 1851, during the political crisis which brought about Palmerston's dismissal, the company wrote a strong protest concerning losses incurred by the ship Hamlet, which had been detained in October at Valparaíso by Admiral Moresby in anticipation of the Central American blockade. If, the company reasoned, El Salvador had agreed to terms in August, why was it that Admiral Moresby had not been informed? Given the obvious negligence of public servants, the company felt that it deserved indemnification.[95] Realizing that the company had a legitimate grievance, Earl Granville demanded an explanation from Frederick Chatfield on January 10, 1852.[96] Two days previously, Granville had decided to recall the aggressive agent. In selecting Charles Lennox Wyke as his successor, the Foreign Office hoped that he would fulfill his duties in Central America "without resorting to compulsory measures."[97]

Two ships, the Hamlet and the Prometheus, marked a turning point

---

93. F.O. 15/74, letters by the company on May 15 and May ___, 1851; Palmerston's notes and letters on May 21, 26, 29, 1851.

94. From Palmerston, No. 34, November 11, 1851, F.O. 15/69.

95. Chalmers-Guthrie Company to Granville, December 29, 1851, F.O. 15/75.

96. From Granville, No. 1, January 10, 1852, F.O. 15/76.

in England's Central American policy. They made Chatfield's retirement inevitable. He had outlived his usefulness in Middle America.

Considering his gift for political analysis, Mr. Chatfield understood the implications of his recall. In fact, it was generally accepted throughout Central America that his recall indicated a change in Great Britain's policy. This, of course, bolstered the spirits of unionist leaders; by the same token, it severely depressed the allies of the British caudillo.[98]

Chatfield's explanation of the *Hamlet* incident was a lame one, to say the least. As Palmerston, the British chargé considered the company shortsighted for having appealed to the United States minister in London against its own government and for having invented stories about him. The August 20 arrangement with El Salvador, he argued, had taken longer to ratify than he had expected — thus, the delay in relaying the information to Admiral Moresby.[99] He dared not admit, of course, that he had no intention of forsaking the use of British ships against the unionist stronghold of Honduras, or for that matter against El Salvador if that state reneged on the August 20 agreement. Later, in England, Chatfield elaborated further on the company's "misinformation" about the *Hamlet* — his choice of words was strikingly Palmerstonian. He had learned that the captain of the ship — a dissolute chap if there ever was one — had sold all of the ship's cargo while in Valparaíso and then had left for China. Another English captain, a witness to the incident, had told him that the *Hamlet* was in desperate need of repairs and could not possibly have made it to Central America. The British government, therefore, was not responsible for the company's losses.[100] And there the case rested.

In hopes that his recall would be temporary, and with it the change in British policy, Mr. Chatfield spent his last months in Central America preparing the ground for a continuation of his policies. The three faithful states (El Salvador, Costa Rica, and Guatemala), taking their lead from Guatemala City, began their campaign to convince the Foreign Office that Chatfield should return to Central America. Their spokesman was Edward Wallerstein, the representative of the peripheral states in London. When El Salvador also selected Chatfield's close friend to represent her in England, it was obvious that Wallerstein would be the instrument

97. "Memorandum of Current Business," F.O., February 27, 1852, F.O. 83/128.
98. Leónce Angrand to Min. of For. Affairs, No. 12, May 6, 1852, A.A.E.P./ CPAC, vol. 10.
99. To Granville, No. 10, March 20, 1852, F.O. 15/76.
100. To Malmesbury, June 28, 1852, F.O. 15/76.

by which the former chargé would continue to exert his influence in Central America.[101] Furthermore, Chatfield recommended three good friends of his to serve as vice-consuls in Nicaragua (Foster had suffered a heart attack recently), Costa Rica, and El Salvador. To which the Earl of Malmesbury remarked facetiously: "Mr. Chatfield seems to have a choice of men for consulships and a choice of places for consuls."[102]

Through Manuel Francisco Pavón, he also assured himself of continuity in Guatemala's orientation. He particularly urged "Chico" to seek a boundary settlement with Belize in order to stop the North Americans. Moreover, he assiduously labored against the renewal of the Belgian Colonization Company's contract which was presented to the Guatemalan government by Martial Cloquet on April 21, 1852. In dispatches to the Foreign Office, Chatfield freely admitted his opposition to the Belgian company and to its port at Santo Tomás.[103] In the meantime, as the French consul observed, *"ce brouillon mechant"* (this wicked meddler) had publicly and thoroughly humiliated Monsieur Cloquet by stating that the Belgian government had recalled him and that therefore he was not authorized to renew the contract. That was Cloquet's reward for nine years of sycophancy to the arrogant Mr. Chatfield.[104] Furthermore, Monsieur Angrand noted, before Chatfield's departure from Guatemala City on May 4, 1852, the English agent had made secret arrangements to block any further attempts to renew the Belgian contract — a very accurate report, as we shall see.[105]

At Chatfield's instigation, according to the French consul, the Guatemalan government acted vindictively toward other foreign nations in the months preceding the Englishman's departure. A Prussian envoy was insulted by a Guatemalan official at Santo Tomás and had received no satisfaction from the government, nor was he able to negotiate a treaty with it. Guatemala, moreover, refused to consider any claims against her pending the liquidation of the British debt; and she also denied the French consul the right to protect Spaniards within her borders. All these acts, Monsieur Angrand attributed to the twisted mind of Frederick Chatfield, a "monomaniac of the worst type," angry at his

---

101. Marcos Idígoras to British Secretary of State, No. 1, p. encl., March 30, 1853, F.O. 15/80.
102. Malmesbury's note to cons. No. 15, to Granville, March 29, 1852; also see Nos. 11 (March 20) and 14 (March 29, 1852), F.O. 15/77.
103. To Palmerston, No. 2, p. encl.s, January 6, 1852; and No. 21, to Malmesbury, p. encl., April 30, 1852, F.O. 15/76.
104. Angrand's No. 12, *loc. cit.*, and No. 13 (May 25, 1852).
105. *Ibid.*

recall and what was being said about it.[106] The American chargé likewise documented Chatfield's distress at leaving Central America.[107]

After arriving in London on June 21, 1852, the ex-chargé to Guatemala and Costa Rica devoted his efforts to counteracting the new English policy toward Central America. Through Pavón and Idígoras, among others, not a single act of his successor went unknown. And working with Edward Wallerstein, as well as by Chatfield's direct correspondence with the Foreign Office, the ex-chargé continued to make recommendations to the foreign secretary. Using "Chico" Pavón as his source, for example, he urged the Earl of Clarendon, who had succeeded Malmesbury in the Foreign Office, to negotiate a secret boundary treaty with Guatemala.[108] In the meantime, Pavón had approached Charles Lennox Wyke on the matter; and Chatfield's successor in turn had relayed the information to London, including the allegation that Guatemala's agent in Washington, Felipe Molina, had been asked by the American government to advance Guatemalan claims to Belize.[109] But Clarendon wisely demurred on the ground that such a treaty would only invite the aggression which Pavón feared from the northern republic.[110] Until his death in 1855, Pavón favored such a treaty, strongly influenced by his good friend *"Don Federico."* Four years later, it became a reality.

With regard to the Belgian Colonization Company, Mr. Chatfield's activities embroiled him in difficulties with the Foreign Office. To begin with, when the Earl of Malmesbury learned of Guatemala's refusal to renew the Belgian contract in April, 1852, he instructed Wyke to remonstrate with the Guatemalan government, maintaining that it had no right to rescind the contract in that manner.[111] British interest in the renewal of the contract stemmed from the fact that in October, 1851, English investors had floated a substantial loan for the Belgian Colonization Company and therefore were vitally interested in the company's future. Guatemala, however, persisted in her stand. Yet interestingly, she displayed a desire to settle with the British investors — an indication of Mr. Chatfield's influence from overseas.[112]

---

106. Angrand to Min. of For. Affairs, Nos. 2 (January 25), 6 (February 29), 7 (March 3), 14 (May 30), and 28 (September 30, 1852), A.A.E.P./CPAC, vol. 10.
107. John Bozman Kerr to Daniel Webster, May 16, 1852, MDCIA, IV, 277-278.
108. To Clarendon, p. encl., August 20, 1853; also Edward Wallerstein to Clarendon, June 7, and July 2, 1853, F.O. 15/81.
109. Wyke to Clarendon, Nos. 22 (July 7) and 37 (November 27, 1853), F.O. 15/79; Wyke to P. L. Wodehouse, December 11, 1852, F.O. 252/74.
110. Clarendon to Wyke, No. 3, conf., January 19, 1854, F.O. 15/82.
111. Malmesbury to Wyke, No. 7, October 30, and cons. No. 9, December 6, 1852, F.O. 15/77.
112. Wyke to Malmesbury, cons. No. 14, December 30, 1852, F.O. 15/77.

What created problems for the ex-chargé was that he made a visit to Belgium in late 1852, ostensibly to undermine the company's objectives in Guatemala. During this trip, he apparently tried to discourage King Leopold and the Belgium government from supporting the company's project. He was received well by King Leopold, who invited him to the palace to break bread with him. Trouble followed when the British minister in Brussels, Lord Howard De Walden, learned of Chatfield's activities. On September 11, 1853, De Walden informed the Earl of Clarendon that the Belgian Company had run into obstacles in Guatemala. Mr. Pavón had laughed at Wyke's efforts in behalf of the company and had said that he had received a letter indicating that neither England nor Belgium intended to support the Belgian company. Pavón had also given the impression that the company was run by speculators and that it was on its last legs.[113]

Following up De Walden's suggestion, the Foreign Office demanded to know from Chatfield if his "line of conduct" during the Belgian visit had been as implied in the recent letter from Belgium.[114] Chatfield, in turn, answered that he could by no means be held responsible for Pavón's remarks; and he argued that Martial Cloquet, out of vindictiveness, had tried to make him the scapegoat in this whole matter by informing De Walden of his alleged activities in Belgium. He denied working against the company's interests.[115] This answer failed to satisfy De Walden. Acting upon his recommendation, the Foreign Office again wrote to Chatfield and insisted upon a categorical answer to these questions: Did he or did he not express an opinion that King Leopold, the Belgian Government, and the English Foreign Office were not in favor of the colonization project?[116] With his back to the wall, the indomitable Chatfield came out fighting. He replied in a manner so reminiscent of his correspondence with small Central American states. In one breath, he denied the charges against him; but in the next, he fully admitted that Pavón's assertions had been correct. Annoyed at the British representative in Belgium, he concluded: "I am aware that Lord Howard De Walden has more than once tried to overthrow my testimony, with respect to the views and position of the Belgian Colonization Company at Santo Tomás, His Lordship having, I am told, given advice to a Mr. Mills in connexion with it, by which that gentleman has lost a good deal of

113. De Walden to Clarendon, p. encl., September 11, 1853, F.O. 10/174.
114. From F.O. (H. U. Addington), September 22, 1853, F.O. 15/81.
115. To Clarendon, September 24, 1853, F.O. 15/81.
116. De Walden to Clarendon, pvt., September 30, 1853, F.O. 101/74; F.O. to Chatfield, October 7, 1853, F.O. 15/81.

money."[117] De Walden caught the innuendo concerning Mills, one of the leading investors in the Belgian loan, and noted "the manner in which Mr. Chatfield can adopt and record in official correspondence matters which can not bear the test of investigation."[118] Englishmen, it would seem, were getting a good taste of Chatfieldian methods and style.

Disgruntled and fighting a losing battle, Mr. Chatfield engaged the Foreign Office in one last battle — the appointment of vice-consuls in Central America — and this in turn involved him in a campaign of denigration against his successor Charles Lennox Wyke. There were two appointments which he did not like at all: first, the selection of Henry Foote to replace "noble" Idígoras in San Salvador; and secondly, the appointment of Edward Hall to the position in Honduras. Chatfield argued that El Salvador's trade did not warrant Foote's appointment. Then came the innuendoes: Wyke had accepted Idígoras' hospitality and then had turned upon him treacherously, etc. As for Edward Hall, he was a mere slip of a boy — a mulatto at that — incapable of holding down the Honduran position.[119]

An excellent representative of the new approach in British diplomacy, Captain Wyke was no mean competitor himself, certainly equal to the task of fighting "the person" who insisted upon naming viceconsuls in Central America.[120] He thoroughly demolished his rival's arguments. It was surprising — and Wyke was right, incidentally — that after so many years in Central America Chatfield could make the shallow statements he had made about El Salvador's economy. Even more ludicrous were the remarks about Edward Hall, the blond and blue-eyed son of William Hall, whom Chatfield hated with a vengeance.

Although previously Captain Wyke had been circumspect in criticizing his predecessor, he now exposed him as the ally of the *serviles* and a man who had done more than anyone else to discredit the English name in Central America.[121] Eyes opened in the Foreign Office, some for the first time. Others, like those of the Under Secretary of State Henry U. Addington, had suspected it all along. When Chatfield sensed that he was losing the battle, he wrote "a very impertinent letter," said Addington, dated January 20, 1854, in which he demanded to know if the Foreign Office considered Wyke's letter about Idígoras "a faithful representation of the case." "By what right, or power," Mr. Addington

---

117. To Clarendon, October 8, 1853, F.O. 15/81.
118. De Walden to Clarendon, No. 130, October 21, 1853, F.O. 10/174.
119. To Clarendon, November 21, 29, and December 20, 1853, F.O. 15/80.
120. Wyke to H. U. Addington, cons. No. 26, October 27, 1853, F.O. 15/80.
121. Wyke to Clarendon, cons. No. 1, January 23, 1854, F.O. 15/83.

pencilled in the margin, "does Mr. Chatfield put any such question to the Secretary of State?"[122] The Foreign Office replied curtly that the instructions sent to Mr. Wyke were those that the "Secretary of State thinks necessary."[123] Frederick Chatfield's career was at an end.

Captain Wyke drove in the last nail. He asked the Foreign Office to compare Chatfield's recent letters on the appointment of vice-consuls with an article that had appeared in the letters-to-the-editor column of the *Morning Chronicle* on December 19, 1853.[124] And Captain Wyke was correct; no one but Frederick Chatfield had the command of the facts cited in the selection. In a brief period, Wyke had fathomed the methods of his predecessor. Since the article reflected Chatfield's final efforts to reverse the trend in British policy which had resulted from the *Prometheus* incident, we shall quote it in its entirety:

> To the Editor of the Morning Chronicle.
> Sir.
>
> By late advices from Central America we are informed that the unnatural war between the several States still exists, to the destruction of all commerce; and that Mr. Squiers, the late United States consul-general in Central America, has offered to the Honduras Government (who are entirely devoted to the United States) a body of Americans to act against Guatemala.
>
> If any of your readers will take the trouble to inquire respecting British relations with Central America, he will be surprised to learn, although a most important country to England as regards her commerce (the goods consumed there being principally British), yet, by the very questionable policy of the British government, the latter are likely to lose all influence there. One of the chief causes of the decline of British influence in Central America is in consequence of not having efficient political agents there. For some 15 or 16 years the British government had in Mr. Frederick Chatfield a most efficient and talented consul-general and chargé d'affaires. During the period that this gentleman acted in that capacity English influence was predominant, and commerce with Central America was both secure and prosperous. Mr. Chatfield's knowledge of the politics, customs, and language of the country, gave him immense influence, which he used as a security for British commerce and enterprise; the payment of the British claims, the reduction of duties, the doing away with all forced contributions formerly imposed on British subjects, and the granting of a Protestant place of burial in Guatemala, will sufficiently evince his efficiency. However, on the late Government succeeding to office, Lord Malmesbury thought proper to replace Mr. Chatfield by a gentleman of the name

---

122. To Earl of Clarendon, January 20, 1854, F.O. 15/83.
123. From F.O., February 4, 1854, F.O. 15/83.
124. Wyke to Addington, cons. No. 7, p. encl., March 24, 1854, F.O. 15/83.

Wyke, a former *protégé* of the late King of Hanover, and holding, at the time of his new appointment, the very inferior (as regards importance) office of vice-consul at one of the ports in Hayti. The policy of the British government in thus substituting Mr. Wyke for an efficient agent, as Mr. Chatfield had proved himself to have been, appears very questionable. Mr. Wyke is a gentleman whom all will admire for his kindness and hospitality to all travelers, yet, certainly, he was not the person adapted for consul-general of Central America, as a knowledge of the language and customs is, of course, essential in one holding that important office, and Mr. Wyke was, unfortunately for British interests, deficient of all knowledge of the language, politics, or customs of the country to which he was accredited; indeed, so very unimportant is the present consul-general considered in Central America that in the beginning of the present year an Englishman was murdered in the city of Guatemala, and some of the unfortunate man's blood was placed in the window of the British Consulate at Guatemala. Mr. Wyke's influence has not been sufficient to cause the murderers to be punished. At the present time, it may be said that the protection enjoyed by British subjects is to be attributed to the very efficient government of the President of Guatemala, General Carrera, whose conduct to foreigners in general must always be a theme of admiration. Too much praise cannot be accorded him for the energy with which he has conducted the government of Guatemala. Another still more extraordinary appointment is one recently made by Mr. Wyke, in placing a young man of twenty years of age in the very responsible office of British vice-consul for all Honduras. This young man has obtained his entire knowledge of the politics and the rights of British subjects in a small retail shop in Guatemala. Certainly, there will appear something extraordinary in Mr. Wyke appointing so very inefficient a person to the office of Her Brittanic Majesty's agent for all Honduras. What protection he can afford to British subjects or commerce, recent advices will sufficiently tell; and indeed, at the present time, with the exception of the city of Guatemala, no Englishman is safe. M. Cloquet, the Belgian consul-general, on his return to Europe, was detained at "Zacapa," in the republic of Guatemala, by the Honduras troops entering that city and pillaging it. The Honduras troops were prevented molesting the Belgian consul-general by their being informed that he was not an Englishman. This state of insecurity would not, I imagine, have occurred had Mr. Chatfield been left at his post. It is well known that many capitalists, both in London and Liverpool, are prevented investing their funds in the mining and other speculations of Central America from the want of security to person and property. It is also reported that the island of Tigre, in the "Bay of Conchagua," is to be given up to the United States by the Honduras Government. This island is important, as being situated in the only good harbour (with the exception of that of Punta Arenas, in Costa Rica) in all Central America. Mr. Chatfield thought proper, some years since, to take possession of it for the British government. The latter, however, at the solicitation of the United States government, gave it up to the Honduras Government. Of course, so important a place (the only safe one in the Pacific) is not certainly to be given to or allowed to be possessed by the United States merely because we have no efficient political agent out there. Certainly, the British Government can afford to have a more efficient agent in Honduras than the present one; a young man whose experience has been acquired as a shopboy is certainly not a sufficient guarantee for British interests.

Time will evince if England is right in succumbing to American influence in Central America.

"Tempus est optimus index rerum omnium."

December 19   POPOCATEPTETL[125]

---

125. *Morning Chronicle* (London), December 20, 1853.

The Brighton Peabody

He looked upon him, in fact, as the Brighton Peabody.[1]
— Brighton *Herald,* October 5, 1872

What with the playful antics of the junior clerks in the so-called "Nursery" and the practical jokes of the senior men, life was not humdrum in the "Old Foreign Office" of the nineteenth century.[2] Thanks to the Hertslets — Lewis and Edward, whose careers as librarian and archivist spanned all but five years of that century — some anecdotes and impressions of the F.O. are available to us. They were recorded in entertaining fashion by Sir Edward Hertslet.

The sensational, as might be expected, stands out in a work of this type. A case in point are the references made to Lord Palmerston, that colorful and exacting taskmaster who was renowned for the quips which he sprinkled generously in his "minutes." Once, when a subaltern in one of the South American legations wrote him a lengthy report, replete with more than a prudent share of suggestions, "Old Pam" pencilled on the docket of the dispatch: "Goose, Goose, Goose."[3] His mania for legible handwriting has also been commented upon frequently — an understandable trait considering the normal schedule of working well into the night. "Life is not long enough to decipher their scribbling," he used to complain; and at times, he threatened to dismiss agents who ignored his instructions on handwriting or who failed to use the proper type of ink.[4] On one occasion, for example, Sir Henry Bulwer had a dispatch returned to him for recopying. Frederick Chatfield had likewise received warnings on his handwriting. Irritated by the events and problems of 1838, Mr. Chatfield answered brazenly that it was too hot in San Salvador to write otherwise. Besides, if he brought a young fellow from England to do his writing, the lad would certainly be corrupted by the environment.[5] Surprisingly, this irritable outburst went by unnoticed.

Sir Edward tells the story of a certain consul who had foolishly avoided paying a debt. By the time the Foreign Office was apprized of

---

1. Brighton *Herald,* October 5, 1872.
2. Sir Edward Hertslet, *Recollections of the Old Foreign Office* (London, 1901), pp. 23-27.
3. *Ibid.,* pp. 76-77.
4. *Ibid.,* p. 79.
5. From John Bidwell, No. 2, March 14, 1838; to Palmerston, No. 33, May 31, 1838, F.O. 15/20.

it, many years later, the obligation had increased to the tidy sum of three hundred and fifty pounds. When the creditor learned that Sir Edward was the offender's agent in London, he demanded payment and hoped that he would be permitted to attach the consul's salary. The whole matter got out of hand at this point; and there were threats of lawsuits which might have involved the secretary of state for foreign affairs and other high officials in the F.O. Finally, however, the case was settled out of court for less than half the amount owed. Weeks later, the consul wrote a "chatty letter" to his agent, containing the postscript: "I'm glad _____'s affair is settled." Angry at the consul's apparent ingratitude, or flippancy, Sir Edward replied scoldingly that if he had been the guilty party he would have written as follows: "My dear_____, I cannot find words to express my gratitude to you for all the trouble you have taken about _____'s affair, nor my sorrow at the annoyance which this wretched affair has caused you and others in the Foreign Office, and I thank you very heartily for the very satisfactory settlement which you made." In due time, the consul wrote such a letter; but, remarked Sir Edward, "it can easily be imagined what sort of value I set upon it considering it had been dictated by myself."[6] This incident actually occurred in 1845–46 while Lord Aberdeen headed the Foreign Office; and the offender, it would seem, was Mr. Chatfield — ironically, the man who never tired of preaching to Central American governments the virtues of paying one's debts.[7]

Another anecdote which contains a familiar ring concerned the retirement of a "high official." "When he made up his mind to retire," Sir Edward narrates, "he came into my room to announce the fact, remarking that a man should always retire when he was at the zenith of his power." Rather arrogantly, he further expressed the view that the Foreign Office might not be able to get along very well without him. But, upon perusing his pension letter, which recited his "past meritorious services," he condemned it strongly as one that might have been written for "a third-class clerk." When apprized of this reaction, the undersecretary of state for foreign affairs remarked: "If he does not like what I have written ask him to write anything he likes and I will sign it." The gentleman in question considered the undersecretary's suggestion as adding insult to injury. The Foreign Office, however, did modify the letter somewhat; and a few weeks later, the veteran returned to Sir Edward's office. "Well," he asked, "and how does the office get on without me?"

6. Hertslet, *Recollections,* pp. 226-229.
7. Alfred Daniell to Aberdeen, p. encl.s and following correspondence, November 15, 1845, F.O. 15/41; also see documents on this case in F.O. 15/42-43.

"Oh, pretty well," answered Sir Edward. The remainder of the visit was even more embarrassing, as the gentleman asked if the clerks in the office had expressed their regret upon learning of his retirement. "This was an awkward question," Sir Edward noted, "for no one had expressed any such sentiments to me, and I was reluctantly compelled to tell him so, but I could see that he felt it most deeply." [8]

◆•◆

For all practical purposes, Frederick Chatfield's public career terminated with the hassle over the appointment of vice-consuls for Central America. Yet in mid-1854, he was called upon to draw up a valuable report on the Mayan ruins in Guatemala at the request of the British Museum and the Foreign Office.[9] Moreover, he continued to manage the Central American loans for a few years after his retirement, receiving the customary fee for his services.[10] As far as political influence was concerned, it waned with the deaths of his two good friends Manuel Francisco Pavón in 1855 and Edward Wallerstein in 1856. Consequently, he had little choice but to settle down to a comfortable retirement; and this he appears to have done quite well. He invested his money wisely in such stocks and bonds as the Delhi, Canadian, and Cuban railways; the Egyptian loans of 1862 and 1864, as well as the Danubian, Turkish, Brazilian, and Peruvian loans. When he died, his estate was valued at from fifteen to twenty thousand pounds sterling. It would also seem that he traveled extensively during his retirement, visiting relatives and friends in Scotland and Prussia, among other places. In his last will and testament, he remembered relatives, three servants, a coachman, and many friends and institutions in Brighton, England, where he spent the last few years of his life.[11]

Although his political influence had diminished, Mr. Chatfield certainly did not abandon his interest in Central American developments during the hectic decade of the fifties. We can safely say that he had strong feelings about the actions of North Americans in Central America and that he vehemently disapproved of any conciliatory policy toward the United States — a retreat from positions which he had labored so hard to establish in nineteen years of service in that part of the world. Let us

---

8. Hertslet, *Recollections,* pp. 136-137.
9. From F.O., May 9, 1854; to Edmund Hammond, May 10, 1854; to Clarendon, and enclosed mem., May 18, 1854, F.O. 15/84.
10. See F.O. 15/88 and 90 on Salvadorean and Honduran claims.
11. Last Will and Testament, Frederick Chatfield, August 13, 1872, probated in London on March 27, 1874.

therefore pick up the thread of Anglo-American relations where we last left it.

After the failure of the Webster-Crampton Agreement, matters took a turn for the worse with the death of Daniel Webster and the victory of the Democrats in the fall elections of 1852. The new administration of President Franklin Pierce, and that of his successor James Buchanan, adopted the "renunciation" interpretation of the Clayton-Bulwer Treaty. The Democrats argued that in signing that document Great Britain had renounced the Mosquito Protectorate, her claims to the Bay Islands, and her rights to lands around Belize which extended beyond the limits specified in the Spanish treaties of the 1780's. In short, the United States had accepted the Central Americans' version of the treaty. England, on the other hand, countered with the "prospective" interpretation, insisting that she had merely agreed not to acquire any *further* possessions in Central America.[12]

Then, incidents which resulted from the unsolved territorial issues added to the strain in their relations. For example, the wrangle between Vanderbilt's company, still occupying the south side of the San Juan's mouth, and the hostile American faction at Greytown served as the background for the celebrated bombardment of that port by an American naval unit on July 13, 1854.[13] It all happened just as Captain Robinson had predicted after the *Prometheus* affair. The filibustering activities of such Americans as William Walker, that "grey-eyed man" of destiny, did not help to obliterate English suspicions that the United States planned to annex Central America, one way or another. We can well imagine what Mr. Chatfield must have told his friends about these events.

Although Chatfield's public voice was gone, his former master in the Foreign Office more than made up for it. In no uncertain terms, "Old Pam" protested any attempt to appease those "disagreeable fellows," the Yankees; and he denounced with equal vehemence the "Shopkeeping Considerations" of powerful British commercial interests, who wanted peace with the United States at any price.[14] On December 31, 1857, he told the Earl of Clarendon that North Americans were rogues:

> and such ingenious Rogues that it is hardly possible to hope that even if the present Questions were settled to their liking by the abandonment of the Bay Islands and of Mosquitia and of part of our Honduras some new Cavils would not be found, or at least

---

12. MTUSA, V, 790-791.
13. Mary W. Williams, *Anglo-American Diplomacy*, pp. 171-183.
14. Palmerston to Clarendon, June 6, 1857, in Richard Van Alstyne, "Anglo-American Relations, 1853–57," *American Historical Review*, Vol. XLII (April, 1937), p. 499.

that by the indirect agency of such men as Walker & his followers some independent North American State would not be established in Central America, in alliance with the United States if not in Union with them, in short Texas over again.[15]

To these remarks, his former protegé would probably have said, "Hear, hear."

Palmerston's opposition notwithstanding, and despite the incidents mentioned, the British government steadfastly maintained the course which "they" had charted after the *Prometheus* affair — a graceful retreat, abandoning Palmerstonian diplomacy in that quarter of the world. Just before learning of Greytown's bombardment, the Earl of Clarendon set down the British position, in answer to the strong stand taken by the American minister to England, James Buchanan. It should be noted that he was willing to withdraw from Mosquitia providing it could be done with "honour," even to the point of accepting Nicaraguan sovereignty to the Indian reservation area — one of Nicaragua's modifications to the Webster-Crampton Agreement. In addition, he made this significant concession:

> Great Britain has no interest in insisting nor does she intend to insist upon the claim to any portion of Central America or to its adjacent Islands, with the single exception of the Belize Settlement with the limits and on the terms in which it was granted to her by the Treaties with Spain of 1783 and 1786 and subsequently recognized by the Republic of Mexico. She makes this disclaimer in order to sooth the way to the immediate fulfilment of the transit & commercial clauses of the Convention in which her interests are seriously involved.[16]

Clarendon's willingness to accept the old limits of Belize graphically illustrated England's desire to repudiate her former position in Central America.

With the Greytown bombardment, and the preoccupations of the Crimean War, the process of retreat remained in abeyance until October 17, 1856. On that date, the Earl of Clarendon and George M. Dallas, Buchanan's successor, signed a treaty which was the lineal descendant of the Webster-Crampton Agreement. It embodied all of the latter's major provisions and added clauses to satisfy the desire of self-government for the municipality of Greytown as well as Nicaragua's wish to incorporate the Mosquito reservation. In other words, the Dallas-Clarendon convention attempted to obviate known obstacles to a permanent settlement of

---

15. Palmerston to Clarendon, December 31, 1857, *ibid,* p. 500.
16. Mem., Earl of Clarendon, ca. August 1, 1854, *ibid,* pp. 496-497.

the Mosquito problem. If it had restricted itself solely to this issue, the treaty certainly would have been ratified.

But the negotiators also included the Belize and Bay Islands questions. With regard to Belize, the United States acknowledged British rights to areas effectively occupied in the nineteenth century — a significant concession which permitted the English to retreat on other matters. And finally, the Bay Islands were declared a "Free Territory" under Honduran sovereignty.[17] This proved to be the stumbling block, for the American Senate insisted upon an amendment making the islands integral parts of Honduras. Due to pride or what have you, the British would not accept this; and so ratifications were not exchanged. In late 1857, the two powers again tried to reach an agreement by sponsoring the mission of Sir William Ouseley to Central America. It also failed.[18]

Undoubtedly, Frederick Chatfield must have breathed a sigh of relief upon learning of these failures. But the situation changed in 1859, thanks to Great Britain's determination. In that year, England reached a territorial settlement with Guatemala concerning Belize — a project which Chatfield had favored and encouraged for many years, it will be recalled. But England also signed other treaties in 1859 and 1860, which were less pleasing to Mr. Chatfield for obvious reasons. By those treaties, she returned the Bay Islands to Honduras and implemented the Webster-Crampton Agreement and the Dallas-Clarendon convention with regard to Mosquitia, to Nicaragua's satisfaction. A territorial settlement between Costa Rica and Nicaragua in 1858 completed the process by which Great Britain was able to withdraw gracefully from Central America.[19] This was a bitter pill for Mr. Chatfield to swallow, especially since the English negotiator of those treaties was Charles Lennox Wyke, later Sir Charles.

—•—

The old veteran moved to Brighton in Sussex County "to pass the winter of his days" and from number three Belgrave Terrace he probably spent many hours watching the waves break upon the shore. On September 30, 1872, the grim reaper surprised the beloved and respected benefactor of Brighton. Upon learning of his demise, the Town Council officially and regretfully noted his death. It acknowledged its gratitude to the deceased for the "handsome Obelisk and Fountain in front of St. Peter's Church" which he had donated to the town. Somewat incon-

---

17. Dallas-Clarendon convention, October 17, 1856, MTUSA, V, 792-798.
18. Mary Williams, *Anglo-American Diplomacy*, pp. 228-240.
19. *Ibid.*, pp. 260-269; MTUSA, V, 801. For an excellent account of the Anglo-Guatemalan Treaty of 1859 and its consequences, see Wayne M. Clegern, "New Light on the Belize Dispute," *The American Journal of International Law*, Vol. 52 (April, 1958), pp. 280-297.

gruous in its modern setting, the monument still stands there today. In speaking to the motion of regret, Alderman Brigden characterized "Mr. Chatfield as the Peabody of Brighton." He had liberally supported "the County Hospital, Dispensary, Eye Infirmary, and other local institutions, and he interested himself warmly in the Society for the Prevention of Cruelty to Animals, the objects of which were not a little assisted by the erection of a Fountain already referred to." "In many other ways," the Brighton *Herald* reported, "he was a great benefactor to the town, making, through his friend and medical attendant, our excellent Mayor, many donations of most valuable books, paintings, and other works of art, to the Free Library and Public Museum."[20] Among the institutions which he remembered in his last will and testament was the Extra-Mural Cemetery, where he lies buried on one of Brighton's gentle slopes, surrounded by luxuriant vegetation and tall, shady trees. May he rest in peace.

A controversial figure throughout his lifetime, forgotten today by his own countrymen, Frederick Chatfield was one of England's most devoted servants. He worked indefatigably to further what he conceived to be her best interests. Perhaps, as the London *Times* once noted, he was a "misguided" patriot. In trying periods of his career, to be sure, he had made many mistakes; he had overstepped; and he had become spiteful, "a wicked meddler" and a "monomaniac of the worst type," — the verdict of his French colleague. Squier knew him during one of those troubled periods and had also referred to him as "a man of small calibre; easily excited, and more by little than great things."[21] An equally distorted picture emerges from the statements of his allies and sycophants, who continually flattered his ego — no small one, as we have seen.

Whatever his faults — and there were many — Frederick Chatfield was not the mediocre British official which his enemies have pictured. Our value judgments of his objectives notwithstanding, it must be admitted that he was talented, imaginative, and hardworking. In another context, he might have been a successful political boss — not a politician, however — a business tycoon, a military leader, a newspaper editor, or even an historian; certainly during his diplomatic career he was all of these things at one time or another. Moreover, certain interesting conclusions have emerged from the study of his career. To begin with, it should be noted that in his day it was possible for a man in the field to mold and influence his country's policy toward a given area; that is why

20. Brighton *Herald,* October 5, 1872.
21. Ephraim George Squier to John M. Clayton, pvt., in Mary W. Williams, "Letters of E. George Squier to John M. Clayton, 1849–1850," *Hispanic American Historical Review,* Vol. 1 (November 1918), 427.

we have applied the adjective "Palmerstonian" to Frederick Chatfield. In the case of Central America at least — and there were flashes of this in his European service as well — the underling helped to fashion the "Old Pam" which history remembers. The techniques were varied; but step by step — and after some failures and disappointment — Chatfield did commit Lord Palmerston to an aggressive, imperialistic stand in Central America. Is it possible that other unknown agents elsewhere might have contributed to this same end? That is a question for students of British diplomatic history to consider. Another interesting observation was the role played by national pride, or the "point of honour," in the acceptance of the recommendations of Frederick Chatfield and Alexander Macdonald by the Foreign Office; and conversely, its part in the retreat from those same policies.

Moreover, there is no basis whatsoever to the frequent charge that Mr. Chatfield was largely responsible for the dissolution of the Central American Republic. On the contrary, he was a positive influence upon unionism — and therefore liberalism — during that government's existence. He recommended and supported financial reforms and contributed handsomely to the 1837 Tariff — measures which were essential to the life of the Republic.

It is true, however, that he aligned himself against unionism once the Republic had been dissolved. He feared that a "more perfect union" would embarrass Great Britain's territorial positions in Middle America. To prevent the reformation of the general government, he developed such doctrines, projects, or practices as the "sheet anchor," the "Guatemalan Confederation," and the use of claims for political purposes. The British Navy did the rest. Before 1848, or possibly as early as 1846, the Foreign Office was not aware of Chatfield's political maneuvers; and it therefore can be argued that England's intentions were not imperialistic in nature. Yet the fact remains that the British government was supporting an imperialistic policy in Central America from 1839 forward. Whether it knew it or not is beside the point. And for the later period, the evidence indicates that Lord Palmerston was not ignorant of Chatfield's motives. He supported him as far as he could considering the vocal opposition to his type of diplomacy in Great Britain.

And there is one final point that should be made. Because Frederick Chatfield worked against unionism from 1839 to 1852, it does not follow that he was the sole cause for the failure of the movement. There were other more basic factors involved; and though the British agent exploited them, he by no means created those factors. Unionism fared no better after Mr. Chatfield's retirement — a point which Central Americans should ponder carefully.

Although this study concentrates on the public career of Frederick Chatfield, I had hoped at one time to present a more rounded biography of him. Certain allusions and clues in the official correspondence suggested the possibility of finding personal papers in England which would throw light upon the protagonist's life during his non-career years. Undoubtedly, I thought, the Public Record Office in London was bound to contain a dossier on him for the year 1826, when he entered the foreign service. Given the exclusive nature of the Second Life Guards, their archives would certainly yield precious bits of biographical information, it seemed to me. And knowing that in 1872 Chatfield had died in Brighton, I fully expected to uncover important documentation there. Before his recall from Central America, moreover, Mr. Chatfield had written a brief sketch of his European career. It looked promising.

Yet, before visiting England in 1958, my optimism was tempered by what Sir Edward Hertslet had written in his *Recollections of the Old Foreign Office* (London, 1901). On pages 245-248, he observed that before 1852 no systematic records were kept of career personnel. Since then, the annual *Foreign Office List* had supplied pertinent official information about career men. It was planned initially, however, to include personal notes about each officer. In 1862, a special edition of the *Foreign Office List* did provide a brief biography of each man in the diplomatic service; but there were so many complaints by the agents themselves that it was decided to suppress the edition. According to Sir Hertslet, only half a dozen copies remained in circulation. Perhaps, I reasoned hopefully, the Foreign Office Library at Cornwall House might have one of those valuable books.

One disappointment after another plagued my search for biographical material — Mr. Chatfield was indeed unknown to his countrymen. As I had already suspected from reading Sir Hertslet's account, there was no dossier marking Chatfield's entry into the foreign service; the Life Guards' documentation was too fragmentary to be useful; I was denied permission to see the Census of 1871, which might have contained significant information about him; the Foreign Office Library did not own a copy of the suppressed 1862 edition, nor did the staff know anything about it; and the numerous volumes on genealogy and what have you in the Bloomsbury branch of the British Museum did not provide a single clue of importance. Thoroughly frustrated, I was also resentful toward the English people for having forgotten such a devoted servant to their country. Perhaps it was poetic justice after all, but this thought held only momentary solace for me.

Finally, and ever so faintly, Clio smiled upon her practitioner. In the newspaper collection of the British Museum at Colindale, I found a lengthy obituary in the Brighton *Herald*. The rest was a question of time as my faithful scouts — wife and daughter — obtained copies of wills, checked the Wimbledon Parish registers, and prepared the ground for my visit to the Brighton Public Museum and Library. It was there that I found the biographical information which has gone into this study — not an impressive amount, to be sure. There were no personal papers in Brighton, we learned; and the estate of Brighton's mayor, Chatfield's old friend who had inherited many of his belongings, had been disposed of at an auction. In short, we did not uncover any family archives in England. Considering Mr. Chatfield's penchant for documentation, it is difficult to imagine that they do not exist. Our protagonist's condition as a bachelor undoubtedly contributed to the failure.

All was not lost, however. The revelations concerning his European career were more than adequate compensation. Aided by the handy registers and indices in the Foreign Office Library, I noted the relevant documentation in the manuscript files for Prussia (F.O. 64), Russia (F.O. 65), and Germany (F.O. 30). The story that unfolded before my eyes was almost incredible. It gave me further insights into Chatfield's personality and especially into his relationship with Lord Palmerston, an unexpected discovery that confirmed a conclusion which I had arrived at after studying his Central American career. Frederick Chatfield was a Palmerstonian agent in every sense. My perseverance was rewarded.

———◆•◆———

Because of the nature of this work as well as of the state of Central American historiography for the first half of the nineteenth century, I chose to draw heavily from primary sources in evaluating Chatfield's public career. Thus secondary studies were used for the most part as guides. Moreover, a review of the literature indicated significant gaps in the history of that area which had to be explored and filled before I could assess Frederick Chatfield's role with any degree of accuracy. It may be of interest, therefore, to future scholars who may embark upon a similar research project to record here some observations concerning the documentary collections which I have perused in the past decade. A few remarks about the secondary literature may also be in order.

By far the leading depository of manuscripts for this study was the Public Record Office in London, an exemplary institution which is devoted not only to the preservation of documentation but also to the advance of scholarship. Without question, the P.R.O. houses one of the most complete and continuous bodies of materials on Central American history for the first half of the nineteenth century. Much of the credit for this should be attributed to Chatfield's interest in the accumulation of documentation — a direct consequence of his devotion to duty and involvement in Central American affairs. To prove this point, we have only to compare the volume and nature of his correspondence with that of his predecessors and successors. Moreover, a quick glance at the "Catalogue of British Official Archives in Central America," September 1, 1851, F.O. 15/72, folios 15-45, which was compiled by Frederick Chatfield and the legation staff in Guatemala City, should remove all doubts on this question. It outlines one of the most comprehensive collections of Central Americana in the world and the bulk of it can be found today in storage places which the P.R.O. supervises in London or its environs.

The general correspondence for Central America — Foreign Office 15 — consists of eighty-four volumes for the period of 1824–1854. Thanks to a special arrangement with the Bancroft Library in Berkeley, California, microfilm copies of those volumes and others in the series are available to American institutions. The universities of Tulane and Yale, for example, have already purchased copies of the film. The F.O. 15 series contains the original dispatches written by agents in Central America to the Foreign Office. Equally important, from the standpoint of the area's political history, are the enclosures. Oftentimes, these include original letters though for the most part they are copies or extracts of the original which the agent referred to in the covering dispatch. They consist at times of an entire newspaper issue, selections or editorials from newspapers, broadsides, pamphlets, or sundry publications which are followed usually by a translation of the whole or a key section. From random checks. I found the translations to be reliable. In Chatfield's particular case, and considering his political inclinations, the investigator must be careful not to accept his statements literally; a check in other sources is indispensable. Moreover, he should not assume that Chatfield correctly evaluated the enclosures — a mistake often made by his superiors which, it will be recalled, permitted him to formulate policy indirectly. As pointed out in the text of this study, the untranslated portions of the enclosures frequently contain valuable political clues.

The general series also includes the correspondence of the Foreign Office with other governmental departments in London and with its Central American representative. Since the dispatches are in draft form, they often reveal, in the scratched-out portions and in the various notes by Palmerston, the real sense of the final statement and the alternatives which the Foreign office had considered. The originals (in F. O. 252), on the other hand, have a set terminology. In addition, the F.O. 15 files contain letters from the Colonial Office, Admiralty, and other branches of government which are accompanied by blocks of enclosed correspondence on a subject of mutual interest. Many of these enclosures duplicate those sent to the Foreign Office by Chatfield, though this was not always the case. For example, the Admiralty's documentation on the Tigre Island episode had some interesting details which Mr. Chatfield chose not to reveal in his account.

The F.O. 252 (Central American Consulate) series, which consists of seventy-four volumes, and the F.O. 254 files, comprising twelve volumes, are valuable supplements and checks upon the general correspondence. Cited in the above-mentioned "Catalogue," these documents at one time were part of the British archives in Central America. They were subsequently transferred to London. The F.O. 252 series, moreover, contains the original F.O. dispatches to Central America as well as Chatfield's correspondence with all governments of Central America, informants in the area and throughout the Western Hemisphere, and British officials of all types. The enclosures are valuable. For the political history of Central America up to 1848, the F.O. 254 materials are indispensable. They provide, for example, governmental decrees and publications of all sorts which cannot be found elsewhere in the world; they were especially helpful in determining the drift of political developments in Central America.

There were other categories of materials in the Public Record Office which proved to be useful for special periods or phases of the Chatfield story. Boxes 7 to 10 in the papers of Lord John Russell (P.R.O. 30/22) threw some light on the *Prometheus* incident. In addition to the files mentioned above for Prussia, Russia, and Germany, I consulted pertinent volumes in F.O. 5 (America, United States), F.O. 10 (Belgium), F.O. 63 (Mosquitia), F.O. 83 (Great Britain, Miscellaneous), and F.O. 97 (Guatemala) which contained volumes 88 and 90, the first on the affairs of Central America and Mosquito, 1844–1851, and the second concerning Sir William G. Ouseley's mission to Central America in 1857. Incidentally, volumes ten to twelve in F.O. 254 also deal with that mission.

Except for the newspaper collection at Colindale, which helped me to survey English public opinion on the *Prometheus* affair, the British Museum in London did not contribute much to this study. Contrary to expectations, the Colindale holdings of Central American newspapers for the first half of the nineteenth century were not impressive; most of the papers deal with a later period. I did utilize, however, the *Colonial Gazette* and a few issues of the *Belize Advertiser,* which are also on microfilm at the Bancroft. Perhaps some day an enterprising bibliophile might like to solve the problem of the missing newspapers, those cited in Chatfield's "Catalogue" of 1851. I was unable to locate them in England.

On the Continent, the documentation in Belgian and French repositories not only complemented the materials found in England but also served as valuable checks upon Chatfield's presentation of Central American developments. At the Ministère des Affaires Étrangères et du Commerce Extérieur in Brussels, I perused fifteen bundles of records (Nos. 2207 and 3393 Bis) on the Belgian Colonization Company at Santo Tomás for the years 1831–1855. I concentrated primarily on political analyses. Moreover, there were two volumes of "Correspondance Politique: Consulats" for 1841–1850 and 1851–1860, and a single volume "Correspondance Politique: Série Générale, Amèrique Centrale" which covered the years 1823–1861. All in all, it was a profitable experience; Martial Cloquet's reports and enclosures were particularly helpful in evaluating the political scene.

In Paris, the Archives des Affaires Étrangères yielded additional materials of a political nature. The "Correspondance Politique: Amèrique Centrale" comprised fourteen volumes, averaging about three hundred folios apiece and spanning the years 1823–1854. The observations of Auguste Mahelin and the enclosures which he sent to the Ministry of Foreign Affairs during the secessionist crisis were especially useful for this study. And yet it should be noted that not all of his letters are included, raising the question whether they have been misplaced or ever reached Paris at all. In addition, there are four thick volumes of "Correspondance Consulaire et Commerciale: Guatemala" which are mainly political in orientation, despite the series' heading. French agents, it will be recalled, were generally hostile to Frederick Chatfield, and allowance must therefore be made for this. Their criticisms were often sent in code which was later deciphered in Paris. Although the volume was less than expected, the quality of the documentation more than compensated for it.

At the Biblioteque Nationale in Paris there were a few choice items in the P. Angrand Collection. These included issues of *El Siglo* (San Salvador) for the period July-December 1852, which complemented the Bancroft holdings of that paper; notes by Colonel John Galindo for the years 1831–1838; and the publications *Nobles de Guatemala,* Felipe Molina's *Bosquejo de Costa Rica,* and *Guía de Forasteros de Guatemala para el año 1853* by J. H. Taracena.

It may appear strange that a study dealing with Central American history should rely so heavily upon depositories outside of the area. An important reason for this, of course, was the anarchy of the period in question, contributing to the wide dispersal of the documentation. Moreover, the disastrous fire of 1889 in San Salvador virtually destroyed the archives of the Central American Republic; and then there were other catastrophes such as the Nicaraguan fire and earthquake of 1931 which further diminished the volume of available documentation — a tale of woe which is well known to scholars of Central American history. With few exceptions — they will be noted shortly — the material has been widely scattered; undoubtedly much of it has fallen into the hands of private individuals or has been sold to foreign institutions. The process of gaining access to private collections, as might be expected, is time consuming and strewn with obstacles of all sorts. Fortunately, I was allowed to use the documents in the private collection of Señor Arturo Taracena of Guatemala City. His holdings are particularly valuable since he is a descendant of Governor Marcelo Molina of Los Altos. Thanks to him, moreover, I acquired the picture of Frederick Chatfield which appears in this volume.

In Guatemala City, I was able to consult key bundles of documents, or *legajos,* in the Archivo General de la Nación, also called the Archivo General del Gobierno. They deal with the period before the transfer of the federal capital to San Salvador and also with the subsequent correspondence between Guatemala and the Republic. Especially useful were the series entitled "Correspondencia de la Legación de Centro-América," concerning Marcial Zebadúa's mission to England, "Correspondencia del Ministerio de Relaciones Exteriores," and "Comisión de Ministros." Furthermore, I made use of five volumes of newspapers in the archives: two on *El Tiempo* (Guatemala City) for the period March 9, 1839, to January 30, 1841, or issues 1-156 with the exception of Nos. 76-100 which are in the Biblioteca Nacional. *El Libro Verde,* bearing the volume numbers 22-24, contains a variety of newspapers for the years 1830–1847. To be sure, there were many more documents in the Guatemalan archives which I might have consulted, but for one reason or another this was not possible.

For my purposes, the Biblioteca Nacional in Guatemala City constituted the second most important repository of materials for the reconstruction of political life in the first half of the nineteenth century, thanks to the extensive Gilberto Valenzuela Collection. Under "Periódicos Varios," bundles 835 to 845, I found a wide assortment of newspapers which spanned the entire period. Complementing these holdings were the annual *legajos* — occasionally they included more than one year per bundle — of *Hojas Sueltas* (broadsides) and *Folletos* (pamphlets). Finally, there were also separate volumes of *Impresos Guatemaltecos* for the period since 1831. No one, in short, can pretend to write Central American history during that era without consulting this priceless collection. Unfortunately, time and insects have left their telltale marks on the documents.

In the United States, there are also key depositories of Central Americana. The National Archives in Washington, of course, house the pertinent diplomatic documentation which, for various reasons, I did not have time to consult nor did I consider it necessary for my purposes. The Library of Congress has an extensive collection of works on Central America and its Manuscript Division possesses a few documents of importance, especially letters by Pedro Molina. Certain universities in the United States have varying amounts of relevant documentation: the Wagner Collection at Yale University, despite its heavy emphasis upon Mexico, contains a few items on Central America; the University of Texas Library at Austin and the Tulane Library in New Orleans possess substantial holdings. The latter institution is especially renowned for its sustained interest in Central American scholarship.

By far the best collection of Central Americana in the United States is in the Bancroft Library of the University of California at Berkeley. In addition to the microfilm series from the Public Record Office, the Bancroft has five volumes of "Central American Miscellaneous Newspapers" which cover the years 1849 to 1855. These include such papers as: the *Gaceta de Guatemala* (Guatemala City); the *Packet Intelligencer* (Belize); *La Crónica* (New York); the Salvadorean newspapers *El Siglo* (San Salvador), *El Rol* (San Vicente), *El Progreso* (San Salvador), *Gaceta del Salvador en la República de Centro-América* (San Salvador), and *La Unión* (San Salvador); the Honduran papers *Gaceta Oficial del Gobierno de Honduras* (Comayagua), and *Gaceta Oficial de Honduras en Centro-América* (Comayagua); the Nicaraguan newspapers *Correo del Istmo de Nicaragua* (León), *Gaceta Oficial de Nicaragua* (Granada), *El Nicaragüense* (Granada), and *Integridad* (Granada); and the following newspapers from Costa Rica: *Boletín Oficial* (San José), *La Gaceta del Gobierno de Costa Rica* (San José), *Album Semanal* (San José), and *El Costaricense* (San José).

Moreover, the Bancroft owns a compilation of "Central American Pamphlets," which comprises nine volumes of indispensable publications for the study of the unionist movement in the late 1840's and early 1850's. Also, there are separate volumes and sets under the following titles: "Guatemala Miscellany, Documents and other Political Material, 1809, 1823–1838" (72 pieces in portfolio), "Central American Miscellaneous Documents" (April, 1849, to June, 1850), "Documents Relating to the Political History of Central America, 1829–1846" (3 vols. in one), and

"Central American Constitutions." Most of these materials, incidentally, came originally from the Squier Collection.

———◆◆———

Though not overwhelming in volume, the printed documentation adequately supplemented the manuscript materials. For British diplomatic documents, the following were useful: Charles K. Webster, ed., *Britain and the Independence of Latin America, 1812–1830* (2 vols., London, 1938); Robert A Humphreys, ed., *British Consular Reports on the Trade and Politics of Latin America, 1824–1826* (London, 1940); *Correspondence with the United States Respecting Central America* (London, 1856–1860), usually referred to as the *Blue Book, 1856;* and the extensive *British and Foreign State Papers* for the years in question. It should be noted, however, that whenever it was possible to consult the original manuscript I preferred it to the printed version, especially on key issues.

As for the American documentation, the following sets and volumes were consulted: *Central America in Congress* (Washington, 1853); *Documents Relative to Central American Affairs . . .* (Washington, 1856); William Ray Manning, ed., *Diplomatic Correspondence of the United States Concerning the Independence of the Latin American Nations* (3 vols., New York, 1925) and his *Diplomatic Correspondence of the United States: Inter-American Affairs, 1831–1860* (12 vols., Washington, 1932–1939); David Hunter Miller, ed., *Treaties and Other International Acts of the United States of America, 1776–1863* (8 vols., Washington, 1931–1948); and Robert N. Burr and Roland D. Hussey, *Documents on Inter-American Cooperation* (2 vols., Philadelphia, 1955). The standard guide for American materials — manuscript and printed — is still Samuel F. Bemis and G. G. Griffin, eds., *Guide to the Diplomatic History of the United States, 1775–1921* (Washington, 1935).

A second category of printed materials on Central America was the travel accounts and publications of foreigners. The works listed below contain pertinent economic, social, and political observations on the Central American scene: George Alexander Thompson, *Narrative of an Official Visit to Guatemala* (London, 1829), which can be found in manuscript form in volumes 1-3 of F.O. 15; James Wilson, *A Brief Memoir of the Life of James Wilson* (London, 1829); Orlando W. Roberts, *Narrative . . . of Central America* (Edinburgh, 1827); Henry Dunn, *Guatimala . . . in 1827–28* (London, 1829); J. Haefkens, *Reise naar Guatemala in 1829* (Dordrecht, 1852); George W. Montgomery, *Narrative of a Journey to Guatemala . . . in 1838* (New York, 1839); Thomas Young, *Narrative of a Residence on the Mosquito Shore . . . 1839, 1840, and 1841* (London, 1842); John Lloyd Stephens, *Incidents of Travel in Central America* . . . (2 vols., New York, 1841); James J. Jarves, *Scenes and Scenery* . . . *1837–1842* (London, 1844); Robert Glasgow Dunlop (pseudonym for Robert Wallace), *Travels in Central America* (London, 1847); Frederick Crowe, *The Gospel in Central America* (London, 1850); Arthur Morelet, *Travels in Central America* (New York, 1871); Julius Froebel, *Seven Years' Travel in Central America* (London), 1859); John Baily, *Central America* (London, 1850); Víctor Herrán, *Notice sur les cinq états du Centre-Amèrique* (Bordeaux, 1853); Manuel Ortiz Urruela, *La Inglaterra y los Estados-Unidos en Centro-América* (Paris 1856); Carl Scherzer, *Travels* . . . *Central America* (2 vols., London, 1857); and such works by Ephraim George Squier as *Nicaragua* (2 vols., New York, 1852), *Travels in Central America* (2 vols., New York, 1853), and *Notes on Central America* (New York, 1855).

Despite their partisanship, the writings and autobiographies of prominent Central American figures are important sources of information in reconstructing the thought and political events of that period. Among these are the works of José Cecilio del Valle, Manuel José Arce, José Matías Delgado, Francisco Morazán, Manuel Montúfar y Coronado, Pedro Molina, and Miguel García Granados. Many of these sets are available in different editions. To this list we should add the historical contributions of Alejandro Marure, in particular his *Bosquejo histórico* (1st ed., 2 vols., Guatemala City, 1837); of Lorenzo Montúfar, whose monumental *Reseña histórica de Centro América* (7 vols., Guatemala City, 1878–1888) is primarily a documentary source; and of Hubert Howe Bancroft since he drew heavily from contemporary documentation for his three-volume *History of Central America* (San Francisco, 1882–1887). These are all basic references for the nineteenth-century history of Central America.

⬤

With some justification — it must be admitted — and because his enemies were articulate unionist liberals and their North American allies, the bulk of the primary documentation paints an uncomplimentary picture of Frederick Chatfield. To his enemies, the British agent was the prime mover of the Republic's dissolution, the fomenter of disunion, and the instrument of British imperialism. The works of Marure, Squier, Bancroft, and Montúfar have perpetuated this stereotype and thus have influenced the studies of later historians in both Central America and the United States. With the passage of time, moreover, further distortions have occurred in the story of diplomatic rivalry. The role of the individual — Chatfield's, for example — and the Central American political and ideological context have been obscured. The charge of imperialism, moreover, has been placed at the doorstep of the British Foreign Office along with the uncritical deduction that Great Britain had deliberately pursued an imperialistic policy since the beginning of Central American independence. That is the interpretation which emerges from the two pioneer studies of Ira D. Travis, *British Rule in Central America or a Sketch of the Mosquito Territory* and *The History of the Clayton-Bulwer Treaty* (Ann Arbor, 1895 and 1900). In her work *Anglo-American Isthmian Diplomacy, 1815–1915* (Washington and London, 1916), Mary W. Williams sketched the same exaggerated picture of British imperialism in Central America.

Some critics have maintained that the above-mentioned works erred because their authors relied too heavily on prejudiced Central American accounts of the nineteenth century. My own opinion, however, is not that they put too much credence in Central American documentation but rather in the compilation of documents by the English and American governments — the *Blue Book, 1856,* is a case in point. Professor Williams, moreover, preferred to use survey, or synthetic, documents from the Foreign Office, perhaps an understandable choice considering the scope of her work. That is not to say, of course, that those documentary sources are worthless; on the contrary, they are extremely valuable if used with caution. Their weakness lies, however, in their lack of depth; they tend to obscure the role of the individual as well as the Central American context. They contribute, moreover, to the unsound conclusion that England must have had imperialistic designs upon Central America since independence. In short, what is involved here is the danger or temptation, which historians face continually, of inferring too much from the effects, or consequences.

In a series of articles written in the 1930's, Professor Richard Van Alstyne viewed British diplomatic relations in Central America from 1846 to 1860 in a more objective light. He qualified and challenged the former imputations of British imperialism, while at the same time demonstrating an appreciation for Chatfield's part in the story. But he approached the problem from the European angle. Perhaps because he was not a Latin Americanist, he chose not to investigate further Chatfield's involvement in Central American politics and thus was unaware of that agent's techniques in formulating British policy. If he had done so, there would have been less need for the present study.

More recently, in *Failure of Union: Central America, 1824–1960* (Chapel-Hill, 1961), Professor Thomas Karnes has evaluated the charges against Frederick Chatfield and his country in a chapter entitled "Great Britain and the Federation." He emphatically denies, and justly so, that

Chatfield contributed to the dissolution of the Republic. But then he also concludes that the British agent was not a fomenter of disunion in the subsequent period. The documentary base for the latter conclusion, however, is far from impressive. Professor Robert A. Naylor arrived at essentially the same conclusions in his article "The British Role in Central America Prior to the Clayton-Bulwer Treaty of 1850," *Hispanic American Historical Review,* Vol. XL (August, 1960), pp. 361-382. In his opinion, British policy and actions in Central America were not guided by political or strategic considerations but rather by the commercial interests of Englishmen in the area. Challenging this thesis of "commercial determinism," Professor Mark Van Aken reproduced some convincing documents from the F.O. 15 files in his brief article "British Policy Considerations in Central America before 1850," *Hispanic American Historical Review,* Vol. XLII (February, 1962), pp. 54-59. And so the controversy rages. My own position has already been stated in detail: the charge of British imperialism in Central America has to be qualified according to time and circumstance.

Controversy also characterizes the literature dealing with the internal struggle for power in Central America. If we recall the ideological issues which underlay that bitter conflict, this should come as no surprise. In a masterly survey "The Historiography of Central America Since 1830," *Hispanic American Historical Review,* Vol. XL (November, 1960), pp. 548–569, Professor William J. Griffith has analyzed this highly partisan literature which still casts a shadow upon modern historical writings. The pro-liberal works of Marure, Bancroft, and Montúfar set the pattern for the present century and, according to Professor Griffith, gave the liberals a victory in the historiographical realm which they were denied in the political arena. To be sure, the sheer volume of emotional and uncritical literature concerning the liberal greats of Central American history supports this generalization.

Yet a qualification is in order if we take into account the serious studies on the Central American Republic. Despite the eulogy lavished upon Francisco Morazán and others, it should be noted that even sympathetic unionist writers like Alberto Herrarte — only one of many — have accepted a defeatist view of the Republic. Undoubtedly they have been influenced by the knowledge of the Republic's failure. In accepting defeatist assumptions, however, they have in effect precluded, or abandoned, any further research on the secessionist crisis. As a result, and almost by default, the conservative interpretation has gained headway. A case in point is Pedro Joaquín Chamorro's *Historia de la Federación de la América Central, 1823–1840* (Madrid, 1951), which is considered one of the most thorough analyses of the Republic. His arguments and facts bear a striking similarity to the propaganda circulated by the conservatives during the secessionist crisis — the power-mad and unprincipled *Morazanistas,* etc. Another recent example is Chamorro's biography of his progenitor, *Fruto Chamorro* (Managua, 1960), which likewise colors the events of the 1840's and early 1850's with a conservative brush and bias. In short, it is my contention that the liberal followers of Marure, Bancroft, and Montúfar have not completely dominated the historiographical scene. Be that as it may, the controversy underscores the necessity of returning to the original documents for a more accurate evaluation of that key period in the establishment of Central American nationhood. Fortunately, a new group of scholars in Central America and elsewhere are now beginning to approach the subject with greater objectivity.

Aix la Chapelle, riots at: 10
Alvarez, Miguel: 85, 116, 202; debates territorial question with Chatfield: 133-35; corresponds with Chatfield about Ruatán: 192-94
"American system": 56, 131
Anderson, Young: 162, 163
Anglophobia: 59, 102-103, 130-31, 189, 224, 247, 316-17
Antwerp: 48
Arce, Manuel José: 59
Arriaga, Pedro N.: 255, 300
Atlantic and Pacific Ship Canal Company: 302, 327-28, 330, 342
Auguste, Prince of Prussia: 9
Aycinena, Juan José: 156, 158, 262
Azmitia, José Antonio: 269-71, 273, 278, 290

Barrios, Gerardo: 211, 212
Barrundia, Francisco: 80, 98, 138, 139, 141, 198
Batres, Luis: 206, 274, 275
Bay Islands: 125; made British colony: 319; see also Ruatán
Belize: 53, 54-55, 57; and Central American trade: 60-62; blamed for Anglophobia, 1835: 102-103; turns down Chatfield tariff proposals: 102-103, 109-110; Macdonald becomes superintendent: 128; territorial settlement: 364; see also British Honduras
Belgium: 47; uprisings in, 1830: 9, 11
Belgian Colonization Company: 352-54
Bennett, Marshall: 73-74, 79, 92, 126-27, 162, 174, 261; gets rights in Guatemala territory: 75; gets grant in Honduras: 75-76; San Jerónimo claims: 172, 195-96, 216
Beschor, Louis: 317, 318
Bidlack, Benjamin: 285
Bidwell, John: 1, 16

Blockades of Central America: 251-52, 254, 256, 258, 297, 308
Boca del Toro: 125
Booth, Charles: 300
British policy, change in: 324, 355; final withdrawal from former Central American position effected: 363-64; see also Central America; Chatfield, Frederick; Palmerston
British Honduras: 53, 54-55, 57; border question: 70; British position on: 72; see also Belize
Buitrago, Pablo: 289, 291, 307, 346
Bulwer, Henry L.: 323, 335, 345; see also Clayton-Bulwer Treaty
Bustillos, José: 228

Canal see Nicaraguan canal
Canning, Stratford: 29, 47
Carrera, Rafael: 138, 141, 214, 292; attacks Guatemala City: 141-142; defeated by Morazán: 142, 160; pillages Santa Ana: 171; agreement with Guzmán: 175; invades Guatemala City second time: 178; overcomes Los Altos: 222; defeats Morazán: 229-30; replaces Rivera Paz government in Guatemala: 248-49; influenced against liberals by Chatfield: 269-71; regime briefly upset by liberals: 295-96; moves against El Salvador and topples Vasconcelos government: 344
Carrillo, Braulio: 161, 165, 247, 250
Castellón, Francisco: 265, 267, 289, 296
Castro, Juan José: 309
Central America, change in British policy towards: 324, 355; withdrawal of British from Palmerstonian policies: 363-64
Central American Federation: 57, 66, 67; unrest in, 1834: 67; fails to legislate against British in Belize:

96-97; finances, and Chatfield's
proposed reforms: 114-18; disruptive
forces: 137-38; financial reform as
cause of disintegration: 149-50;
forces behind failure of: 151-56;
constitutional weakness: 152; growing
power of states: 154-55;
congressional attempts to avoid
breakup: 157-61; Morazán resigns
presidency: 176; plans for reviving at
Sonsonate meeting: 272-273;
Sonsonate meet fails: 273, 276;
Pact of Nacome clears way for
revival: 292; *see also* Unionists
Chad (English minister): 29, 31
Chalmers-Guthrie Company: 348-50
Charlotte Louise, Empress of Russia:
3, 4
Chatfield, Allen (father): 5
Chatfield, Frederick: 15; birth and
education: 6; brothers: 6
European career: disappointment with
post at Meml: 1-2; consulship at
Meml: 3-4; sends intelligence on
Belgian uprising: 10-13; policy on
Belgium: 13-15; argues with Foreign
Office on pay: 8, 17, 18-19, 27, 40;
instructed to write directly to
Palmerston: 21; increasing sympathy
for Poland: 24; increasing dislike for
Russia: 25-26; appointed consul to
Warsaw: 27, 28-29; arrives in
Warsaw: 32; early days in
Warsaw: 34-36; formulates anti-
Russian policy: 36-41; Nesselrode
demands recall: 41; recalled from
Warsaw: 42; final interview with
Paskevich in Warsaw: 44-46; first
meeting with Palmerston: 47-48;
goes on reconnaissance to Prussia:
48-51
*Alliance with Central American
Federation:* appointed consul to
Central America: 51-52; studies
Central American situation: 53;
arrives in Belize: 66; arrives in
Guatemala: 67; opens treaty negotia-
tions with Zebadúa: 68-70, 71;
meets Morazán: 71-72; formulates
Doctrine of Mutuality: 72-73,

103-104; aids liberals in interest of
British: 85-86, 112, 117; arrives in
San Salvador to observe federal
congress: 89; turns against Galvez:
90-91, 92, 93; formulates program
of reciprocal annoyance: 91; moves
to force reopening of treaty
negotiation: 93; gains objectives in
federal congress, 1835: 96-97;
instructed to abandon negotiations:
101; returns to Guatemala: 102;
blames Belize for anglophobia:
102-103; recommends tariff program
to Belize: 104; tariff proposals turned
down by Belize: 109; British reaction
to program, 1836: 110; proposes
Central American financial reforms:
113-19; ambushed by Indians:
123-24; feud with Macdonald, origins
of: 128-30; debates territorial
question with Alvarez: 133-35; seeks
Macdonald in Dearing affair: 145-47;
aid of British navy: 143; opposes
acts to protect British interests in
secession crisis: 161-63; suggests
British aid to federal government:
165-66; pro-union stand, reasons for:
167-71, 175; begins to shift position
on Central American Federation:
171-74, 189; proposes loan to federal
government: 172, 175; breaks with
federal government: 178; prepares
Palmerston for changing allegiance:
191
Period of imperialist policies to 1840:
attitude toward Central American
states after break with unionists:
189-92; recommends direct intervention: 192, 208; corresponds with
Alvarez on Ruatán: 192-94; builds
alliance with *serviles:* 194-200; takes
offensive against Los Altos and
Salvador: 200-201; goes to
Nicaragua: 205; activity in
Nicaragua: 207; and jailing of
William Kilgour: 211-13; increasing
feeling against Chatfield: 213; anti-
unionist strategy: 214; exploits
British claims: 216-18 *see also*
Claims; maneuvers against Los Altos:

218-224; defends actions in Guatemala: 231-32; friction with Carrera: 233-34; returns to England on leave: 234, 235-37

Period of imperialist policies, 1842–1852: returns to Central America as Consul-General: 250; restores alliance with *serviles:* 253; proposes "Guatemalan Confederation": 254, 262-63, 274, 278; influences Carrera against liberals: 269-71; justifies events leading to collapse of Los Altos: 273-74; works against success of Sonsonate meeting for federation: 276-77; proposes plan for control of Pacific coast: 282-85; fears U.S. intervention, urges strong measures: 293-94; decides on occupation of Tigre: 301; organizes anti-American propaganda: 312-14; consolidates control of San Juan: 318; deals with worsening relations in Honduras and Salvador: 321-23; proposes English-American superintendency in Central America: 345; role of economic interests in recall: 348-50

Recall and last days: recalled from Central America: 336, 351; works for continuation of Central American policies: 351-52; continues efforts to influence Central American policy: 353-55; reports on Mayan ruins: 361; last days in Brighton, death: 364
Chatfield, Mary (mother): 5-6
Chatfield family: 5-6
Chinandega Pact: 253, 261-62
Chiquimula: 75
Chlapowski (Polish general): 23, 24
Cholera in Central America: 121-23
Cholera in Europe: 20-21, 22
Claims: 64; origin of: 114-15; Chatfield proposals for liquidation: 117; Chatfield holds states responsible: 172; San Jerónimo claims: 172, 195-96, 216; Chatfield's use of for political purposes: 216-18, 263, 284, 304-5; and Mosquito Shore protectorate: 244-45; settlement forced by blockade: 251-52, 256, 258; Chatfield

forces issue in Nicaragua and Salvador: 258-59; Chatfield proposes taking islands as liens for: 297
Clark, Francis J.: 293
Clayton, John M.: 339 *see also* Clayton-Bulwer Treaty
Clayton-Bulwer Treaty: 311, 323, 324-25
Cockburn, Francis: 66, 76, 78, 91-92
Colombia *see* New Granada
Confederation of Central America: 267
Conservatives *see* Serviles
Convention of Santa Ana *see* Santa Ana Convention
Costa Rica and "Mosquito Question": 127; secedes from Central American Federation: 160; treaties of alliance, attitude towards; 183; Morazán overthrows Carrillo: 250; revolution overthrows Castro: 309; conservatives recapture government: 310; signs treaty with Britain: 310
Crampton, John F.: 332-336

Dearing, James: 145-47
Debts *see* Claims
Declaration of Managua: 307
de la Tijera, José: 257
Doctrine of Mutuality: 72-73, 103-104
Durán, Jauquín: 255
Durham mission: 42, 47

Eastern Company: 84, 116, 132, 162-63; gets extensive rights in Guatemala: 75; gets grants in Petén: 77
Effective occupation: 55, 56, 57
Electra (ship): 200
El Salvador, invasion of: 175, 177, 181-82; attitudes towards treaties of alliance: 183; Treaty of Quetzaltenango with Los Altos: 185, 200-201, 203-204; invaded by Ferrera: 187-88; forces under Morazán defeated by Guatemala: 229-30; British blockade: 297-98; agreement on claims after blockade: 308-309; rejects claims settlement: 312; reaches agreement with Chatfield: 348
Escobar, Bernardo: 111

Fead, William F.: 329, 330
Federation of Central America *see*
Central American Federation
Ferrera, Francisco: 161, 181, 187-88,
204, 263
Flores, Juan José: 309, 346
Fonblanque, Thomas: 27
Forced loans doctrine: 135-36, 139-40,
164
Foreign debt *see* Claims
Foster, John: 149, 205, 206, 289, 346
Frederick, Robert Charles: 239, 243,
244
French influence: 64, 65, 164, 292
see also Mahelin, Auguste
French treaty fails: 165
Fugitive slave issue: 59

Galindo, John: 71, 77, 79, 101, 116,
143-44; gets grant in Petén: 77;
opposes Chatfield, proposes mission
to Europe: 81-82; sent to U. S. and
Europe: 85, 106-107; failure of
mission: 111; occupies Boca del
Toro, reopens Mosquito question:
125; denounces English aggression:
130; opposes Chatfield in James
Dearing affair: 145-47; death: 244
Galvez, Mariano: 66, 73, 80, 95, 112,
138; campaign for governorship of
Guatemala: 82; wins, loses federal
election: 90; recommends strong
anti-Belize program: 108-109
Geilgud (Polish general): 23, 24
Goméz, Ignacio: 294
Gould, Thomas: 74, 79
Green, James: 317, 318, 327, 342
Greytow *see* San Juan del Norte
Guatemala: 54; grants import rebate to
Spanish house: 79; anti-British
feeling rises: 82-83; Indian uprisings:
138-39; unrest in: 141; proposed split
into two states: 154; revolution of
1838: 160; secedes from federation:
178, 181; attitude towards treaties of
alliance: 183; Chatfield recognizes
sovereignty of: 194; agrees to meet
Chatfield's terms: 197-98; requests
British guarantee of peace: 199;
requests British intervention to

guarantee peace: 206; intercepts arms
for Los Altos: 215; invades, overcomes Los Altos: 222; proclaims
independence: 279; liberals briefly
upset Carrera government: 295-96;
negotiates with U. S.: 298-99;
"center" states prepare action against:
322-33; *see also* Galvez, Mariano;
Los Altos; Rivera Paz, Mariano
Guatemalan Confederation: 254, 255,
274, 278; failure of: 256-59
Guerrero, José: 292, 296
Gulf of Fonseca: 282, 283
Guzmán, Augustín: 175

Hall, William: 68, 139, 141, 142, 245
Herrera, Próspero: 64
Heytesbury, William A.: 29, 31, 33
Hise, Elijah: 294, 298-300
Hise-Selva Convention: 300
Holdship, George C.: 162, 168
Honduras, grants land to Bennett:
75-76; and "Mosquito Question":
127; secedes from Central American
Federation: 160; attitude towards
treaties of alliance: 183; negotiates
treaty with U. S.: 300, 302; *see also*
Mosquito Shore; Tigre

Idígoras, Marcos: 276, 309
Import and export trade: 61-62
Irving, John: 64, 65

Jáuregui, Felipe: 174, 261, 304, 310,
312, 319

Kilgour, William: 211-212
Klee, Charles Rudolph: 78-79, 132,
140, 141

Land grants: 75-78
Lawrence, Abbott: 330-31, 335
Liberals: 67-68; first disillusionment
with British: 60; program and point
of view explained in 1835 pamphlet:
98-100; split among: 138; and
secession crisis: 155-156; upset
Carrera regime briefly: 295-96;
see also Unionists
Lindo, Juan: 292, 321

Livingston's code: 138
Loan to Central American Federation proposed: 172, 175
Loans, forced *see* Forced loans
Los Altos: 154, 161, 214, 295-96; secedes from Guatemala: 154; attitude towards treaties of alliance: 183; supports unionist policies: 184; Treaty of Quetzaltenango with Salvador: 185, 200-201, 203-204; threatened by Guatemala: 215; continues action for federal union: 220; invaded, conquered by Guatemala: 222

Macdonald, Alexander, and Mosquito protectorate: 128-29; issues ultimatum against interference with woodcutting: 129; and "Trujillo-Ruatán" Incident: 170; lands forces at San Juan de Nicaragua: 239-42
Mahelin, Auguste: 113, 124; instructs vice-consul not to represent British: 224-25
Manning, Thomas: 257, 260, 289, 292
Meany, Carlos Antonio: 74
Mejía, José Antonio: 162
Meml: 1
Miller, Thomas: 92, 107
Molina, Felipe: 221, 273, 345
Monroe Doctrine: 56
Mora, Joan Rafael: 310
Morazán, Francisco: 68, 71-72, 137, 158; elected president of Central American Federation: 90; and foreign debt: 117-19; steps down from presidency during debate on territorial question: 133; drives Carrera into mountains: 142, 160; resigns presidency: 176; defeats invaders of El Salvador: 181-82; elected governor of El Salvador: 184; defends El Salvador against Ferrera: 187-88; refuses to retract ratification of Treaty of Quetzaltenango: 204; prepares invasion of Guatemala: 225; invades Guatemala, is defeated: 229-30; overthrows Carrillo in Costa Rica: 250

Mosquito Shore: 54, 74, 125, 282; woodcutters expand into: 126-27; Macdonald's projected protectorate over: 128-29; Chatfield announces British protectorate over: 134; Palmerston rejects protectorate: 144; measures to establish protectorate: 232; Macdonald commission and Mosquito expedition: 242-44; British acceptance of protectorate policy: 245-46; boundaries announced by Foreign Office: 285, 286; British plan to occupy: 287; British-American negotiations, British withdrawal: 227-38, 339
"Mosquito Question": 126-27
Mutuality doctrine: 72-73, 103-104

New Granada: 285, 286
Nacome, pact of: 287
Navy, British, committed to Chatfield: 218; Electra appears off Nicaragua: 200; Blockades Central America: 251-52, 254, 256, 258, 264-65
Nicaragua, secession of: 149-50; attitude towards treaties of alliance: 183; asks British guarantee of peace: 207; government changes: 213; blockaded: 252, 264-65; blockaded second time, yields to Chatfield's demands: 265-66; attempts to block British occupation of San Juan: 287-90; declares Mosquito territory a department: 288; signs truce recognizing occupation: 291; negotiates treaty with U. S.: 300, 302; British land at Trujillo: 305; *see also* Mosquito Shore; San Juan del Norte
Nicaraguan canal: 236, 293, 325; contract awarded to U. S. company: 302
Nicholas I of Russia: 39
Nichols, Robert: 232, 233
Nuñez, José: 149, 161

O'Reilly, John : 107

Pacific coast, plans for control of: 281-85

Pact of Chinandega: 253-54, 261-62
Pact of Nacome: 287, 292
Padilla, Mariano: 273
Pais, Jerónimo: 269-71
Palmerston:14, 359-61; and Belgium:
    13, 15; Belgian and Russian policy:
    42; statement on recall of Chatfield
    from Warsaw: 42-43; first meeting
    with Chatfield: 47-48; reacts
    favorably to Galindo mission: 108;
    opposes force in Central American
    negotiations: 108; rejects
    Mosquito protectorate: 144;
    begins to favor Chatfield's point of
    view: 170-71; refuses direct
    intervention: 200; opens ways to
    imperialistic policy: 218; commits
    navy to Chatfield's use: 218;
    conversations during Chatfield's
    leave: 235-37; and occupation of
    San Juan: 287, 289-90; rejects
    Chatfield's use of islands as claims
    liens: 298; supports anti-liberal
    moves: 311; evacuates Tigre island:
    311-12; dismissed: 334; drafts
    apology for Prometheus affair: 335
Paskevich, Ivan: 20-21, 22-23, 33, 34,
    43-46
Pavón, Manuel Francisco: 255, 264,
    274, 275, 283, 305, 306, 352, 353
Penal code: 138
Petén: 77, 84, 105, 106, 134
Petén grant: 162
Poland, Russian policies in: 25, 33,
    37-39, 44-46; Russian behavior in:
    37-39
Polish uprisings: 15, 20, 23
Postal communications: 113
Prometheus-Express incident: 328-29,
    335-36
Prussian army: 49-50

Question of Honduras *see* British
    Honduras
Quijano, Manuel: 239-242, 244, 263;
    abduction of: 242, 247

Reid-Irving House: 64
Republic of Central America *see*
    Central American Federation

Rivera Paz, Mariano: 181, 194, 213,
    248-49
Ruatán: 54, 60; strategic importance:
    63; "Trujillo-Raután" incident: 170;
    British land, pull down flag: 179-80;
    Chatfield-Alvarez correspondence on:
    192-94
Russia and Poland: 25, 37-39, 44-46

Salazar, Carlos: 203
Salazar, José Gregorio: 68, 96
Salvador *see* El Salvador
San Juan de Nicaragua *see*
    San Juan del Norte
San Juan del Norte, British landing at:
    239-42; British determine to occupy:
    287; British-Mosquito forces occupy:
    291; reaction to occupation: 291-92;
    outbreak of Nicaraguan sailors at:
    317-18; Chatfield consolidates British
    control: 318; Chatfield tariff
    rescinded, declared free port: 326;
    municipal government established:
    327; negotiations for settlement:
    339-43; American bombardment of:
    362
Santa Ana Convention: 183-84;
    failure of: 185-88
Santo Tomás: 63, 76, 163, 320
Secession crisis, 1838–39: 151-56
Selva, Buenaventura: 300
Selva, Raimundo: 317
Serviles: 67, 154, 181, 182; Chatfield
    consolidates alliance with: 194-200
Skinner, George: 132, 195-97, 199
Slaves, emancipation of: 58-59
Squier, Ephriam George: 301, 302,
    303, 321, 314
States rights doctrine: 155, 156, 183;
    States rights triumphs over unionist
    efforts: 185-88; Chatfield recognized
    leader: 225; propaganda on
    Guatemala: 226

Tariffs: Belize places 5% on Central
    American goods: 59; Central
    America levies 5% on imports from
    Belize: 63; Guatemala grants rebate
    to Pacific traders: 82; British
    Honduras exacts new tax on wood:

97; Central America repeals rebates on exports: 101; Chatfield proposals on: 104; Central American tariffs: 109, 111, 112; Board of Trade rejects Belize wood tax: 110, 126; Central America drops 5% levy: 120; tariffs at San Juan: 318, 326

Taylor, Zachary: 311, 323

Tigre (island): 283, 297; occupied by British: 301, 303, 306; Honduras cedes temporarily to U. S.: 302; reaction to occupation: 306-307; Palmerston agrees to evacuate: 311, 314

Treaties: Chatfield negotiates commercial treaty with Central America: 53, 65, 69-70; cause of failure laid to Belize: 79; negotiations end: 133, states sign treaties of alliance before Santa Ana Convention: 183; commercial treaty with Guatemala proposed: 278, 280; U. S. signs treaties with Central American states: 298-300, 302; Costa Rica signs with Britain: 310; final settlements in Central America: 363-64; *see also* Clayton-Bulwer Treaty; Webster-Crampton Agreement

Treaty of Madrid: 55

Treaty of Quetzaltenango: 185, 200-201, 203-204

Trujillo, British landing at: 305

Unionists: 155; urge convention to reform central government: 182-84; failure of, 1839: 185-88; unionist propaganda: 226-28; movement gains impetus from Quijano affair: 247-50; gains momentum from Chatfield's claims action: 259; plan Sonsonate meet to reconstitute central government: 272, 273; meeting fails: 273,

276; Chatfield maneuvers against Representacion Nacional: 343-48; *see also* Liberals

United States: 275, 285; negotiates treaty with New Granada; reacts to occupation of San Juan: 291; negotiates treaties with Guatemala, Nicaragua and Honduras: 298-300; demands explanation and apology for Prometheus incident: 331; apology made: 335-36

United States of Central America *see* Central American Federation

Vanderbilt, Cornelius: 302, 328-29, 330

Van de Weyer: 11, 12

Vasconcelos, Doroteo: 296, 297, 344

Vaughn, Charles: 106

Vera Paz: 75, 105

Verveer, John: 63-64

Vervier: 9

Vigil, Diego: 176, 182, 193, 202-203

Walker, Patrick: 246, 291

Wallerstein, Edward: 351, 353

Walsh, Robert M.: 341-43

Warsaw: 32-33

Webster, Daniel: 330, 336

Webster-Crampton Agreement: 337, 338-39, 341-42

Wellington, Arthur Wellesley, Duke of: 101

Witt, Count, Prince of Warsaw: 32, 33, 35

Woodcutting problem: 55-56, 58, 92, 126, 128, 129

Wyke, Charles Lennox: 336, 341-43, 353; exposes Chatfield's alliance with *serviles:* 355-56

Zebadúa, Marcial: 59-60, 64-65, 68-70

Zugapango: 123

A native Californian, Mario Rodríguez received his undergraduate and graduate degrees from the University of California at Berkeley. He now has in press a synthesis of Central American history to be published by Prentice-Hall and Company, and is engaged in a project concerning the life and times of José Francisco Barrundia (1787–1854), a controversial figure whose public career spans four decades of Central American history. To study the impact of this Guatemalan politician, the foremost ideologist of liberalism in that area during the first half of the nineteenth century, the historian has been awarded a John Simon Guggenheim Fellowship in History which will take him to Central America for the academic year 1964–1965. He also held a Morse Fellowship in History from Yale University (1958–1959) which allowed him to do research in England, Belgium, and France.

Dr. Rodríguez is a Professor of History at the University of Arizona, having joined the faculty in 1960. He is a frequent contributor of articles to scholarly periodicals and since 1959 has been a contributing editor to the *Handbook of Latin American Studies*.